D0173021

NINE FACES OF CHRIST

A NARRATIVE OF

NINE GREAT MYSTIC INITIATIONS

OF

JOSEPH, BAR, JOSEPH

IN THE ETERNAL RELIGION

DEVORSS *Publications*

Nine Faces of Christ
Copyright © 1980
by Eugene W. Whitworth

All rights reserved. No part of this book may be reproduced
or transmitted in any form without permission in writing from
the publisher, except by a reviewer who may quote brief
passages for review purposes.

ISBN: 0-87516-665-2

First Published in India in 1972 by
Great Western University & Darshana International
Moradabad, India

First U.S. edition published in 1980 by
Great Western University & Wiechmann Publishing
Seattle, Washington 98055

First DeVorss Publications edition, 1993
Fourth Printing, 2001

DeVorss & Company, Publisher
P.O. Box 550
Marina del Rey, CA 90294-0550

For more information,
please visit our website: **www.devorss.com**

Printed in The United States of America

AUTHOR'S PREFACE

You are about to begin an emotional experience – so be prepared! To help you, let me set out the basic thesis on which this work was created.

Research indicates that inside the Great Religions throughout history there has been a learned, secret, initiate group who work for the good of all mankind against false priests, bigotry, and self-complacency.

Research has failed to produce a single official historical point of record of there having lived and been crucified the man Jesus. You must accept him on unofficial records – that is on faith alone. Is this not pure mysticism? Yet, do you not believe His promise to you: "All that I do, you can do, and more also!"?

These two threads of mysticism – supported by the study of more than four hundred books on the lives of AVATARS and the Great Religions – gave the basic thesis for this book.

The central character is not Jesus.

Incidents similar to those told of His life are used in this book – but they are similar also to reports of AVATARS in other religions. The central character is not Jesus. There is no historical and official documentation of His life, remember.

There is some documentation of the life of a man who was crucified fifty-six years before the reported birth of our Lord and Savior. This man was said to be the Messiah by his supporters, and to have risen from the dead. In the sparse and strange records his name was Joseph-bar-Joseph, or Jeshuau-Jeshua (which might be better if written Jeshua-U-Jeshua).

The central character of this story is Jeshuau-Jeshua, or Joseph-bar-Joseph, overlaid with the documented and reputed powers of the Anointed Ones (Christ means "Anointed") of the Persian Magi, and the powers of the Avatars of many of the other religions.

Now, here is the strangest of paradoxes - a veritable mystery of the ages. If you take Jeshuau, or Jeshu for short, and place him in the framework of the life of the times about eighty years after his crucifixion - you have a story like that of our Jesus. If you go further and give him the training of the Essenes, the Magians, the Brahmins and some of the religion of Hermes-Thoth of the Egyptians - you have created a character which resembles our Christ.

Yet, many things about the life of Christ are not explained to the satisfaction of the world at large. If this work is to do its best in the hands of thinking man, it must contribute something to a better understanding of all men and all religions. If to the character which already resembles the Christian's Christ, we add the attributes of the Eternal Initiate, the candidate for Mastership or Adeptship, in all of the Ancient Religions known to man:-

You have an exact duplicate of the Christian Christ - created as a character *not of fiction* but out of the common pool of the most sacred beliefs of the men of all major religions. You have in truth The New Age Christ created out of All Faiths by Universal Yoga.

Isn't it strange that in the Great Religions of the World we find the deeds and personality of the Messiah - a strange, almost metaphysical foreshadowing of the Christ? Isn't it strange that from the lives of Great Avatars we take acts much like those said to have been done by our own Savior? Indeed when Christians come upon this fact and are not prepared for it, it can be most upsetting - especially in a world disposed toward scientific skepticism.

Add to this another uncomfortable truism. Some acts of Christ as reported in the New Testament are enigmatic, seemingly unreasonable when put to the test of logic.

Yet - and here the mystery compounds itself - when seen from within the thoughts of a Great Avatar skilled in the mystical *knowing* of the advanced Initiate, all His acts are clear and logical indeed. Such an approach is surely permissible.

You are about to begin one attempt to use the Golden

Thread of Secret Training, which seems to form the common core of every major religion, to suture scattered ideas into a unity of logic that is understandable and acceptable to all men everywhere, and to all faiths.

The central character of this book is the Eternal Initiate, the Great Candidate of All Religions. It is hoped that as you read you will become so emotionally involved in the problems of this Great Initiate that as he approaches initiation after initiation in his preparation for the Final Effort on The Cross, you will feel that *you* are there.

It is hoped the reader will love the Eternal Initiate with complete understanding, knowing *why*.

If there is truth in the unrecorded story of the Great Cabal, the central character of this book can be no other than the Great Candidate For Eternal Initiation – the Spirit-Self *of the one who reads*!

Eugene E. Whitworth
San Francisco, California,
June 15, 1972

CONTENTS

FOREWORD

You should know if you will profit by reading this book before you begin. Here are tests you may place upon yourself.

Can you tell *for certain* the exact difference between a dream and a vision? Can you *positively* and unerringly distinguish the difference between actuality and reality? Can you say *positively* that you have all the answers to religious and moral questions?

If your answer to these questions is *yes*, read no further, for this work is not for seers, saints, egocentrics, bigots or those who know beyond doubt the answers to all things for all ages.

Have you ever talked face to face with your Lord and Savior? Have you ever heard from His lips the Truth as He taught it – un-warped by the misinterpretation of overzealous missionaries? Are you able to find the True Christ-Faith in the remnants of someone's excessive zeal for organization, doctrine control and centralization of thought? If your answer to these questions is *yes*, except it be the last one, read no further, for this work is not for visionaries, fakirs, or prophets.

Do you know all about the private thoughts of a Messiah who became a Christ? Are you positive you can read in a thrice-translated work the inner, sacred purposes of the greatest mystic who has lived in the flesh in 2000 years? If you are, read no further, for your mind is either closed or you need no training that can come from the pen of man or Master.

Have you secretly yearned for more than is given you through established and powerful orthodoxy, or the so-called infallible priests? Have you felt the upsurging evidence of immortality *within yourself*, within your very cell-body felt the upsweeping power of the spirit-body? Have you felt your higher self rise within you like the true Serpent of Wisdom, only to be lulled and piped to quiescense by the flute of your supposed superiors, as the Hindu pipes the cobra back into the basket? Have you ever wanted to cut the bars and crush the wall of your socially-ordained, culturally-hypnotizing prison? Have you wanted to let the magnificent, secret, inner self – the Serpent of Wisdom – bear your higher consciousness to the furthest reaches of time and space? Have you longed to know the Truth behind the supposed truth? Have you felt upon your flesh the upsweeping of God's own arms as He raised you out of your earth-bound cells to some magnificence of self which is near unto heaven? Have you wondered about the meaning behind the meaning of many of the sayings of our Lord and Savior? If your answer to these questions is *yes*, read on, read on indeed! For this book may perhaps answer some of your yearning, re-orient your wandering thinking, re-establish your faith in the *apparently unsound* orthodox.

Have you longed to have for your own the sacred, secret wondrous training of the Initiate Adepts of all ages? Have you wondered at the power of these Students through the ages? Have you been puzzled at how closely the powers and abilities of these Adepts resemble those reputedly used by the Divine Initiate, who is said to have lived in the time of Herod and Pontius Pilate? Have you felt within yourself the urge toward the mastery of these secret techniques, and truly believed that you could master them, but because of cultural hypnosis accepted defeat and the ideas of your "superiors" that you lacked the capacity and ability to use these powers for the good of mankind without hurt to yourself? If your answer to these questions is *yes, Oh, My God, YES?*, then clutch this book to your heart – for this is the breath of spiritual life to you.

Read then of the mystic's AVATAR. Imagine as you read that you are within the mind of the Great Initiate, and you may surely find that this book is your own memoirs – the story of your own inner, sacred, eternal self......

1

JOSEPH,
MY BELOVED FATHER

There is little true historical evidence that there lived one Jeshuau, sometimes called Joseph-bar-Joseph, a man who became a Messiah. Therefore, for centuries men, especially the doubters, have questioned my life and my birth, even as I questioned in my early youth. Even to me, the one involved, the concept of Virgin Birth was unbelievable when first I heard it. Then I, even I asked, as men have rightfully asked through the ages since, "Who is this man? And from whence came he, in truth?"

This mystery and many more shall now be unfolded, if it be the will of God. Verily, I say unto you, "That which has been written about the life of anyone who became a Christ is neither false nor true." How this may be will be made plain as my life unfolds. But mark you, that which is now to be written shall be more true than false! Know the truth for the truth shall set you free. But is it not harder to compress great truth in a small book than to keep fishes in a basket from which to feed the multitude? Truly this, my first effort as a writer, may leave much to be desired in style and form. But the eternal verities lie not in style or form; the eternal verities lie in the magnificence of the power of our Almighty Father and there only do they lie. Read and note well the true meaning of the concepts. Read with eyes open, mind alert, heart afire and spirit radiant with

1

the quest for truth. Know it is the Father within who does the work, both my work in explaining and your work in understanding the sometimes hidden spiritual message.

The very beginning, as I knew it, revolved around the moving human temple which was my beloved father, Joseph. In my early life there was much stress due to my mother, Mary. Verily, there was much mystery and within my heart there was often misery and doubt. For from a very early age I realized my sweet, beautiful mother did not believe I was the son of my beloved Joseph. Yet she held that my brothers and sisters were of his flesh, and his blood and his lineage. Her manner was strange and veiled. It hurt me that I should be set apart as not of the flesh and sinew of my beloved father.

My mother, Mary, was a strange and forceful woman in spite of her small stature. She was willing and able as a worker and very powerful with her small hands. She preferred to read from her precious scroll of history and The Law, and would sit for hours and read and re-read the passages which spoke of the one who was to come, - the Messiah, he who would return the Jews to their rightful place. My first clear memories are not of her tending me and my needs; they are of her reading in her pleasant voice some of the passages from history that spoke of the Messiah to come. These she read over and over and over to me.

Another memory is her chanting of the services of the Jewish temple. These she knew well for her uncle was a high priest, her aunt a priestess. My mother had been destined to be a priestess of the faith until she met and became enamoured of my father, Joseph.

Joseph sang songs that were lovelier and far more beautiful, and his voice had a deep vibrancy that made even the birds and the animals stop and listen when he sang or spoke. His songs were never mournful as were the chants of Mary.

His songs came from (this I found later) the Essenes of Nazar, a sect that accepted only Gentiles and permitted marriage. This Order was small but very powerful because of its many abilities. They called themselves the Brotherhood of God, but the people of our village called them the Nazar-Essenes. This was shortened through disrespect, and often laziness, to *Nazar-ines*. This may explain to some why there is no record of Nazareth, a town or village, until many years after my time on the earth; for the Nazar-Essenes lived outside our village a thousand paces in a quadrangle of cultivated land with many buildings; the estate which they held had for centuries been called in Aramaic, "Nazar" that is to say, "Non-physical."

The quadrangle housed all of the celibate members of the Order but many of the most powerful men had large families who lived outside the walls of the compound. Only the Initiates were allowed to enter the compound. Many men came from all parts of the earth to be initiated into the Brotherhood and taught by the heads of the Order. My beloved father, Joseph, belonged to this Order and was one of the three members of the Supreme Council. Membership in the Order was his because he came of Aryan stock, as indeed also did Mary, and his membership in the Order was to him as dear as life.

From my earliest memories I know I adored my father beyond all belief. The sound of his voice was a thing of joy. He was, as I remember now, a tall man with auburn hair and gray-green eyes. When he stood beside my mother she would fit under his raised arm. Often in his joy, for he was gay with magnificent happiness (which you will understand later), he would put his arm over the head of Mary and look around in a bewildered way and say to us, "Children, where, oh, where is your beautiful mother?"

There was always a roar of laughter for he made us all laugh with glee. Then he would pretend to find her and hug and kiss her as if she had been truly lost and she would blush with her own joys and her own delight. Joseph was droll and tender and loving and gentle, but there was something in him that was so - so *universal* that even as a five-year old I began to sense his true magnificence. He was a strict disciplinarian and stern when we failed in our task. He was more stern still if we failed in our promise or our trust. To him duty could be equated with life, and the first evidence of obedience to

3

duty was in keeping our promise and our word.

My beloved father was also *fey*. He was a *Hanif*, a joyous mystic. He could foresee events, as I remember, from my earliest times. He always told us of his pre-visions in a light manner, usually in a little pattern of rhythm and rhyme. Perhaps I can recall an example over the many years-Oh!, for instance, the one he told before my seventh birthday:

"Joseph-bar-Joseph will soon be seven.
He will give the Jews a lesson at eleven!
For how to save their religion will seem simple,
When he whips the money maniacs from the temple!"

How my brothers and sisters chanted that at me for days and days. How joyous and innocent it seemed when Joseph first recited it in his resonant voice.

Secretly I thought Joseph loved me more than he loved any of the other six children, and he loved me from the bottom of his heart as his son and companion. In this way he loved me more than Mary loved me. She always seemed to love some potential me, never the *me* of the moment. And in my early youth this bothered me greatly and caused me much grief and concern and doubt; but Joseph loved ME. He taught ME his trade of wood mechanic and home builder from the time I was five.

One day he told us that I was to get a hammer and a saw, in one of his clever little rhythm-rhymes. (It was not until much later that I understood the initiate wisdom behind the apparently indifferent funpieces.)

"Joseph-bar-Joseph will lose no teeth from his jaw
Until he has mastered hatchet, hammer and saw!"

Over and over he repeated the jingle until it was part of my very being. It was not until later that he could use the other children to repeat and repeat his messages until they were driven into the very fiber of being. And he was not wrong!

At the next feast day I received a very man-sized hammer and saw. I was put, and hard put, to heft the heavy tools; but I loved the fact that I was given man's tools with which to do man's work. Carrying my tools, I could then go with Joseph any time he went into his shop behind our home and I followed him everywhere I could.

4

Many times as we worked upon the furniture he made for sale (he assigned me important tasks to do, not play tasks), he would talk to me about the religions of the world and the history and the religion of the Jews. He would often talk of the True Religion of God and seldom did he ever leave off a discourse without repeating, "Religions of all history are sewn together by the secret inner golden thread, for there is no religion higher than Truth." Even before I was six I knew that my father was deep in ancient and important wisdom, a veritable tower of knowledge, and a humble man who attributed all of his abilities to his God and his secret training.

How very much like a God on earth my beloved father was, was not made clear to me until after my fifth birthday when one of the men from the compound came toward us in the workshed, his tunic bright crimson from the blood that squirted from his wrist. His hand had been almost completely cut from his arm by the head of a broadaxe that arced from its handle as it was being used to trim timbers with which to build an addition to the Essene Hall of the Assembly, which was their temple. Joseph turned to me and called for my help. I scrambled up on the unfinished table we were making, and at his direction held the severed hand in place.

He said quickly and without tension in his voice,

"Joseph-bar-Joseph *now* must learn to be about his Father's business,

And even at the sight of blood, he shall know no dizziness."

The way he looked and spoke made me curious and keenly alive to everything that went on in the next miraculous seconds. Joseph set the bone and the flesh correctly and was careful with the tendons and with the artery that was spurting bright crimson upon us both. In a moment his body was straight and still and he said in a commanding and vibrant voice, "Almighty, Indwelling God, *Heal!* Heal instantly and perfectly! I command you, *Heal!* For it is the right of God to heal!"

Over and over and over he said the words. Then I noticed that from his hands a tingling passed into mine and into the mutilated flesh of Johanan, the Essene. I

5

stood very still and quiet with my eyes almost closed against the sight of the blood, but I clearly saw the blue-white or silvery-violet flame that licked from Joseph's forehead and touched the head of the injured man. Then we all seemed to be wrapped with a violet light and the noises of the distant villages were shut out. There was nothing in the world it seemed but that light! Though I was fully conscious of what was happening, it was as if time had been stopped and I was caught up in a power greater than I had ever known. We all seemed to be sustained in the power, suspended between earth and sky and held motionless in time. My father seemed to be speaking from far away and, as I watched the hand, it began to move in my own. First, the bleeding stopped and the flesh sealed over and healed before my eyes! I had watched buds of flowers open in the strong sun and this was like a bud opening, but in reverse.

Suddenly, Johanan, the Essene, took his hand from mine and looked at my father. In his eyes was an adoration such as I was to see many times later, "Joseph, you are indeed the worker of miracles!"

My beloved father shook himself, as if he had been asleep standing up, and said quietly, "My Brother, you know well that it is not I who does the work but the Father who is within us all. Go forth healed, Johanan! Tell no common man lest we all be scorned or stoned by those who cannot believe."

Johanan, the Essene, muttered a prayer, bowed to my father in reverence and walked quickly back toward the compound looking not at his path, but at his hand!

I was looking at my father and, even as young as I was, I knew I stood in the presence of a great master, a True Man. He saw my utter amazement, put his arm over my head, as he sometimes did my mother, and chanted in his funny way,

"Has anyone seen little Joseph-bar-Joseph?
Where could he have gone, do you supposeth?"

Something of Mary's doggedness was in me too, and I knew this man was more than human. In my five-year old brain was a plan - I wanted to be like him and heal! Something within me suddenly made me grow up, for here

6

was the meaning and purpose of life, and this indeed was my Father's business. With all my heart and forevermore I knew I adored this big, ambling, laughing, rhythmic father. But more, I wanted to *know* and to *do* what he knew and could do. I wanted to know all about him and his work, and I knew he could teach me.

"Teach me how to do that!' I said.

My father looked at me and stopped his clowning and his eyes were large and puzzled--and a little fearful, I thought. "My son, I would rather teach you than anyone in all the world, but I have taken an Oath of Secrecy and am not permitted to pass on this learning to anyone who has not joined the Brotherhood and taken the Oath of Secrecy himself."

" I will take the Oath," I said.

In my eagerness I moved about and almost fell from the unfinished table. My father laughed a long, deep, merry laugh. Then suddenly he stopped and looked at me with great love and deep understanding. "Why not?" I did not know if he mused aloud or merely thought it. "It has not been done in the past but could not a man be both father and master to such a son? There is neither precedent nor rule,--therefore a vote of the Assembly of God....." He stroked my head gently and said, with great intensity: "It shall be, if it be the will of God.'

He put me down and we went to work. We worked side by side as we did in years to come and from that moment I was a man full grown. I had purpose and meaning and loving guidance, and a burning desire to be as good as my adored father. Many days later I was to know what he had done. He had told me nothing of his efforts during the hours and hours of talking to me as we worked in the shed.

One morning my mother waked me earlier than daybreak and in the flickering light from a taper she dressed me in a clean robe, tied a colored sash around my middle. She was in tears. I did not realize that something very important was about to happen until she set out my sandals and told me to put them on! Only on matters of state would I be required to put sandals on my tough little feet. Even as I bent to catch the latches she burst out crying and left the room. A moment later I heard her remonstrating with Joseph and then his gentle but firm reply.

"They may *not* take him and it will break his heart!'

"Beloved, it will happen if God wills it. He is a *mighty* little man now and his mind is set."

"But he is so little, and will be with fifteen-year old ruffians."

"Twelve to sixteen-year olds, my beloved, but not ruffians. For no ruffian could stay an Essene longer than one meal after he was found out."

"He is so little, so young!"

"I know he is small and young but he is *tough*! And he is wise beyond most grown men. He will be in good hands there and in our hands here. We will let it be enough that he and I wish this thing to be."

Mary wept, and then said to my father the words that created torture and doubt in my mind for years. "It is alright for you to talk but remember, he is not your child, and I am his mother. He is in *my* keeping!"

I heard the power of decision that came into Joseph's voice and tone as he answered her firmly yet gently, "He is my son, Mary, and he is in *our* keeping. Let us be silent on that subject."

I walked into the room as if I had not overheard and Joseph looked at me with eyes filled with love. My mother burst out sobbing and ran from the room and Joseph winked at me solemnly. "Mothers do not like to see their sons grow up too soon."

Without another word we walked toward the compound and I strode beside him manfully matching two strides to his one. Suddenly he said, "You heard what she said?"

"Yes. Are you not my father?" I looked up into his eyes and read there love and a strange agony of mind.

He smiled and said gently, "Son, ask me this question in ten years and I will be able to answer you well, in terms you will understand *without doubt*. For now, let it be enough that I call you my son."

My panic was quieted for I trusted him completely, and I knew that he would never tell me a lie for any reason whatsoever. We were silent as we walked the remaining distance to the compound gate over dusty trails. We then went directly toward the hall of the Assembly, the largest building on the entire place.

Into this compound at Nazar no woman was ever permitted to go, and no child! I was very proud to know that I, at least, was considered no longer a child as the doors were pulled open by men in long robes of beautiful linen. When we entered the large hall I knew I was expected to be awed by the sober men in long robes who sat in silent stern-faced attention as my father outlined his plan and his reasoning. The members of the Order were restless as my father rose to his feet, his face determined and his auburn hair towering over his shorter companions like a banner. Even though stern, his face was also pleasant as he looked around and his eyes rested for just a moment on Johanan, the Essene, who stood beside an upright post.

My father began in his stimulating voice and the Assembly was soon hushed and breathless. His words are still clear, for my destiny was waiting upon his acceptance by his peers.

"My Brothers, what I am here to ask you to sanction is unusual. There is no precedent in history and no rule in our Order to guide us. Whatever we do here must be with the permission of the Elders and by the unanimous vote of all. We are making precedent and history. I propose to induct my five-year old son into the Order and place him under the Oath of Secrecy. Then, and then only, I may teach him of the Initiate Truths and the techniques of healing which he has asked of me. But what I hope will come of this action is that the Brotherhood will make a way for a father to teach his own son by lowering the age of entry from twelve to five. Then any member may be father and master to his own son, if he wishes to be."

"Could any five-year old know enough to enter our Order?" This was said by a grave older man; his tone was not argumentative nor heated but inquisitive.

"Perhaps not." When Joseph said this--my heart sank! "Surely not, unless he was possessed by the Spirit

9

of God and made wise beyond his physical years."

"True, Brother Joseph, when the Father works within, all knowledge is the province of man! But how can we determine that this child is advanced enough to enter our Order? Or any child? According to the rules of the Brotherhood, any man beyond the age of twelve may enter and study. But he must know enough to pass the test at the end of the first year."

"We can test him!"

"But how? We have no entrance test! Only exit tests!"

"Good! Let us test him orally,--he knows not enough of characters and ciphering yet--on any subject within the first year of our studies."

"Would that be fair to him?" It was Johanan, the Essene, who asked this.

"Perhaps not to him, Johanan, but certainly to the Order. We demand of him more than we would of any ordinary twelve-year old because we wish to be certain of his capacity before we change the rules of the Order for his benefit. Is it not just that the individual give much to the Society?"

"As you will it, Brother."

But the older man suddenly spoke sharply, "Do you suggest that we test him on the material of the first year? Would we not then be testing him for the level of a thirteen-year old?"

"Yes, but so be it!"

My father said this. He patted my shoulder and left me to stand alone in the center of the Assembly Hall. He walked over and sat upon the spotless floor, placing his back comfortably against the upright post beside which Johanan stood. I felt his eyes upon me and in a moment I saw the silvery-violet flame. It leapt from his brow and seemed to touch me with warmth and love. It took away my trembling and gave me great courage and peace, and a fierce inner determination to succeed.

A short, burly man with small tawny eyes walked toward me at a nod from the elder man. His brown hair was wavy. His face would have been pleasant, but now it was set in a grimace of pleasure. His actions were like one who has just captured a bird and is about to make a meal of it. Later I was to learn that he was Master of The First Year and a wise and just man, though stricter than others. But at the moment he seemed to me to be a hurdle.

"Well, boy!--child, can you tell me this? Where did the Jewish religion come from and how was it founded?"

I looked at him in utter defeat and despair and amazement for I saw in his aura the answer he wanted. But that answer was not the truth, and I knew I knew the truth. The true answer came from some deep well of certainty within me. I also realized that this was not the answer I was supposed to give to pass the test. I looked at my father helplessly and would have run for comfort to his loving arms but the blue-white beam held me to my spot. I felt the tears coursing down my cheeks. They were tears of frustration and also tears of fear. For I could not lie and yet I knew the answer that would get for me the one thing I so greatly desired.

"Well, child," the old patriarch looked at me kindly and I bolted straight into his arms. He folded me gently in his arms and said, "It is nothing to fail, child."

"Oh, Sir, I know the answer he expects. But I also know the truth. If I speak not truth when I see it, I wrong the teachings of my father. If I speak truth I shall not pass this test."

"By my faith!", he exclaimed, and many shuffling feet stopped as men turned back from leaving the assembly hall. The old patriarch laughed gently and motioned the departing men back. His hand stilled the buzzing in the hall. "Hear, Brothers. Verily this fiery one is caught on the horns of a dilemma as fine as any in our philosophy. Master Habakkuk, with your gracious permission, may I try to get your answer for you? Good! Now, child, go back to the center of the hall and face the Brothers!"

I did as I was commanded by such a gentle voice. "Now, my child, answer the question in two parts. First, give the answer you think Master Habakkuk wants you to give; second, give the answer you think is the truth, as you say."

I flinched, for I did not *think* it was truth, I *knew*! I

raised my eyes and looked at the group and remembered the courteous address my mother had drilled into me.

"Sir, Men of Learning, Adored Father. In the aura of my Master of The Lion's Eyes, I see that my answer should be thus: The Jewish religion was founded by God Almighty in his contacts with Adam, Noah, Abraham, Jesse, and especially with Moses to whom God is supposed to have given the Ten Commandments, carved in stone by flames on Mount Sinai, forty years after the Israelites came out of Egypt."

He of the tawny eyes nodded affirmatively. "That is our external religious history, son, and only an Initiate knows the true story."

"My father has taught me that no religion is higher than Truth, Sir. I now tell you truth, not as I think it is, but as I know it! Verily the Jews have no religion that is truly theirs and they have never had in all history. Throughout the years they have taken bits from the more advanced tribes around them and from the stronger cultures in which they were held captive. From the Chaldeans, Hittites, Uranians, they took freely the story of the creation of the world and man, and so also the story of the Flood. From the Mittanni they took their beliefs of heaven, hell, God and the angels. Also, they took the Nordic strain which is in the veins of the descendants of Jesse, for the ruling house of the Jews is not Semitic in origin but Mittannic-Nordic, not that is to say, Jewish but Gentile. The Ten Commandments they have taken by violation of the Truth, boldly from the sects of men of Indus, who knew it not as the law of God but as the virtuous way of good men. The Jewish story of the coming Messiah to be born of the Virgin and over whom a star shall hover at birth, turning night into shining day - all this has been taken from the ancient beliefs of one of the tribes of Media, a faith founded by a Persio-Median, Zoroaster, who lived a hundred centuries ago."

I finished and looked at my father. His head was comfortably back against the post and his eyes were closed but on his face was a smile, and I know he was pleased with me. Johanan, the Essene, was staring, amazed, yet also pleased. The Patriarch, who was later to be my teacher in the Torah, was nodding in rhythm to my words for they had tumbled out of me in a most compelling rhythm and force.

I could not understand the sudden burst of expressions of amazement from members of the Assembly. A few of the men hurried out of the hall and returned with many of the Brothers. Soon the hall was so filled with curious men that some sat at my very feet on the vast floor and more were coming in every few minutes as I went along. They were hushed and quieted by those who were in the hall who seemed to be enchanted by my childish treble and the ideas which flowed from me with such perfect rhythm.

I do not recall all of the questions. They all dealt with Jewish Bible history as known to the external sect and as taught by the Rabbinical scholars of that and earlier days. But not one question could I answer only as Master Habakkuk *seemed* to *wish*. Yet he seemed more and more pleased with me as time went along. In truth, I answered as his aura indicated, and then explained the Truth to keep my father content with my answer.

One question I remember well for it was a trick question. "Who was Moses and what did he do?"

"Master Habakkuk, the answer you desire from those of your class is that Moses led the Israelites out of Egypt, opened the Red Sea with his staff, caused the seas to close on the armies of the Pharoah, and then led the Jews for almost forty years toward the promised land. He also is reputed to have received the Ten Commandments from God himslf, and then was lifted up into heaven."

"That is the usual answer, Master Joseph--bar-Joseph."

"You also know that there were three Moses."

"*Mo-se* is merely the Egyptian word of ancient times which means 'child', or 'child of', and is found in our Talmud as *Mosheh*. The first *Mosheh* was a young man in the days of the mighty and righteous Pharoah Amenhotep IV, who became the first true mystic priest king in history, and changed his name to Akhnaten. Young

13

Mosheh was trained at the University of the Sun God, the god *Re* in Heliopolis. When the mighty Pharoah died his mystic religion was overthrown by the powerful priests of Amun and the followers of the true religion were sent to an abandoned fort of the *Hyskos* near the city of Avaris. Here the followers of the One God organized themselves and chose *Mosheh*, whose Egyption name was Osarsiph, to lead them. They founded a confederation and brought forth a covenant that said they would make no graven image of God, nor worship one; they would give no respect to sacred animals.

"At first the warrior *Mosheh* was successful in regaining much of Egypt and was helped by Semitic tribes in bondage to the false priests and also by the *Jebusites* from *Canaan*. But the tides of war changed and the armies were destroyed and the allies were scattered into the grasslands of the Sinai region. A few were pursued through the grasslands near the Jordan River. Here the first *Mosheh* disappeared. One warrior priest, a commander from *Shechem*, fled with his warrior comrades into the center of the Sinai Peniinsula and he became *Mosheh* of *Shechem*, that is to say, the Child of Egypt from *Shechem*. These were *Canaanites* and soon conquered the small tribes of the area and imposed upon them the God of War, *Isra-el*, who was symbolized by the calf made of gold. Either the first or the third *Mosheh*, or Moses, took the Hebrew bonds-people from the delta region of Egypt, with livestock, and retreated south through Goshen and then out into the southern part of the Sinai Peninsula.

"Soon this Moses set up a written covenant and laws for the priesthood and the laymen of the survivors of Atonism of the mighty Pharoah Akhnaten, and this was called the Book of the Covenant. It was based on the agreement of Avaris and included most of the elements of Atonism, including universal circumcision, dietary and sanitary rules, and a law prohibiting graven images of God and tested rules and statutes against theft, murder, false witness, covetousness, adultery, and respect for family and parents. This constitution was merely dedicated at the ceremony of Mount Sinai and the Ten

Commandments came from the mighty mystic Pharoah
Akhnaten, not from God.

"By the end of forty years the two segments under
the two Moses, two personages, had been re-combined.
Then there was trouble with the golden calf, and they
came under either a third or a fourth Moses. But it is
clear that we have at least three Moshehs, one true
Egyptian and two others; one Canaanite, another
possibly a mixture of both. Later, the Levites, who were
nought but the inheritants of the priests of Aton, made
the three Moses into one figure, adding myths to give the
weak tribes a reason for unity and strength. Not one of
the Moses was a great religious leader but each was a
great man. The mystical past of the composite Moses was
added later by the Levites and the scribes and has no
substance in the records."

There was a strange pause when I had finished
talking and no one seemed to want to ask me questions.
My last, but one, question was asked by my father.
"From history, what do you conclude concerning Truth
and religion?"

"That religion is only part of Truth. Religion is
usually shown in formal ways, in organizations meant to
control thoughts and actions of men. But at the core,
within every accepted sect of religion, there is a golden
thread. This is the secret and hidden sacred tecniques
and powers which make men able to perform the
miraculous. This is the wondrous golden core of Truth,
which I wish to learn."

There was much debate between the members of the
Order and then a question was flung at my father. "He is
not of an age to be responsible, no matter how bright! If
he is not responsible to his word, how could he take an
Oath? If he was to break it, we of the Order could not
under the laws of the Brotherhood touch him in
punishment! What do you suggest to answer this
imponderable?"

My father opened his eyes and looked steadily at his
questioner and said simply, "Ask him!"

They did, and verily, this is the answer I remember.
"Sirs, my father has told me that I must take an Oath in

which I promise that my life shall be forfeit if I violate that Oath. To gain the knowledge of healing, I would risk my life. Do you not remember the story of Abraham and Isaac? *That* father was willing to sacrifice his son to obey the command of his God and keep His favor. Let then, my father be responsible to punish me if I break my Oath, and bind him by special oath to slay me if I break mine. You may as well bind him for I know, and he knows, that he would slay me anyway."

Master Habakkuk said simply, "My Brothers, I have tested him with questions to the fifth year level. I am as satisfied with him as I could be with any eighteen-year old student."

There was a vote and my father was instructed to bring me next morning at sunrise, for I was to be placed under sacred oath and he was to be bound, as my words had indicated. He smiled and there was loud cheering as many men crowded around me to ask me questions. I slipped between them and made my way to my father where he lay back against the upright post. I rushed into his arms, clambered upon his stomach, and whispered my urgent needs in his ears. He roared with laughter as he led me quickly toward the door.

"Brothers, your questions must wait. I am not surprised that the child is hungry, for we have been here since before sunrise and it is now past mid-afternoon. He has been answering your questions for three quarters of this day and it is time for relief and food."

Soon we were at the back of the Assembly Hall where steaming food appeared on the tables, and hundreds of men were already eating. I sat between my father and the old patriarch and ate with manly delight until my stomach was stretched. Then I realized that I was tired and very sleepy, and fell asleep with my feet in the lap of the patriarch and my head in the lap of my father.

2

MARY,

MY BEAUTIFUL MOTHER

Unknown to me at that time, I had sown the seeds of my greatest glory and also of my inevitable crucifixion by men. To both my rise to glory and my greatest trial, my mother, Mary, contributed her fair share. Even as I stood before the Brothers in the Assembly Hall of the Essenes of Nazar, her training and her personality were part of my being and gave rise to much of my surprising knowledge. From my mother I imbibed many things including an impatience with the stupidity of the Jews; a belief that they were destroying their own religion and country; a restless verbal *drive* that relentlessly drove home my convictions in face of opposition; and a sharp and agile mind, coupled with a memory that was extraordinary and detailed.

Yes, the strong hands and the strong opinions of my mother had been with me in that ordeal. Ordeal it was! And yet it was an experience of singular bliss. From it also I was to realize two things, both expanded and proved later. The first was that, under stress, I could rise in a sort of physical-mental scale of octaves. It was something like a feeling of an emotion or an excitement that lifted me to an unbelievable pitch. In this high state I seemed to come into a strange harmony with the universe, and to be able to tap limitless knowledge and to see clearly things that I could not know of my own personal experience. The second thing, I found, was not so pleasant; this mood or feeling seemed to require an enormous amount of energy to sustain it, even for a short time. When the mood or feeling left me I was always ravenously hungry and also exhausted. It was as if my vital energy could be called up to perform the unbelievable, but it then left me depleted and completely without energy.

The feeling or mood itself was filled with amazing pleasure. When it was upon me I felt as if completely isolated and sufficient unto myself, as if I were a superman with a superintelligence. But it was also like expanding or floating in space and arriving at an abstract bliss in which there was no sensation or effort. It was gracious to feel and glorious to experience. When in that exalted condition I could see with amazing acuity and observe infinite detail, and in later experiences, found that I could seem to be in more than one place at a time. My mind seemed to be separated into strange physical aspects so that I could see my surroundings, places distant, and also things not purely of the physical world. Yes, all this was accompanied by that indescribable and blissful feeling of langour into which any man might long to escape from the trials of the physical world. Always, following hard upon the blissful period of ecstasy, there was that brutal and punishing hunger and exhaustion. It had the effect of clamping a hood of black upon the rioting colours of mind. It seemed to crowd my mind into dark crevices so that even the light that reached my eyes could hardly register, and all was seen through a veil darkly. I seemed to be suddenly unworthy even to live, and to be enveloped in a black despair.

I do not know how I got home after falling asleep in the laps of two high priests at the Assembly Hall of Essenes of Nazar, but I was awakened for our evening meal. I stumbled to the table and could barely hold my heavy listless body up to eat. James, a year younger than I, sat and ate with dignity and that tidy carefulness which mother trained into all her children. I felt depressed, useless as if a great weight was in every cell of my body and as if my mind would not function. Even though I was ravenous I could hardly lift a lamb stew and goat milk curds to my mouth; and food, in which I usually delighted, tasted as if filled with straw. Yet I could not get enough to satisfy my craving.

My mother was tense, critical and tearful as she moved in her kitchen, over which she usually presided with such calm and serene delight.

"Look at Jeshuau now! I told you it would be too much for him. He can hardly move, he is so tired. How can you expect him to carry on his studies at the Temple? And also at the Brotherhood? He's too young! I tell you, he cannot do it!' Her tone was sharp, her features drawn.

My father answered in his kindly voice, "Beloved, he is lethargic. I know the feeling. It comes from excessive mental effort of a special kind. He will not normally experience such an energy drain as today and certainly not in the training of the Brotherhood. He will continue to go to the Temple for training on the Sabbath and two other days in the mornings only. He will train at the Brotherhood the other days of the week."

"Do you expect one so tiny to be in school all the time?"

"No, only from sunrise to sunset four days a week."

"What will they teach him?"

"What he has asked to learn, and more!"

"What, Joseph? Exactly what will they teach my son?" Even in my lethargy I could feel the tension in her almost hysterical insistence and my stomach knotted at her distress.

But my father laughed in his pleasant way. "Ah, when you take the Oath, I will tell you, Mary."

"Oath!"

That was all she said but her tone made it clear how she felt. There was a long silence but I could see the stubborn set to her chin. Detached as I was, possibly because I was physically unable to participate in the emotional tensions of the moment, I detected that strange something in the behavior of my mother that caused me to worry and to wonder. It was as if she resented Joseph's interest and his influence over me and my destiny. In the years to come I felt that she thought he should be an outsider in the intimate relations between the two of us. This night, in a dim way, I began to notice this but of course at that time, and for years, could not understand its meaning. But I suffered for, and with, my beautiful mother.

She seemed to be caught in some emotional trap which she could not speak about to me and from which she could not free herself, or even ask help from God or man. I loved my mother and it hurt me that she was not happy with my father and me. But I knew that I wanted those studies in the Brotherhood with the very strength of my life, and was certain that my father had made up his mind that I should have them right away. Yet he never spoke quickly or forced his will upon my mother. He won point by point over all her logic and persuaded her from her purely emotional stand by gentle laughter and loving firmness.

When it was right for all concerned he could not be swerved from his decision and eventually she yielded. Yet as the years went by and my studies raised me to understand how truly great my father was, I wondered that she could, for one moment, oppose his divine will.

I was excused from the table and took my dessert of three dates to my pallet with me. But I was too tired to stay awake and eat them.

Once, much later, I roused to hear my mother's fierce whisper from her camel's hair padded bed in the far corner.

"You know who his father is, Joseph?"

And I was reassured by Joseph's patient and sleepy answer, 'Joseph-bar-Joseph is the first born son of an adoring father."

"Oh, Joseph!"

The anguish of her soul and bitterness of her life seemed to be twisted into those two words, and I felt a pity for my troubled mother, a pity that I could not understand but which lay around my heart with fear.

"He hasn't the strength for such an ordeal". She whispered it but now even she was sounding a little sleepy, I thought.

"Beloved, today he answered questions that only an

eighteen-year old should answer. In the normal school he will gain strength along with his knowledge. More important, he will gain his life's work and inner peace."

"I know what his life's work is to be! And so do you!"

"Have you told him?"

"You know I cannot. Not yet for years!"

"Then, is it not best that we help him go the way he wishes now?"

"The poor child, - such destiny - the only hope for our nation -"

Sobbing, her words were lost and I was too tired to listen or finish chewing the date in my mouth. I swallowed hard and dropped into sound sleep from which my mother's gentle but strong hand awakened me. She bent and kissed my cheek and pushed the hair up from my forehead and I smelled the fragrance of blossoms that was always about her.

My mother's eyes were large and deep blue in color but in the early morning light they looked purple and seemed to be filled with flecks of fire, like a cooking fire reflecting from the top of a goblet of grape juice. Her skin was so fair, it was whiter than the linen she wore or the scarf which kept tidy her soft curly light brown hair. Later, when my learning was great enough, I realized that she could have been a direct descendant of the Nordic strain that came into Egypt through the conquered Mittannic tribes. As she bent over me her lovely face showing her concern I felt a great tenderness for her even though I could not understand the cause of her strange actions. I put my arms around her to comfort her.

"My son, my son, too soon you are a man."

Father was moving about the kitchen area and I could smell the brewing mulberry leaves from which he made a savory drink and the bread baking on the top stones of the oven hearth. But my mother did not seem in a hurry to release me, and clung to me with a fierceness that was new to her. Usually she was quick to start to teach me numbers or words or sentences which she had memorized from the temple work given her by the priests

21

of the family, for she was the eldest daughter and the third child of Levi, youngest brother of Zacharias. In these training sessions she often said to me over and over, in Aramaic, Greek or Latin, "You are the hope of the world!" She whispered this to me on this morning but did not let me repeat the words before she added, "You are the only hope of the Jews!"

I held her tightly for she seemed to need the feel of my arms and I whispered back, "I will study hard, Mother! I will be worthy!"

I think she started and gasped. She pulled back and looked hard at me and long into my eyes. Then, without a word, she handed me another clean robe, fastened at the waist with a bright blue cord. My sandals were dropped to the floor from the third shelf of the rosewood and cedar wardrobe.

My mother was tidy and neat and her house was always in perfect order. The stone floors and the stones of the cooking fire and oven were washed the afternoon before each Sabbath. The three rooms of the house were swept daily. No food dropped on the floor was allowed to stay and she would not permit goats to come into the house, as did our neighbors. Even tiny lambs had to be kept outside in shelter.

She walked to the distant stream daily to wash clothes during all the years when her family was growing; and daily also she went with a tall pitcher, of Grecian design, to the fresh water well at the edge of the compound. Here, as was the custom of her day, she met all of her friends and neighbors and chatted with them. It was at this well, over the years, I heard my mother's innermost convictions poured out in debate with woman and with man.

Years later I was to realize that my pretty mother was politically minded and, since she could not debate in the square or at the temple, which were the strongholds of men, she turned the village well into a debating place. There, in her woman's realm, she took on and defeated many wise men and spread her own political thinking throughout the village; and finally, throughout the central part of Galilee.

22

Mother had been raised in a family of high priests and from her infancy had heard the facts of political and social changes and the personalities and causes behind them. In her beautiful head she had a mind as keen and as retentive as any man, even my father. And in her small body she had a heart that would have fitted any lion of Judah. Nothing would have pleased her more than to have organized an army to sweep against that injustice which she called, "Roman tyranny and tax!"

Standing in her tidy robe, small and fair, she seemed an easy match for any man. As her fame spread, important men came to meet her challenge at the well and went away convinced. Sometimes she made enemies; - men who tried to silence her by pressure from the authorities because they thought she was too outspoken in her opinions. But she would never back down and once defied an overly officious Centurion. My mother's political interest came out of her family and also out of the times. Many times I heard her use history to prove her point and say such things as: "My grandfather was twenty when Pompey came as the pretended peacemaker between the Maccabean lines. But he turned conqueror and made our land a vassal of Rome, destroying the religious and the political liberties the Jews fought and died for under Mattathias Maccabee."

The Roman power overthrew the Jewish national independence sixty-three years before I, Jeshuau, was born. Thirty-seven years before I was born, when Mother was yet twenty years in the future of births, the unspeakably cruel Herod (later called The First, and, The Great) was made King of Judea by the Roman Senate. Three years later and seventeen years before my mother's birth, Herod had conquered Galilee and, after a long seige, had recaptured the sacred city of Jerusalem.

One of my mother's adversaries shouted in his wrath, "Herod, The Great, was a zealous builder. He built amphitheaters and the Royal Palace, forts, castles, and magnificent cities! He builded Caesaria in Samaria from sand dunes of the sea. He even rebuilt the Citadel of the Temple!"

"He was a builder indeed! He built a licentious

passion for ten wives, and into his flesh he built the loathsome disease of which he died. In his last days he built a hell upon earth by slaying Antipater, Alexander, and Aristobulis. And then, not satisfied with killing these sons, he also ordered the murder of his wife, Mariamne. He ordered a new bath for himself at Callirhoe east of the Jordan, but even the healing waters could not save him. The only things he did not destroy in his life were the palm trees of Jericho, under which he retired and died on April 5, A. U. C. 750. That was three years ago!"

"You remember the dates too well!"

My dear, beautiful mother pulled herself up to her tiny height and placed her hand upon my head, "I should remember, for your great builder has built himself an eternal condemnation by ordering the destruction of all male children born in Bethlehem in the year of Jeshuau's birth. We had to take the child to Egypt for seven months and dared not return until that Great Roman died."

"The tax of Rome is nominal and we are allowed religious freedom!" One debator challenged.

My mother's eyes flamed like two blue lances.

"True, each tax is nominal, but the poll tax and the property tax are not all! The right to levy import taxes is sold to the publicans yet we must pay all of these taxes even if we cannot find wherewithal to buy food. I say, any tax is a shame upon our history! And, of course, we have religious freedom. That is why our High Priests of our Temples must go and ask our Roman conquerors for the use of the Jewish sacred robes when we want to hold a religious service! Have we freedom because they do not tell us what to believe and when to go to worship, when we cannot hold a service without begging for the vestments of our priests? Have we religious freedom?"

"But that is necessary so they can be certain there will be no priests led to revolt, sponsored by the Levites."

"Oh, I see! Even as it was necessary to slay all the innocent children born in Bethlehem to prevent the rising of the King of the Jews?" With this, my mother stooped and hugged and caressed me. The many times I heard her use this argument, I never knew her to fail to turn to me with adoration and caresses.

In my mother's opinion the very bad political situation, in which conquerors strutted over the provinces and controlled the ritual vestments of the Levites, was not as bad as other conditions of the times. Many times when the long shadows of evening brought the cooling shadows to the heated arguments of the well, she would say something like this: "The fate of the Jews lies not within the hands of the tax-eating Romans but within the hearts of the Jewish people. We are all fools, weaklings and idiots! We have forgotten and deny the brotherhood of man in the service of God which made our people great and could make us great – even in these days. We fight each other over trivial ritual matters. This is our ruination; it is the touch of a loathsome disease which will burn our country's body and destroy our people as a nation. Through history have our prophets and priests not said that our only salvation is in unity? Have they not warned us that the Temple shall be destroyed and the people scattered when factions and disobedience arise? What are these great differences? Have not both modes of thinking been with us since the return from Babylon?

"Verily, the Chasidim, that is to say 'the pious', who returned from the exile, set themselves too firmly against all heathens and all laxities in the enforcement of the Levitical laws. And they deserve to be called the 'Perushim', meaning 'the separate ones' in derision out of which grew the term 'Pharisees'.

"The opponents naturally retorted that they were satisfied to be merely the Tsadiqim that is to say, 'the righteous', and out of this grew the Sadducees. These have, over the years, become the ruling Jews of the church, the high priests, and the higher class of society. What if the Sadducees deny the resurrection of the dead and deny that there is reward or punishment after death? Are there not items in the belief of the Pharisees that are just as imponderable?

"Do not the Pharisees insist upon an angel or archangel for every hair of the head? Do they not insist

25

upon an ascending scale of their Levitical purity, that is to say, separation from all that is profane or even sensible? Is not the Chabher, the highest of their four degrees of purity, the 'associate' of their organization, a synonym for one too pure and too punctilious? To them, has not the written law been insufficient to guide the daily conduct of man? Have they not over the years expanded and made comments and expositions upon the law which is known now as 'The Oral Law' or the traditions of the Elders? Has this not in turn given rise to the conceited, arrogant scribes who have made a vocation of copying the Written Law, teaching and mouthing it? And also learning the Oral Law so that they can spew it into the minds of the younger generation? Are these supercilious Scribes not a guild within the party of the Pharisees? Proud and boastful because their learning has brought them honor, and because they are usually called up to deliver the discourse in the synagogues of our people. Are not almost all Pharisees hypocrites, lacking humble and God-fearing men who are not puffed up because they are pure?

"The Zealots, another party within the ranks of the Pharisees, has risen within the last forty years. They grew under the rule of Herod, the so-called 'Great'. They would use force and the sword to bring about the reign of the Messiah, for whom we all wait. They, and they only to my mind, make complete sense. They are constant to their watch-cry: We will recognize no lord by Jehovah! We will pay no tax but to the Temple. We will have no friend but a Zealot! Given time, they may save our poor nation. But unless they do, the Pharisees, the Scribes, and the Sadducees will kill our nation with stupid rivalries that have no just cause. They will bring ruin upon our people, pulverize our Temple, and spread our believers through the entire world to have no place of their own-for a time-and a time!"

Often we would walk back through the warm night from the well and my mother would be transported into an ecstatic daze. And as my years of maturity approached, her influence had spread across the land until learned men came to sit and hear her. In my earlier days they

26

came merely to bait and bother her and she was often able to change the opinion of man and was proud when she could do so. She knew, as did all the people of my time, that the Jews were facing desperate days unless they changed their hypocritical insistence upon the Levitical laws. She always hoped that the Zealots would help her put forth the true Messiah.

"You expect the Savior of the Jews to be born just in the nick of time? That is a belief in miracles!" One Rabbi taunted her.

"I do not believe in miracles, Learned Rabbi! I *know* they exist. Have I told you the story of my uncle, the ancient and venerable priest, Zacharias? And his beloved wife of fifty years, the childless Elizabeth?"

Of course she had not, and this was indeed one of her favorite tales and it never failed to impress. So many times did I hear it that I had it memorized before I was six, though for many years, I thought it was just a story of her fondest imagining. But this indeed was the story of a miracle. I tell it here with all her delightful and picturesque embellishments.

"This miracle began in the first week of October, 748 A.U.C., and my uncle had passed his sixtieth birthday in the service of the Temple as a priest. This morning he had been selected from the priestly Course of Abia as Superintending Priest. He was to be honored with the Office of Incensing on the Golden Altar of Incense, glowing red with coals, very near to the heavy veil which hung before the Holy of Holies. Since he was a priest, and not of the Levites, he had come from his home in the south country in the hills of Judea. For he did not live in the Ophel quarter of Jerusalem, nor yet in Jericho. And all of us who knew him were proud, for his kindness and love were known in every mind and every heart.

"Where Zacharias stood, we knew God was present. We waited without the Temple gate until the three blasts of the silver trumpet wakened the city to life, and began the Morning Sacrifice with the massive gate of the Temple opening with the first light. For the priest on watch from the highest peak of the Temple had signalled the first-light sign. And those who had been washed and

27

purified, according to the ordinances, were in the Priestly Course under the direction of my beloved uncle. He had made the inspection of the priests and the courts of the Temple and had cast the lots to select the Course of Priests in the Hall of Hewn and Polished Stones. All was in readiness and we who loved him were great in the congregation, even before the organs of the Temple summoned us all to service.

"How glorious he looked as the celebrant Priest, bearing the golden censor, standing alone within the Holy Place and lit by the glow of the seven lights of the candalabra. How glorious indeed were the robes of his Office! And to the left of the altar was the table of the Shew Bread. To his left, that is the right or south side of the altar, shining with beauty, was the golden candlestick. How serene and confident he looked as he stood waiting for the special signal to spread the incense on the altar. The priests of the Course and people had withdrawn in reverence and were prostrated before the Altar of the Lord, offering their unspoken adoration. Zacharias saw the incense kindled and was about to prostrate himself in worship and then withdraw; but he stopped and his eyes were fixed upon the right or south side of the altar and between it and the golden candlestick.

"He suddenly stopped and stood half crouched but absolutely transfixed by what he saw. It was clear that he was troubled in his mind and that a great awe fell upon him. Thus standing, he was unmoving while the prayers of the people were offered, and our gaze was fixed upon the still form of beloved Zacharias. How great was our expectation and our dread as he at last turned and moved forward as one who walks in his sleep, to stand at the top of the steps which led from the Porch of the Altar to the Court of the Priests. For standing thus, as was the tradition, he was to lead in the priestly benediction which was given unto Moses thusly:

'The Lord bless you and keep you!
The Lord make his face to shine upon you and be gracious unto you!
The Lord lift up his eyes to you and give you

peace!'

"But this benediction which is spoken daily in the Temple before the meat offering, he could not speak! - though his neck strained, his jaws worked, and his eyes rolled with strain. Nor could he lead in the chant of psalms of praise and there were no words to accompany the joyous sound of music as the drink offering was poured out.

"All the priests, and then the people, realized that something of marvelous power had been shown to him in the sanctuary. He tried to show by signs that he could not speak. Nor could he speak for nine months thereafter.

"For he had seen the awesome form of a most beautiful angel, who spoke to his ears only and was visible to his eyes only. And the angel had said to my uncle, 'Zacharias, show no fear before me, but know that the barren wife of your youth, though now weighted with years, shall conceive and bear a son. And when her time has come, you shall call his name Jehochanan, that is to say, 'the Lord is gracious'. Great shall be the joy and gladness for he shall be filled with the power of God even from his mother's womb. He shall drink neither wine nor strong drink but shall lead the way wherein many of the children of Israel shall return to the Lord God. He shall have the power of prophecy and shall turn the hearts of fathers to children, and make the disobedient understand wisdom'.

"But Uncle Zacharias was fearful and asked for signs that this miracle was indeed from God.

"'I am Gabriel,' the angel said, 'I am sent from the presence of God to speak to you and bring you glad tidings. And the sign of my justice shall be this: You shall be unable to speak from this instant until the day that all these things are performed and you shall know this is all from God.'

"And when Aunt Elizabeth was delivered of her son, her friends would have called him Zacharias after the father, but she would not so name him. When Uncle Zacharias was asked what name he chose, he took a slate and wrote the name that the angel had given, and the dumbness fell from his lips. His first words were: 'Indeed the name shall be *Jehochanan*, that is to say, *John*.'

"Such is the power of God and the miracles he can and has delivered to save our nation and the Jews. But an even greater miracle occured during the sixth month of my aunt's pregnancy – a miracle that shall be told in due season."

Always, when she reached this point, my mother's eyes were upon me as if she spoke of something hidden that I should understand. From a very early age I was made to expect some marvelous thing that she would relate, – in a time, – in a time! She would often say to me when I asked her to tell of the great miracle, "Wait a time with patience for the story is meant for grown men and is not meant for the very young."

Such was my beautiful mother, strong, wise, clever, yet as tender at heart as should be the priestess of a temple. For no woman was ill or in labour but that my mother was there, her strong hands and her keen mind soothing away pain. Thus, through the years all Nazareth, as our village came to be called, adored, respected, loved and admired my mother. And what she spoke was believed and what she suggested was done for she was a power and a treasure such as walks seldom upon the face of the earth.

After she had hugged me and caressed me, my beautiful mother went into the room with the kitchen fires and left me to pull on and tie my sandals. I combed out my knotted auburn locks with a tortoise shell no redder than they. Then before I hurried outside to wash my face and hands, ears and neck in the stone basin at the right of the doorway, I looked closely at my family for I loved them dearly. I adored the sight of my beautiful mother playing with my brothers and sisters while she bathed them. It was all the more pleasing when she and my father laughed and played with us all and glorious indeed when they joined in singing joyous or religious songs. My mother singing in her sweet clear soprano, holding Mary-Beth, that is to say, Mary-Elizabeth, named for my mother and her aunt, mother of Jehochanan. Mary-Beth was the youngest at the time I went forth to the compound of the Nazar-Essenes, and she was then not a year old. My father would cradle Jo-Jo, that is Joses, who was a year older than Mary-Beth, on his breast; and bounce Jim-Jim, as we called James, upon his lanky knee. But I was a whole year older than Jim-Jim and stood upon my own, loving each one with an intensity and a passion that hurt my small breast.

Though I have written of my family at the time when I went forth to the Assembly Hall, in later years the scene was even more joyous and loving. For Simon, whom we nicknamed Zim-Zim and the people about called Simon of Nazar - I know not if this was for the village or street upon which we lived - Simon was born two and one-half years after Mary-Beth and a full two years before Da-Da, which was our loving name for Juda, the fifth son of my parents. The second daughter and the seventh child was eleven and one-half years younger than I. She was named after Mother and my grand-mother and was called Mary-Anna. We loved her very much and called her Mary-A to fit with Mary-B, for Mary-Beth. My youngest sister who was born when I was seventeen and away in Brittanin, was called Mary-J, or sometimes merely Eena for her name was Mary-Josephine, and she was named for my mother and my father.

This morning I tiptoed to the rawhide cot, over which a mattress of grass was laid and on which Jim-Jim slept so soundly. I touched his flaxen hair and was surprised that his lively blue eyes did not open in his smiling face. But he slept on and I turned to the hand-hewn rocking crib which held Jo-Jo. He lay with his head pushed against the upper slat and his rear raised above the coverlet and leaned far over against the side of the crib. And I smiled to myself that he could sleep thus on his neck and knees, and yet sleep so soundly. I touched him gently and whispered my love for him and for all this house. For I knew that I was going forth into a world of men of purpose and was leaving behind my hours of sunny childhood and aimless play.

3

SECRETS OF THE ESSENES

After my beautiful mother's last tearful outburst of emotion, we stepped out of our home in the pre-dawn cold. Even though it was almost mid-June and I was three weeks beyond my fifth birthday, I shivered in my cotton robe and pulled it more tightly about me. Neither my father nor any of the Aryans wore a headdress unless they were to be long in the hot sun of the unshaded desert. The crisp night wind touched our hair and it went through mine with sighing fingers as if the air itself grieved with my mother - that youth was flown too soon! We walked swiftly along Nazar Road which led from home to the big gate on the east side of the compound of the Essenes. But the silence of the sky-lit village turned into a bustle of purposeful activity and sound as we were passed through the ever-vigilant guard at the huge gate and entered the compound. Here all was a-bustle, though it was about three hours before sunup.

Many groups or platoons of men moved in many directions but there was a master design in everything they did. Each twelve-man squad had a leader who seemed to direct as well as help do the work. Several squads were busy sweeping the very road on which we moved within the compound. Others moved swiftly bearing baskets of fresh-smelling bread or fruit. Even a few squads were busy doing exercises, either stooping, squatting, jumping; or the favorite, which was to throw themselves face down upon the ground and then raise themselves twelve times, supported only by their toes and hands.

Everything was done in lovely rhythm. Every move was accompanied by the sound of words, or a rhythmic chant. Those who swept the streets counted rhythmically in Aramic, Hebrew, Greek, Latin, and even Egyptian in turn, or said the alphabet of each in turn. Each man answered with fervor the leader, and I felt that they strove to formulate a harmony of movement and sound, and all in a pleasant, resonant and vibrant voice. Each letter or number was said with a timbre and resonance of sustained tone that created a thread of living sound. Each man seemed to strive to make his voice more perfect than the others. One squad walked the way with us, and in five languages they repeated:

> Blessed, oh, blessed is the Lord,
> The God of compassion and All Love,
> Who has given me knowledge of Truth
> And wisdom to tell forth His wonders
> Unchecked, both day and night.
>
> Blessed, oh, blessed is the Lord
> For whose burdens I yearn,
> And in whose goodness I trust;
> On whom like a living rock,
> My faith is founded in Truth.
>
> Now that I know His Truth,
> Now that I look on His glory,
> And have wit to understand them,
> I will always tell forth His wonders
> Unchecked, both day and night.
>
> I give thanks unto my God
> And extol Him as the Rock,
> The firm foundation of faith
> And will gladly tell forth His wonders
> Unchecked, both day and night.

I was so enchanted with the beauty of the rhythmic phrases, repeated in many languages line by line that I quite forgot myself and stepped through the giant doorway into the Assembly Hall and glimpsed at least a thousand white-clad figures kneeling upon the polished floor of the Assembly. But not more than a blink could I look for a firm hand put me back into the night.

"Not too swiftly, my son. Wait here a time in patience until the Brotherhood is ready and the Master calls."

I stood alone in the darkness surrounded by the sweet cadences of many tasks being done with rhythm and energy. I realized that this was but a perfection of the technique my mother had used to teach me over the years; a way to help learn the greatest possible amount in the shortest possible time.

I startled when a pleasant voice near me said, "Child, should you not pray?"

I recognized the voice of the Master of the First Year, Habakkuk. "I would like to pray, sir, but I am too frightened."

"Fear not, my child, for in all things I am always with you."

Somehow, these were the perfect words for my moment in aloneness and strain, and I found myself praying silently inside my own self for strength and for guidance. I felt the warmth of the presence of the Master Habakkuk although he was a dim outline in the faint glow of the skylight. But only a few minutes went by before the door opened and a voice demanded,

"Who comes to this sacred portal?"

"One who seeks Light, Truth and Wisdom!" my father said.

"Is he prepared?"

"He is! He is come of a Holy Family, and is clean and healthy in body and mind."

"Let the Candidate be admitted to the Hall, there to await the call of the Gracious and Perfect Master."

A moment later I was inside the vast assembly hall, but there was not a person in the place! The overwhelming roof was supported on rows of enormous upright columns set about ten paces apart. The light of a taper, that had been thrust into my hand, reflected from these columns endlessly it seemed, but the enormous room

34

was empty and silent. The only sound was my quickened breath and the thudding of my heart. I moved aimlessly into the hall and at last sat in the center of the room and stilled the beating of my heart. The taper burned out but still there was neither sound nor motion. I wanted to cry - to run to the arms of my beautiful mother but the thought of my father's look of disapproval kept me still. After a while my physical self began to calm, my mental self began to ascend and I felt at peace, and safe.

Daylight began to filter through the openings high up near the roof. These were covered with screens made of translucent goat's bladders and let in light while it kept out dust and wind. But I sat still, my mind turned inward to my heart, my eyes upon the light above, until my father spoke to me.

"Arise, follow me!"

I looked for him but my eyes were light-blinded and I could not see him in the dark interior of the room. But I moved swiftly to follow the sound of his voice and my trust was complete. A hand steadied me and guided me to the man-sized steps which led down from the center of the room. In the dark my little legs were hardly long enough to reach but we followed the steps down, then struck a level path along which we walked hand in hand. Soon the path began to rise, and then to curve. Then we came upon steps which wound upward in the blackness. When it seemed that my legs could carry me no further, we came upon a level area, took forty paces, and I was shown by pressure that I should kneel.

To my surprise my knees did not strike bare ground but a cushion. I knew from the fragrance around us and the absolute blackness that we were within earthen rooms or a long cave. The air was still as it never is under the starry heavens. There was that pungent darkness that is found even in dry caves beneath the ground.

Before I could get my senses oriented, a voice boomed out of the blackness, "Who presents himself to the Botherhood?"

"The Candidate who shall be nameless if he pass not or test."

"Is he prepared to bind himself under an Oath for

life and to which he makes pledge of his very life?"

"Are you prepared to bind yourself under an Oath for life, and to which you make pledge of your very life, my son?"

"Yes, Father!"

"He is ready, Perfected Master of Light!"

"It is well! Let the will of the Brotherhood be done and the Oath administered!"

A voice trembled through my body with liquid notes, reaching ears like warm honey reaches the tongue. My father's voice was more wonderful and more resonant but this voice was a thing of melody and beauty, so fine and pure that its very sound waked the heart. I was so enchanted with the very sound of that voice that I did not actually hear the first part of the Oath, but remembering later, I think that part of my Oath, which can be now revealed, went thus:

"I, a poor, lowly and unnamed Candidate, do seek admission into the Brotherhood of The Elect, the Brothers of Light, and bowing myself humbly before the Perfect Master, do promise and bind myself for all my life to the following Oath and each of the several items of the Covenant.

"Above all, I will honor my Almighty Father in Heaven and serve Him.

"I will obey those who have rule over any land in which I may be. For under my Father, which is in Heaven, nobody has the rule of man for long without the aid of the Almighty Father.

"I will obey all my superiors in the Brotherhood of Light. If exalted by my Brothers to position of authority, will never misuse that authority or abuse anyone of lesser stature or power. Either as a Voter or Elector of the Brotherhood will my demeanor and worthiness be an example for others to emulate.

"I will deal justly with my fellow man even as I deal justly with my Brothers.

"I will live as an example of a true and pure heart and exercise justice and honesty to all men. I will harm no man either by impulse or under influence of other men, or by duress. Rather throughout my life, in secret or

36

sunlight, I will shun injustice and show mercy, and ever undaunted and untiring I will further the cause of justice and of Truth.

"I will preserve my mind from impure thoughts, from baseless impulses and I will preserve my hands and soul from the stain of unjust gain, or even just gain at the cost of my fellowman.

"I will studiously prepare myself in body to be strong and healthy, in mind to be firm and original, in memory to be agile and retentive, and to be faithful unto death in all the assigned duties of the Almighty Father or the Perfected Father of Light.

"I will strive to pass the tests of the four levels of the Brotherhood, and will be subservient and obedient unto all the requirements of my Elders or Brothers in daily activity.

"I will contend not with my Brothers or anyone and if I am smitten upon one cheek will yet turn the other in pity and in love.

"I will claim no power or credit of my own even as I will claim no income or property knowing that all goods, talents and capacities come from the Father which is in Heaven, through his perfect love; and all I can do, others can do, and more also, for it is the Father within which does all works.

"Therefore, I will hold myself to be the child of no man but of the Almighty and Everlasting Father which is in Heaven, and will accept as His Representative on Earth, the Father of the Brotherhood of Light."

To here, I was in full accord but the next phrase caused me to stop and my voice would not follow the chanter. The phrase was, "I will leave and disclaim the house of my father and mother and will never marry, have intercourse, or procreate children. I will leave and disclaim the house of my father and mother and will never marry."

Three times he repeated the words. I could not say them. It was as if a hand had stopped my mouth for I remembered the love of my beautiful mother and the joy I had of my brothers and adoration I had for my father. The voice of the Patriarch asked, "Do you not wish to go on?"

"I do, Sir, but I will not swear to forsake my family, my father and my beautiful mother. Nor will I swear not to bear children, for above all things, I love them! But I will keep your other commandments in love and obedience, Sir!"

There was a long pause and then something of a chuckle in the darkness. "Cantor, let that clause of the Covenant be stricken from the Oath, if no Brother objects. At this juncture, it has little validity anyway."

I thought I heard a ripple, a sigh of smothered laughter from many men but the beautiful voice continued with the Oath: "I will turn to the Brotherhood for guidance, spiritual, physical and mental, and for support and maintenance and satisfaction of all my wordly needs. And I promise that if he is in need I will never deny to a Brother aid, help or defense, though I may lose my life in his behalf.

"I will at all times faithfully interpret and explain anything of the laws of the Brotherhood but never in any other spirit than I, myself, have received it from the trained and Holy Elders. And I will faithfully preserve the goods and the properties of the Brotherhood and hide and take care of the archives, books and learning devices of the Brotherhood. And will reveal, never under any circumstances, to any outsider the place of the treasures, or the names of the angels with whom the Secret Master of Light has held communication.

"I will at no time, even at the forfeit of life, under travail or torture, betray or reveal any secret of the Brotherhood of Light to anyone who has not been prepared to receive it by the vote of the Sacred Order of the Perfected Ones.

"To all this, I bind myself for life; and, except for this, no Oath shall be sacred. And all promises shall be kept with 'Yea' or 'Nay'. But to this Sacred Oath, I bind myself for all my living days! And, if I break this Oath, I shall deliver myself into the hands of the Sons of Light, to have my bowels torn out with a sword, my head dismembered from my body, and my flesh strewn upon the earth for the eaters of flesh."

The voice stopped and I thought the Oath was over, but it was not. The Patriarch demanded, "Brothers, will you accept this Oath and thus bind the Candidate to the Sons of Light?"

"Yes, Master of the Perfect!" The sound must have come from a thousand voices, echoing in the cavern.

"Say, Candidate, who comes now unto the Brotherhood?"

"Jeshuau Joseph-bar-Joseph!" My father whispered in my ear and I said the name aloud.

"Who vouches for this Candidate's honor and holds himself to suffer the fate if the Candidate breaks his Oath and delivers not himself to punishment?"

"I, Joseph of Nazar, an Essene of Nazar!"

"Sponsor of this untried Candidate, why do you place your life in jeopardy for his performance of his covenant?"

"Because........", – the tension of nerve and mind seemed to have reached its highest point. But I was not prepared, as was any Candidate, for what happened within the next few breaths. There was a sound, a sort of rumble, which filled the air and then began to shake the very earth. The pad upon which my knees rested jumped even as my heart and my ears were appalled at the mighty sound. There was at the same instant a blinding light and my being leapt up in terror and in ecstasy. My body was instantly bathed in warmth which was a balm to my excited senses, a peace in the turmoil in my mind. Suddenly my startled eyes were filled with the blinding glory of the rising sun which rested as an orange-gold disk upon the eastern hills.

The entire end of a giant vault had suddenly been dropped away and I was facing the new sun and its rays poured down upon me like shafts of burnished spears hurled at me, and at me alone. I was in the mouth of a gigantic cave and was kneeling beside but slightly in front of my father. The Patriarch, the Secret Master, was seated in a golden chair and dressed in golden robes, his face toward us, his back to the sun. The sun surrounded him in a magnificent halo of light, so breathtaking in its sudden magical appearance that I felt

39

transfixed with emotion.

But the tension was increased even more. As if the word my father had started to speak was their signal, a thousand beautiful voices continued in unison: "This is my Beloved Son in whom I am well pleased."

An instant later a thousand voices spoke out of the darkness behind me in the recesses of the cave: "This is my Beloved Brother, for whom I will lay down my life."

Within the cave around me as far as the light would let me see, there were ranks or squads of white robed figures, each kneeling, each crossing his right hand over his breast, his palm over the heart. And the feeling mounted as an eagle in the sunlight. The first chorus of those around me began a chant in glorious voices. When the cadences dropped at the end of a phrase, the distant voices picked up the thought as a running cannon. The way it was done it was solemn praise to the Universal Master of All, followed immediately by a strain of praise to the Secret Earthly Master, who was a symbol of the Brotherhood and also of the Universal Power Come to Earth. This was a *Pean of Double Joy.*

Oh, Father Which Art In Heaven,
  Oh, Father Which Art On Earth,
All Hallowed is Your name;
  Revered is Your holy name;
Your sacred Kingdom is come,
  The sacred Kingdom is Yours
And Your will may now be done
  And the Father's high will may be done
On earth as it is in heaven.
  On earth as it is in heaven.
Give us this day our daily bread
  Give us this day our meal of love
And forgive us our trespasses
  And forgive us our trespasses
Even as we forgive those who trespass against us.
  Even as we forgive Brothers who trespass against us.
For great is Your Kingdom,
  For great is Your Power
Eternal is Your Glory
  And we are Your children

40

Forever and forever, Amen.

And love You forever, Amen.

Truly I say unto you, that the sound was a thing of moving beauty and the symbolism of the sun as a heavenly representative of the Universal Father and the Secret Master as the Earthly Representative was itself a poem. The moment was of such beauty and transcendent power that I felt lifted up into another dimension of enjoyment. All of the personal love and devotion which I had felt for my family now became a universal love and devotion, poured out upon these Brothers. Love for each was pouring from me, not a personal love but an impersonal love that was boundless, and I thought that surely I had reached the greatest possible heights of joy but more was yet to come in other ceremonies and other initiations.

From that moment on, every second of time I spent with the Essenes was devoted to improving the physical, mental and moral qualities of my being. No time was wasted. Yet there was never a feeling of hurry. When the ritual of the Oath was finished I was admonished that Essenes expect constant improvement upon all levels of man's behavior and told to present myself to Master Habakkuk for directions and instructions in languages, numbers, sciences and deportment. To Master Horenhab, he of the golden voice, I was to present myself for instruction in voice, music, speech and rhythm. To my father, Master Joseph, Master of Masters, I was to present myself for history and religious instruction of the Jews and also for the history and sacred religious instruction of the Brothers of Light.

We then rose and made our way back in squadrons of twelve, with a leader, toward the Assembly Hall. I realized that we had gone underground beneath the entire village of Nazar and up a tunnel inside the hill overlooking the eastern valley, and then into an enormous natural cave which might have held every house on the lovely hillside. I found later the magic of the earth shaking and sudden admission of the sun was accomplished by dropping a wall of rocks from the mouth of the cave into the lip of a cave below. Later, we carried the stones back up the incline, and placed them in

41

position for the next initiation. And this very effort was done with chanting, counting and recitations in many languages. It was said to be an exercise to improve our strength, especially our backs and legs. Even the first day I was not allowed to miss the exercise and was given rocks to carry up the steep incline that were almost, but never quite beyond my strength.

When the sun was well beyond the center line of day we heard the silver tones of the gong which called us to our midday meal which was called the Feast of Love. We all began to assemble toward the Assembly Hall but by way of a roofed structure that had no sides. Here we entered and took off our work clothes and walked through the building clad only in a fly in front and rear, tied with a string about the waist. At the other end of the building we came upon a trough which was kept filled by Novitiates who ran from the stream a hundred yards away bearing two buckets of water. Since the bathing form was higher than a man's head, they had to climb up a ladder before they could dump their buckets and race back toward the stream.

We took a quick bath and walked on to our own rack and towel where we dried, and then donned our white robes. Then we assembled in squadrons for entry into the Assembly Hall. But on that first day I had not yet earned the privilege of bathing or eating with the Brothers, both being considered sacred. Indeed my first Feast of Love was a lesson in itself, as with everything else within the compound.

At my first meal I was guided to a table in a far corner to the right of the Secret Master, but far over in the corner. Two of the Brothers who had seated themselves at the table before I arrived got up and moved away. I was left completely alone, not in sight of my father without stretching, and out of view of the Brothers.

Master Habakkuk merely said, "Sit there! Keep your head bowed. Do not eat until the Master of Light speaks to you and tells you you may eat. Sit still!"

I sat at the lonely table, and while the table was low the bench was high, and soon my legs were asleep and I wanted to squirm. I sat still while long passages from the Manual of Obedience were read in Aramaic, Greek and Latin. Before the reading was over I had the passage memorized. It ran:

"Every person who may desire to join the Community of The Elect must pledge himself to respect the Father and his fellowmen, to live in accordance with the rules of the community, to seek the Father diligently, to do what is good and worthy in sight of the Father and in accordance with what he has commanded through Moses and through the prophets who are his servants; to keep far from evil and cling to good, to act truthfully and righteously and justly and walk not in stubborness, guilty at heart, lustful of the eyes, or doing any manner of evil in thought or deed whatsoever; to bring into the bond of mutual love all who have shown their ability and willingness to carry out the Statutes of God's Perfect Brotherhood."

After this special paragraph there was a Blessing read in Hebrew, Egyptian and then Greek. It ran:

"Father in Heaven, Bless these Brothers in the Eternal Covenant which will stand forever; and open to them from heaven the Perpetual Spring of Faith Unfailing.

"Favor them with all manner of blessings and make them privy to that sacred knowledge which is possessed by the Holy Being.

"Bless them with Perpetual Spring and withhold not from those who thirst the Living Waters of Truth and Right.

"Bless and keep them from all evil and destroy the frenzy of the damned.

"Bless and keep them from every corrupting spirit.

"Favor them with salvation and cause them to delight in peace all abounding. Favor them with the holy Spirit and with loving kindness and understanding, and keep them in truth, health, and the Eternal Covenant.

"Bless then with insight into Eternal Truth and give peace between each man, even unto his offspring, forever."

When these blessings were said over and over in

43

three languages, I had them memorized. But I was not ready for the hurt of hunger and pride that came. For Novices in blue clothes, which was the color of work robes, came into the hall in squadrons, carrying fragrant fresh bread, jars of savory vegetables and lamb, and also freshly cooked fruit. They also put down before me a bunch of ripe grapes and each grape lured me like a friendly eye. The fragrance was almost overpowering, so was my hunger, and I resented having bccn told not to eat until directed to do so. I looked around from under my lashes and felt all the more hurt that no one was looking at me, or cared if I disobeyed.

My little heart rebelled and my stomach began to roar its resentment at such treatment. Wasn't the order silly? Why was such a useless order given? There could be no cause not to eat - everyone else was! My hunger and my rebellion mounted until I thought of leaving the bench and running home to the arms of my beautiful mother. I could explain to her that it was foolishness to starve to death when food sat on the table and grapes almost reached for one's mouth. Then I decided I would stay, but I would not even taste their old food. And before my eyes the hot foods and the vegetables and lamb began to look cold and to be covered with that film of grease known only to lamb dishes!

Unperturbed by my rebellious self-pity the Brotherhood ate in silence or with a minimum of talk, and during the entire meal one of the Brothers stood at the far end of the hall and read from the Torah in Hebrew and Greek, and he also started in Latin, when the Perfected Master raised his hand.

"Brothers, are all finished? Then let it be known that the son of Joseph has passed his first test in obedience! Joseph-bar-Joseph, you may now eat!"

I dared not raise my head for there were huge tears of self-pity in my eyes and I was disturbed that my good hot food had grown cold. I pretended to say my personal prayers while I squeezed the tears from under my eyelids. But then I found I was truly praying in my heart, for strength and stamina to learn to heal. I heard a small click and looked to see my plate of foods taken away by a young Novitiate. I could not speak but a moment later a bigger platter of food was placed before me piping hot! And I fell to eating with a will, with a great joy in my heart for I had seen that my father half rose to look across the room, - to my indignity! I knew by the look in his eyes and the slightest of nods that he was pleased with me. I ate steadily while the Brothers ran through a series of prayers to which I did not listen and did not memorize, but soon my little stomach was filled and the ordeals of the day seemed bearable again.

The prayers were finished as I finished my meal and the Secret Master said, "In humility, let every man carry the plate of the Brother to his right to the scullery and wash it well!"

It turned that the Perfect Master came to my table and took my plate and carried it to the scullery. "Sir, I should carry yours!"

"No, son, this is our lesson in humility. For not even the Lord of the Brothers of Light is above his duty to the Order or above the most menial of tasks. Remember that!"

Every move was used to train the body, the mind, the heart, the morals or the spirit of the Brotherhood. How swiftly and how simply they taught. I had been taught the need for obedience without argument or justification of authority. I had been taught perseverance in spite of personal desire or hardship, and I had been taught true humility and service, all at a single meal. And my training had not yet begun or, verily, had it? How could one say when his official instructions began in the Brotherhood of Perfection: Each assignment, duty, detail or act, could be and usually was for the purpose of training someone along the line. The training stopped not until the Secret Master himself was reached. And at times he seemed to be the intent of all training and of all effort. For the method of precept and example was employed fully. But there was ample time spent under personal discipline such as lettering, composition, ciphering and art. No concept was either to small or too large for the deliberate use of the Brotherhood.

Each week each man of a squad was expected to give

45

a resume of what he had learned that week and woe betide him who missed the implication and the spiritual value of some of the physical drills. I was assigned to a squadron of new men and our first duties were to sweep every inch of the street of the compound, and do it daily. This we did while rhythmically chanting our alphabet, counting to one thousand and doing mental sums, or repeating well-known maxims in any of the five languages, and at the command of our leader.

Our leader was a man of the desert, Ishmaul, a broad man and medium short, like myself. But he was dark of skin and brown of eye, and as time went by I came to know that he was a *Hanif*, a natural mystic, a man who had sudden insights into things beyond the physical or mental. He was, as most mystics are, a man of powerful and contagious joy, but his moods ran from the prankish to the harsh disciplinarian. But in any mood, he did ten times the work of the other twelve in his squad. We came to love him and to fear him with equal candor, for each month we were to tell each member of our squadron how we felt toward him, and our reaction to him was of no apparent consequence to him. Under Ishmaul's rule, I was granted no special favors but had to do my share of whatever work was assigned to the squad, and to do it to the utmost of my skill and with all the strength of my little body. When it came our turn to carry water for the daily Bath of Love, I was given two buckets of small size. But as the weeks went by and my strength increased, Ishmaul gave me ever larger buckets to hasten the development of my strength.

"Reach! Reach! Do all you can, then more! For progress lies not in doing but in the reaching! He who does not overreach himself every day will never grasp heaven!"

One day in my second year, just a week after Simon was born to my beautiful mother, I was carrying water when a sudden flash of insight came to me. During our rest period I cut a curved branch from a willow tree, notched it and tied a leather thong at each end. These thongs I then tied to the buckets. Using this crude yoke, I was able to carry the two regular sized buckets. I was so proud and expected a compliment from Ishmaul but he said nothing and did not seem to notice my improvement. But the next day on our rest period, he crept to the bank of the stream and tested my yoke. He then tied two buckets on each side and tested that. I pretended to sleep in the shade of our special tree, but inside, my heart was eating me with anger. The next day he brought two enormous buckets holding almost three times as much as an ordinary bucket and, during our rest period, he crept down to the river to try the yoke with that enormous weight. But still he said nothing except that on the day before the fifth Sabbath he told me to bring my yoke to the Assembly Hall. This was the time of the quarterly report to the Brotherhood and he called me forth to demonstrate that I could carry much more weight safely with a crude yoke. He then took the yoke and connected it to his enormous buckets, carried them himself and then asked the Masters to test the yoke. This was done and the Sons of Light voted to have two hundred yokes made of special wood, and curved at the neck so that it would not hurt the bone. And our squadron was taken from its water carrying assignment and assigned to make the yokes under my father's skilled direction.

Ismaul then gave me full credit for the invention of the yoke which would allow the transport of water in half the time and with half the effort, thus freeing squadrons of Brothers for other work.

But I felt a deep remorse at my bitter anger at his testing my yoke and told the Assembly, "Sirs, I would like you to know, Ishmaul of the Desert, did test and try the method and his mind and skill prefected its use. He deserves more credit than I for I saw no benefit to the Brotherhood but only to myself."

The Secret Master stroked the gray strands of his long beard and nodded. When Ishmaul protested and said that the credit was mine – for credit at that time of training might determine if we were allowed to progress in the studies, the Son of Man raised his hand and said, "Brothers, let us make the accounting thus: We will then render unto Bar-Joseph that due which is his; and unto

Ishmaul, that due which is his! Thus the Holy Order of the Father shall have no contention."

The work was long but it was not really hard and the studies were easy; well, all studies except writing and composition. I could never cipher with great ease and beauty and it was as if I could not speak when I tried to write down my thoughts. Such effort! But in two years I had mastered all of the learning of four years and even more. For this I deserve no credit. My mother and father had taught me well. And the Father in Heaven gave me a mind that was agile and a memory that was as prodigious as it was accurate. This was the marvel of my preceptors. Once I was called upon in strange emergency.

It was the habit of the Brotherhood to pay all its debts to the other compounds for lodging, food, materials, and other things, once a year. On this year I had been assigned to the Stores and Accounting Master that I might learn of such things. I had seen the scroll on which all our accounts were made before it was sent to our scroll keeper, Baradas of Hebron, and to the other compounds, at such places as Bethany and Mount Carmel. Our Brother was killed by a lion in the Samarian desert and the scroll was destroyed by its claws and teeth. I was asked if I could recall the exact items on the scroll and all columns. I meditated on it for an hour, then in a frenzy of haste recreated the scroll exactly, entering the amounts into each column and recalling accurately whether the amounts were due in Roman or Jewish money. This was most important, since if we received Roman coin or if anyone demanded it, we were compelled by Roman law to pay in Roman money. Also involved was our belief that the Brotherhood must be exacting and careful to meet every legal requirement so that no criticism might befall our actions.

Jewish laws require that everyone attend the local synagogue of the Temple of Jerusalem on the Sabbath and on certain religious feast days. Our Brotherhood was most punctilious about attendance although we were not basically of the Jewish faith, as were some of the other compounds. Some of our compounds, particularly near the northeast tip of the Dead Sea, were entirely Jewish.

Furthermore, the religious instruction of the Jewish faith we received within our compound was more intensive than that received even in the synagogue. In fact, one of the tests for those who wanted to rise to be Masters, or teachers of the Brotherhood, was based on our saying,

"He who can teach the teachers of others,
May teach the lowest of our Brothers."

To be allowed to start at the lowest grade of teacher in our compound one was required to subtly, but effectively, teach the High Priest at the Temple at Jerusalem. Before one was allowed to attempt this, he must be able to teach his own Rabbi. What he taught had to be within their own faith and their own belief and was to be done without arousing prejudice or antagonism, and with complete respect for the priest and his belief.

When I decided to attempt this, it led me to the amazing discovery of the White Brotherhood.

4
SECRETS WITHIN SECRETS

My beautiful mother never accepted my success in the Brotherhood with ease. Often, when I would relate some trivial incident, I would find her eyes looking at me with wonder at what she saw. As the years went by, she grew more and more direct in her challenge of my father's authority over me. At times she seemed to intimate that I was not his son. But when she found me staring at her in disbelief, she burst into tears and left the kitchen. Outside of this seldom felt but brutally confusing tension, she loved me with a tenderness we of the Brotherhood reserved for the Eternal Father.

Once, however, her political beliefs brought her to openly challenge my patient father with: "You don't seem to care if the Messiah never comes to our people! There is no hope for our nation until the One Who Has Been Foreseen comes to redeem our people from political slavery."

My father then turned to her and, using questions, put over his point. One of the things I had been taught by him was that a truly initiated man never makes bold statements but wins his points with questions.

"Are you sure, beloved, you know what I truly think? Could it be that the future strength of our nation lies not in the redemption of the Sadducees, Pharisees and Zealots? Could there be some value in the common poor man? Could it be that the worth of the ordinary man is greater than that of the priest or Rabbi? Can there be some exceptional worth in the poor? Could it be that they may inherit the earth? Could it be that they are secretly blessed because they are meek and strive not with destiny? Could it be that in their humbleness there is more power than in the Roman legions? Is it possible that the strength of the people may be loosed by Essenes because they make no effort to compel any person, or to guide the life of any other man? Could it be that the Essenes may gather the poor as a shepherd gathers his flock? Could it be that he who would be King of the World must raise up the humble, exalt the poor, and be a citizen of the kingdom of the meek and lowly?"

I saw the tremendous impression his words made upon her and how her blue eyes wandered to me in speculation.

But from that moment on, my mother seemed less resentful of my father and his relations with me and at times seemed almost to tolerate his authority. She was very insistent that I attend the Tabernacle of Nazar as much as possible, which was two afternoons a week in addition to the Sabbath when all the Brotherhood went out of compulsion and command. Personally, I thought it was a waste of time and so did many of my Brothers. But it was part of my duty and we were careful of duty. The Rabbi Borrenchan was a small man, very florid of face and nervous and seemingly sickly. He was not a brilliant man though he was studiously learned, therefore, he was conceited and opinionated. He was most jealous of his position and his prerogatives and was, therefore, subject to flattery. Because of my mother's almost hysterical insistence, backed by instructions from my superior, I spent the extra time required to take extra instruction in the Jewish religion from the "Orthodox priests of the Great Religion." With my amazing memory I soon was helping the Rabbi and my father gently chided me that I was teaching him as his Master. But my father loved the situation for he taught me more of the Jewish religion than was found in the Torah or other Books of Laws. He helped me clearly see that the Jews were their own worst enemies and were, in their very striving to "live by the law",

51

killing their own hope of doing so.

He often said, "Man lives not by the letter of the laws but by the spirit thereof. God gave the laws in spirit. Man makes fetters of the letter of the laws!"

Perhaps the time I most resented spending with the Rabbi Borenchan was before the annual trip to the Temple in Jerusalem for the Paschal Feast and the registration of the ones who had come of age. Each male who had reached his twelfth birthday before the Feast of the Passover was required to present himself to register and to be tested by the priest on his learning in the religion; for he came to Age of Acceptance at thirteen years of age.

How strange that the Feast of the Passover and the strict Jewish religious law should make possible a moment that was so important in my development. For before my twelfth birthday, I had made up my mind to attempt to become a Master, or teacher, in the Brotherhood, which required that I teach the High Priest of the Temple. This was no easy matter and many more failed than passed that test. The High Priests were deeply learned in the narrowness of their laws and they were impatient, arrogant and proud, even verily as men are who inherit power or place.

First of all, the candidate had to pass the required test of the priests and become a Son of The Commandment. Then, with Brothers in the audience to watch and check him, he had to entrap the most learned men of the Jews and teach them in their own beliefs. Only when his Brothers unanimously agreed that he had succeded could he then be given the title of *Rabboni*, that is to say, Master, and teach his own Brothers.

Many things fed into this decision I made to become a teacher, but perhaps no one thing was as important as the attitude of my beautiful mother towards my cousin. He came from the hill country of Judea in the high and rugged land south of Jerusalem when I was nine, just by my birthday. Aunt Elizabeth wanted him to have children around him and did not want to raise him in a house with one old woman since she was past fifty when he was conceived. She especially wanted him, for some reason I could not then understand, to come to Nazar and join the

Brotherhood, even as I had, and live with us.

Jim-Jim was eight, almost; Jo-Jo was almost six; Mary-B was nearly five; Simon was two; and there was room for an almost grown boy of ten. My mother was delightfully eager about his coming and my father was pleased. For we loved our family and all our relatives were always welcome for any length of time. Uncle Zacharias had died suddenly and we knew not why.

Jehochanan arrived with an Essene caravan from Bethany, and passed his initiation that very day on the strength of the fine record that I had made with the Brothers. That night he came to my mother's table for the first time, his eyes big, brown and shy. John-John, as he became to us all, was big and, even at near ten, he was like a grown man who had a serious mission. He moved slowly but relentlessly and he was soon loved by everyone. He was a natural leader and gathered all about him in love. He also was a natural preacher and talked in a most interesting manner for hours about the most insignificant things.

When later his mind was filled with the beginnings of his lifetime beliefs, he held men so fascinated they even forgot to breathe. From the moment he came into the house he and Mother were often in whispers and in conspiracy, and then would look at me with eyes of strange tenderness and great awe. Verily, John-John was as gifted and possibly more gifted than I. He was calm and very bright and my mother's merest suggestion to him was as much as a divine order. He gave to my mother the adoration she deserved and which we were taught was reserved for the Secret Master, who represented the Eternal Father on Earth.

Aye, like my father, John-John was a *Hanif*. He walked in constant contact with his personal Father in Heaven. Frankly, I even envied him for, from the earliest days of his life, he seemed to know exactly what he wanted to do. Everything he did was to prepare himself to do that thing which he had come to do. He was so self-contained, so assured, so certain. I was perhaps a little jealous of his relationship with my beautiful mother. Not jealous of the love he took, for there was always love

53

and affection to spare, but jealous of the understanding which seemed to be between them. So burdened was I with this that I came down with a catarrh, an illness which was never heard of in my father's house. He came to see me and sent me immediately to the Secret Master with these words: "Go! Unburden yourself! For your cell-self feels it has sinned, or your body would not take a cold!"

Before our venerable Patriarch I trembled but confessed my jealousy and my confusion over my mother. He listened fully and then he said, "Son, your mother bears a great burden of belief which she surely will tell you when you are a little older. Wait that time with love and patience. Now arise, and go forth to work. These sins are forgiven you by the Father! Go!" I went forth and my catarrh was gone, and never did it come again nor was I ever ill.

On my tenth birthday, John-John and I were accorded a most important honor and privilege. The Brotherhood took recognition, partly in jest and mostly in earnest, of our outstanding record. They voted to permit variation from the rule that no one could be a full Brother until he reached his twentieth birthday. At the meeting John-John stood beside me, big and deep-chested, with a calm face brought to intensity by large and rounded eyes in an almost olive skin. We shared the same bed and were taught by the same Rabbi and by my father. But we were assigned to different squadrons in the Brotherhood and saw each other only in passing. John-John tried, in everything he did, to take my burden, to lighten my way, to make my path more peaceful and easier. But on this day we stood shoulder to shoulder sharing an honor never before granted. We had passed all the mental tests of learning the Masters could devise, and were physically developed beyond our ages. Sometimes we would dispute with each other to sharpen our own belief and to learn to express our convictions better. We were grown in mind and emotion but I think the thing that caused us to be given the honor was our Love Bath improvement, which caused me to learn of the White Brotherhood, and almost cost John-John his very life.

We were always trying to work out ways to do more

of the physical work of the Brotherhood in less time and with less effort. In three months after he came we had devised and built a windlass and belt that lifted the rocks of the Initiation Wall back in place. It could now be rebuilt in one hour by ten men, whereas it had before required a thousand men almost the same time.

A while later, still flushed with our success, we saw that the creek, from which we carried the water for the Love Bath, circled close to the upper corner of the compound, then swung far out and came back in a sweeping circle to cut across the lower edge of the property. We also noticed that once water was placed in a siphon it would continue to flow until stopped by some outside hand. Using our rest periods, we carried rocks to make a dam across the bed of the creek; then filled the creek with straw filled with clay, thus making a fairly deep pond where there had been merely a purling stream. We then cut and fitted the joints of many hollow canes into which we could thrust two fingers. We then curved the cane by fastening it, while green, between pegs on the ground.

When all was in readiness we had a cane stretching from the pond across the roof of one building and ending in the trough from which the water was taken by spigots for the daily bath. We fastened the canes at the roof by means of a belt of leather and also at the trough. But to start the siphon, we had a special idea. I was at the trough ready to cap the cane as soon as it was filled with water. John-John, up at the pond, was to slowly fill the cane with water, then dive down and fix the end of the curved cane to a stake in the center of the pond. Thus anchored, it would be safe from falling, and the water could run through to the trough. There, with a wooden plug, we could stop the flow of water any time we desired or start it by the simple removal of the plug. We had done it all on our rest periods over many weeks and were in readiness; but also over-eager and, therefore, unwary.

When the canes were full of water, John-John went into the water and sank with the curved cane to set it in the stake. He surfaced, called to me to release the plug, then dived down to inspect the end of the siphon, to be

55

certain no mud or dirt was flowing in.

It was the mode of our Brotherhood that at no time was our nakedness to be an offense to the Father in Heaven. We wore around our waist a cord of seven strands of twisted flax and in front and back, over our private parts, had flags of linen. I knew not that his flag had caught in the siphon trapping him under water by the strong cord around his waist. I knew only that suddenly the water stopped flowing and something like a blue light touched my head and told me of his hazard. I sprinted to the pond and dived in even in my work robe and moments later had pulled him free and pulled him to the bank.

But he had been under water too long - and John-John was unconscious. I carried him over my shoulder and water streamed from his mouth and nose, and I felt greatly confident that the healing my father had taught me through the years could save his life. I tried to revive him but it would not work, and panic gripped me.

From the instant that John-John came into danger, his mind seemed to make some magical direct connection with my own and his thoughts, his feelings, his agonies were upon me. I felt the pain of the pressure of the water in lungs and stomach, the agony of the lungs bursting for air, and at last the utter anguish of the separation of his spirit from his punished body. I felt the separation as unbearable pain in every nerve and cell of my body and my thoughts were snarled in terror at the thought of losing him - for death to my own self would have been kinder.

Death itself did not frighten me for in the Brotherhood we were taught that to die was but to be born into the spirit world where the pangs of flesh could not enter. The thought of losing him and thought of my beautiful mother's desolation if he departed threw me into concern - not for the dead, but for the living. I picked him up as we did the sacks of wheat from our field and, with him over my shoulder, ran back toward the compound, calling at the top of my voice for help. I saw suddenly in the middle of the compound, near the upper gate, the figure of my father and he came across the yard toward me. I put John-John down upon the earth in the shadow of the bathing trough.

"Oh, father! Help me! Help me! John-John is dead! He has drowned and he is dead!"

How strange my father looked to my excited eyes. Like himself - yet different. It was as if he floated over the tan earth, his feet scarcely touching the dirt. Yet he was strangely translucent as if the sun shone from deep inside his flesh. He moved with a calm deliberateness that caused me to urge him to greater speed for he seemed to be completely detached and almost indifferent. But his face was so calm that I thought he had not heard me as he stopped at my side and looked down upon the pitiful sight of John-John. He moved his hands in a token of blessing. Then he said calmly to me, "See, he is not dead. He only sleeps. Wake him!"

"But, sir! I have tried! I have failed!"

"That sin of failure is forgiven. Try again, with full knowledge and strong will as I have taught!"

Obediently I turned back to John-John. His face was ashen and his flesh was rigid as I kneeled beside him, stretched him out upon his back. Then, out of my well of love, I lavished my thought energy upon him and willed him to be alive. I did all that I knew, recalling all that my father had taught me but John-John did not move nor open his eyes.

"He is dead! I cannot awaken him! He is dead!"

"He is not dead! He's asleep! Wake him!"

Again I tried, in terror if I failed, in pity for myself and my family; but all my training was as naught.

"He is dead! No man can save him now!"

"*You of little faith!* Try with the faith of a mustard seed! And miracles will fall around you!"

"Oh, Father!" Tears were streaming from my eyes so that I could see him only as a floating vapor and I was sobbing so that I could hardly see. "I have failed - no man - no man - can save him now!"

"No *man* can ever save him, my son, for it is not man but the Eternal Father who does the work. Death is but a deeper sleep. Command your physical self! Command your Divine Self! *Raise him to his feet!*

"I cannot!" I collapsed upon his stiffening body.

I felt the fingers upon my shoulders - that gentle strength with which I had been thrust out of the Assembly Room and guided from harm or controlled as I approached for my Oath, or guided in my healing studies - was now fierce and cold. I felt the blow upon each cheek that rocked my head from side to side.

"Stir your faith! Deny you not your divinity! Think! Why have you tried to save him?"

"For - for our love for him - his love for us."

"Personal reasons!"

"For what reason can I save him?"

"Answer from your learning!"

"F-f-f-for an eternal principle to which I am detached but I cannot see - ." I would have collapsed again but the fingers were like steel bands upon my shoulders and slowly my panic-filled mind saw the reason I had failed. "I-I will try again - willing that he be saved to serve the Eternal Father and his fellowmen."

The hands were gone and I felt a great loneliness. "Father. I'm afraid!"

"Put out fear! For if fear is in you to the size of a mustard seed, your faith is as nothing, and you cannot command your Inner Divine Presence."

I sat very still and breathed in the way I'd been taught - to still my physical self. The hysteria dropped from me and I felt the warm flow of my father's presence. I worked on my mind and my emotions and my consciousness. At last I was able to poise in the sphere of complete indifference to my personal feelings, or love - to sit in spiritual equipoise between the antipodes of heaven and eternity.

Verily, I had known from the beginning that a man in hysteria or fear, or a weakling faith, could not do the Master's work. But as I calmed my outward mind and sank within, felt a warm blue-white light that seemed to flow from my father's presence into my head. I was filled with a glow, a radiance, power, and suddenly *I could not doubt!* I knew with a knowledge beyond mere belief, with a certainty beyond all reasons, that I had the ability to heal and to save my cousin! I held my self still for a dozen breaths, then rose and stood over the body.

"Father in Heaven! Let Your will be done! He sleeps! Let him now awake!"

Some of the power, the glory, the energy of the Kingdom leaped from my head and body, touched John-John and enveloped him with a flash of blue-white fire. I took his hand gently but determinedly and with absolute certainty began to pull him firmly as if to help him rise up to his feet. First there seemed to be an image of him rising within the purple haze around us. It seemed like the shimmering image seen on a hot desert, and this image stood upon its feet, while the body still lay upon the ground. Then, as if I lifted by my will, and guided by my hand, the body came to its feet and moved into the shimmering form. At that moment, his big eyes opened, he sighed a mighty shuddering sigh and gulped for air. The living blue-white fire from my body continued to bathe him as he gasped several times. His ashen skin began to change to ruddy color, then slowly to smooth olive.

"Thank you, father," I said over my shoulder, for I knew that but for the disciplined help and living fire my father had given me I could not have saved John-John.

But - my father was not with us! I looked around for him but John-John collapsed and I turned back to him; but he was merely weak and gasping for the energy from air lost for too long a time. He sat upon the earth and panted but I could do nothing to help him and turned back to look for my father. I saw him - not near the upper gate but just within the lower gate which opened to the trail from our house. He was running toward us and near the Assembly Hall he was joined by the Secret Master and other teachers. He stopped at my side and now he looked like himself - not like an image. He saw my look of appraisal and his eyes locked with mine, and his thoughts and his hand signalled me to silence. He nodded and his face was placid and calm and when he spoke there was a note of laughter in his voice.

"John-John, tell me - what do you think?
Will you ever want another drink?"

John-John sat for a few breaths in stunned surprise at such levity. Then he laughed aloud. "Uncle Joseph, this day I have just been too well baptized in water, but I also have been baptized in living flame."

We explained about the improvements which we had made and merely said that John-John had almost drowned in our efforts. As I looked around at the faces of my Brothers I saw that only three would really understand what had happened. These were my father, the Secret Master, and Johanan whom my father had healed of his severed wrist years before. There was more interest in the improvement than in John-John's near-death, and we were cheered by the squad assigned to carry water. Two squads were set to work making the dam permanent and the hollow canes more secure.

But I marvelled much in my heart concerning the things that had happened. Yet, when I tried to express my thanks to my father, he held me with his level gaze and said, "The greatest sin is to doubt your divinity! Do not thank me, thank the Father Eternal, for He alone can do the work of miracles!"

Two subsequent items caused me to ponder long, to question myself and perhaps, to doubt. I hurried home to tell Mother, Jim-Jim, Jo-Jo, Mary-B and Simon about the wonderful thing my father had caused me to do - had, in fact, done through me. My beautiful mother listened quietly and there was no doubt shown on her face that this had come about.

She said, "How wonderful, Jeshua! Joseph could not have helped you as you imagine."

"Why couldn't he?"

"Because he was there on the bed asleep! When we heard you call for help, we could not even wake him!" Jim-Jim said.

"That's right! Jim-Jim and I were playing there on the high place when we heard you scream for help and saw you carrying John-John from the pond near the upper gate."

"They told me what was happening and I tried to wake your father but he would not awaken!"

"He was very still - very still - and did not breathe."

"Still!" Jo-Jo said, "He was stiff and rigid!"

"We tried to awaken him," Mother explained, "then ran to the lower gate to get help. We were there talking to the guard when Joseph came hurrying by. When we tried to tell him what had happened, he merely hurried on saying, "Yes, my love, I know!" But, how could he know? He was so sound asleep!"

I did not know. And it bothered me greatly until I resolved to face my father with this mystery. But my challenge did not even cause him to blink, yet over his eyes came a mist as if he retired to some distant height beyond the clouds of my unknowing. For a long time he looked at me, his eyes seeming to see through my head and far out beyond. I knew he turned over in his mind his response, and that I could only wait.

Suddenly, he said, "My son, it is good for you to ponder how a man can be in two places at the same instant. It is good for you to wonder why he could not be awakened and why he was very stiff and rigid. But I cannot yet tell you whether it will *do any good for you to ponder* or not." Suddenly he smiled, that wonderful smile that untangled cords of doubt and wonder and made my heart resonate to his very being. In a sing-song he added,

"Though you chain me and you bind me,
And you beat me with a stick,
I will not say one word more than
White Brotherhood and Order of Melchizedek."

Oh, how very much I loved my wise and wonderful father at that moment. He told me with those humorous lines that he could not tell me anything about Orders in which he had taken Oaths of Secrecy and he told me the names of the Orders themselves. But I knew that nothing would cause him to say more.

So we applied ourselves to learning more about how to heal by the use of the mind and will. That night I was again exhausted and ravenous. When I had eaten and fallen asleep against John-John's patient shoulder, I was excused and went to bed. As I lay in a torpor I heard Mother speaking softly to John-John and to my father.

"Jeshua has now raised from the dead! Is that not proof enough of his divinity? Can there be further

61

doubt?"

"My beloved, is not every man inwardly divine?"

Afterwards, my father treated me with the same attitude, except that he was a little more severe with me in my training. My beautiful mother and John-John treated me with a new intensity and seeming conviction. In their minds and behavior I read a strange reverence for the healing which I knew my father had done through me, but which they attributed to some special power that was implied as mine alone. From that day onward it seemed that John-John and I were brothers of the mind, each knowing the other's wish and physical-emotional reaction. It was as if our minds were connected in some magical way. This connection at a later date was to change my life in its most crucial moment. But these things were many happy years ahead, and half a world away as we stood on my tenth birthday before the Assembly. No moment was ever lost for training and in delightful jest our Brothers were practicing on us the arts of debate and speech. We did not know that they were jesting.

It was the custom of the Sons of Light that everyone, even the lowest level of the apprentices, should have the right to vote for or against anyone who came up for the Fourth and final level and was voted the precious right to membership in the Brotherhood. For such a person could then hold office and, if qualified, could teach or administer the affairs of the compound. And every full member of our group at Nazar had a chance of becoming the Secret Master, the representative of the Eternal Father on Earth. Thus, as we stood elbow to elbow, attired in new robes and new sandals, the vote of anyone, even the newest recruit, could keep us from membership, - and we knew it! Everyone could argue for or against the action, and not until all had been heard was the final vote possible.

We were completely unprepared for the events of the day. The Secret Master demanded to know if any opposed our admission or wished to be heard. All the members of both of our squadrons arose as one man and said, "We wish to be heard in our opposition, Sir!"

We were completely surprised for we thought that our companies bore toward us a great affection and fondness. The Supreme Master stroked his gray beard and looked stern.

"This is most unusual, for your opposition was not spoken in the annual analysis of these men. Nevertheless, speak! On what evidences do you base your opposition?"

"Why, Sir, on what other records but their consistent failure in attempts to make improvements for the Brotherhood?"

John-John was so angry that he turned livid, and I feared that he would take physical action for he was ever a forceful-minded and direct individual.

"Have they not made many improvements?"

"Aye, Sir. But have they not failed more times than they have succeeded? Remember, Sir, when the mad bull charged through our compound, and John tried to invent a method of guiding a running bull by holding to its tail? Then Joseph-bar-Joseph came to his aid but in all his scheming failed to deflect the raging bull which missed the river gate and crashed through the wall. Did he not cost us three squad days to repair that failure?"

Oh, the Brothers began to laugh, and then roared! For we had indeed been unable to head off or turn a running bull until it had damaged our wall and gone free into the river.

"Honored Sir, did they not fail in their attempt to improve a method that the Brotherhood uses to carry water into the desert?"

"My memory fails on that point!" The Patriarch said from behind his hand.

"Oh, Sir, remember when John was poured so full of water he dripped like rain-drenched moss for a month? In fact, Sir, even to this day he has seldom been seen to take water lest it spout from his ears!"

The Brotherhood rocked with laughter and applauded with their joy. But when the jesting had run its course, Leader Ishmaul rose and addressed the Assembly.

"Brothers, these Candidates for Membership in our

Holy Order of Eternal Good are but half the necessary age. But they are each three times as energetic as the normal man. Each, Sir, is ten times as smart, twenty times as clever and one hundred times as beloved." He stopped and surveyed us, his dark face grim in thought, for he was ever a taciturn man and compliment was not ready to him, not nearly as ready as was good action. At last he said, "'Impossible' is connected with these two – and membership in our Order – for I say, it would be impossible for our Order to do itself greater honor than to accept them in full Brotherhood and love."

The Brotherhood gasped, for this was indeed the highest compliment that could be paid – that we graced the Brotherhood! There was much discussion, and the final decision was as just and concise as it could be. We were to be made Special Provisional Brothers with all rights except the vote in the election of the Supreme Master. This was to last until we reached the age of twenty when we were to be given all rights and privileges of the Fourth Estate of Brotherhood. Meanwhile, we were accorded the privilege of serving in the Officerships, and we were given one month to decide what special area we wished to work in. I already knew for there had never been any doubt in my mind that I wanted to be a teacher. And when I had acquired more of the skill of my father, I wanted to teach the methods of Divine Healing to everyone.

The month was filled with much work and with practicing how we would make our statement, our statement of Life Duty Selection to the Assembly. At last the day came and we stood before our Brothers. John-John was older than I and he was asked first what he would like to do for the Brotherhood for all the rest of his life.

"Sirs, I should like to go before Jeshuau Joseph-bar-Joseph to make ready the minds of men, and preach unto them the good tidings of great joy. I would like to cry unto men and make straight the path and lay down the hill, for divinity and healing comes now to mankind. I would give my life unto preaching the beliefs of the Brotherhood, that the Messiah comes and the time to repent of the false faith and turn to the true faith of the Sons of Light is now upon us."

The Brotherhood was stunned by the beauty of his words and the height of his fervor. But when he spoke, no man could keep his heart from hearing. At last they burst into applause that rocked the hall. It at last died down and I was asked to state what I wished to do for the Brotherhood for the rest of my life.

"Sirs, I would follow after Jehochanan, son of Zacharias, and bring unto all men everywhere and for all times, the Truth, Light and Love, and teach them to minister and to heal that the glory of the Sons of Light and the magnificence of Heavenly Father might be known unto all men. I would teach the Brotherhood and all mankind some of the healing and divinity of my Father."

There was no applause – only a stillness that tore at my heart. I thought I had failed. But suddenly there was a rustle of movement and, as one body, every Brother rose to his feet and, as they stood, looked down upon me, lips parted in a smile of understanding and happiness. In every eye there glistened tears. Never before had it been known that the Brotherhood stood to honor anyone who selected his Life Duty. But my choice was made, and I had to prepare by special study to instruct the High Priests of the Temple of Jerusalem in their own religion.

Great was the excitement and hard the task and I found the teaching of our narrow and opinionated Rabbi of little interest. But at Father's suggestion, I continued to read and speak at the synagogue at Nazar. Great were all expectations, and greater still were my doubts.

5

BEGINNING OF MYSTERIES

Questions surged in my mind. They beat at my consciousness. They turned me in my dreams and made me stumble when I walked. Everyone thought that I was deep in my preparations to meet the learned priests of the Temple. Indeed everyone who knew my task was interested but, of course, this was limited to the Brotherhood.

My mother did not know the reason for my intense studies but thought I was suddenly turned orthodox in Jewry, and was secretly pleased with me. Of course the Brotherhood hoped that I would succeed for what a faith it would give in the Order, to know that a twelve-year old Essene could be Master to the mightiest priests of the Jews. In the beginning, verily, I harbored a thought of pride, the pride I would take in such a conquest. But soon, by gentle questions and mere suggestions, my father and the Patriarch of the Brotherhood made me see that there was a higher opportunity, a greater responsibility, a higher destiny. Yet I know not how they made me feel this for never one word of this greater duty passed their calm and gentle lips. It was as if I took the meaning from their unspoken thoughts. How this could be was one of the many questions that surged in my mind. Indeed, I studied hard upon the orthodox thoughts of the Jews. But I was not truly concerned for in two years I could have memorized every scroll of the laws of prophets and almost did. My beautiful mother often said that I knew more of the books than did her father and her two elder brothers, and all three were priests.

But the questions in my eager mind could not be answered from the writings of a narrow people. They could be quenched only by drinking of the living water of the knowledge of pure truth. And, at that moment, my father was the spigot behind which all of the knowledge was locked. I knew that there was no way I could get him to open more than he thought was best for me.

How was it possible for man to be in two places at one time? How was it possible for that man in one place to be firmly asleep, so firmly asleep that he could not be awakened? And, in the other place, to be compelling, masterful, and capable of divine action and anger? I hinted the question to my superiors in the Nazar Essenes, Ishmaul and Habakuk. Both answered with a flat statement that it was impossible. I said no more for I did not want my quarterly report to be unfavorable for deviating from the established beliefs. I was curious about the Great White Brotherhood and the Order of Melchizedek but I dared not mention those names to anyone of my squadron. However, my annual review and rating brought me to the presence of the Patriarch. Something drove me to speak to him about so strange a subject.

"Sir, do you know of the Great White Brotherhood?"

His eyes did not flinch, his brow did not wrinkle, but I felt a sudden surge in his emotions and if my father had not painstakingly taught me never to fear I would have fled from the place.

But he was quiet so long and sat so immobile that I stammered, "Do you belong to the Great White Brotherhood, Sir?"

"To which of the twelve?"

His words took me by surprise so that I couldn't find words. At last I pressed on, "Maybe I dreamed it, or imagined the name, Order of Melchizedek. It bothers me that I know nothing about them, Sir!"

"You would not dream about them unless you wanted to know."

"Sir, how could I find out about them? Should I ask someone?"

"Son, you might. But the answer would be the same from every man. He who does not belong might say he does but could not help you. He who does belong would never say that he does."

"Why?"

"These Orders are secret and more sacred than your breath. No man can ever admit he belongs. For the instant he starts to admit it, that instant he ceases to belong." My look of incredulity brought a touch of a smile to his lips.

The Patriarch was old, for many said that he was in truth the Son of Righteousness, hidden from his enemies in our compound. But he seemed quite young when he smiled. His skin was translucent and he seemed to be wrapped in a serenity and radiance that knew no age. And my father was the only other person who was so serene, and so radiant.

I blurted, "But, Sir, how could the Order be filled - h-h-how could the younger men be - ?" I stopped short when I saw the look of amusement. "Sir, is there no way I can find out about these organizations?"

"It depends."

"Sir?"

"Son, when you came to the Essenes, you were asked if you would take an Oath on which you would stake your life."

"Yes, Master."

"Would you be willing to risk your life to gain knowledge of these Orders?"

"Without knowing anything about them first, Sir?"

"Yes."

"Without knowing anyone who belongs to them, Sir?"

"That too!"

"Without knowing what they teach, or what they stand for?"

"Yes. That, and more also!"

I hesitated, but not for long. My father had taught that fear was a trap that stops all hope of progress. "I would risk my life, Sir!" He sat quite still for a very long time and I dared not move. I almost held my breath.

At last he spoke. "Then you have my permission to mention this conversation to your father."

That was all. Nothing more. He instantly turned to other matters, such as my lack of skill at ciphering and composition and gently urged me to improve them. I promised to try and was dismissed with a silent nod.

I verily was silent and deeply puzzled, all that day and all the next, until after the Tabernacle studies, I arrived at the shop to work with my father and learn from him about the religions and about healing. He was doweling a lovely panel of sun-bleached cedar when I came in. It was very exacting work but such was my impatience that I blurted, "Do you belong to the Great White Brotherhood?"

"Which of the twelve?"

His hand at that moment pulled the paneling into exact alignment. It was as if he had been expecting my question.

"Yesterday, the Master gave me permission to speak to you about -."

"Explain to me in three sentences: What is the difference between the Pharisees, the Sadducees, and the Essenes concerning the Messiah."

"The Pharisees, the Sadducees, oh, these interpret the scriptures of the prophet literally and physically. They expect a physical Messiah who will save their nation. The Zealots believe to prepare his coming by use of force. The Essenes interpret the prophecy as scriptural allegories and consider them to be divine secrets earnestly proffered."

"Whence came the beliefs of the Orthodox Jews and of the Essenes?"

"Both came from the Priests of the Sun and the time of Amunhotep IV, the Egyptian priest king, and were transferred to the Jews by the High Priest, Moses."

"Since they came from the same source, why are the beliefs not the same?"

"The Jews have strayed toward the physical. They would make Divine Law that law by which the culture is ordered and controlled. The Essenes have leaned toward the spiritual, but order and control the culture by supervision of training and of daily activity."

"Which is more perfect?"

"That which is nearer to the spiritual."

"Of Pharisees, what is their dominant trait?"

"Withdrawal, unfortunately coupled with hypocrisy; they pretend to follow to the very limit the ancient laws. In truth they are but proud and arrogant and keep to themselves from pride and disdain."

"Of the Essenes, what is their dominant trait?"

"Withdrawal too, but they retire in order to follow their beliefs more fully. No man is permitted to join who has not taken an oath to keep their beliefs secret and not reveal their sacred teachings. They also believe that by withdrawal they may live the purer life needed to ready their eternal souls for bliss after death."

"Like the Pharisees, the Essenes are withdrawn?"

"Yes, but without hypocrisy."

"Should we say, "With less hypocrisy?" son, or do you think the Essenes are perfect?"

"Oh, no, Father, they do not include women, and fear them, saying that women are emotional and seldom faithful to one man. Therefore, the priests of Zaddok have no offspring and must surely die out."

"Is this wise and just?"

"No, Father, perhaps in all history it shall be probably more short-sighted than the false belief of the Jew in his superiority because God spoke to his ancestor on the mountain. We know from records that God did not give the Ten Commandments but that "Mosheh" took them from the early Egyptian laws!"

While we talked we finished the careful doweling and began to assemble the loose boards into one tightly held whole. My father assembled my ideas into one sudden and massive idea. "Have not the Essenes four steps in their learning? Is not a lifetime of work and learning required for the average man to attain to the height of the Fourth Degree? Is it not all they can expect to master with continuous effort? Therefore, is not our Order carefully adjusted to meet the demands but stay within the reach of the average man? Yet, once in a while, a special one comes, one who has limitless capacity to learn, an insight which cannot be taught. Such a one learns as if taught by angels. The mind of such a man may go down with the details of his life or upward to the laws of heaven. If such a blessed one turns his mind to the Eternal Father, he soon becomes purified – weathered – ready! – just as these boards which make up this mighty table top were first weathered in shadow, then tortured and bleached in the desert sun. No board knew its destiny but, now, in its perfected place, it holds all other boards in true harmony and with great strength. Could these tried and tested boards not resemble the members of the Great White Brotherhood?

"The learning of man goes back to its supreme source. It is how he interprets the eternal wisdom and governs his thoughts and actions. As the Jew has turned to physical laws and to human control, the Essene has turned to spiritual laws and human control without coercion. Could it be that a still higher learning would turn to spiritual laws free from all control of mind or being? Could it be that a higher learning would turn to training all of the people rather than those who chose to join the Brotherhood? If so, would they who are members thereof be in hazard of property and life?

"To raise the question from the physical, let us look upon this table. As long as these boards were unselected and unassembled, no man could physically destroy this table for it was only in mental form. That which exists only in the mental and spiritual realm cannot be destroyed on the physical. Therefore, what greater safety for a great secret Order than this – *It was never assembled or it never was known.* In organization there is physical strength but is there mental and spiritual strength? When the Master of Righteousness took from the failing hands of the Maccabees the Zaddok priesthood and made it into an organization like unto a church, he built into the Essene Order the seed of its own destruction. If anyone sets a limit upon an organization, measured to the height of the ability of the common man, does he not measure it to a shroud of mediocrity, to be worn even throughout eternity? Of such proportion are all churches

71

which found their faith on belief that their powers came directly from God. This includes temples and synagogues."

He was silent while we placed the heavy smooth sandstones upon the surface of the table and began to grind and polish the wood to an exacting tolerance and a high gloss. When we were finished, I knew the surface would be one beautiful, masterly made, inlaid whole.

"While an organization is death to the exceptional mind, it is birth and security to the ordinary man. Therefore, he must be protected and used for the benefit of all mankind. But, he who would know true divinity, must never admit any limit upon his freedom or to his abilities or skill. He must, in the end, become his own teacher and his own priest, for to him all other teachers or priests must be false. Could it be that a person becomes a member of the Great White Brotherhood the instant he can personally become his own spiritual teacher? Could it be that there is no *physical* organization to which he may belong, yet he may be a member? Could it be that man may rise by the drive of his own being ever higher and higher, until he commands the very angels themselves to do his bidding?"

There was a silence except for the sound of the heavy sandstones moving backward and forward under our hands. Over beyond the compound, upon the flat area in the curve of the river, I saw the squadron which was serving in the field gathering to return to the Assembly Hall. Beyond our house on the sudden small hill that formed our back yard, I heard a lark carolling from the top of a tamarisk tree. The fragrance of bread came from the hearth where Mother and Mary-B were baking. This was so earthy, so familiar, so beloved, yet I was haunted by a feeling that my father was telling me more than I could grasp. And yet, even that was not enough!

"Father, how could anyone be in two places at one time?"

"Above the Essenes there may be a Great White Brotherhood. Above, or intermingled with the Great White Brotherhood there may be an Order of Melchizedek. Above them all, there may be that other Order which is too sacred to be named, too holy to be limited, too wondrous to be defined. If there is, do you suppose those who have earned the right to know would call it the Order of No Name, or simply, the Order of the Sun? And do you suppose that if there are such Orders, and I have not said that there were, they would not have some special training program to aid their candidates?"

The thrill that went through me was like a sudden chill. My wonderful father never failed to teach me by raising my mind and my emotional understanding to a new level. And the promise of his words was like honey to my tongue.

"Go, son, go find John-John and you two prepare yourself with a warm robe and a heavy blanket. Tell your mother that you are going for three days into the far fields so that she will neither worry nor wonder: then come quickly. Neither you nor John-John have undergone the three days of trial in the rock manger of the Isolation Grotto. This you must do, according to the Perfect Master. Today, your mind is ready for that experience. Go!"

Normally it was the custom of the Essenes to put each Candidate through a severe series of trials, one of which was his death and resurrection to the world of movement, light, sound and feeling. We had been told by many of our Brothers that it was a gruelling experience. Now, suddenly, it was our turn.

We presented ourselves to the Master of the Caves, wound through the narrow tunnel under the compound, climbed the steps in the underground tunnel, and came to the first crypt. It was not much larger than a man, cut in stone, and another giant stone was arranged so that it would roll into place. In the depths of the cavern no sound came, and from the tunnel to the mouth of the cave there was a fresh movement of air. When John-John was safely placed upon his stone bed, I was taken onward to the darker recesses of the grotto to another manger. I was told to wrap myself in a blanket and lie upon the smooth stones where so many other Candidates had lain. A moment later, the stone was moved into place and I was alone in the depths of the earth. There was neither sight in the blackness nor sound in the grotto. I stretched my hands and could touch the cool stones of the back wall and the front wall. Above me I knew there was a stone roof, a little higher than my reach when standing. It was like being closed in a tomb except for the openings at the tops of each side through which air could come. The crypt was much like a feed trough at the front of the stall where we fed our cattle. This was of stone, not wood, and it was longer and deeper but it was also closed on two cnds and almost closcd on both sides. The series of experiences that awaited me in the hours to come reached beyond all written words to relate. How then, could one who was ever poor at composition make you feel the magnificence of the mystery? The experiences themselves must have been only in the mind. No physical body could have risen from that tomb-like crypt. Yet the experiences turned into a greater reality than the stones upon which I lay with my arms flung out to each side so that my body formed a cross.

The events came by stages which were well marked and set apart. Yet each melted into the other. The events were trivial but the total effect reminded me of threshing in a strong wind, where no straw is large, but soon they have built into a stack that covers a broad area. The first stage was physical. I was acutely aware of the cool stones, of the rough wool of the blanket and the warmth of my cotton robe. I found the heel holes gouged in the stone and I touched the rough texture of the rock with my finger tips. Then the feeling of sleep began to steal over me and it rose like a gently warmth from within my being. How long I slept I do not now know but suddenly I was wide awake, aware of the feeling of hunger in my being. My stomach panged, growled and churned, and my head throbbed until I could count each shuddering heart beat. A calmness then began to settle over my being and with it the physical sense of sleep. But the sleep was intermittent, or intertwined with all the other experiences. Slowly I began to weary, a-straining at my physical senses. There was no light, nothing to hear.

My mind began to turn inward and drifted toward an indefinable but definite second stage of my experience. In

74

the second stage I seemed to be all mind. I recalled my lessons over the years, re-said the Psalms of the Essenes, and at last turned to the teachings of my father. Then I recalled the words and actions of my beautiful mother and how she had made me worry and wonder. But at last I turned to the special teachings of my father concerning the learnings of the Initiate and recalled with exactness each point of his years of careful instruction. Then, out of all I selected these as being the most important: He had taught me how to breathe so that I enhanced the power within my body. Then how to become still, calm, and at peace, and increase this relaxation with every breath. He had taught me never to make a positive or antagonizing statement if a question could be used. Under no condition could an Initiate argue, condemn or find fault, but must look for the good and the beauty in everything.

One could never show his prowess or ability or take money for work in the sacred field. Nor could one ever force ideas upon another even knowing he was right and knowing the other was wrong. For a higher law operated in this relationship which could make the right wrong, and the wrong right. No matter what the emotional, mental, or religious plight of anyone, the Initiate could not give aid until asked to do so. He must never attack the faith of anyone, or undermine his confidence in his faith, nor could he give a good faith to replace a bad, until he was asked to do so. Every man must earn his own way by physical work. Teaching was a privilege for which no pay could ever be taken.

But my father had given me instruction in a still higher plane. It was clear that nothing could be done of one's own self except that it become the channel for the use of the Universal Power of the Father, who is in heaven. Therefore the Initiate could have no emotional participation with anyone, that is, he could be neither attached nor detached to anything or any person beyond the requirements of his Life Duty. However, these duties required a certain amount of love and it was the duty of the Initiate also to meet this quota of love and attachment. Yet no matter what the relationship, no personal opinion

75

could be imposed upon another by use of the will, or by thought, or by crafty persuasion for personal gain of any kind.

Yet, there had been higher teachings. And dimly in my mind I realized that my wonderful father had guided me down a rocky highway and never let me stumble. No man could reach the summit of *learning and Knowing* who did not become his own teacher and his own priest. Organization was death to the exceptional mind, but birth and security to the mediocre mind. Success is not important, – doing is all that is important. For duty is more important by far than achievement or success. Thoughts are things of weight and substance. Properly used and controlled, they can kill, cure, destroy or save. And this was the basis of his wonderful healing, which he taught to me.

With all my faith in my own religion, I must never be blind to the value of another's faith, for no religion or church or group had all the good, or all the knowledge. And there is not, nor ever will be a religion higher than Truth! Oh, how he had repeated this to me, "There is not now, nor ever will be – a religion higher than Truth."

And within the framework of truth there were symbol pictures which had meanings made clear only to the mind that continued upward on the spiral of learning. Beyond the religion of the Jew, for instance, was the faith and practice of the Essenes. Above the Essenes was a mythical Brotherhood. Above this, the Order of Melchizedek. And still above this, an Order so sacred, so secret, that it was given no name. As I thought upon these things I grew more and more excited, more pleased with my training, and grateful to my father. But with this excitement and carried by it, there came an exalted exhaustion of memory and brain so that my thoughts began to slow down, and to spin out of the control of my conscious will.

Suddenly, I would find that I was not thinking upon the subject of my deliberate choosing but upon something that had slipped into my mind and would not be rooted out. In fact, it began to seem that I had two minds, one obedient to my conscious control, and the other obedient to its own truth. I fought for control but there was no sight or sound on which I could orient myself and, as soon as I drifted toward rest, my mind would spin off to its own delight. At last I had wearied until I could not think, nor could I even move my fingers to touch the cool stone. I lay as if suspended in time and space, neither thinking, nor not thinking.

Suddenly a rainbow of light, jagged and fast as a lightning stroke, slashed through my head in colors so strong that I saw them with my physical eyes. It was so beautiful that I cried out with the joy of seeing the vibrant rainbow of color. Surely, anyone who has seen such glory would know why the rainbow is said to be God's promise to man. I was gripped and held by the flashing beauty of light and my thoughts were utterly stilled in fascination so that I could not think or move. Somewhere in the primal essence of my being I was enormously aware of the oncoming experience but in no way prepared for the turn it took. Instantly, without warning, the color was covered as if with a blanket of gloomy black. It was as if soot had been thrown upon a radiant fire. The stunning shock rocked my senses and made me a little fearful. Out of the smoldering soot rose phantoms like nightmares. Every doubt or weakness in my mind or character seemed to well up in a horrifying physical form to accuse and plague me. Devils of black doubt and terrible depression raked and tortured me. My very bones hurt from the impact of this emotional ordeal. I tried to escape but was almost unable to move, and could only curl myself in a small ball, cover my head and shake with sobbing! But the demons came on and on, goading me with a remorse for things both done and undone. I wept in pity for myself and then in detestation for my life. I moaned with the pain of seeing myself in pitiless truth, pounded upon the stone and shouted for relief from the torture of those inward visioned memories. But there was no relief, no help, no interlude, until my strength failed and I fell into a torpor of exhaustion and could no longer think or see.

Later, it could have been a moment or an eternity, I was jerked awake by the gay singing of a lark and the lowing of cattle. The sound was so clear and beautiful I laughed aloud and then wept to hear. Ears denied sound had brought memories made sweet by the hunger of time. Then I began to hear voices, whispering at first, and there were words well spoken, and songs, then many voices carolling in full-throated happiness. The sound was more than a heart could stand of happiness, and again I wept for the sheer joy of weeping, until I was again exhausted and seemed to sleep.

My waking was like a jolt of landing. I felt as if I had fallen from a height and every cell of my body was tingling as if it had been asleep and now waked to painful life. In that mystical recess of being, I felt the presence of my wonderful father and Secret Master. They seemed to be helping me to rise upward, upward, ever upward. The emotional upsurge within me was like a warm bath of flame, beginning inwardly to rise slowly from the center of my being toward my heart. The fullness of the pressure was beyond pain or joy. It was limitless expansion that leapt beyond sense and then suddenly thrust inward and outward at the same time. A blue light seemed to explode out of my heart, transfer to the center of my chest and then surge relentlessly upward, ever expanding as it rose. The upward moving light rose of its own energy, just as it had come into being of its own creation, without parent in desire, mother in emotion, or father in thought.

I knew nothing of what to expect and lay as one in a sleep, lethargic, suspended, immovable. All events seemed to be happening to another person. The rising light touched my throat and the sound of singing and joy filled the manger. Then the surging light reached my head and the crypt and cavern of the grotto was lit with a wondrous light. I could see - I could see unbelievable details, even the very particles that held the stones together. Even as I looked, I felt that I stood outside the crypt enwrapped in a violet mist. But I was held to my petrified body inside the tomb by a cord of silvery white. Sight had become all important. I saw beyond the confines of the cave, beyond the barriers of time. It seemed that I saw that which neither had been, was, nor was yet to come, and yet was all three. And I was aware that both my father and the Patriarch were beside me. It was as if they had lifted me out of myself and now held me against the pull of the silvery cord which led back to my body inside the crypt. Then I saw the tall gray haired young man who looked so much like my father who came toward me through the purple mist across the endless ocean. He stepped from his sailing ship and held out his hand. He spoke, and his words thundered through space.

"I am a tin man. Come with me to Brittanin and to see Caer Gaur or the Stonehenge in the Town of Glass.

How sweet, how inviting was the smile on his face and oh, how I wanted to go with him! But I found that I could not move forward. The pull upon the silvery cord was now growing greater and greater. I cried out with the pain. But I was torn from the hands of my father and the Secret Master and was pulled backward toward my prostrate body in the manger of the grotto.

My conscious senses began to awaken. I was dimly conscious of falling and striking my body and then being absorbed by it. In my physical body I felt again that tingling in every fiber as if a million needles had prickled my flesh. Then my consciousness grew until I was aware that my eyes were open and there was not absolute blackness in the crypt. But the light was so faint that I could not be certain that I saw the flickering with my physical eyes and I thought that again my senses had spun out of control in yet another direction. But at last I was certain for the nerves of my eyes began to screech their protest. Yes, I was awake!

I heard the sound of voices singing in the grotto, joyous harmonies of the beloved *Psalm of the Essenes*. Their words were:

Oh, I give praise to the Heavenly Father
For he has fashioned a wonder from the dust
And shown forth his mighty power
In that which he moulded from clay.
He has made me to know the deep, deep Truth
And to understand his wondrous works.
He has put into my mouth the power to praise
And on my tongue the words of psalms

79

And given to my willing lips
The readiness of songs with which
To sing his loving kindness
And constantly, both night and day,
    Recall his might and bless his name.
    Recall his might and bless his name.
I will show forth his glory
To the sons of men.
And in his abundant goodness
My soul shall greatly exult.
    Knowing that in his hand is bounty
    In his thought all knowledge
    In his power all might
    And all glory and all truth.
He has given to my willing lips
The readiness of songs with which
To sing his loving kindness
And constantly, both night and day,
    Recall his might and bless his name.
    Recall his might and bless his name.

The carolling Essenes had stopped afar to sing and to let my eyes become adjusted to the light. By stages they advanced and the singing grew ever louder and louder until the group was outside my crypt, and the light was streaming into the upper part of the manger. The pain in my eyes had become ever less but still, was great when I heard the grunts of my Brothers straining to lift the stone that closed the tomb. As the stone was raised and rolled away, the light from the many tapers came in upon me, flooding the crypt with light. Dimly, through the tears in my straining eyes I could see the Brothers banked in great circles that extended beyond the light. There must have been a hundred of the advanced Essenes in their shining white robes. As they saw me they began singing in sweet joy the *Song of Rising* and the words were:

    Sing for the Lord of Heaven
    Has to mortals given
    The love for which they've striven
        That glory which they desire.
    Sing for the Lord of Earth

Has proved to man his worth
The value of human birth
And the glorious inner fire.

How good were my Brothers, how sweet to work through their rest period so that they could bathe and dress early, struggle through the tunnels and up the long stairs to greet me on my waking from what was called the tomb. But how unreal their solid physical forms seemed, how inadequate was the human light to one who had seen with higher sight. My eyes had beheld the realities greater than their too, too solid flesh, and a light more adequate than a million suns. How very unreal the actual seemed! How actual the insubstantial was in my memory. The singing rose to great height and then into shouts and hurrahs as I stepped forth from the tomb. A dozen eager hands reached to help and steady me. Then practiced hands whisked away my robe and my blanket and I was bathed with water from enormous jars, jars which they had carried all that way, then rinsed with cold water, and then with special spiced oil and it was lathed upon me.

"Behold the robe of your glory!" Master Habakkuk said these words and held forth to me the coveted new linen robe, snowy white and glistening. When I had clothed myself I was handed a golden goblet, filled with milk into which honey had been dissolved. Even as I drank, the energy flowed back into my limbs. Soon I again began to touch the actual which was around me. The exaltation and joy of each of my Brothers was communicated to me, for only they who had passed through the experience were permitted to come to see the Candidate risen from the dead. They knew something of the sensations that no words could convey and I felt their good will like the warmth of a fire. Truly at that moment I learned the meaning of Brotherly Love.

John-John had been awakened from his crypt by another group, even though he had resisted his awakening. So great was his pleasure in the experiences of inward withdrawal, that from that moment he was changed. As we moved along in stately processional returning towards the steps and the exit from the cave,

81

he whispered, "Oh, such bliss! I want to be a Therapeut!"

Within the Essenes there were some who married though this was not approved in every compound. There were also those who loved to withdraw into the solitude in complete retirement from mankind, to meditate and pray in constant seclusion. These sought the far places of the desert and tried to live undisturbed in their constant contact with the Indwelling Being. Such were called Therapeuts, and most were indeed devout and holy men; much admired by all the others.

We were led into the midst of the Assembly Hall just as all the Brothers assembled for the Feast of Love. We stood before the Secret Master and my father for blessings and special prayers and to learn the kiss of the Brotherhood by which we could make ourselves known to all Brothers in all lands anywhere. And as we were taught, my father's eyes were upon mine as if he searched my very soul to see if I had garnered understanding and wisdom from the experience.

As I worked with him under the direction of the Secret Master, I whispered to him softly, "Thank you, father! It was more real than actual flesh! I have at last........oh, I know at last how one may be in two places at one time."

A hint of a smile touched his fine lips and, as he embraced me in a practice demonstration, he whispered in my ear, "Are you sure you know *how* it is possible for a man to be in two places at one time? Is it not rather that you know now that a man can be?"

6

THE

FOUNDATION STONE

OR ROCK OF FAITH

How true was my father's mind, how relentless his drive for perfection in the Sacred Learnings. Yes, I knew that it was possible for a person to be in two places at the same time but, as he showed me, I did not know how this was done. Suddenly, the "how" became the driving problem of my life and my father was taciturn and silent. He would not speak with me about the experience I had had nor about the techniques of further study. He listened with interest but made no comments when I talked about it. A grin twisted his lips when I told the story of the impossible man who said he was a "Tin Man" and wanted me to go to Brittanin to see Stonehenge in the Town of Glass. But though I saw a flicker, almost a mockery, he would say nothing.

I reasoned for myself that there must be a technique by which one could learn to use and control the sense of being in two places at the same time. Surely then, it could be taught! But if my father would not teach me, to whom could I turn? My problem grew until it was like a goad that made me accomplish every assignment of allotted work in half the usual time, master my learnings with exacting thoroughness so that I could have leisure time to meditate and to dwell upon the problem. My father continued and increased his teachings in the religions and in philosophy and healing. But he spoke no more of the Great White Brotherhood or of the Order of Melchizedek.

When I dared to suggest that we discuss the things that bothered my mind, he said: "It is good to be driven by the goad of a strong inner stress, for to him who desires greatly, much shall be given swiftly."

Thus, for two years my conscious mind was driven hourly by the strange unanswered questions. Shortly after my twelfth birthday, we were working alone in the big house high on the hill at the end of Marmion Road. It overlooked all of the village, the tabernacle, our old house, the compound, and beyond to the river, and the valley filled with herds of cattle and rich fields. Hoping that the vista had mellowed him, and knowing we were alone, I said, "Father, how can I learn or go further in the desires of my heart if there is no one to explain the problems of my mind?"

He smiled, and we continued the building. But at sunset when we walked together down the dusty road in the May day, he said quietly, "My son, much has been given to you, yet more is to be given. But know this – your inner development cannot be hurried. You are now in the cycle of mastering the things of earth. Later, I will be of more help when you must master the things pertaining to heaven. Know this and remember it well: When the student is ready the Master will be there."

Truly, I should have been concerned with the things of earth for the time was fast approaching when I was to face the priests of the Temple in secret trial of my skill at teaching. The trial would come in the Month of *Nisan* for we would be at the Temple during the day of the Paschal Sacrifice of the Passover, generally spoken of as The Feast, meaning, The Feast of The Unleavened Bread. This would be in the month now called April. Since my birthday fell in May, I would still be twelve years of age. But to meet the Jewish law I had to register before I was thirteen. Verily, the time was upon me.

A large company from our village had planned to go up to the Temple. There were many reasons for going, some merely for the pageantry and the holiday but many said they wanted to go and see my admission into the rolls of the Temple. I had a rather flattering popularity among the Orthodox, since many times on the Sabbath I was

84

permitted to either read, translate or explain the Law as read from the scrolls in the synagogue. Somethimes I was even encouraged by Rabbi Borrenchan to talk on the history of the religion of the Jews. Of course, I told back the things my father had so carefully taught me. But I was young, slender, a little short for my age, and made a nice impression with my auburn hair and blue-gray eyes. There were many among the Orthoox Jews who believed that the Rabbi had trained me, and listened to me for that reason. There were some who listened because they liked my looks. There were some who listened in admiration to the very things I said. Rabbi Borrenchan, by inference, took full credit for my training and at the last minute decided that he, too, should go up to the Temple and present me to some of the priests with whom he had studied.

Within the compound many things were astir, for a large number of the Brothers wanted to go and see me either fail in my trial or reach the summit of glory for a twelve year old. The judgment of the Patriarch was taxed but at last all was done so that the compound could be well run and yet the Brothers might go with me. This put them all to extreme activity preparing, for instance, their traveling robes. It was a custom of our Order that when we travelled or went among the Orthodox we wore poor clothes and patched robes. Sometimes when a robe was not sufficiently shabby or patched, it was rent and then patched so that the wearer might look poor. This gave our Order the name of "The Poor". Our reason for wearing such patched clothing was that we should never appear to have authority or affluence and thus have no help towards forgetting our vow of allegiance to humility and obedience. Indeed it was a goodly company of the Orthodox and the devout which readied itself to travel. As the time for departure drew near my beautiful mother's attitude toward me became ever more marked and confusing. Her treatment of me showed that she was tense and disturbed. Yet I knew she loved me, possibly the best of all.

One day she announced her desire to take all of the children along to Jerusalem ...indeed a most unusual decision. When my father asked why, she glanced at me significantly and said, "Joseph, you know they should go and see this. Never before and never again in all history will such an event be recorded!"

For a moment I thought that she had heard of my coming trial of skill with the High Priests and was prophesying my success. But it soon was made evident that she thought she herself was coming up to some special trial. Further, this was something that involved me and I could tell that she faced it with both pleasure and dread. I wanted desperately to know what this task was but her emotions about it were so strong that I dared not do more than hint that she might explain, or to suggest that if she explained she might not be so tense and preoccupied. Each time I did, she looked at me with eyes filled with love and adoration, caught her breath in desperation and burst into tears. John-John was usually at her side to comfort her and to look at me with brown eyes filled with a most inscrutable light.

Father treated mother with great patience and with endless love, as was his nature. The contrast was great. Her great agitation showed against his composure, like an angry patch against a calm cloak. Many times I heard her weeping in her bed at night, and sometimes her fiercely whispered demands.

"Joseph, Joseph, why can't you tell him? I am so inadequate!"

"Beloved, to that one on which heaven imposes a heavy burden is given the skill to manage and the strength to carry it."

"I must! I will! But I am so afraid, Joseph. No, I must wait...I...I will tell him on the journey."

Yet she feared her decision. Sometimes when I looked up suddenly from reading in the firelight – or when she came to the shop to talk as we worked and I looked up quickly from my work – I would surprise fear mixed with love and adoration in her eyes. But when I smiled and winked or threw her a kiss, the fear was gone to be replaced with a depth of love no man child has ever deserved.

We planned carefully. The distance was great and

hardships were prepared for. Taking the children made an exceptional burden upon my father. John-John, Jim-Jim, Jo-Jo and I could, of course, walk. Jo-Jo was already nine years old, and a strong and brilliant boy who could do wonderful things with his hands and carve wood into beautiful figures. For the other children we decided to take a black and tan ass called Big Bray. He was louder than any other two in our pasture. For Mother and Marianna, who was just over one year old, we chose to take a large tan ass, docile and trail-wise and of pleasing gait. For our sleeping blankets, food and special offerings for the Temple, we chose a jinny of very great size, well tried on the trails and good with burdens. But she had a young colt which had to follow for it was still suckling. Mary-B and Simon were supposed to ride Big Bray but they were on and off, the minxes, like thrushes on a tamarisk twig. And the colt grew tired with much frisking, and waving its over-sized tan colored ears, and soon was riding in their place, strapped to the pack saddle of Big Bray. Father carried Mary-B when she grew tired, and John-John and I took turns spelling Simon's short fat legs. With little sleep because of the last minute details, we were ready to move out before the first light of the ninth day of *Nisan*. We all left our homes when three blasts upon the silver trumpet at the tabernacle echoed from hill to valley.

Rabbi Borrenchan caused much concern when we stopped for our midday meal at Jesreal. He wanted us to change our plans and go straight southward. We had planned to swing eastward to the highway flanking the River Jordan because there was more dependable water and a better terrain. But he was very hard to convince. He was a dear man, but firm in his belief that he knew the right and that anyone who disagreed with him was either bereft of sense or deliberately sinful. Such is often the attitude of small minds or of men of low learning, while he who is great knows that there are more things than can be compassed by the average mind. I knew that my father would neither argue nor take that shorter route through more difficult country. Also I knew that his refusal would hurt mother for she held the Rabbi in high esteem. She seemed to be proud that he was coming along to show me off, and claim credit for my development.

The momentary conflict resolved itself, for a party of youngsters had hurried on ahead because they wanted to leave the highway to search for special stones on the northeastern slope of Mount Gilboa. They were to join us again on the highway before nightfall and go with us to the first night's camp at the Well of Barsun. Thus our path was determined and we swung eastward toward the Jordan. Great was our joy and voices were raised in song to lend wings to tiring feet and legs. When the songs had all been sung, we turned to chanting psalms in unison, thus preparing ourselves for the high moment of religion that was to come. It was a devout and high spirited company that approached the valley of Barsun, that is to say, Son of the Sun, and prepared to camp at the Well of Travellers. Soon our camps were ready and fires made and our family had eaten its evening meal of barley cakes, baked lamb, hard curds, honey and dried dates. Then the entire company gathered at the well to sit in small bunches and talk, sing or banter each the other on the events of the day.

As was her wont, my beautiful mother came from our camp, a short distance away, to fill her pitcher with cool water at the well. She was so very popular and deeply loved that all eyes turned to her where she stood, slender, fair and lovely in the coming night.

Someone called aloud, "Mary of Nazar, tell us a story!" Soon the cry was taken up by three hundred throats for she was noted for her ability to hold, with gripping stories, a multitude. She was pleased but when her eyes fell upon me sitting near John-John, Mary-B and Miriam, the daughter of Rabbi Borrenchan, she seemed suddenly quite nervous and irresolute.

Many times she hesitated before she said, "Would it please you to hear a story about the promised Messiah, He Who Is To Come?"

Indeed, in all Israel no other subject could have been more popular. Every sect, even those that fought each other, believed that the Messiah was to come as promised in scripture. The clamor was instant in

88

beginning and continued long. She still seemed nervous and finally turned and placed her pitcher at my knee and it was as if she nailed me to the spot. Strong hands lifted her to the stone rim which surrounded the edge of the well so that she could be seen in the firelight by those at a distance.

"This is a true story." The way mother began caused the whole company to laugh. It was all the same to them whether mother told a fanciful tale or quoted the Commandments.

"This certain woman was much concerned and pained inwardly in her heart for she bore a secret which had been given to her by the angel Gabriel. Deep in her heart were hidden words spoken by the Voice of Heaven, that out of her maidenly body should come the promised Messiah. She had borne a son, named him as directed by the Angel of The Lord, and of course had fulfilled the first obligation of the covenant between the All-Father and Abraham when the child was circumcised on the eighth day. But, as all women will, she would change from complete faith to no faith in the angel's words. Thus it was that she was sorely perplexed and concerned when the time came for her son's redemption. And when her time was accomplished and she must needs go through the purification, great was her anguish of mind and soul. This was the first-born. According to the Law, the first-born son is to be given unto the Lord, but may be redeemed of the priest for the sum of five shekels. The earliest time of this presentation of the redemption price is thirty-one days after birth. Time and time again she had looked upon every part of his tiny body to see if she could find any blemish that would disqualify her son for the priesthood. For, as you know, he was truly the first-born of the priesthood. She often dwelled in dread upon the possibility that the child might meet with rejection, or by accident of death should not be redeemed.

"But she would not relinquish him for his own redemption until after her own purification. The time for purification of the mother of a son is forty-one days under Rabbinic law. It is of course eighty-one days for the mother of a daughter. But she was not wealthy and could not make a special trip to the Temple. Thus she waited for the first Feast days, since it is lawful to delay either the presentation or the purification within a sensible season. Though she might have foregone her own presence in the Temple and been purified by the offering of a friend at the Temple, she refused. For in her heart of hearts was a belief that a miracle had happened unto her.

"How she trembled with fear, and also delight, as she approached the Temple at last and entered the Gate of the Women on the north side of the Court of Women. Indeed, she had to hurry, for out of the lofts of the Temple the organ began to announce that the incense was about to be kindled on the Golden Altar, thus summoning those who were to be purified and blessed. She quickly dropped her poor-offering into the third of the thirteen trumpet-shaped chests. For she was not of such wealth that she could afford a lamb to substitute for a turtle dove or a pigeon. Indeed, a dove was more than she could afford. But she was soon arraigned by the ministering priests with others inside the wicket on the right side of the great Nicanor Gate, right at the top of the fifteen steps, which let from the Court of Women to the Court of Israel.

"But the short purification service did not cleanse her heart or clear her mind. She wondered if she should find the High Priest on duty and tell him of the annunciation of the Angel of The Lord. Or should she retire with her precious burden - say nothing to anyone about his birth! But if she spoke and was not believed, what ridicule would be hers! What vicious tongues would do to the tender life she held to her aching breast! Yet if she did not speak, would she not be denying the infant all his divine rights and condemn him to the life of an ordinary man? What should she do? So torn was her soul and mind that the tears fell upon the bright face of the infant in her arms and in her agony it was as if spikes had been driven into her breast.

"Knowing not what else to do she resolved to speak to a priest and at least have someone to share her burden or strengthen her faith. But before she could put her new resolve into action, the purification was finished. The priests went within and the other women streamed past her. She was forced out the wicket and wandered aimlessly out toward the Court of Men where she thought to meet her husband of ten months. The women left her and she felt alone, as if all the world and heaven too had deserted her in that stony courtyard. A priest in his vestments came hurrying by, possibly late for a sacrifice. Yet even as she strove to make her voice sound, in order to speak to him, he saw her despair and stopped.

"'Daughter, in tears'?"

"She struggled, but could not speak and merely wagged her head. The priest rushed on smiling, possibly thinking to himself, 'The emotional weakness of women!'

"Torn with the anguish of her weak faith and her holy burden she fell upon the stones in the far corner of the Court of Women at the meeting of the raised stones. There she bitterly whispered to the Heavenly Father her anguish, 'Father, forgive my weakness or kill me for lack of faith.' She placed the gurgling child upon the raised shelf and said, 'Father, remove my doubts for all time, or destroy me forever! This child is either the Messiah or he is not the Messiah! If he is verily Your Son, let it be told by two tongues other than mine. If he is not Your Son, not the awaited Messiah, let my heart be stopped in my breast!' This she said in a whisper only because she feared lest some curious stranger hear her bewilderment and accuse her of blasphemy. She was still kneeling thus when her husband found her and quickly moved her to the Redemption. He raised her to her feet and supported her upon his arm and urged her toward the officiating priest in the alcove next to the Sacred Altar. There, with much doubt, she hurried. But as they went through the side corridor of the court, a black cloud covered the sun and hid out the midday light. It was as black upon the earth as it was black within her doubting heart. But soon she knelt before the priest and received the benediction. Then she handed up her son to the priest, giving up her first born to God. The cherub waved his hands in delight and the cloud that was before the sun dissolved.

91

"The prayer was said in bright sunshine!

"But before the Amen an ancient and venerable figure, a Chief Officiating Priest, known and loved in town and sanctuary, came as quickly as his weight of years would allow.

"Where is the one who was to come? Where is the Messiah?" He cried out in his eagerness.

"The officiating priest stopped, for the ancient Simeon was noted for his piety, his justness in all his relations between God and man, his fear of God, his humility, and above all, for the promise made in a vision in his youth that he should behold the Messiah before he would be permitted to die. He was the strongest of the Orthodox priests in the belief that the Messiah was soon to come. Through almost a hundred years he had waited and watched for the fulfillment of a vision of prophesy from God. With near-sighted eyes he peered upon the cherub and cried aloud and fell upon his knees. Then he rose and praised the Heavenly Father and took the child. Praising God in the Highest, he walked directly to the Golden Altar and placed the child thereon."

The company gasped and mother said: "Oh, you gasp here beside the well of Barsun.

"Imagine how much she gasped, kneeling before the altar. For she knew that only that which is consecrated and sacred could be placed upon the Golden Altar. She cried aloud her doubt but Simeon, the priest, heard her not.

"Verily, Simeon fell upon his knees before the altar and so did the other priests, and he worshipped and prayed and cried aloud, 'Oh, my God, You have been ever good and are now truthful to Your servant. You promised that I should see the Messiah! Now I may lay down the weight of my years, cease my longing and watching, and die in happiness! For thus, Lord, You have kept faith! Now, let Your servant depart in peace, for my dim eyes have seen the Salvation of Man, and my gnarled hands have held the Treasure of Heaven. Here is the glory of Israel, the Light unto the Gentiles. The Messiah that *is* come!"

"Having thus spoken, he rose and came back with

the smiling cherub. The bewildered mother held out the five shekels to redeem the child but Simeon placed his hand upon the money and pushed it down.

"'Holy Mother, you cannot buy back the Messiah!'

"The heart of the woman rose within her and almost broke, and tears flowed down her cheeks with joy and despair. She knew joy to have the promise of the angel confirmed, despair at the words which implied that she would not be able to reclaim her smiling child. But before her heart could burst, Simeon bent and placed the child in her arms.

'Mother, into your arms I place the Salvation of Man! Minister unto this Instrument of the Divine Will!'

"The woman rose and left Simeon. Her husband guided her toward the corner gate for they were intending to retire to Bethany, three miles away, there to rest before returning to Nazar. They had reached the gate itself, and within the woman a great doubt and turmoil was again rising. She reasoned thus: Simeon was old, bereft of good sight, possibly bereft of clear sense, perhaps he had a lapse of memory due to age.

"Thus doubting in her heart of hearts she stepped into the gate and was one pace only from the outside when a great cry caused her to stop. It was the voice of Anna, the admired prophetess, daughter of Phanuel of the tribe of Aser. She was beloved by all in the Temple for there she had dwelled many years, serving God and praying and fasting. She never left the Temple grounds but foresaw events. She had been a widow for eighty-four years, but had known her husband for seven. Thus of great age and wise, she had foreseen the coming of the Messiah into the Temple, and had waited at the Central Gate. When he came not, she turned to her inner sight, followed the cherub and stopped the mother with a mighty shout, lest she go forth from the Temple grounds. Anna's great cry brought a multitude of persons and they crowded close to see when Anna prostrated herself upon the stones, and gave thanks to the Most High that she was allowed to see the Messiah. A few scoffed, but all who knew the prophetess and loved her, knelt down and gave adoration.

93

"And Anna rose and spoke to them saying, 'Oh, look you well upon this babe, and behold wherewith God fulfills his promise with a savior for down trodden Israel! Verily, look upon the Redeemer!'

"Many wept. Others pushed close. And some reached to touch the child. But when Anna knelt to pray, she commanded all to do likewise. And the husband and mother passed quickly beyond the Temple grounds, and were lost to the curious who endangered the child. And as they went to Bethany, the mother rejoiced in her heart, praying that she be given strength, wisdom, power and knowledge equal to the task of ministering unto the human needs of the Instrument of Salvation."

My beautiful mother stopped talking. From afar the desert night birds stirred their orchestra of love to serenade the stars. Not an eye in our company was dry and my own tears came down my cheeks. For a long while no one dared speak lest his voice betray that he was choked on tears.

But at last Ishmaul said in his direct way, "We shall not sleep for curiosity unless you tell us who the woman was!"

Mother stood near me, her hand upon my head, peering down into my eyes in the firelight. "If you do not know, let it be a puzzle in your heart until we reach this well on the return trip. Then, if you will it, I shall tell you an even greater miracle and the name of the mother. And the name of the son!" My mother touched me with love and stooped to kiss my brow. I felt her warm tears fall upon my hand. She turned quickly, picked up the tall pitcher, then was gone into the dark beyond the firelight.

"Oh, did she not speak the dream of every man? Oh, Israel! Israel! Where is thy expected Deliverer? Long, long have we waited for Him whom the prophets foresaw!" Rabbi Borrenchan said.

Perhaps he would have said more but his comments got no response from the company. Men's hearts were too full of the mystery of the story my beautiful mother had told, to be led into either a political or Rabbinical discussion. Beside, the day had seen them march almost twenty-one miles and some were mildly tired. Others refreshed by the break in their daily routine of life, planned to sit up all night to pray, or to quietly chant psalms around the central camp fire.

John-John and I slipped from the circle and went to our blankets and I have seldom seen him more pensive. Soon, with that lust for sleep known to the young, he was in his private dreamland. But I lay for a long time thinking of my beautiful mother and wondering in my secret heart of hearts why she treated John-John and Jim-Jim with more intimate and more human love......when I was certain she adored me more than either. Idly I wondered about the Messiah, and then about the technique by which one could be in two places at one time. And then thought fleetingly of the best way to trap the attention of the proud and haughty High Priests and hold it long enough to teach them.

The touch upon my shoulder was strong to rouse me from deep sleep. We were soon under way, saddled and moving with the very first light. In the cool of the morning we moved briskly and the animals trotted almost without switching. By a little after sun-up we had covered almost half of the twenty miles we expected to march that day. We put the donkeys to grass with loosened cinches, and sat down to our own breakfast of nuts, dried dates and cold barley cakes. Under the heat of the sun our pace then slackened and we were toiling in the heat of high noon before we reached the camp on the Jordan. We watered the animals and rested throughout the afternoon heat.

Thus without incident, except when Mary-B almost stepped upon a puffing adder, we arrived at Bethany on the 13th day of the Month of *Nisan* and stopped for a day and a half. The ceremonies in the Temple did not begin until the evening of the 14th, therefore we had two days for the women to clean and wash and make ready. The men also repaired harness or garments and many took from their packs the intended sacrifices. All birds were carefully fed and watered. The gifts of metal were polished with industry and great love. When the Orthodox Jews were thus busied, the Brothers slipped

95

out of the company and went to the compound of Essenes beyond the Mound of Bethany. There they were welcomed by the salutation and embrace, enjoyed a Bath of Love and a Feast of Love, and the goodness of fellowship and worship in the Assembly Hall. Soon they were helping the Brothers of Bethany in the customary and beloved menial tasks and telling of my forthcoming trial.

The beloved Patriarch arranged that many of the Brothers could go to the Temple at Jerusalem to watch me either succeed or fail in my attempt to teach the High Priests. Others went ahead, but my father delayed our arrival at the Temple until sunrise on the 15th.

How could anyone express the awe and the inspiration of the first sight of the crowded streets of Jerusalem and then the mighty Temple. Bands of people were moving down the roadways into Jerusalem from every direction. The bands ran from ten to three hundred, moving as groups upon the streets. Few companies were as large as ours as it moved through the cool pre-dawn toward the Temple. There was an overspilling and intermingling of individuals, yet each band kept its identity and was a thing apart.

The streets of the city were filled with groups walking and singing to the rhythm, or to the thrilling beauty of the bird-like flute. Though Jim-Jim was not as skilled as Jo-Jo at singing, he played the flute with a perfect beat and many a skirling flourish that embellished the melody and he was very popular with our company. Jo-Jo and Mary-B sang, each in a firm, sweet and loud voice, and soon earned the title of "The Larks." Young as they were, they led the singing of the company as we wound through the hillside streets of the city.

We had been told that the Temple was big. Someone had said, "Bigger than all the village." But, we were not prepared for the sight! Surely, words can never relay an experience. We came suddenly up out of a twisting ravine and turned back upon the shoulder of a hill. There, before us, rose the Temple! It looked like a veritable island, rising abruptly out of a sea of deep valleys, enormous walls, palaces, streets, houses. We had been told that within its gigantic courtyards more than two hundred thousand people could move and worship. But knowing that its base measured a square over one thousand feet, could not begin to hint at the immensity which struck the wondering eye. The structures of the Temple rose on top of the mountain, which, coming abruptly out of the valleys around it, seemed to float the Temple and the Sanctuary in the palm of God's mighty hand nearer to the heavens. The structures seemed to strive upward, each on the other reaching toward the heavens. Terrace rose upon terrace, mighty buildings of snowy marble, and glittering gold probed upward in search of the highest, pointing like man-made fingers to the purpose of man's existence.

Our company moved on, silenced by that splendor. Coming from Bethany to the east, we passed by the northeastern corner, not far from the Tedi, a northern gateway into the Sanctuary. But, by custom, it was closed. We turned southward along the roadway paved with enormous stones, went over the tunnels which led from Ophel, which is to say, the suburb of the priests, through the Huldah Gate to the outer courtyard. We passed the Susa Gate and entered at the Gate of Gentiles near the southeast corner of the outer courtyard. From just within this gate, which was raised by eleven steps in the enormous wall, we saw the northwestern corner of the Temple, and my beautiful mother pointed at the frowning stone fortress.

"How we need our Redeemer! The Romans garrison their troops in our precious Castle of Antonia, once the home of our priests. Here they hold the sacred vestments of our religion, and unlock them only at the will of Caesar!"

Our steps led to the southern colonnade over the eastern end of which rose the lofty tower known as The Pinnacle. From high on this tower, the priests kept morning watch and announced the sunrise and thus seemed to be at eagle height above the vertical sides of the valley of Kedron. The eastern-most of the double colonnades around the inner court was known as Solomon's Porch. Within this area the meetings of the first or lowest of the three Sanhedrins, that is to say, the

97

Temple, were often held. The second Sanhedrin, like a court of Appeals, was held in the Court of Priests. The highest of the Sanhedrin courts, called the Great Sanhedrin, was held in the Hall of Hewn Stone, a nearby court of great reverence. We went beyond the porches of the colonnade toward the Chol, that is to say, the profane place where the Gentiles retired during the Holy Feast. It was in this area that a market place was located and also many, many Jewish money changers. On a terrace twelve steps higher than the Court of the Priests was the Sanctuary itself. Here, in separate chambers considered sacred, all things necessary for the sacrificial services were kept. The Sanctuary was set off by a two-leaved gateway. Beyond this area, the Holy Place had the Golden Candlesticks at the south, the Golden Altar of Incense in the center, and the Table of the Shew Bread to the north.

"Look at the Veil! My father once said that it is the duplicate of the Veil of Mystery used in Egyptian mystery temples." Mother was silent for a moment and then she added in awe, "Beyond the Veil is the most holy place. It is empty except for a piece of rock, the *Aben Shekinah*, or Foundation Stone. It has a double meaning: It is the Rock upon which both the Jewish faith and Temple is founded. But it is also said to the the Rock which covered the pit...the Rock on which the world was founded at creation."

The size and the beauty was so overwhelming that my heart was as heavy as a rock within my breast. How could an unknown Essene hope to instruct the wisest of the priests who founded such a faith - held the Rock upon which the world was created - built such a structure of magnificence? I felt like David against a thousand giants! But now, the giants even held the Rock and I had no stone to throw.

7

ABOUT

MY FATHER'S BUSINESS

"Grandeur!" my father said, his eyes upon mine and I am certain he read my mind. "Beyond that curtain is indeed the rock upon which they found their faith! Found their church! Found this Temple! But it is only physical grandeur! Their rock can be destroyed with a sledge hammer blow, and the faith of man deserves a firmer base. Truth is not founded upon such physical evidence – it need not be!"

As he talked, some strength and resolve flowed back into my weak knees and my heart was less heavy in my breast. But as the days moved by the hours were more and more filled with the overwhelming sense of the pressure of people. Tribes and men of every description milled about in the Temple courtyards, packed themselves into a mass of shuffling people and moved with unthinking acceptance the way they were directed. They, too, were overawed by the size and the color of the Temple, stopped to marvel and tremble before the Rock, that supposed physical evidence of the firm foundation of their faith.

The activities were so arranged as to keep the masses moving much of the time and the assistants and the priests pointed the way from the stage of one function to that of another. Imposing as the coming functions were, I began to have a sense of the complete futility of them. Surely men with intelligence would soon see through the show and the panoply to the rigid bone of an ancient belief, once vital and once alive.

The first two days were the traditional days and were the same as they had been for many, many years. Mother was greatly impressed, for the entire message was concerning the magnificence of God in keeping and caring for his chosen people. This theme was repeated over and over, in one place or in another, or in the prayers of the priests who thanked God for making the Jews a superior race. During the first two days the Passover was eaten, the Chagicah, or Festival Sacrifice, was offered. Also the first ripe barley was rushed into the Temple. This was very theatrically done for it was supposed to be devoted to the use of God, and be made into the Ohmer of first flour and waved before the Lord. The ceremony seemed to me to be slightly foolish. For it was obvious that the barley had not been just to eat but had in fact been kept outside the Temple wall to be rushed in at the moment it fitted into the ceremony. This was to impress the onlookers that the first and best should be returned to the source from whence it came. Unconscious of their overweaning pride and lack of God-fearing humility, the priests represented that God source from which all power and all things of nature came. They compared most unfavorably with the Secret Master of the Essenes, who refused all honor, all power, and all prestige!

A new complication began to bother me. My beautiful mother was constantly at my side. She whispered to me many interesting bits of information about the Temple and she pointed out certain of the High Priests. But she would have interferred if I had attempted to involve the High Priests. With her present, I dared not try. Many of the Essenes grew tired of following me about, decided I had lost my courage and ceased to look upon me with either pride or compassion. Try as I would, I could not lose my mother, for she would command me to wait if I went ahead and would wait if she went ahead of me. My father saw my difficulty and I knew his resolve cost him a heart twinge. He knew that the only way I could have my chance was for him to take Mother away and he would then miss my attempt.

100

At the end of the second day he said, "Mary, we've fulfilled our duty. The boy is registered and we have seen this so many times. Let us come tomorrow for the first of the half days and then leave for the village the following day."

Mother did not really want to do so, but carrying Mary-A was not easy and the children did complicate movement and attention. Thus it was that I rose early on the fourth day and slipped out of Bethany Camp and made my way toward the Temple, alone. I knew that according to Talmudic tradition the priests of the Temple Sanhedrin sat as a Court of Appeal from the close of the morning to the time of the evening sacrifice. During the Feast Days, however, they followed the ancient tradition and came out upon the terrace of the Court of Priests to talk to the pilgrims and to teach them of the law and of behaviors seemly in the sight of the Lord. Since my mother had been at my elbow during my registration, this was my only chance at the High Priests. Here was my chance, my only chance, and I had to take it.

The terrace was in fact that portion of the court which was raised above the level of the common floor and set apart by a row of flowers in pots, placed upon a knee-high stone barrier. There were also two parts to the lecture. The priest to give the lecture to the public was first honored by his colleagues and by learned Doctors of Law. He gave a scientific lecture carefully prepared with much research. This lecture was given behind the flowers and, if in hearing, was arrogantly assumed to be above the level of understanding of the common people.

The very method seemed to me to be insufferably proud and a little stupid. For is not the purpose of the teacher to teach those who need learning, not those who have it? With arrogance the priest discussed the same subjects again by moving to a seat at the border of the flowers and speaking to the common people. The formal talk was supposed to be carefully researched and put together with painstaking effort, in order that it should be as accurate as the laws given by God, as they said. All common people were forbidden to question the priest and these, ignorant of the fine points of the law, could

101

not cross the flower hedge to sit upon the terrace, though it might be empty of priests.

Fortunately, the High Priest of the Temple Sanhedrin was talking on this morning and, since I was early, I got a seat upon a stone at the flowers. I could hear everything he said to his colleagues and it was not very deep, though he quoted endlessly from the Pentateuch and Talmud. To support his thesis, he said, "To know God is the only purpose of man's existence." However, he talked mainly in the general theme: "Unless we know God, how can we serve our fellowman?" And did not cling to the central premise as any Essene would have done. His talk was nothing original but he stated and proved from references that man must give all to God - obey the laws, do good always, turn to the priests for guidance. The priests then had the duty of directing men in the way of the Lord.

When this shallow and presumptive talk was finished, the priests debated at length upon some very fine points of law. Then the High Priest moved out to his seat and prepared to lecture to the general public. Now, after a general lecture it was supposed that anyone could ask any question he might desire. However, one had to be most careful for it was easy to anger the priest! If the priest was offended, he who was guilty, was an outcast from his own people. Thus there could be nothing in the procedure that was original, and unless there was something original, how could I teach the High Priests?

When the priest had moved out, I looked upon the sea of faces of men and women seated on the stones of the court. I saw not one, not one of our people, not a familiar Essene. Even Rabbi Borrenchan, who had been so prominent at my registration and so boastful of my learning, was nowhere to be seen. But my mind was made up and I would not turn back. I listened carefully while the priest talked about men's duty and small things in daily obedience, the need for attendance at the Tabernacle, and that it was man's supreme duty to search for God, cling to the good and forego sin. When his loud talk was finished there was a period of simple questions easily answered.

102

But without support from my friends I still had to make my attempt. I swallowed hard and asked a calculated but apparently simple question. The High Priest's first reaction was to laugh and this relieved me for I knew he did not detect my deliberate trap. Thus, spurred with a little courage from a little success, I felt better.

"Sir, what is sin?"

"Oh, my little redhead, such a question! At your age! Has not your mother taught you the meaning of sin?"

He was expansive and good natured and I said, "Sir, she has tried but she fails in consistency. She tells me that doubting the word of a Rabbi is sin. Is it a sin to doubt?"

"Not to doubt, but it is a sin to doubt the servant of God!"

"Oh, Sir, have I indeed sinned just now since I doubted you and your conclusion to your lecture to the priests on the Terrace?"

"That could be mere disagreement, my son. In what way did you disagree with my conclusion?"

"Sir, before your conclusion in your secondary thesis, you said, 'Man must know God to be able to serve his fellow man.' I wondered if it were not more important that man should serve his fellowman in humility and kindness in order that he could come to know God. Did I sin in wondering and doubting your word?"

"No, son – well, no!"

"I doubted you and did not sin?"

"No, son, no!"

"Then, doubting even a High Priest is not a sin. Oh, please, Sir tell me what is sin?"

"Well, stealing is a sin."

The entire crowd was inching forward upon the stones and straining to hear and silencing anyone who dared breathe loudly or scuff a stone. "Oh, Sir, I am sorry that I do not understand. If I take and eat the sacrifice, do I sin?"

"Yes, you certainly do!"

"Would all of my offspring live in sin thereafter?"

"Oh, yes, indeed!"

"Then, do the Jews live in sin, in shadow of such a theft?"

"No!"

"But the ancestor of our race took and ate the sacrifice when he wanted food!"

"Yes, but that is different!"

"Sir, then sometimes stealing is not a sin? There are exceptions? Oh, this is what puzzles me - is there no sin that has no exceptions?"

The High Priest turned in his chair and looked at me with knotted brows. For a moment I thought he would like to shatter me with a blow.

"Incest is a sin; adultery is a sin."

"Oh, oh yes, Sir! My mother has said as much, yet is it not true that one of our greatest ancestors lay with his own daughters in both adultery and incest? Yet, we reverence him as the great founder of our race."

Beads of perspiration began to form on his forehead and his smile was very tight and his lips were set and thin above his long beard. "You have taken special exception in each case, son."

"Sir, forgive me, but is there no case to which some exception may not be taken?"

"Apparently not, son."

The crowd roared with laughter at that and I pretended to be embarrassed. "Sir, you joke with me. Would it be impertinent for me to show from your own words spoken out on the Terrace that there is one case, and one case only?"

"From my words?" The sentence was jerked from him in surprise but I took it as an invitation to proceed.

"Oh, oh, you want me to recall them to your mind?"

"Yes, yes, of course!"

"Sir, in the *Kallah*, that is, in your careful scientific discussion to the priests you said 'To know God is the sole purpose of man's existence!'"

"Yes! But what has that to do with sin?"

"But, Sir, is the statement true?"

"Of course, it is true!"

"Do others agree? Will your other priests agree to

104

this statement that it is true?"

I was hoping by this method to involve them in a discussion - and it worked! Some thirty priests and Doctors of Law came to the hedge and stood looking down upon me. They agreed that knowing God was the purpose of man's life. I turned back to the High Priest.

"Sir, your thought seems to be accepted as wisdom." I rose and walked to the puzzled and almost angry priest and stopped at his knees. "I want to thank you for helping me with my puzzles and making me see so clearly. Is not that a sin, and that only, which causes any man to miss in his attempt to make connection with his God?"

I waited until the murmurs of approval died down and the priests had ceased to comment among themselves. "Sir, are there any exceptions to this definition?" I turned toward the other priests. "Good Sirs, have I not re-stated his own conclusions correctly but in my own words? Is there an exception to this definition of sin?" The High Priest looked with some concern at the faces of the other priests but no one spoke, and he relaxed and put his hand upon my shoulders.

"Manachi, I say he has carried your own thinking to a higher level. What say you?"

The High Priest, Rubin Manachi, patted my head and said with great tolerance, "I say that he is indeed a bright young man! I would talk with him further but it is time for morning sacrifice. I shall be busy until the evening sacrifice. Also tonight with Roman authorities. Take him to Ophel for the night! Find from whence he came. Locate his Rabbi that we may learn if this wisdom is of God or devil. Tomorrow we will meet with him and his Rabbi and we shall all test him. He is clever and of good deportment. Sometimes the wisdom of the Lord flows from the mouths of babes." Rabbi Manachi rose to leave, then stopped and said to the group of young priests, "Let the Great Sanhedrin know. Tell Hillel and also tell Shammai of this amazing child and invite them to come tomorrow to guide our formal questioning. And Gamaliel, treat this child with more than your usual rigorous courtesy, lest you offend the Lord and me!"

When he turned away a short, dark faced priest of

about twenty-five years took me over-firmly by the hand and led me toward the tunnels which led to Ophel, or the priests' houses. But the old priest came along, he who had been talking with me. We passed through the tunnel. In about fifty strides we came into an open court, very long, along the sides of which there arose the apartments of the priests. I was hurried directly to the apartment of Gamaliel. He was fierce and forceful but a careful, correct priest who spoke with some authority to his fellow priests, all who had accompanied us.

"Someone must let Hillel know that a prodigy has been found. Who wants to go and deliver the invitation to the President of the Great Sanhedrin? Fine! You go! But don't be surprised if the liberal old fool falls upon his knees and thanks God for sending the Messiah to liberate us!" There was humor in his voice, tinged with a bitter mockery that made it furious. I felt the undercurrent of struggle in him and in the group.

One said, "You should not speak disrespectfully of the President of the Great Sanhedrin."

"No matter what his power now, soon he will be set aside by the growing power of Shammai."

"That traditionalist! He is so rigorous in his interpretation of the laws that he feels that the laws delivered by God should not be changed to meet the changing conditions of man! Ha! He's a smart scribe but he is only vice president of the Great Sanhedrin."

"He will be more! Wait and see!"

There was comradeship and teasing in the words and the manner of the priests. But there quite obviously was an equal and serious tension which indicated the friction into which I was caught. The departing priest turned to me and spoke, and I could tell he was deadly serious.

"Lad, pray that you are questioned by Hillel, not by the scribe Shammai. Shammai cannot believe that anyone who is not a scribe can know anything about the laws of God. And if he has some knowledge it must be because he was taught by the devil."

Gamaliel turned to me and snapped, "A question, boy, were you taught by the devil?"

I looked up into his set, fiery, mean eyes. "Sir, you

106

offend my teachers, Rabbi Borrenchan, my mother and my father! They taught me in the tradition of the Faith as taught to them by you priests."

As the tedious day wore on I found out much about Shammai, the scribe, and about Hillel. Shammai was trying to oust the liberal priests from power. There was much secrecy and much in-fighting on the part of the scribe. For the liberal Hillel wanted to bring the Law of God to man in terms of man's understanding, not as adamant and inflexible rules of conduct. Shammai was a legalist, anti-humanitarian, and fought with treacherousness and tenacity, brutality and mercilessness. He was all the more frustrated because Hillel seemed to hold him in check without effort and without hatred or force. Gamaliel turned to a priest. "Go find the Rabbi Borrenchan of this village called Nazar. See that he comes tomorrow at the command of the Great Sanhedrin. And get from him a report on this Joseph-bar-Joseph which shall be for my ears alone."

"For your ears alone, Gamaliel, until you can rush over and report it to Shammai, eh?"

We had a meal of over-rich food late in the afternoon. I was soon tired of the narrow strife-filled minds of the priests. When the meal was finished I laid back upon a pallet of thick carpets and promptly went to sleep. Inactivity was strange to me and boredom was something entirely new. The food was too heavy and indeed the day had been a strain. Sometime during the night I was covered with a fine light fur robe against the night chill but did not fully awaken until almost the first light of the 19th day of *Nisan*, the fifth day of the Feast of The Passover. Soon I was bathed in a tiled tub and we had a breakfast that was again too heavy and grease-filled. As I ate I longed for the robust taste of the baked barley cake and the feel of hard milk curds and good fruit. But the queasiness in my stomach may have been because I was tense and nervous, for I faced a rough trial, a fact that Gamaliel called to my mind quite often with a gloating manner and threat in his voice. We hurried to the meeting.

I first saw Shammai, the scribe. He was a short,

thin man with sallow skin and sharp features and there was a small ring of black hair upon his head and it seemed to support his bald pate. His eyes were brilliant, perhaps too prominent and too brilliant. I also saw the great teacher, Hillel. He was tall and gaunt, yet he seemed expansive, and would be said to be big. His face was high in color, near to florid, and his gray and brown beard was as wide as his massive chest. His hair was like a shock of sun-darkened wheat upon his head and he seemed to have a radiance that was like a halo. His eyes were wide-spaced, and strangely like my father's. Before him stood the short, nearly cringing figure of Rabbi Borrenchan. But the eyes of the Master Teacher seemed to be focused through and beyond the Rabbi's head.

"I have taught him with care and his mother is a most devout woman. If the devil has invaded him it is certainly of recent time." Borrenchan said this in a tight voice.

My test began in a formal manner but I could feel the thoughts of hatred and frustrations shooting from Shammai toward Hillel. The President of the Great Sanhedrin sat as if wrapped in impassable spiritual armor, holding all the world in the spell of his expanding love. Only a false man could have failed to return his outpouring of love and it was obvious from their auras that Shammai and Gamaliel were hurt by his very benevolence. They swung upon me with a battery of questions which were unkind. They asked them in such a way that the answers would have had to be tarnished by acceptance of a black belief. Such questions as: "When did you first know that the devil was in you?"

"In the beginning, did you resist the devil? Or did you let him have his way without a fight?"

"What is the law of the devil?"

When they first started asking such unfair and prejudiced questions, I did not answer, and they grew almost gleeful, as if they were having a great success at my expense. At last, growing tired of such juvenile and unfair questions, I decided to bring them to a stand, for it was apparent that they had cowered the other priests and doctors, all except Hillel and the young priest who stood up to Gamaliel, whose name I found years later to be Nicodemus.

I could expect no champions so I said suddenly, "Sirs, Shammai and Gamaliel, you have asked many, many questions to indicate that you know much about the devil and his works. If God occupied your thoughts, as he should in your position, could you then be so pre-occupied with the devil?"

Both men gasped, and a flurry of comment went among the hundred or more priests and doctors.

I looked out into the court but among the many persons that were sitting on the stones, I saw no Essenes except about seventy-five dressed in the blue robes and hoods of the probationary step. It seemed useless anyway, this attempt to best the great minds, so I threw all caution to the sky and said, "Sirs, do you consider your questions either dignified or fair? Are you asking me to answer questions that are nothing but a trap? Questions so worded that a simple statement will not suffice, and an hour's dissertation would be wasteful of your time and mine? Are not your questions designed to trap and discredit me and my teachers? Would I not need a learned champion to answer you? Since I have never known anything or thought upon the works of the devil, may I conclude that you have? I am a farmer's boy and have heard the saying, 'How can that cow be with calf who's never known a bull?'

I faced them firmly with defiance. "May I know, Sirs, do you wish to test me fairly or defeat me by any means? Do you strive against me to increase your prestige in the Great Sanhedrin?"

For a moment there was a deadly hush, setting on top of indrawn breath. Then President Hillel began to laugh, loud and joyous! The terrible tension was broken and the priests joined in a gale of laughter, and at long last my two antagonists began to laugh.

Hillel reached out and placed me on his ample knee. "Ho, this is indeed a Jewish Roman Candle! He lights up like a sky exploding! But, son, you must learn to control that waspish tongue! These learned priests have done you a favor. They have deliberately been the devil's

109

advocate to provoke out of you the truth. Have they not proved to all, gentlemen, that his knowledge comes not from the devil? Therefore, we may proceed on the assumption that it comes either from man or God?" He shook me gently. "Now that this is established, shall we talk together as friends?"

"Sirs," I turned toward the two priests, "I was taught to turn the second cheek before striking my offenders. I pray you forgive me, for I was indeed not wise enough to see that you are my friends in disguise, not foes of my welfare. For your friendship and help, I thank you!" A wry smile came upon their faces but they came near me and were neutral, if not kind.

We talked then at length of the law and of the symbols by which the law may be taught to common man and of means by which young men, such as myself, could be encouraged to learn. As we talked, the greater doctors asked me fair questions. I was able to answer them sometimes rather well, and they seemed to be pleased, and it became obvious that I was to be successful in my trial. Rabbi Borrenchan came forward to stand beside me. When he saw that the men of the Great Sanhedrin approved of me he began to expand, smile and nod his head. I loved the man, the benevolent and unlearned Rabbi and was secretly pleased to see his eyes glaze when I gradually raised the discussion to the higher principles of harmonic law. Soon I was talking to the listening priests on the relationship of physical laws as the disciplines or stepping stones by which man could reach the spiritual laws, above doctrine, above creed, above temple, above church.

I saw my mother hurry into the court, her beautiful face pale and distraught. When her eyes met mine, relief flooded her face and she hurried over to the border of flowers. But there, true to the training and tradition, she stopped, daring not to come inside the border. She stood in some agitation until those behind her caused her to sit upon the stones so they could hear and see. Soon I forgot her and all else for the great teacher, Hillel, had carried the discussion into the finest realms of my knowledge. He was so like my father, so insistent, yet so

110

patient, so wise, yet so humble. And love spilled out upon all, enveloping me and lulling me and it was apparent that Hillel only understood the metaphysical principles of the Law.

At last, he asked me a question that stopped me and for which I could not immediately think of an answer. As I stood in meditation I felt two rays of blue-white light strike me in the forehead. One came from somewhere beyond the border in the midst of the court and the other from the forehead of Hillel himself! Suddenly, as if borne up into another level of consciousness, I knew the answer!

"Sirs, you asked, 'What is the very highest principle of the law?' Is it not that it releases and makes free and is not in any way a binding force? It may be that law in the physical level may bind man and make him an unwitting and unwilling prisoner to culture and social mores. It may circumscribe his actions and even his morals. But, at the spiritual level when properly understood, he who obeys the law is above all control. He is above cultural and social mores. He is truly above all the controllable actions and morals. Though he is neither unwittingly a prisoner, nor unwilling to perform the law, he has risen above all law to infinite freedom. Has he not become totally spiritual? Can that which is spiritual be controlled by physical laws?"

There was a long hush, and then the most astonishing thing happened. From beyond the flower border, there was the sound of hands clapping, and soon the priests and the doctors were applauding too! I was deeply pleased but then blushed for I was certain that Hillel could read my thoughts, even as my father could. I thought perhaps I had succeeded but when I looked into the court I was dismayed. For in all the space there were no Essenes, except those of the lower order. There seemed to be no one who might know and report my success to my Brothers. Therefore, my chance of becoming a teacher was almost gone, and I was sad in heart. At last the Great Sanhedrin was satisfied and Hillel rose and led me to the Teacher's chair. There he stood me upon the seat and turned to the group in the court.

111

"Behold Joseph-bar-Joseph from the village of Nazar! He is a student of the synagogue and also an Essene. We find him rich in knowledge and wise, able to make intuitive connection between ideas and facts, and to reason in the difficult realm of abstraction. In him, we are well pleased."

The great teacher stopped and waited for several seconds. I saw in the far court several of my Brothers in white dress and without hoods. They came slowly into the court. My heart leaped, then fell, for it was clear that they were all too late. They could not now see my effectiveness and judge for themselves whether or not I had indeed taught the priests. I found Hillel looking down upon me in a most understanding way and I'm sure he read my mind. For that great teacher stepped to the fore, spoke again, as if he said his message to the heads of my Brothers, especially. "Let us say that he has been most excellently tested, except that his red hair set fire to his tongue, we find him most pleasant." He edged forward and raised his voice as if to be certain that the Essenes heard him clearly. "Let it be known that he has taught us at the Great Sanhedrin and taught us well. Let it be said that this proves that the Great Truth of God is not written in scroll or found in temple, synagogue, or in a body of highly trained men. It is found only within a just, upright heart."

The great Hillel turned to the priests and doctors. "Do you not agree that he has taught us of these things pleasantly and well?" There was a chorus of agreement and the Great Sanhedrin broke up to carry out the duties of the Temple in the morning sacrifice. My beautiful mother came to me quickly, tears streaming down her face, and she was both laughing and crying as she swept me into her embrace.

"Oh, Jeshua, how you have dealt with us! Your father has long since come back looking for you! We hunted for you with all the company and when you were not found, we hurried back to the Temple in concern. I was afraid something had happened to you!"

I put my arms around her and kissed her gently. "Why would you worry about me, Mother? Wouldn't you know I would be with you or going about my Father's business?

How strange was the thing that happened next. If subsequent events had not proved the rightness of my sensitivity, I would not dare report what happened. How foolish it seems to write, "I saw thought." Yet, this is what happened.

One of the novices came near to us. He was tall, even as my father, and his entire face was hidden by the hood, which some novices wore. His side was turned to us, his left side, and he stood about ten feet from mother and me and somewhat closer to Hillel. He stopped and stood very still. Someone bumped him and he did not sway. Then, there seemed to rise from his head a blue-white light. I watched it grow in intensity until like a spiritual serpent it struck across the distance and touched the head of the President of the Great Sanhedrin. Hillel was speaking to many people and smiling but he turned away from them and stood straight and very, very still. A new light of great delight came into his eyes and he looked at me with a sudden and different awareness. He seemed to think for a few seconds, then closed his eyes and stood very still and completely unmoving. A silver-violet thread leaped from his head to that of the Novice. I saw the pulsing ties, like two spiritual ropes running between the two men, binding them into a single unit of supreme understanding. I saw and I knew that they exchanged knowledge, and that the exchange was caused by and concerned me.

Quietly the great teacher opened his eyes, saw me looking at him, and smiled. The Novice moved without looking back. He even walked somewhat like my father. Hillel came purposefully toward me, and talked to my beautiful mother, even with the duties of the Temple clamoring for his time, about my possible future studies. Mother, of course, asked about the possibility of my entering the training of a Rabbi.

The great teacher encouraged the thought, then he added, "In the reaches of the desire, there is sometimes the thought in every advanced mind and soul that he may be selected to work for a mystical Brotherhood or that he

113

may be of the Order of Melchizedek. If such mystical things were true, they alone would be better training than that which is needed for the priesthood."

My mother paid no attention to the words he said for he said them with an apparent humor. But I heard them as a man dying of thirst hears the bubbling of water. He saw the look upon my face and his eyes signalled for me to be silent, and his lips talked evenly to other things.

Soon he was gone out of my sight and hearing but not out of my life. For to me, he would ever be the living, walking, laughing symbol of love. I was to hear many times in my training, one of his maxims, "Do not unto others that which is hateful unto you." But, with all his openness and love, at least on the physical level, I had noted a mystery about him. How marvelous was his understanding that he could conquer with love. But what of the strange intertwining of thought messages between him and the Novice concerning me?

Mother was most anxious to depart from the Temple and we hurried toward the Bethany Camp. Though she scolded me gently for worrying her, her eyes told me how proud she was, and also of a new height of that more than human adoration that worried and confused me. We reached Bethany after the company had gone ahead toward the first camp which was on the Jordan about seven miles beyond Jericho. It was a long march for one day but they had left us the two largest mules and we rode swiftly even through the hot afternoon and caught them in camp well before sundown.

John-John, Jim-Jim, Jo-Jo, Mary-B and father were waiting the meal for us and my ears burned with the glowing reports that mother gave of how Hillel had treated us because of me. The youngsters were excited that their brother should dare to talk to the High Priest and by nightfall had spread the tale through the augmented company. But not a Brother of the Essenes came to talk with me and I could tell nothing from my father's inscrutable face. Therefore, in deep sadness I concluded that I had failed, insofar as they knew, to pass my trial. And in my heart I was bitter, for indeed Hillel had said that I had taught the priests, in the hearing of

114

my Brothers, and they had joined the company by sundown, but had not even spoken of me.

We started at first light the next morning and passed the point of East Mount Sariaba where the Jabbok River of Perea comes into the Jordan, well before midday. We rested for a time and pushed on to make camp near the Jordan before the great heat of the afternoon. The next day was a short easy march to the well of Barsun.

My exploits in the Temple were forgotten as many came to remind Mother of her promise to tell more about the miracles and the woman of our village. Excitement grew in the augmenting group from *Cana* and the new Roman town of *Tiberias*, and *Jotapata*, *Magdala*, and as far north as *Chorazin*, Capernaum and even *Gischala*. They all decided to make a short day in their march to stay and hear Mother's story which concerned the promised Messiah. And verily it was a huge group that crowded close upon the earth between the camp fires near the well when the night shadows began to settle across the wilderness. When Mother came to the well for her night pitcher of water, a chorus of voices urged her to hurry and begin her story. She carefully filled the pitcher and placed it at my knee, as if to hold me to the spot.

A hundred men offered to lift her to the stones beside the well while she was so slender and light that I might have done it myself. She stood straight, slender and beautiful in the firelight, and there was a strange and piteous smile upon her face, and tears - yes, tears in her eyes. Many times she looked at me almost in doubt, or fear. But at last she threw back her shoulders and began her story. It was that very story which was to change my destiny.

"Beloved friends and comrades of the journey! The time has come to make known to the world that which cannot longer be hidden! The Scriptures have foretold the coming of the Messiah, the Redeemer of Men. You all await his coming, do you not? Then listen to my story *well*! I know that the long awaited Messiah has been born to man. The Scriptures have already been fulfilled. And there is come out of the house of David, the son of God!"

115

8

THREE WAYS
OF VIRGIN BIRTH

An exclamation of surprise, mixed with pleasure, went up from the throats of the people in the large company at the way my beautiful mother began her talk. She was known and popular with all in our village and they had spread her fame among the others of the company. Rabbi Borrenchan sat next to me in the firelight and I saw his pleased smile as he glanced at me. My father's eyes came slowly around to lock with mine and I noticed that John-John had fixed his eyes upon mine with that strange adoration he and Mother seemed to share.

"Do we not all expect the Messiah?"

"Yes!"

"In Malachi, it was written long ago: 'Behold! I will send my messenger and he shall prepare the way before me and the Lord whom ye seek shall suddenly come to his Temple, even the messenger to The Covenant. And he shall sit as a refiner and purifier of silver and he shall purify the Sons of Levi and purge them as gold and silver, that they may offer unto the Lord an offering, and righteousness.'

"You remember also, from the Prophet Isaiah: 'And he shall judge among the nations and shall rebuke many people and they shall beat their swords into plowshares and their spears into pruning hooks. Nation shall not lift up sword against nation, neither shall they learn war any more. And there shall come a rod out of the stem of Jesse, and a branch shall grow out of his roots; and the Spirit of the Lord shall rest upon him, the Spirit of Wisdom and Understanding, the Spirit of Counsel and Might, the Spirit of Knowledge and of the fear of the Lord. And he shall not judge after the sight of his eyes, nor reprove from what he hath heard. But with righteousness shall he judge the poor, and reprove with equity the meek of the earth; and he shall smite the earth with the rod of his mouth, and with the breath of his lips shall he slay the wicked; and the sucking child shall play on the hole of the asp.'

"I say again, these prophesies and others have been fulfilled! Even now, one walks among you who has come of the lineage of Jesse, out of the loins of David, by the way of a virgin undefiled and pure. Let me tell you her story; for although you all know of Jesse and David, I alone know the Perfect Virgin. She is, and was, a girl of our village, a daughter of priests. This is her amazing story.

"This maiden was raised as a holy gift from God. Her parents saw to it that her feet touched no unconsecrated ground until she was seven, and she was made a bride of the church. All her youth was attended with great care and good tutoring, and she grew into womanhood a little lonely, and much given to mystic thoughts. Long after she reached the age, she was not chosen by any man. Not until long after she was fifteen did one come to claim her and pay the dowry for one so mystical and so well kept. At seventeen she was chosen by a great and learned man, of sweet disposition and humble mien, and he was twenty-four when they were betrothed. After the betrothal he went forth to another city for a building job and after four months of his absence she was greatly lonely and went often into the sanctuary of her father's house to pray.

"There, one day, her sight was blazed by an angel. Standing straight and tall and in a mighty brilliance, the angel said, 'Hail, Virgin, highly favored! God is with you! Blessed are you among all women!'

"But the maiden was sorely troubled and terrified lest the vision should be false. But the angel said, 'Fear

117

not, Virgin, you have found favor with God. Hear the will of Heaven! Ye shall conceive and bear a son. He shall be mighty and shall be called the Son of the Almighty! And the Supreme God shall place him upon the throne of his ancestor, David! He shall reign over the House of Jacob forever, and there shall be no end of his kingdom!'

"But even as the angel was speaking, and the sanctuary was filled with his brilliance and echoed to the glory of his tones, the Virgin's mind began to waver and slip away from Divine Consciousness. How soon she dropped from a high meditation into a human attitude of mind. Doubt, shame, fear, yea even terror, began to hammer at her consciousness. Her mind wrestled with such questions as: Was this indeed the Angel of God? If he was a messenger of the Most High, by what sign could he prove himself? If she, a virgin untouched by man, were to conceive and bear High Heaven's child, would man believe and worship, or would man shame her and accuse her before the world? Would her beloved put her away with a Bill of Divorcement? If so, would he do it before two witnesses who would keep her in faith, or would he do it in public before the Gate, or within the synagogue? If he believed her not, would her neighbors? Would then irate neighbors, believing themselves right and justified under the law, stand her to public trial and condemn her? Then stone her to death, according to custom? Indeed she had cause to fear on the human level and no assurance of her future. Verily, the anguish of her soul was great but she was also secretly pleased at being chosen, and she partly believed. Had not her father and Anna, her beloved mother, many times assured her that before her birth she was envisioned as the chosen of God? Had she not, in sacred ceremonies, been dedicated to Him in body, mind and soul? Even as a woman is wedded to an earthly husband, had she not been wedded to the Most High? Her feet had touched no unhallowed soil until she was seven years of age and her life ordained.

"Were other maidens so carefully tended and so fully purified for divine purpose? Even as she reasoned thus, she began to see that she was chosen as the instrument of the Lord before her own conception. Her ordained and divine use was a juggernaut that rolled over her human doubts and frailties. Humbly and in gratitude she fell upon her knees and bowed to her service to the Divine. Yet, will the human mind not always be curious? Will it not keep asking,- How? Why? When? Even of the Divine? She asked of the angel, 'How can I conceive since I have known no man?'

"The angel smiled and said, 'Behold, it is no mystery! You shall be raised into your spiritual, radiant body, together with all the faculties and powers of womanhood! The thought power of the Highest shall overshadow you and the Divine use of thought force shall form the seed and place it in your womb. You shall know no man but only the touch of the thought, shadowy as a Holy Ghost. But when your Radiant Self has been brought into your physical self, you shall conceive in the flesh of this Divine Thought! Therefore, shall you give birth to a Holy Being which shall be the Son of God! This Son of God, you shall call by this name' The angel whispered into her ear the name and it meant 'Redeemer!'

"The angel said, 'Know that with God, nothing is impossible! Recall that your aunt was barren all her life but in her old age has conceived and is to bear a son!'

"It was done even as the angel said. And as truth of her vision, she arose and hurried to the house of her uncle in Judah, as directed by the angel. But she spoke the name of her aunt, and her aunt was filled with holy thought. Her aunt gathered the trembling virgin in her arms and cried in a loud voice:

"'You are blessed above all women; even as the fruit of your womb is blessed above all men! And blessed among women am I that the maiden who is to be mother of my Awaited Lord should come to me. And blessed is the babe in my womb for even as your voice spoke my name it leapt with joy. Dry your tears and do not fear, Virgin of God, for because you believed, the awaited one shall come forth!'

"The Virgin saw that her uncle also knew and she wept and cried: My body and my soul is devoted to the Most High; and my heart magnifies the Lord. Without regard to my unworthy and low estate, He has chosen me for His handmaiden and henceforth all generations of men will call me blessed above all women. He that is Almighty has done to me great things, and has shown His mercy, together with His strength. He has put the proud from their high estate and exalted those of low degree.

"In order that no man might condemn her, her aunt and uncle did witness her purity and attest it. Then they kept her from that moment in sanctuary and seclusion and allowed no man to approach near unto her, that her character should be above reproach, and her name be good upon the lips of all mankind. They sent a message to her espoused love to where he worked building a temple. Near the end of four months, he came to her at her uncle's house for, only then, was his work finished.

"How frightened was the virgin as he stopped in her presence and she looked upon him with eyes of love and wonder. Could she really know what he would do, or say, upon finding that she was almost four months pregnant? What would he believe? But she and her aunt and uncle told him all, saying that he should know and that, if he believed them not, he should examine her body before he put her away with divorce. But he stood very still, his eyes upon her in an inscrutable way and was neither moved to blame nor reproach. He heard the aunt of the virgin declare upon her honored word that the maiden was yet a virgin, and no man had come near her in the time. But neither was he moved to acceptance, praise or jubilation. He looked at her with eyes that seemed to be filled with adoration and love, yet he spoke not a word but turned away with tears in his eyes and left the house.

"The virgin knew not what he felt nor what he believed, and wept in her anguish and cried aloud to the Almighty. Thus she resolved to die and refused food and water. And at the end of two days she stood in the sanctuary and cried with bitterness. Then she heard a sound and felt the arms of her beloved around her, his sweet kiss warm upon her face and his tears mixed with hers.

"'Beloved, never did I doubt you, for I knew before you knew and there were things between me and my most

120

High God that I had to pray upon and give thanks for. And I could not speak for the joy of your blessedness and the wonders of His Creation!'

"When the lovers were reconciled and the aunt and uncle of the virgin were come into the sanctuary, he said forthrightly to all, 'Verily, I do not believe she has conceived as has been told.'

"When the aunt would have protested and defended the virgin, he stopped her with a silencing look. 'Woman, hear me! I know this maid is yet a virgin for I have proof more wondrous than tongue can tell! But I know whereof I speak. There are three ways of virgin birth. Here me yet further with complete understanding. If she were a harlot rather than a virgin, still would I marry her, so great is my love for her! Yet, if I loved her not at all and she were defiled and common rather than pure and virtuous, still would I marry her for such is my duty to my promised word. Know this! I love her and I know she is a Virgin of God! Yet I do not agree upon the way this holy maiden conceived! With this opinion clearly stated, openly so there shall be no secret belief in me to be cause of misunderstanding, I place my love and my name at her feet and ask this maiden to decide! If she still wills it, let the marriage be this day, this very hour, here in this sanctuary made divine by her prayers, her tears and her presence!'

"How great was the maiden's joy and the sweet hour of nuptials was appointed and she became his bride. That evening, four persons and three miracles sat at the bridal supper- a barren woman who became fruitful at the promise of God, a virgin who conceived at the command of God, and a bridegroom who rose above all human doubts; and with them the two unborn sons who were to influence the future of all mankind. Though she came to his home and his bed, the bridegroom knew not the maiden until a son was born from a virgin, thus fulfilling the promise and the prophesies.

"Thus it was that when her time was near, a journey must be undertaken from their home in our village to Bethlehem. For the Roman Caesar had called for a registration of all Jews in the city of their birth. And

121

Herod, The Awful, required the act be done without delay. Thus she was big with child when they came into the little town of Bethlehem. But they were late for she could not travel fast and there were no rooms in the Inn or the home of good folk of the town. Thus it was that the bridegroom went to the Essenes and was granted permission to use the Grotto of their secret ceremonies. And thus it was that she brought forth her first-born son, wrapped him in swaddles of cotton and linen and placed him in a manger within the Grotto. All unknowing of the events outside, she cared for the Son of God. Yet other miracles were happening.

"Certain shepherds watched the flocks meant for sacrifice at the Temple. Suddenly an angel stood before them in the fields where they lay wrapped in blankets against the chill of the night for it was near first light of May 23. A splendor shone all around and the angel said, 'Fear not, for I bring you tidings of great joy to all peoples of the world, for all time! This very hour there is born in the City of David, The Awaited, The Saviour! And that ye may believe and know that this be your sign, ye will find him wrapped in swaddling clothes lying in a manger.'

"Even as the herald angel spoke, a multitude of heavenly voices spoke forth praises to God the Almighty saying, 'Behold the Messiah! Who will bring glory to God the Eternal! And on earth will bring peace, good will toward men!'

"And the shepherds left their flock and hurried into the town and found the virgin mother, the bridegroom and the child asleep in the manger. The shepherds told their story abroad in the crowded town and the virgin mother was puzzled and pondered in her heart why the birth of the Son of God was so lowly and was thus announced.

"When the eight days were passed, the child was taken for circumcision and he was given the name announced by the angel before he was conceived in the virgin's womb. And when the days of her purification, according to the Mosaic law, were come, that happened which I told you at this well. Simeon and Anna came upon the mother, proclaiming in loud voices that they had foreseen and now behold the Messiah!

"I promised to tell you who was the woman at Nazar! Verily, she was that same virgin who conceived of The Most High and bore a Son of God and called him by the name the angel spoke! That woman who was that virgin is now within the ring of these camp fires! That one who bears the angel-given name now sits in the firelight at this camp! Verily, I am that woman! The Virgin who bore the Son of God! And he was named Jeshuau, and is called Joseph-bar-Joseph, and he is that Divine Messiah for whom you wait! And at his side in the firelight is John, angel-announced son of my very Aunt Elizabeth, wife of Zacharias! Proudly I swear to you that I am the mother of Him that was to appear and is now come in the flesh and walks among you! Behold the Son of God!"

In all that vast company not a breath stirred the desert air, not a person moved lest the enchantment of the tale be broken. Rabbi Borrenchan wept and nodded and wept some more. My mother stood in the glow of the firelight seemingly borne up and set free, radiant beyond the fullest dreams of man. Yet, her eyes sought mine with a strange pleading and a strange terror. John-John sighed as he sat beside me and his eyes were aglow with a light of utter adoration. But my surprise was complete and my heart was too full with wonder to let me move.

My beautiful mother was lifted down and stood hesitantly near the well, her eyes fixed upon mine. I saw in her face that strange terror which I had seen and my heart leaped out to her in spite of my confusion and my embarrassment. I smiled at her, trying to show across the distance my love for her and I rose to my feet to go to her. But she sped eagerly across the firelight and into my arms and clung to me trembling and sobbing.

"Oh, my son, my Divine Son! I should have told you! I have tried many times. Oh, how unwise and unworthy I have been!"

I could not speak. At that moment tears were in my throat indeed, but with her words my mind was frozen by the staggering implication! I was poised above the deep abyss of doubt. For my beautiful mother was the most

123

imaginative and mystical woman and a fabulous teller of tales. I knew she might invent or improvise for the sake of her story. But in her eyes I saw that she truly believed every word of the story she had told. In her trembling terror and her words, I sensed her dread that I might be displeased with her story, or doubt her word. I patted her.

"Beautiful Mother! You're the finest and most worthy Mother! Too wonderful even for a Messiah!"

The children stood and looked up at us with owl-wise eyes, both proud and shy. Mother, on seeing them, laughed through her tears at the expressions on their faces and swept them into her arms all at once! Soon, in the business of being a good mother, she regained her composure and soon was laughing with us all. But from that moment on, I sometimes surprised in the eyes of my brothers and sisters, that same look which had previously been only on John-John's and Mother's face. In a few minutes the pilgrims of the expanded company began to come to thank her for the story, and for magnificent entertainment! But each visitor looked at me with either curious, baleful or worshipful mien.

Much later, when most of the camp had strolled past our fire or stopped to chat, we were able to settle down and try to sleep. But the buzz of voices persisted as many sat at their own campfires and discussed the story. Even as we lay in our desert beds, many of the pilgrims came and stood beyond the glow of the embers of our fire and I could see curious eyes peeking into our camp from all directions.

With little sleep, we were eager to leave the camp by the first light. But many came, bearing burning torches against the blackness and talked with Mother and asked her questions. We ate quickly and started upon the trail but still many came to talk with Mother and to ask me questions as we moved on in the early morning light. We swung westward past *Mount Gilboa*, northwest of *Jezreel*, and when we stopped for our midday meal, *Mount Tabor* loomed up against the wilderness to the north.

But I did not want to talk to the many curious pilgrims. I wanted to talk to my beloved father. I needed

124

his help and his stabilizing opinions and, most of all, I needed his wisdom. For I was beginning to realize that Mother had been telling what she thought was true.

We were almost back to Nazar before I realized that my father was deliberately making it impossible for me to talk to him alone. He was intentionally leaving me with my inner questions. Those restless questions seared in my mind and flamed to a white heat. I was so plagued and distressed by the inner thoughts, doubts and suspicions that I found myself only half listening when talking even with the Elders of the company. I paid little attention and not too much respect.

Mary-Beth was tired from the long walk and John-John and I decided to rest her by carrying her on our shoulders. John-John took her first and carried her for a while. When I reached to take her she drew back. I was surprised but not ready for the deep hurt of her direct words.

"Should a mortal like me weigh down the Son of God?"

I felt the words like a blow in the stomach, and for a moment was stunned to silence and stillness. Beyond John-John's face I saw the deep eyes of my father and read there a kindness that answered my great need.

"Mary-B, is it not well to test the Divine? Must not that which is divine truly bear all the burdens of human flesh? And yet more?"

Mary-B thought it over for a while and tossed her cottony curls in the desert sun. "Well, I do love him as a brother, even if he is the Messiah!" With the directness of a child, she came into my arms and sat astride my neck, and we trudged on in the afternoon heat.

My father never spoke but to guide or teach. His words had been a warning preparing me for the hard tests to come. My heart was torn by the questions that rode the shoulders of my mind, even as a cushion to the cross. Was I indeed divine? Was I, as Mother thought, the Son of God, born of a virgin undefiled by man? Yet another wild question plagued my thoughts. What had Father meant when he told Mother that there were three ways of virgin birth? The more I pondered these things and wondered, the more I knew I had to talk with my father. But he always was with someone and we could not talk alone.

Mother apparently unaware of the burden she had dumped into my heart, seemed like a bird, gay and uncaged. She moved with a new energy, and she was more animated than I had ever known her to be. I could see that she had at last done that thing which she felt compelled to do, yet had put off, bearing the burden of postponement within her heart. One good thing had happened. Now when she and John-John looked upon me, I understood somewhat the strange adoration of their eyes. It was not love or lack of love for me. It was humble adoration for that God-essence which I represented in her mind. I realized that as long as she thought of me as the Messiah, so long would her radiant adoration be turned upon me.

But I asked myself- what would happen if she found that I was not divine, but merely human? I knew how her life turned around the thought of her own careful preparation, her birth and training to serve as the handmaiden of God. Without this secret thought, this magnificent purpose in her life, her life would indeed be worse than nothing! How clearly I saw that my own divinity, truly even my own verbal acceptance of divinity as the Son of God, was necessary to her continued faith in her own belief. The moment I denied that divinity by deed or word, the moment I evaded her idea of God in human form, or the moment I failed in the tests of divinity,- at that moment, her life would become a failure, her dreams purposeless, her life futile, her hopes denied. That moment - my beautiful mother would be better off if she were dead.

Because of the love I bore my mother I knew I could never deny to her, or in public, that I was divine, born from God into human form, the Son of The Most High. To have done so, would have been to destroy my mother utterly. It would have been kinder to drive a dagger into her heart. For now, to deny my divinity would be to betray her to the fish-wives and the tattle-makers. And in our village her reputation would be torn to bits. She

126

would be treated as a wounded fox in a wolf pack. All love and admiration would be withdrawn from her and she would walk a lonely road. No, I could not deny the divinity without crushing my beloved mother into an early grave, or leaving her empty-hearted – and better off dead.

But – could I claim divinity? If I accepted her claim for me, would I cut myself off from my own brothers? From my family? From my fellowmen? Or worse, would I cut myself off from the Initiate Path which I longed to tread? Would I then be forever barred from learning more about the Great White Brotherhood and the Order of Melchizedek? Only my father could answer. And he was deliberately avoiding me. Near enough to fend for me if others were unkind but far – too, too far from me.

The more I turned my thoughts inward, the more confused I became. And I began to ask myself questions that I could not answer. If I was divine, why had I not known it directly? Was not the divine all knowledge? If I was divine, why did I not have all skills and all abilities, including composition and ciphering? For was not the divine all learning? If I was divine, why was John-John more beloved than I, and why was I not beloved by all men? Was not the divine all love? If I was divine, why was I not tall and handsome as my father, or broad and powerful as was John-John? Was not the divine all beauty? If I was divine, why did I not understand the meaning of the vision of the Man of Tin? Was not the divine all revelation? If I was divine, why did I not understand all of my own inner emotional conflicts and counter loyalties? Was not the divine all truth? If I was divine, why could I not stay in the radiant condition of mind, such as was mine in deep meditation in the manger of the Grotto during Initiation? Was not the divine all glory? If I was divine, why had I lost self-control at the time John-John was in trouble? Was not the divine all courage? If I was divine why had I not understood- or, at least, immediately mastered the technique of how one could be in two places at one time? Was not the divine all power? If I was divine, why could I not raise John-John from death? And why, why had I lacked the healing ability, even after my father's long and careful training? Was not the divine all wisdom? If I was divine, why did I have so many human weaknesses? And so many frailties, so many burdens? Was not the divine all divine? If I was divine, why did I not completely understand what my father meant when he told my mother that there were three modes of virgin birth, or what he meant when he told me that he would be able to help me more when I must master the things pertaining to heaven? Was not the divine all understanding? If I was divine, why was my father avoiding my questions? Was not the divine all commanding?

Mary-B put her palms over my eyes so that I could not see the trail. When I came to a halt she laughed and said, "You haven't heard a word I said! And I've been talking and talking! You've run away from everyone, even John-John couldn't keep up! Do you think we should wait?"

I took her from my shoulders, put her on the ground and rumpled her cotton top. I kissed the peach colored cheek.

"Heh, I'm proving that I'm divine!"

She did not laugh with me, but stood looking up at me in all seriousness. "But you don't have to prove it! I know! It shows!"

"How does it show, Mary-B?"

"Wherever you go, good things are there, and where you walk, beauty grows. When you speak, the whole world listens! Not just little girls like me, but important men! And not just men and women, for even the larks forget to sing, and little ground squirrels sit up to hear. When you smile the whole world is happy and when you frown, it wants to cry. If you say something is to be, it always happens. If you think hard upon any problem, it always solves itself. When you're near, everyone is filled with a strange peace and happiness. By such things, we all knew you were divine before Mother spoiled our secret last night!"

I looked down into her eyes, so blue and deep, holding the wisdom of my father and the fire of my mother. No words would come, so I touched her gently with the tip of my finger on the nose, and at last she smiled. "Maybe- maybe you are the one who is divine! Suppose?"

John-John caught up to us, his big body moving swiftly and his face covered with a broad smile, and sweat. "Phew! You darted away like a frightened dust whirl. And I don't blame you for out-distancing those chatter-boxes. They're all over our family, asking everyone questions about last night. As if they couldn't see that you are divine."

"How could they see it, John-John? In what way do I show it?"

"In every move, and every word!"

"Mother should know. She always notices!"

"Indeed she does. Every word, every move."

The first of the company was near us then, and the shouts and banter went up. For a while I walked with some of the Essene Brothers who talked of trivial things, or chanted the prayers and songs. But as soon as I could I hurried ahead to try to untangle my twisted thoughts.

Had my mother pointed out my traits to the others of my family, making her eyes see divinity in me for them? I had seen her by the force of her logic, her beauty, and her outflowing love, persuade learned men to her opinion. If she had used such tactics daily upon members of my family, they had small hope of not being convinced. Already I knew I could not turn to Rabbi Borrenchan, for he was deeply under her spell and was one of the secret Zealots who awaited the coming of the Messiah, hoping that He would lead Israel into throwing out the Roman conquerors. I could not turn to the priest for counsel. If my mother had implanted the idea of my divinity into the minds of my family and her friends, I could not hope to find truth reflected in their eyes unless my mother was completely right in what she said and what she thought. For verily, under her sway, they would all see me as divine and as the awaited Messiah. Then I wondered if I could turn to my Brothers within the compound. I thought upon it and decided that I could not. They walked with me now yet said nothing either of my success at the Temple or lack of it, or of Mother's story of the

Immaculate Conception, They were attentive to me and kind but this was in our daily training. We talked only of trivial daily matters, or said our prayers, or recited enmasse our Psalms of Thanksgiving. Truly, I could think of no way to turn but toward my father and he would not give me opportunity to talk with him - not alone. Yet I knew he loved me well and also that anything he finally said would be of great importance and of Eternal Truth.

At the turn-off, we took leave of those pilgrims who were going on north toward *Cana*, *Capernaum* or the other towns. It was only our own goodly company of about four hundred who sang as they walked briskly into the winding streets of our village. We stopped at the top of the ridge and looked down. Our village was placed upon the smaller hills on the side of a mountain. It was a beautiful sight, with the houses resting like dream scenes upon the hills and the river circling lazily in the wide valley, seemimg to cozy the compound and the fields of the Brotherhood against the edge of the valley. With many goodbyes and much banter, individual families turned toward their homes. The Essenes and my family stayed together until we reached our yard. Then the Brothers left us with a silent salute of love and blessing.

But I could not arrange to be alone with my father. Jim-Jim and Jo-Jo were with us in unharnessing and currying the animals. Then they went with Mother and Mary-B down to the rocky basin in the river to wash our travel clothes. In the carpentry shop where Father went to work, he had John-John and a stream of visitors all afternoon. Thus the moments sped by until it was time for the evening meal. We were all together then until bedtime. It was a lovely evening. Mother was so sparkling, so radiant, so spontaneous, so free! Her wit was flashing and her energy soared. Her love poured out upon us all. She was unburdened and joyous.

When we had gone to bed I heard her happily whisper to my father, "Oh, Joseph, Joseph! I am so glad that it is done at last! Hundreds from all over the nation now know the truth. And already believe in his divinity. I feel so free!"

"Beloved! You told a convincing story and you were so beautiful that no man could doubt you for long!

"What about my husband?"

"Who adores you more than he?"

"He adores, but does he fully believe?"

"More than fully. He truthfully believes."

"Oh, Joseph! Some day you will know how wrong you are!"

"Meanwhile, pretty wife, do I not already know exactly how right you are?"

"But you don't believe that he is the Son of God."

"God in human form?"

"Is there any other God?"

"Unless you know there is, would you agree if I told you?"

"The Initiate Way! Remember, I went that way for six years."

"Could it be you stopped too soon?"

"I stopped when the angel appeared."

"You were never curious to know exactly how that came to be?"

"How else but that he was sent from God"

"God in human form, Beloved?"

"Is there another way? To me, there is only one way. It had to be God in human form!"

"In this your belief, would you have me concur if it ran against my own true knowledge?"

"If you only believed!"

"Beloved, I know! I know I adore you, woman, is that not enough?"

"What if he does not believe, because you won't?"

"How does he feel about it?"

"Oh, he is unassuming and modest. The story was a shock! He cannot yet accept the true story, but in time he will. Oh! He will! He must!"

"Shall we say, 'He must if God wills it'?"

"Oh, Joseph! Joseph! I know you do not accept. But you will see, my darling! You will see!"

9

MYSTERIES

OF THE MAN OF TIN

Questions stormed through my mind. I could not lie still and tossed and turned upon the pad. When all were asleep I eased out of bed and into my robe. I moved toward the kitchen door but my eyes were drawn through the doorway of the big bedroom. In a shaft of moonlight I saw my father and mother up on the big bed. Father's left arm was under her head which was pillowed upon his shoulder. A gleaming white duck's feather had escaped from his down pillow and now lay upon the side of my father's head, above the right temple. It was as bright as a candle's gleam in the moonlight and it moved each time my mother's breath passed across it, quivering but not falling away. I looked upon them with great love for they were so beautiful in the bright glow and they looked so strangely content, each with the other.

But the thoughts in my own disconsolate heart drove me out into the moonlight, around the house to climb the mound until I stood at the very top. From there I could look down upon the town, the compound and the curling river. They seemed so very solid, so sure, and my own doubts so unsubstantial. How could I be divine when I felt so inadequate, so insecure? I wrestled with these questions until I could bear the strain no longer. Then fell upon my knees weeping.

No sound of footsteps told me of his arrival, but my father stood beside me, and his radiance was strong in the moonlight. But his feet did not seem to touch the ground as he stood looking down upon me.

"Oh, Father, am I divine?"

"Only your heart may tell you, Joseph-bar-Joseph!"

"Oh, Father, don't leave me in the black doubt and suspicion?"

"What do you think?"

"I- I truly love my mother, but I'm afraid to believe. She - she's so imaginative. She - She's so very persuasive, so - so convincing. Even if she imagined every one of the events, including the Immaculate Conception she would be able to make the whole world believe her story. I am confused! I ask you - *am I the begotten son of God?*

"Are not all men begotten of God?"

"Yes, in the long view. But am I divinely begotten?"

"You must answer that!"

"Oh, Father, I can't!"

There was a long silence. I broke it, driving ahead in my restless search for answers to my burning question. "Mother mentioned that you told her that there were three ways of virgin birth. I wanted to ask you if-"

"Yes, I saw on the trip that you wanted to ask me many things but could I let you throw your burden of curiosity away? Other than curiosity, is there now in your life any emotion strong enough to drive you to that height of passion which is needed to achieve that which you so strongly desire?"

"Can't you guide me in this? Can't you tell me, what are the three ways of virgin birth?"

"My son, how can I tell you and be true to my Oath as a teacher? If I were to tell you all, would not this apparently kindly act rob you of the will and strength to support your spiritual drive? All I cannot tell, but I will tell you a little.

"Virgin birth is usually thought to be the result of the Most High God placing in the womb of fleshly woman the seed of life. Some even think that God must take human form. This would indeed be a miracle. And this is the thing your mother believes happened before you were born. This would be one way to bring about virgin birth,

133

but this is only the first of three ways. The second mode of virgin birth lies in the act of raising the dormant pristine spirit of man out of the mother body in each human cell. This is the virgin birth known to the Initiate who must experience this birth of spirit out of the eternal manger of living cells. You, yourself, have worked long to accomplish this very birth. Perhaps you have achieved this. Is not this birth of the Spiritual Self out of the flesh self into which it is eternally crucified unless raised by purity, power, will and love - is not this truly also a virgin birth? You see why I could not accept your mother's belief?"

"Father, what is your belief?"

"Does it matter what I believe, or, even what you *believe* only? If the whole world called your mother a liar and you a fraud, this of itself, no matter how strongly believed, would not make truth out of their error. Yet, if the whole world believed you were divine, preached it from every housetop and at the crossroads, this of itself would not make you truly divine. However, if or when you know beyond belief that you are divine, no one, no, not even I, can convince you of anything else! When the lark sings his song, he knows he is the chorister of heaven, even while he sits upon a clod of dung. When you are to become the divine voice of heaven, you will know and no one will ever change that knowing. But until you truly know, no one can force that conviction by expressed belief. You will know out of your inner self!"

"What then, am I to think? Did Mother make up her story? Did she lie out of her political interest in the coming of the Messiah?"

"No, son, your mother is incapable of lying!"

"Then, she was right?"

"Does it follow that, if she did not lie, she is right?"

"N-no, but what else can I believe? If she did not lie, she must have told the truth!"

"If she told the truth, insofar as she saw it, would she be lying if the greater truth lay not in the interpretation of what she saw? Could there not be a higher interpretation of the very event she reports?"

"How?"

134

"Could it be that there is a third mode of virgin birth? Could it be that the third mode would explain these same events as greater truth?"

"*If* there is a third way, what is it?"

"Would it not be better for you to wonder, to strive, and at last to come to true knowledge? Would not that be better than being burdened with hear-say knowledge, for hear-say knowledge could, possibly would, delay your development. Will you not, when you have searched and found and understood the third mode of virgin birth understand exactly what happened in your mother's case? Then, will you not know beyond all doubt all about your own possible divinity?"

Through clear eyes, I saw the greatness of my beloved father, how wise and how kind he always was in seeming not to coddle. Long ago I had detected the method of my father's teaching but now I began to detect a purpose, a deliberate intention to make me strong and able. It was as if I were treated as the legendary Good Sword and was being tested and tempered in the fires of trials and knowledge. I was always allowed the sweet personal choice for it was never of the faith of my father or of the Brotherhood to force opinion upon anyone. But in the very fervor of my passions, I was given only the slightest pointer toward the spiritual pathway to solution. Yet always I was given that pointer at the darkest moment when without it I might become hopelessly lost. Yet it was always up to me to fight through to my own mental goal and emotional stability.

When I turned to thank my father, he was gone without a sound of footsteps. I followed quickly, now calm in my heart, knowing that a full understanding and a complete answer to my great question could come forth in the future. I ducked into the bedroom quietly and as I passed the door to my parent's room, I was stopped cold! For my mother's cheek was still upon my father's shoulder, and he still lay in blissful comfort. Still, for he had not moved! He could not have moved. The downy feather still lay upon his temple, still trembled gently with each of Mother's breaths. That bright feather was ample proof that once again my father had been in two places at one time!

Even as I stood transfixed by wonder, Mary-A whimpered in her cradle and Father stirred, ever so slightly. The feather drifted down to the floor in the shadow of the bed. When Mary-A was again quiet, I sought my bed and was puzzled over the question: – had this ability to be in two places at one time something to do with the third mode of virgin birth, and my own divinity? Was the feather a thing of chance, or was it special guidance? Searching my reason in this way, I fell asleep, deeply aware of my beautiful and forceful mother's effect upon my life and the equally great counter effect of my wonderful Initiate Father.

Morning came and we were soon on our way to the compound. But even the cadenced song of the lark could not raise my spirits in the first light of that beautiful dawn. For I must now face my Brothers! How they had expected me to succeed in my trial, and by what strange circumstance had I failed to prove myself in their sight. But it was of our faith that one should never worry over failures that could not be helped. Yet my heart was heavy as we went into the near gate and separated to go directly to our assigned squads. All morning I worked at the assignment given but my thoughts were in such a turmoil that I was chided by the Master for inattention. Our lesson was a story about Pharoah Thutmose I and it was read to us from the scrolls in Egyptian. When we came to the time of the questioning however, I knew the answers as if I had written the story. But the sense of failure was upon me. I felt hollow as if my heart had dropped from its place, leaving a void.

From the class we went to our morning work and at midday hurried back from the fields to the Bath of Love. We slipped from our work robes, bathed, and then took the Seven Sacred Paces to our clean robes. When we were dressed we went into the Assembly Hall for the Feast.

I had hardly spoken or been spoken to and could hardly raise my eyes to see the many eyes that I felt looking upon me. The prayers were said, the Psalms of Thanksgiving were chanted, and we fell to silent eating. When all was finished, I wanted to run, even as once before I had wanted to run. But my name was spoken by the Secret Master who had called for a report of the Committee of Observation.

My father stood forth and said, "Brothers, the Committee of Observation and every Brother in this compound failed to be able to see the trial. Not one of us can from personal knowledge vouch as to the outcome. Due to most unforeseen circumstances, it was difficult for the Brothers to be near without betraying their curiosity in the discourse. However, there happened to be at the compound in Bethany, a group of the Secret Masters from many compounds. They donned the habits of Apprentices to our Brotherhood and were led to the Inner Court by one Joseph of Arimathea. Lest the hearsay report of the great Hillel should not be enough to satisfy us, my half-brother hurried here from Jerusalem that he might report his first-hand observations"

My father sat down and the Secret Master rose. This was indeed unusual. We of the Brotherhood looked upon the Secret Master as the earthly representative of God and treated him as such. He was entitled to every courtesy and honor and, except at the end of meals when he washed his own dishes to prove his humility, he seldom or never rose in ceremonies. Now he stood and the very act made us attentive. But he began with the word used by the Brotherhood to introduce a most important idea or an outstanding personage.

"Know!" The word had its effect and the assembly was as if a trumpet had sounded for silence. "Brothers, know! Over seas and plains and desert, one has come to us. He is our Brother. A man of the Temple as well as the Brotherhood. An advanced Initiate who has gone beyond the place of the Secret Master and is now a Master-At-Large. The entire world is his compound. Brothers, he who comes from afar, Joseph of Arimathea!"

As one man, the hundreds in the hall rose to their feet. From the far end of the table of Masters came a tall man. He was familiar. He was as tall as my father and they were about the same build. But he was a little darker than my father. As he moved towards the center of the table, I saw that walk which I had seen in the Temple, the one who was in the blue robes of a Novice. As he turned his face towards me, I gasped! For it was the face of the Man of Tin in my vision in the Grotto!

"Know!" His voice was much like that of my father, full, resonant, strong and filled with melody. "Know, Brothers! I came swiftly from the shores of the Isle of Celts, across the sea in a lightly loaded ship, hurrying to the Temple at the call of the Masters of Light. There I was told of one Jeshuau Joseph-bar-Joseph who strained the bounds of man's learning in religious matters. In council, we were told that he was to attempt the almost impossible: - teaching the High Priests! The circumstances were not kind. The Brothers of this compound volunteered to stay away from the Inner Court and miss the test, lest they seem too curious and betray the Candidate to the priests. We, of the Master's table, donned Novice robes and went to see this reported prodigy. We were sorely disappointed."

He paused, threw his hands in the air and let them fall in defeat. Everyone laughed but me. My heart stood still, aching for the next word to explain his meaning. "Yes, sorely disappointed! But- in the priests, and in the High Priests of the Jewish religion. They didn't even ask him one question to cause him to stop to think. The answers were in their ears before the questions were formed in their mouths. And at the last the magnificent Hillel, the President of the Sanhedrin, and the former Secret Master of Babylon, pushed the questions into the rarest areas of philosophy and the most refined thought. Then, upon seeing some of the Brothers in the passageway at the far end of the court, he called that they might hear, saying that the High Priests had been taught. But meaning that even he, the greatest living mind on Jewish religious matters, had been taught. Jeshuau Joseph-bar-Joseph, we submit, successfully passed his test!"

Joseph of Arimathea stood silent and the Secret Master spoke. "You of the Brotherhood, who gave up your place, are to be thanked and commended for your unselfishness and wisdom. What is the will of this gathering?"

There was a silence before John-John spoke. "Let us accept him as our Master and teacher. For this is his due and his right!"

No one moved- no one spoke. I looked into the faces of my Brothers in concern. At last Habakkuk, Master of The First Year, spoke out in his direct and bold manner.

"Most Worshipful Secret Master, there is no doubt in our minds about Joseph-bar-Joseph being a teacher. He has been teaching us all since the first day he came here but five years old. No mind here but could learn from him. But we all have heard the story of his conception of a virgin undefiled. Many of us believe that the Messiah is near. We wonder if it is appropriate that we vote to accept that which may have been divinely sent for our good."

There were many murmurs of agreement while Master Habakkuk shifted from foot to foot. "I say we don't need to vote! Anyway, he is and always has been our teacher. Let it be without vote – as the Will of God!"

Instantly, there was wild cheering. As it went up from my Brothers, I felt my heart soaring with their acclaim. Even when the beloved Secret Master raised his arms for silence, my Brothers continued to cheer. But soon their natural obedience and training caused them to pause and his voice could be heard above the tumult.

"Beloved Brethren, this is a most unusual request! Am I to understand that you are voting to have entered into our record and thus made binding upon our hearts, the words, 'Jeshuau Joseph-bar-Joseph, not by vote of his Brothers, but by the Will of God, has been chosen to lead the Essenes?'"

"Yes!" Master Habakkuk shouted the word, and the cheering started again and it continued for some time. When at last it quieted I could not see my Brothers. My eyes were so filled with tears of relief and happiness that I was blinded. When at last the cheering died down, the Secret Master said, "It is the will of the Assembly. Let that be enough for all men. Joseph-bar-Joseph, stand forward to receive your Jewel of Honor."

I walked to the center of the front table and stood happily in front of the Patriarch. He took from a wrapping a bejewelled medallion, a thing of rare beauty and deep meaning. It was carved from new gold or, as my Brothers said, "Living Gold." It was a rule of our Order that no such medallion could be cast or pressed in a mold, for each new Master was to be honored as never one was honored before. Therefore, the carved gold and the jewels were new and different from any other Master's medal. For each new Master was to accept the jewel as his badge of office and no one could even touch it except a more advanced Master. The new Master accepted the Jewel as a holy trust and it was hung about his neck upon a golden chain made strong enough to last for a lifetime. For it was placed upon his neck by his Superior. No one could remove it, not even that Superior. If a new Master removed the medallion, or permitted it to be removed, he symbolically forfeited the right to teach.

I looked with fascination upon the carving, set in chips of diamonds, ruby and jade. It was the lion's paw of the Tribe of Judah, grasping the hand of fellowship and drawing it upward, as if from the grave, through torches of learning and scrolls of The Law and The Prophets. Never, indeed, had there been a Jewel more beautiful and my heart leapt up as the Secret Master held it up for all to see and admire. It represented all that my Brotherhood could offer in the way of prestige. It opened the way for one to eventually become a Secret Master, a representative of God on earth.

"Jeshuau Joseph-bar-Joseph, will you accept, with this Master's Jewel, the responsibilities of a Master?"

"I will."

"Brothers, is there anyone present, or known to you, who has any objection to the bestowing of this Jewel, in token of a life-time contract?"

"No! No! No! No!"

The words thundered from all the throats in the Assembly Hall but one- or was it two? My father had spoken against the acceptance. Also Joseph of Arimathea. And the silence and surprise in the Assembly was great. I looked at my Brothers who sat in bewildered immobility, looking from me to Father, the Secret Master, and then Joseph of Arimathea.

140

"Let those who object to this contract, speak."

My father rose from his place, came around at the end of the Master's table and stood to my right, even as Joseph of Arimathea stood to my left. Between them and the Secret Master I stood at the center of a triangle formed by three bodies.

"To the contract, no objection. But there is information which both the Brothers and the Candidate should have before the Jewel is bestowed. Hear the words of my half-brother."

"Brothers, know that the honor which you here bestow upon Jeshuau Joseph-bar-Joseph is but a step in man's upward struggle toward ultimate truth." He reached up and took from his neck a medallion so beautiful, so jewel-studded that it lit his face. As he removed the Jewel from his breast, a gasp of despair went up from my Brothers. But he merely smiled.

"Thank you, Brothers, for caring lest I break my contract. But as the student progresses, he truly finds that there are more rules he may break and fewer he wants to break. At the very last, the only discipline left to a Master-At-Large is that which he wills to impose upon himself. He cannot then break a contract with our Order for there is none. It has been substituted for a contract with all mankind. Therefore, I may remove my Jewel that you all may see. Behold, this is a thing few men are privileged to look upon for it is held by not more than twenty men in all the world. It is bestowed only at the meeting of the Most High Masters of the Essene Order. Gladly would I give it up for the opportunity which is available to our young Brother. Know, Brothers! I came not on the business of our Order alone. I am empowered by one who represents himself as the spokesman for the Great White Brotherhood." He had to stop for the noise of whispers of astonishment that ran through the Assembly.

"Yes, by that very same so-called Mystical Brotherhood, I am instructed to say, a Master of Masters is needed in the world today. He must be one of great power, one whose knowledge is adequate for the problems of the Age. He must be willing, and must have searched

141

for the Great White Brotherhood earnestly. It is reported to have come to the notice of someone that Jeshuau Joseph-bar-Joseph spoke of such an interest, and also wanted information on the Order of Melchizedek. To whom did he speak? Does it matter when you cannot even think the words without that being known? At least, so it is said. But I am told to say that Joseph-bar-Joseph has been carefully observed for years by those who have authority and power, or claim to have. He has been screened by the Masters of Men. His power, his knowledge, his integrity, his ability, his humility, his willingness, his aptitude, and especially his courage and persistence. With all these, the Masters were impressed. They also looked into his spiritual development and found it good. And they decided that he should be approached and given an opportunity to risk all, and, if he failed, gain nothing, not even a noble death. Yet, even if he is successful, he gains only that which he must forego until a time more glorious.

"If he is willing, under these terms, to accept, he must also know- in addition to accepting this uncertain, in fact, unknown assignment- that he must do certain things as preliminary. Among these are that he must learn the religions of the Brittons, the Hindu, the Parsee, and finally, he must master the Mother of Religions, to be found in Egypt. He must learn the outer religions, even as the Essenes must know the Jewish religion. But, before he can earn the right to go upward in his assignment, he must also earn the right and be initiated into the Secret Inner Religions of each of these countries. He must prepare himself to synthesize, out of their teaching, the greatest religion of all times. Then he must present himself as will be directed for further assignment, or for abandonment.

"If at any place he fails, he must not return to Mastership in the Essene compound. He must leave all things, even father and mother, and follow after his unknown, so far mythical, guides. If he wins, he may at worst know something more about the mystical Great White Brotherhood, the Order of Melchizedek, and possibly others still more advanced. At best, after all his work, he may be invited to go farther in the interests of mankind under the blessings of the Masters of Men. Public mention of these Orders is most unusual. But I was told to say that never before has the interest been shown in one individual, and no one before has had the necessary qualifications to deserve the public support which is here offered. It is discussed with you who are Essenes for it shall be to your everlasting credit and glory if he succeeds. For if he is ultimately successful in all trials, he may be crowned with the success denied until now to all men. You, each and every Essene in every compound, will share the Eternal Glory.

"Behold, Jeshuau Joseph-bar-Joseph, in my right hand is the priceless Jewel of The Master Teacher of The Essenes. It promises a life of service under contract. It promises known and valued friends. And here in my left hand is the Jewel of The Master of The World. This you cannot wear, may never earn, and under it in my palm lies nothing. Nothing but the last great hope of our people. Come! Choose! Take one of the Jewels, and live or die by your choice."

Joseph of Arimathea stopped speaking and stood still. There was no doubt in my mind what I wanted to do. I would take my Master Teacher's Jewel and stay with my friends and family. Why should I forego all the joys of a known and valuable life? Why should I risk the problems and strains of an unknown life, a mysterious assignment, a reasonless situation?

My eyes fell upon John-John; his face was so radiant and expectant that I felt the glow of his emotion like a burning coal close to my skin. My Master Teacher, Habakkuk, stood with his eyes aglow, looking at me in a dark-eyed happiness I had never seen before on his face. My father stood near Joseph of Arimathea and his face was a mask of apparent calm; such calm, indeed, that I wondered if his was physical indifference or divine abstraction. There was no hint of excitement or strain, no apparent emotion of any kind upon his face. And I thought I knew which choice I had made, even as I moved forward. Of course I would take the Teacher's Jewel. Consciously I had thought out all the reasons why I would

143

benefit by taking that lifetime contract between my own people and myself. I had gained all the heights available to my faith and my race. I was certain the choice was good and willing to abide by my decision. I reached out toward my uncle's right hand to take the gleaming Jewel as my very own. But I thought of the White Brotherhood and of the mysterious Order of Melchizedek. I felt curiosity immobilizing my hand and my mind. Then I felt the warm lash of blue-white power from my father's head. It was joined by force from the head of the Secret Master, and then by the pull, lashing from the head of Joseph of Arimathea. It was as if three living serpents of white plunged deep into my being. It was as if a living golden rapier was thrust through my forehead into my brain and there touched a pathway of glory into brilliance like exploding suns. The radiance reached my heart with a sweet compulsion.

My will was not set aside. Had I willed, I could have completed my half-started motion. Indeed, my own personal will was part of the reason for my subsequent actions. It was as if my own will was suddenly raised to a higher plane and my understanding soared into a wider universe. But the total effect was that my brain was by-passed and my conscious will was set aside in order that my subconscious will might come into being. I then saw, with a great clarity, the only possible choice I could make. For he, who has once seen the face of God, may thereafter walk in Light eternally remembered by every cell of his being. I knew my choice was not for myself, alone. It was, indeed, not even for those of my immediate family whom I loved. For I saw clearly that my body, my life, my very existence was not my own to use as I willed. It was the property of my fellowmen. They had full right to my skills, which came seemingly from the universe and, at times, poured through my brain.

Suddenly, I was changed in my stance and in my intentions. I saw, as one sees from a distance looking down. I saw myself reach out and take the Jewel of The Masters of The World gently into my two hands. I seemed to be looking upon myself, yet *feeling* and *knowing* within my flesh to a higher degree than ever before.

144

The Jewel glowed within my hands with a light new and strange. It throbbed and pulsed with a life of its own! Slowly, I brought it toward my face and I saw myself kneel. But I also felt and saw the Jewel as I brought it toward my face. I kissed it with reverence and respect, and felt my lips tingle and my body glow with the power within it. I opened the clasp of the golden chain, rose slowly and put it around the neck of my beloved uncle. Carefully I fastened the Jewel of The Masters of The World back to its rightful place. Then I took his big, rough hand and kissed it. And in my soul there was a great joy and a great pain. For I knew that this was a moment of trial safely passed. This was and had been designed to be a testing of my intentions and the strength of my interest in advanced metaphysical training.

My unseen masters had made this a choosing of pathways, a difficult and dangerous choice. But I was never more to doubt that he who would walk the Path of Enlightenment must desire that above all things else. It was also clear to me that he who wishes to know great happiness must understand great sorrow. He who would be Master of Men must first be servant to man. He who would be served by God above must first serve his fellowman here below. I had given up everything for a mere hope on the winds of the future and I was abundantly glad.

Joseph of Arimathea clasped me to his breast with a joyous laugh. He let me go and my body was aglow with a strange new sensation. I was so caught up in my ecstasy that I could hardly hear the sound of my Brother's cheering. It seemed far away and unimportant, yet very important. That which had seemed to be the archstone of my life until now was become but a stirrup stone for mounting to a greater height.

I knelt before my father and heard his glorious voice speaking his words and they were simple and proud.

"This is my Spirit Begotten Son. In him I am well pleased!"

Before the glorious voice had stopped vibrating in the hall, my Essene Brothers had surrounded me in a rare moment of emotion. For it was not our way to indulge in

145

emotions, but they were filled with that amazing upsweep of joy which had come upon me. It was as if they sensed the universal rightness of the decision which had been made. Perhaps, in some dim and indistinct way, they realized that I, of myself, had not made the decision. It had been made by a Higher Order than my puny physical self. Probably, it was this realization that brought such display of emotion from them. But it pleased me in my human heart to see the tears in the eyes of my Brothers. I took some, at least, to match the tears of sadness in my own eyes at the thought of separation from those who love and adore each the other. Truly, the joy of communion of Brotherhood is passing strange.

John-John moved toward me through the crowd, his eyes glistening with joy and pride. He swept me into his arms, then held me aloft in his boundless strength, laughing up at me through tears in his throat and droplets distilled by my own sorrow and joy speckled his shoulders before he set me down.

"Now, will you believe that you are truly the divine Son of God?" His mouth was near my ear so that I alone could hear. "Will you admit it before these waiting Brothers?"

"Is it right that I shall announce my own divinity?" I whispered back, laughing at my jest.

"But, of course not!" He was quite serious. "I will announce it!" He turned and would have done so but I tugged him back and begged him to be silent. My jest had shown how very deeply he felt, how convinced he was of my divinity.

I could see that my refusal to let him declare his belief had hurt him and I added urgently, "John-John, John-John, not now! It would embarrass my wonderful father, no matter how much it would please my beautiful mother. Don't you see?"

"When may I?"

"Sometime - sometime!"

I said this, hoping to turn to jest. But he was set and would not yield to humor. Cautiously I added, "John-John, if ever the time comes, you shall be the first to know. I promise you that."

146

He held out his right hand in the clasp of Brotherhood and I took it. In that solemn moment there ran between us a unifying energy. It turned into a secret contract and it sutured us into a unity. From that moment onward, I could know his thoughts and feel his pains and joys. Through time and distance I could know his higher mind and his more intense emotions. Our melding of hearts and lives was so complete that we had little use for words with which to communicate one to the other. In the future years I was to know his soul-twisting loneliness which sent him into the deserts in search of his Eternal God. And I was to experience with him his moment of Divine Revelation which sent him from his beloved peace and quiet into the strident centers of men. I was to know that he went toward his death in order to announce the coming of the Divine Messiah. How sweet indeed is the Brotherhood of man.

We left the hall after a while and Joseph of Arimathea was at my left. John-John was beyond my beloved father on my right. We moved across the compound side by side, matching strides with the Masters. And again, there arose and floated between us a wonderful sense of Oneness, a unifying purpose which seemed to make all of our intentions and all of our purposes but One. These four lives seemed to have been molded into a single larger form, our minds seemed to have embraced a single goal, a dim, distant and darkly seen goal, but important to all mankind.

As we climbed the hill toward our home on Marmion Way, I saw my mother on the flagstones of the courtyard above us. A great wave of love went over me and, for a moment, I was perplexed. How could I have so easily chosen to leave her when I loved her so very much? I had an answer that was as instinctive as a bird's homing flight. But how could I, who had never been gifted at ciphering or composition, explain that fine line between love of home and family, and love of all mankind? I knew I would immediately leave my beautiful mother, whose questions and concerns revolved around my said-to-be miraculous birth, and my supposed divinity. I loved her all the more for her deep conviction and her care.

I loved my brothers and sisters more, oh, much more than most boys seem to love. How, then, could I be joyous at leaving them? It seemed to me that I had loved them to the greatest possible limit of the human heart, but now, I found that I loved them even more. My love was lifted and exalted until the entire community became my family. Then my love rose higher and moved outward toward all the points of the horizons of the world. I loved my family not less, but more! But love for my family was but one little candle lit in the chambers of my heart. Now, by the candle I could see that they were but the center of my love, not its total content. Suddenly, I was all aglow with the lighting of a thousand candles, each throwing a light equal in importance and each making more intense the light of all the others. And it seemed that the light was too bright, too big, for my heart to contain. It spilled outward as from a great height down upon the entire world. In its light I could clearly see, with eyes both spiritual and physical. I could see that every man was my brother. I could see that every girl was my sister. I could see that every woman was my mother. Yet I could see only my wonderful father as my father. To me, at that moment, there was no Fatherhood except that which walked at my side.

I tried to capture that belief. To hold it alone against all other thoughts, but I could not. And that was bothersome to me. Had my mother so planted in my mind the counterthought that I could not recognize truth? Even as I wondered I reached out to take the arm of my father in love and tenderness and in gratitude. But a confusing thing happened. Even as my right hand moved, so did my left. I found myself holding to Joseph of Nazar and also holding to Joseph of Arimathea as if each were my physical father. And in my mind echoed a question: Why! Why! Why! Why!

10

SECRETS

OF THE MAN OF TIN "

Once my decision was made to strive for knowledge in the Secret Brotherhoods, events began to pile upon events. When we had finished my last supper with my family and friends, I was admonished to dress myself in my poorest clothes and make certain that I took with me no metal thing whatsoever. I was also forbidden by my beloved father henceforth and forevermore to bind myself with belts of the skin of animals, but only with fibers or the skin of a sacred serpent which I alone could kill. I dressed quickly, but not before promptings from my uncle and my beloved Masters of the Essenes of Nazar. I embraced my mother, and looked with longing upon my brothers and sisters whom I loved so very much.

Would I see them again? The way was long, the path dark and unexplored, and my life was forfeit to any mistakes. Would I look again upon the bright eyes of my loving family? Even as I puzzled, I was urged along. Outside I was swept into the parting embraces of The Secret Master, and my teachers. It was the embrace of Brotherhood, and it waked a longing in my heart to stay in the safety of my home and my Compound. But magnificent horses waited for us. I was mounted and on my way while the embrace of Brotherhood by my father and Master was still as warm upon my breast as were the tears on my cheek.

But the desert wind both cooled and dried my tears

as we galloped over the hills toward the desert in the light of a rising moon. Our pace was fast, and in two hours the horses were tired and winded. But then there loomed up a tent and fresh horses, and in less than the time it took us to drink a welcomed broth, our saddles had been changed to even swifter horses. We changed mounts three times and sped on under the moonlight. Just at daybreak we changed again, and by sunrise we were on the trail of a rim of low hills and looking down upon the Mediterranean Sea.

By midday I was saddle weary and sleepy. But the pace continued as we crowded time on our move toward the country of Chem. At last we pulled up on hills overlooking Arimathea, a city which had been built by my Uncle and his family. It clustered around wharves and sheds in a small cove which made perfect harbor for many ships of cargo and commerce. We rode directly to one of the wharves and beneath the towering bows of the Merchant Ship "BRITANNIN". She was massive! Her high prow and forecastle gave her a look of majesty and seaworthiness that was reassuring to my land-born heart. Two lofty masts rose out of her great length and reached for the sky. And even as I looked up in awe and wonder, I saw men toiling in the sail ropes and yard arms high above.

My uncle did not speak. I thought, therefore, no man aboard knew whence I came nor whither I was to go. I was to marvel because of this when subsequent events showed that persons half way around the world knew and had made preparations.

Lines were cast off and the gang plank drawn in before we had taken twenty paces upon the gently swaying deck. A man stopped bellowing orders to those above and on the deck fore and aft and came toward us.

"Captain James of Bruton, this is Jeshuau of Nazar. Feed him and let him sleep a while. Then make a sailor of him".

"Aye, Sir. How old are you, boy?"

"Thirteen"

"Thirteen, *Sir*!" Captain James of Bruton bellowed at me, "Show your respect to your ship's master!"

I was dimly aware that my uncle walked aft toward the owner's cabin and left me entirely at the mercy of the tempestuous Captain.

"Respect, Sir? Would you have me respect you out of fear or out of love?"

I did not see the blow. But I was knocked forward from my feet by a blow on the back of the head. As I lay dazed at the feet of the Ship's Master, I faintly heard the words that passed.

"Who is this smart one, Sir?"

"Jeshuau of Nazar. Take him below and feed him and let him sleep. Then make a sailor of him, Nicodemo."

"Aye, Sir."

Rough hands grabbed my shoulders and heaved me to my feet. My knees would have buckled but a strong arm grabbed me and slammed me upright against the edge of the forecastle. In a few seconds my thoughts cleared and I could focus my eyes into those of Nicodemo. His eyes were blue-grey and very bright, and they burned into mine with a strange intensity made of questioning and of commanding. I fought to still my reeling senses, then stood straight. A grim smile came upon the face of Nicodemo as he turned and made his way toward the galley. I followed because of the command in his gesture.

I was fed black bread, boiled barley, and cold baked fish with leeks and squash. It was a rough fare, but I was hungry beyond belief. Yet could hardly eat what was placed before me so sleepy did I become as soon as my stomach was filled. A youngster came for me and took me down into the musty hold of the ship. I was handed a dirty blanket and shown a stretch of deck upon which no man had left his blanket. This was to be my bed!

I lay down, fully intending to weep for myself and my foolish decision to risk all I had gained for some unknown goal. I could not weep. My head hurt, and the deck was hard. Yet, somehow, I knew this, even all this, led toward my final goal. Somehow this was part of my training in that mysterious Great White Brotherhood, and in the ancient and sacred Order of Melchizadek. I drifted into sleep even with the exciting calls which controlled the running feet that pounded above my head.

151

A moment later, it seemed, Nicodemo stood over me, shaking me severely. It was brutal when compared to the gentle persuasion of my mother, and anger flared within me. I was awake enough to stumble after him to the deck of the gently swaying ship. The gentle breeze kissed my face with dawn's freshness, and I realized that I had slept through the night and it was now daybreak.

How beautiful was the scene. The blue Mediterranean held the *"Britannin"* like an airy fleck of foam in a huge blue cup. The weaving water seemed to curve upward toward the horizon on all sides, and from the east a ray of sunlight rolled a ruby carpet into the azure water. The ship was a strange thing, powered by the breeze that slanted across our bow and filled the immense sails like happy cheeks of hurrying squirrels. There was the indescribable and lonely call of gulls floating aft the stern, and the rhythmic lapping of waves upon the hull. High above, like the teased strings of a muted lute, sail-ropes made loving sounds to the kissing wind. Embracing all was the salt-clean fragrance of the gently running sea.

We passed the mid-deck and went up to the raised aft deck, and still further up to the tiller-deck. From there we could look down across the decks of the ship, even out across the bow toward the horizon.

"There is a rope and a cask for lifting water. There are stones for scrubbing. Scrub this deck, then report to me at the tiller."

I soon had lifted several casks of water, washed the deck, and rubbed its scarred surface with the heavy stones. Aching in every joint, I walked proudly to Nicodemo:

"I have scrubbed the entire deck, Sir."

"Good. Now scrub it twice more."

Again I hoisted the heavy casks and washed the deck, and scrubbed it hard with the heavy white stones. Carefully, I did it twice. Then I reported the fact to Nicodemo who was standing beside the tiller arm looking at me with hard eyes.

"Go below and bring me food. When you have eaten, scrub this deck three times more."

Three times more I lifted the heavy casks, flushed the deck, and scrubbed it with the heavy stones. When I had finished I could hardly rise from the deck so cramped were my muscles, so tired my body. But I started all over again, and scrubbed it for the seventh time. I then carefully sloshed the deck with clear salt water, and put the stones back in the holding racks. Then only did I limp toward my hard-eyed tormenter.

"I washed the deck a seventh time, Sir."

"Why?"

"To please you, Sir."

The blow caught me on the side of the head and sent me reeling a half dozen paces, "To please me! Boy, have you learned nothing in this day of drudgery? You do not work to please me. You work to carry out my order- and that only! It may not please me to give the order, nor you to execute it. You do exactly as you are ordered, and you do that only. Is that clear?"

I nodded dumbly.

"Good. Now, scrub that deck again. Then go below for food, then find me, wherever I may be. I will show you how to tie a few knots- at least enough to hang yourself!"

For the eighth time I scrubbed the deck. At last I stored the stones away and holding to the rail, kept my aching legs from buckling until I could walk on them again. Painfully I crept down for food, and was cursed by the galley-man for coming so tardily. Grudgingly he fed me, skimping on portions, and grumbling all the while. I ate swiftly, finding no joy in the loneliness of the meal, and no pleasure in the taste of the stingily-served food. I climbed the ladder to the deck, the tasteless food knotted in my stomach, and sticking in my gullet.

What manner of life was this? Fury was in every man, a subtle hatred of all things - even himself. Only one thing was respected - the order of the Ship's Master. Yet, it seemed that even against this structuring of behavior there was grumbling. No man loved any other. There was no joyous cooperation in the doing of work - but each man was an island of resentment unto himself. Why? Why would men live without brotherhood and love?

153

I leaned against the rail of the "Britannin" and looked out toward the lip of the cup of my world. The sea was a brassy color under the fury of the Mediterranean high-noon sun. No cooling breeze stirred in the lines above, and the sails hardly filled but flapped a little, as if loath to do their work.

Nicodemo was found at last, sitting on the deck in the shadow of the jibsail, as far forward as one could go in the bow of the ship. Beyond him was the bow-sprit, and the two-faced carving of a god, holding a new-cut sprig of all-heal in an apron of gold. We spent the broiling afternoon learning to tie knots and make them tight, until my fingers were as sore as my back, and my head was aching from the endless raps I suffered from Nicodemo's back-hand and knuckles. For each time I made a slip or an error, I was cuffed.

"Boy, think. Keep your mind on the knot. Your very life depends upon it."

"How can I concentrate in my fear?"

"In moments of terror you must be able to bring all your faculties to one point. Your eternal life depends upon it!"

Time after time, hour after hour, I tied whatever knot I was commanded, until I could do so even when the punishing knuckles were hovering above my head. When at last I had tied the thirty seven knots each seven times at great speed and without error I felt pleased with myself. But Nicodemo merely grunted and said.

"Go eat. Then to rest. In four hours you go on the tiller crew."

I turned away, with still some pride in my accomplishment, but the snarling voice stopped me short. "Boy, you'll never make a sailor. You are stupid and you are awkward."

I fought down the choler that rose in my spine and made the nape of my neck bristle with my fury. I held his bitter eyes with my own for a dozen heartbeats, then turned away. But his voice cut again like a lash across my back.

"Besides you are a weakling. You have neither endurance nor strength."

154

Before I could take another step his voice struck me again. "You are a physical coward."

When I was slapped awake the "Britannin" was yawing and pitching in the running troughs of a rising sea. Still the sails hung almost limp and no breeze stirred the sultry anger of the night. I was hurried to the tiller deck and placed opposite an enormous Egyptian sailor whose name was as ugly as his constant mood, Skakus. In the running sea it was our job to hold the tiller wherever we were directed by Nicodemo. When the movement was to be to the starboard I was to push. When to the port Skakus was to push. With the ship sloughing into the quartering troughs we were constantly having to correct her sluggish progress. The huge tiller-handle pressed hard upon our straining arms at all times. We could not rest for an instant. Shakus, too, was inclined to meanness. When he could do so he let go the tiller-handle so that it would slap at me with the crushing force of an onrushing wave, bruising my chest and arms, and staggering me before I could regain my footing. Within a very few minutes I was bruised and aching, and sweat was streaming from me. Across the tiller-handle Skakus grinned at me in merciless mirth, staring down from his enormous bulk and height like a devil from Mount Olympus. He stank with a swinish sweat, and with an oil that was worked into his hair, and with the foul breath of one who craved and drank too much Roman grog.

When at last the bruising trick was over, I stumbled toward the galley for food and then hurried toward my blanket to lie down. As I passed the waist deck, four powerful forms blocked my path. I tried to step around them, but they cornered me. I tried to cry out. A calloused hand was clapped over my mouth and my arms pinned to my back. I tried to kick, my feet were swept from under me, and I was slammed against the rail so violently that my senses spun.

"Put him in scull." It was Skakus, and his voice rasped with anticipation. "Let him kill himself or learn to handle boat. Otherwise he kill us all."

A moment later I felt the narrow scull being lowered with me in it, and we hit the water with a wave-breaking splash. The scull danced into the waves with a drunkard's lurch, throwing me against the side of the "Britannin." Before I could cling, a contrary wave caught the light boat, and I was rolled to the other side. The huge bulk of the "Britannin" slid away from me. I was caught in the full force of a hard-running sea. The scull sloughed wildly under me, and began to settle cross-wise to seas. I realized that I might be rolled over, and grabbed for the sculling oar. I fought desperately to right the boat and head it into the rough sea troughs. When this was done, I thought to cry out, but the "Britannin" was a dozen rods away. I fought hard to control the tricky scull and to row it toward the "Britannin". But precious minutes were wasted while I tried to learn the trick of steering the slender boat while rowing it. At last I learned, after waves had swept me with spume and wetted me with spray. Then slowly I began to close the distance between me and the ship. I fought and strained until the breath came hard in my dry throat, and realized that my strength would never last for that desperate run. I almost collapsed for a few seconds, rowing only enough to keep the bow pointed into the waves. Then, rested a little from the fury of the strain, I began to row moderately. I set a pace I could hold for hours, and continued to row with a dogged but space-consuming stroke. With agonizing slowness I gained on the ship until at last I was within two scull lengths of the stern. I could see the white wake made by the rudder as the tiller was pushed about far above. But I could not approach closer, for the sudden flash of that wide rudder would crush the shell of my light scull like eggshell.

I had been let off on the starboard, and hoped to find lines dangling there, so I forced the skittish little shell into the out-boiling wake of the ship, and drove hard to cross the troubled water. A swift running wave slammed into the bow of the scull and spun me about. Instantly the wake slammed into the stern and spun me back again. For a moment I thought the scull would tip, but it righted itself and nosed into the relatively sheltered water beside the big ship. I rowed cautiously now, making little noise, but shivering with the eagerness of my hope that the lines would be dangling to the water. I found a line trailing in the water. To this I fixed the bow of the scull and tested to see if the little craft would pull. It did so and I decided to climb the line and then pull the craft up. I had not gone halfway up the line before the scull, whipping about without my weight, began to pound the hull of the "Britannin" with each and every wave. The racket was enough to wake any man on the ship. I climbed frantically to get above the rail. I had just dropped to the deck when the entire ship's crew seemed to converge around me, led by a swearing and angry Nicodemo.

While he glowered at me the scull again crashed against the side of the ship, and the sound was like that of a huge drum. I backed away from the rail and then stepped forward and began to pull the line until the scull was lifted from the water. Straining against the weight, I brought the boat up until it could be lifted aboard the ship. Only then did I turn to face the waiting mate.

"Who gave you permission to go over the side?"

"No one, sir."

"Why did you go?"

"I don't know, sir."

"If you were put over, it will mean twenty lashes for every man until we find the culprit for 100 lashes. If you went of your own free will – God help you from the Master's wrath. Speak, Boy. Were you put over? Or did you break the Master's law?"

Skakus stood in the front ranks of the crowded sailors. In the sky light I could see plainly the animal fear upon his snarling face. Could I tell? Should I tell? Should I make certain that the law of the ship punished those who had recklessly risked my life in the high-running sea? I knew I would not do so, no matter what punishment might be in store for me. I was not accustomed to this brutal world, and I could not understand a world that was moved by fear and hatred rather than love. But I had not sunk so low that I could not show love and compassion. I bit my trembling lip and said nothing.

"Your answer, Boy."

"What shall I answer, sir?"

"The truth, Boy."

I felt the tension in every sailor aboard the ship who was near to me. The tension so intense that they seemed to forget to breathe.

"The truth, sir? When I went over the side I did not know it was against the order of the Master."

"Is that all you have to say, Boy?"

"You asked for the truth, sir."

The blow struck my head and smashed me against the railing. My senses spun but I did not fall. "For your insolence you shall be stern-hauled for quarter of a watch. Skakus, Dobbun, Romulus, rig a line and stern-haul - but let him tie the knots, and if one fails, let him drown. Hurry. Hurry."

A line was slapped against my chest and then passed around my waist. Despite the urging of a dozen voices to speed, I concentrated only upon the knot, and tied a bowline saddle around my legs, and then around my upper chest close under the arms. Each knot was worth my very life and I tied it well and tested it thoroughly before going to the next, despite the urging to speed. Then I was picked up by the sailors and rushed sternward. There the line was measured so that I would trail fifty feet behind the ship, and I was hurled outward into the dark sea. I turned slowly in the air, and fought to strike the water feet first, and was only partly successful. The air was knocked from me, and I sank into a seemingly endless sea. I fought myself to the surface, and had just managed to gasp a breath when the line tugged me backward and forced me under again. I fought the water until I had oriented myself to the pull of the rope, then I pulled upon the rope to bring my head above water. I had time for a fast breath before the next wave slammed me under again. I realized in sheer panic that if each wave broke over me, I could never last a quarter of a watch. I could not last out ten such punishing onslaughts of twisting, crushing water. The panic gripped me and I felt myself grow stiff with fear.

There seemed to burst from the center of my heart a small blue-white flame. It moved to the center of my chest and darted upward with spear-like thrust that burst with a golden brilliance into the chambers of my brain. It was as if I could see myself in the water, being dragged by the merciless line through a torturing sea. But I also was conscious of the fact that my stiff body was now pliable and warm. My mind and muscles were not frozen with fear. Instead, I felt the wisdom of a thousand and the strength of ten thousands.

Slowly I began to swim, until I was guiding myself over the waves, and letting myself sink into the less punishing troughs, For a few minutes I fought all the time, then I realized that I could coast down into the troughs, and needed to work only as the wave was coming toward its crest. Then a few powerful strokes would lift me over the wave and make it possible to coast for several restful seconds. A great joy came over me, a joy of self-dependence and personal worth. It was with grim inner triumph that I saw the sun at last tip the hills of the waves with gold, and spread a path into the murky, rebellious water. I had conquered my fears, but more, I had conquered my own self, I had made my fear-drained body function to a higher level than it normally could.

When I was hauled up to the stern-deck the grim-faced sailors eyed me with enmity, and Nicodemo stood spraddle-legged looking at me with contempt-sharpened eyes. Without a word he turned and left, and I was roughly shoved toward the galley where I sat shivering and drinking pots of hot water sweetened with honey. At last I began to warm up and was given food before I went to my blanket to sleep. As soon as my hair hit the blanket, I was asleep.

How long I slept I do not know, for I fell into one of my strange periods of complete exhaustion. I awakened to the sickening realization that the deck of the "Britannin" had dropped away, and I was sliding across the planking. A moment later I skidded into the side of the hull with a frightful force. Before I could come out of my daze, the deck of the ship twisted about underneath me, and then dropped away in the opposite direction. I slid across the deck, whirling slowly, and crashed again into the inside of the hull. This time I caught hold of a stave-post, and when the ship lurched again, I held on until I could regain my sense of direction and balance.

I pulled myself up and held to the clamp-rail and slowly became aware of the sounds out on the weather decks. Feet were pounding and voices calling, but they were dim and faded into the howling fury of a storm. The lines snarled as the wind slapped them about.

The companion-way seemed beyond reach as I clung to the clamp-rail and tried to walk toward it. The ship twisted and turned like a living thing under intolerable torture. It rolled so far that it was inmpossible to stand on the slanting deck, and I was almost torn from the clamp-rail. The ship then crashed into a wave with a violent shudder that sent squeals of protest through every beam and brace. Yet even as it squealed in agony, it rose to attack again the oncoming walls of water. I was jarred and battered in trying to hold to my feet.

At the top of the companion-way I found that the hatch was battened down and I could not raise it. Even with my shoulder against the wood, I could feel the water pounding against the frame. I braced my self against the hatch, wedged between stair rung and hatch-cover and, waited. It seemed hours before there was any change in the squealing of the timbers. Then it grew worse. But suddenly the battened hatch gave to the pressure of my shoulder. I waited until the tremendous force of a wave had roared over it, and sprang out with all the speed my cramped, sore muscles would permit. The hatch was hardly back in place when the wind snatched at me, followed a moment later by the whiplash of a wall of water that broke over the bow. I was slammed to the deck, but clung to the under side of the hatch until the brutal wave let me go. Then I scrambled to my feet and grabbed for a better hold on the hatch. In the half light of early dawn I looked about upon the utter destruction of the upper part of the ship.

Broken lines hung from splintered yard-arms, howling in the wind, and lashing their wet lengths across the waist-deck of the "Britannin". Not a sail was still intact, but tatters fluttered from every rope and every davit. I waited for a passing wave, then lunged across the deck and grasped the rope-whipped forward mast.

160

There, lashed in the network of ropes was Skakus and Dobbun, clinging for life in the hardrunning wind, and bleeding around the head and shoulders from the lashing blows from the wet ropes. I clung while a wave broke over me. And when the water drew back to strike again Skakus yelled:

"Tie yourself. You'll go over!"

"What happened?"

His answer was stopped by a roaring wall of water. When it was gone he roared above the waves, the wind, and the groaning ship. "Cyclone struck without warning. No one can move. Tie yourself."

I began to tie myself, then stopped. Something urged me forward, something compelled me to go toward the bow of the ship. I ran between waves to the ladder leading from the waist deck to the forward deck. Seven times I clung to the rail or a clamp-rail before I could force my way forward toward the bow of the ship. The bow was raising, and then sinking, thrusting itself under water for seconds at a time. And it was clear that danger lay ahead, but I could not turn back. I inched along until at last I saw why I had come.

There, pressed against the bulkhead was Nicodemo, held by a spar and part of the top mast, broken and splintered, but bound together in the form of a cross. He was only dimly conscious. Each time the wave rolled by and the bow of the ship climbed toward the sky I could see that he struggled against the weight of the cross. He was too weak to lift it. I had to be careful, for if I unpinned him at the wrong time, he would be washed overboard. Before I touched the spar or the mast, I rigged a line around the rail, and tied it under his arms and legs in a saddle. Then I got down beside him and waited for a wave to break. Together we struggled to raise the crossed timbers, and were helped by the onrushing wave. The cross was tipped upward, stood for a moment as an ominous shadow over our bodies, then tumbled backward into the raging sea. I clung helplessly to the rail until the wave had passed. Then, I inched Nicodemo along the deck, passing the rope that lashed him from place to place along the rail stanchions. At long

161

last I had drawn him down to the companion-way and to the waist-deck of the ship.

But my strength was failing. The battle in wind and wave had lasted over an hour, and exhaustion was making me stupid and slow. I suddenly felt flash over me a roaring fury at the needless destruction of the good ship "Britannin".

I straightened up, and holding to the companion-way rail took a wave full in the chest. A great exhilaration rose up, and I commanded the storm to be gone. Over and over I yelled until my voice was hoarse. Then suddenly the ship lashed into the sea, and did not lurch upward with its normal violence. Within a few moments the waves had rolled beyond us, the wind had died to a gentle zephyr, and the "Britannin" drifted in a quiet sea.

Nicodemo half stood and half hung to the rail of the companionway, looking at me with inscrutable eyes. Behind me I heard the slow, bone weary tread of Skakus and Dobbun. Soon the sailors began to appear from the stations where they had been caught by the sudden fury of the unexpected storm. Untying Nicodemo, I carried him toward the officer's cabin, guiding the listless movement of his feet until I could put him down upon his cot. He sighed and stared at me from over-bright eyes, but said nothing-not even a thank you for his life.

Certainly there had been no thought in my mind of heroics in what I had done, but I did not expect the results that followed. The sailors refused to work a watch with me, and were driven to it because of fear of the Master of the ship. They blamed me, in whispers, for the sudden storm. And soon they were hissing at me when we passed on deck.

"Jonah! You devil's mate!"

Within three days we had cleared most of the debris from the deck of the ship, and had new sails and lines upon temporary masts and spars. We kept on running in a northwesterly direction, passed through a narrow gate between Africa and Gaulicia, and ran on northward. Many days later we came in sight of a low-lying headland and the lookout sang loudly, "Land's End ahead, Sir.

Straight on the beam."

We sailed westerly around this cape, and then turned northeasterly. By nightfall we were past Trevose Head, and in the night the sailors grumbled because we were sailing in narrow straights between Dearcountry Point and Lundy Island. Before morning all hands were rousted out to shorten sail, and at daylight we nosed in toward an apparently impassable marshland. As we came close to shore I saw that there were many broad channels weaving like silvery coils into the low lands. As we eased around the wide turns, pushed by a persistent breeze, the way was sometimes so narrow that we could have stoned the land far below our bow and not over eighteen inches above the water of high tide.

All day we moved inward until an hour before sunset the lookout called, "The Mendip Hills, Sir."

A look of pleasure came to the face of Skakus and Dobbun. They spoke at once, each saying apparently the same thing.

"Yinnis Writtin," Dobbun said.

"Glastonbury," Skakus said. Then he added. "Look you, the mouth of the Brue!"

There, coming down toward us was a ship exactly like the "Britannin". As we came into the mouth of the river, it came out into the slough called Meare Pool or Sea Basin. In that near-sunset passing began something surpassing strange in my life. Golden light, strong and strange, came from a bank of golden clouds, and was mirrored in the waters of the river. The air was fused into a pink glow, welding water, earth and sky into one magnificient totality. Our sister ship passed almost in boarding distance of our starboard, and on her decks was a scene of great beauty. When first I beheld it, my body was melded and fused with a sweet music, music that never could completely die for all the rest of my life.

On a golden rug in the center of a square made of purple velvet ropes supported on stanchons sat a small and beautiful young woman. She was dressed in a simple garment of shimmering green, and around her shoulders was a fleecy cloak of purple and gold, iridescent in the golden light. All the richness of ornament and trapping was as nothing compared to the girl herself.

She was pure beauty. Her oval face was fairer by far than my mother's face. The crown of gold upon her head was so light it was almost silvery. Two braids hung down across her shoulders, the golden-colored hair ending in fillets of pure gold upon which there had been set large jade scarabs of lustrous green.

I stood at my watch on the tiller-deck, and could see her clearly on the deck of the owner's cabin of our sister ship. As I looked at her my body was suddenly rigid. Longing for her seemed to swell inside my heart. I seemed to leap across the gap and kiss her lovely cheek in utter adoration and deep love. She seemed to me to be all that woman ever was or could ever be. She was my mother, my sweet sisters, my aunts, and all lovely women I had known. And yet-yet-she was more. A rising tide of delight in my physical body made strange music upon the strings of my being. In response to this new stirring, I kissed her again. Not in reverence and adoration upon the cheek. But in manly vigor upon the ruby, heart-formed lips that smiled at me from beneath her jade-green eyes. I kissed her with all the passions of the world of a lonely man-and I saw from her looks that she knew I had done so and was pleased.

In an instant I was back in my body, and the ships were passing almost silently on the still waters of the River Brue. Yet I knew that a thing of great importance had happened to me. Even as I stood in the rags of a sailor, dirty and tired, I was suddenly purely clean, vitally alive, and vibrant in every cell. I was aware of my emerging manhood and pleased with it-oh, far more pleased with it than I thought my mentors would approve! Yet, I knew that there was also a spiritual and endless pull from my inner being to this silent, beautiful, guarded and smiling girl.

Even when the ships had moved apart, and she was lost in the distance, I could still feel her. I could even see her! It was as if every cell of my being had been stamped with a cameo of her beauty and her warmth. Somewhere from the distant hill beyond the landing pier of Glastonbury, a Sommerset robin sang to the end of the

164

day, and its notes floated on the air like a song in a sweet dream. From that time on I was not to hear the song of a robin but that I saw again the vision of eternal and feminine grace. Never, never, I was sure, had there been such beauty. I would have stayed lost in my dreaming of her but for the landing call. The great ship became a battleground of feet running to bring us safely into the wharf.

When the big ship had been made fast hundreds of local Cornishmen began to come aboard and carry away the cargo to the markets of the burrough, and to other towns and markets throughout Sommerset and the Salisbury plains. Most of the sailors were given permission to leave the ship, and I was ordered to go with them. Not one would walk with me, but I was close-packed between them and by listening learned much. This series of sloughs was in fact a sluggish lake in the Sommersetshire low lands. To it and the area was applied the name Meare Pool. The lake of many arms fed from the River Brue into the sea, and at the sweetwater line on this tidal river was the village called "Yinnis Writtin". Some called it "The Crystal City", still others "Glastonbury" or "Fort of Glass". One called the entire village and the sweeping countryside, from Salisbury Plains to Mendip Hills, "The House of God".

On hearing this my flesh became suddenly alive. What did these ruffian sailors know of the House Of God? Was not this what we called the inner and sacred part of our Brotherhood of the Essenes? Why, then, should this strange place be so named?

We trudged along the quay, passed the friendly and smiling, fair-haired people of the village who were on the river fishing, and went far along the river before we turned suddenly inward toward the hills, and began to climb the edge of a strangely abrupt hill. We had not gone far before we all stopped and sat down to rest. Nicodemo came near to me, still limping a little, and he sat down heavily.

"Aye," he said to no one in particular, "this is named rightly, the Weary-All Hill. We are weary, all."

When we rose to go I stopped in amazement. Two

165

things came to my view. First of all, "Yinnis Writtin" was
on the lake side of an island which was clasped in two
arms of the wide, slow river. Second, the rising ground
beyond Weary-All Hill was like a man-made mound, a
pyramid of enormous size with the top truncated over a
large acreage. From where we had rested we could see the
trails that laced the sides of this apparently
man-designed mountain. I pressed forward eagerly, my
curiosity pulling my tired legs. Before we reached the
first of the lacing trails Nicodemo turned and snarled at
me.

"Boy. Upon this mountain is a sailor's rest. Only
sailors may stay there. Look. Across this vale, that
branch of the Brue, and upon yonder swale you see the
Giant Oak? Go there, build yourself a hut in which to rest
yourself and wait without fail until we come for you. Do
you hear, Boy?"

"Yes, sir."

I was turned from the well trodden path toward the
distant Oak which loomed big in the swale a thousand
paces long. I made my way down into the verdant valley,
waded across the sparkling arm of the River Brue, and
drank my fill of its purling sweet water. Then I trudged
disconsolately toward the towering Oak, knowing in my
heart the misery of failure, and the torture of loneliness.
Painful was the thought that my uncle had deserted me.
He had left me in the hands of a ruffian crew, had not
even spoken to me when the long trip was over. For this
had I given up my Master's Jewel? I climbed the low swale
to the Oak and sat down in its spreading shadow near the
expansive trunk. I was tired, and it was only one night
and a quarter day since we had tied up at my uncle's
wharf. But I could not continue to sit. I had been told to
build a hut in which to rest myself, and to wait until
someone came for me. What had I learned upon the
"Britannin" but that obedience was the first law of my new
world. I looked for material, but there was none. At last
I saw, growing in the Branch of the Brue, very tall
reeds. They were pulpy and strong but pliable. I
gathered them in by the arm full and trudged with them
up to a spot about forty paces from the enormous Oak.

There, toiling without food in the midday sun, I began to build a small hut, by weaving the reeds together after burying the butt-ends deep in the ground to hold in place against the wind. When the almost water tight skeleton was finished, I brought long leaves of a water-corse and wove them from the top downward so that they would shed the dew and rain. Then, through a hole I had left in the top, I wove longer reeds together to form a cupola, open to the passage of smoke and air, but proof against rain. When I had finished the sun was setting and I was hungry. But I was also proud of my rude hut, made of my own skill and my own hands. I left my blanket and pack inside the hut and hurried down to the Branch of the River Brue. There I found water succulents aplenty, and trees of wild fruits and vines of sweet berries. Hurriedly I wove a large basket of small reeds, and filled it with food for the next day. In the growing darkness I made my way toward my home of reeds. The gathering darkness made me lonely. I found three stones to serve as a hearth and hunted for dry limbs to make a fire to cheer me. I let tears flow down my cheeks for pity of my own loneliness and my rude surroundings. But as I looked into the flames leaping from my own hearth, saw the bulging basket of food, and felt the warmth of my own home – my pity was dried up.

Then in the flames I saw again the Golden Girl upon the rug of gold, and again in my longing and adoration I kissed her ruby lips, and she was pleased. As the days came one upon the other, I laid in stores against the cold ahead, gathered nuts and acorns, brought up cords of wood and did all things to protect myself and my home. At first I longed for companionship, but as days turned to weeks, I almost began to dread the thought of someone coming for me to take me from this paradise into the beastly ship. If my uncle had in truth deserted me, I came to thank him for it. My only concern was that I did not seem to be progressing toward my promised goal of knowledge about the White Brotherhood and the Order of Melchizadek. Each night, each morning, and each noon I prayed that I might continue on the road of service to my fellowman. Thus, truly I say to you, did I continue for

167

twenty weeks by my reckoning and no man spoke to me, and I to no man; but I had grown beyond fear, beyond loneliness, beyond criticism of my self or my fellowman. I had turned inward to the resources my own heart devised, of which comtemplation and meditation were chief, but visioning the Golden Girl was sweetest.

Each day at sunset I placed a palm-sized stone upon a walkway that was eventually to curve from my doorway to the towering Oak, for this was my calendar by which I reckoned the days. I had placed the 147th stone the night before, when at sunrise I heard the music of pipes and drums coming from beyond the Oak. I ran to its giant trunk. There was no person in the entire swale, yet the music and cadence were growing ever louder. I stood in utter delight at its beauty, but in complete bewilderment as to its source. Then, even as I looked, the earth beyond the Oak began to rise, and it folded back on all four sides until there was an opening like that of a cistern or a well flanked with giant stones of granite. Then, out of the mouth of the cistern marched in perfect order and rhythm the magnificent sight of a body of Druids.

First there came the heralds and guides, glorious in yellow robes and ruby supertunicas. Second came the lesser priests in the grades of Eubates, in saffron and green. Then came the body of the priests of the grades of Bards, in simple tunics of many colors, like those worn by men of travel, and each priest carried a lute, or had the symbol of a lute embroidered upon his overtunic or upon his cape. Then came the mighty Druids. Even in the way they walked there was recognized majesty and might. They moved in conscious union, a masterly brotherhood - like soldiers of the spirit who had conquered all foes. Each was kingly in his tunic of white and blue, with his robe of green and blue, and his cape of purple velvet. Upon the head of each was placed the jewel-encrusted cap of blood-red color.

Last came the Arch Druid and his 12 Chief Druids. They were most resplendent in tunics of white or green as the grade might indicate, and cloaks of royal purple velvet. The procession circled round, and in circling ranks, surrounded the Mighty Oak against which I leaned for my legs had grown too weak to hold my excited heart. Then at a signal from the staff of a Chief Druid, all sounds stopped and all knelt upon the grass of the swale, circling round me. I knelt too, for I knew they merely worshipped the hightest God whom they adored more intensely by praying before the largest Oak in a grove. When the prayers and the ceremony had been said, the assembly rose and the sound of piping and drums fed them back into the mouth of the cistern.

Nothing was said to me. Neither hello nor goodbye, not even a "stand aside you distract our worship". No eye recognized me. No face lighted in greeting. It was as if I did not exist for them. How can I say how great was my longing to be with and of them? My heart was at first full with hope and gratitude that they had come for me. But as they disappeared into the stones of the cistern my heart grew empty as a crushed acorn-cup. When they had closed down the stones and I stood upon the sun-flooded swale near the giant Oak, I felt the tears upon my cheek. After a short time I turned to contemplation, realized that it was neither bad nor good that I was thus forgotten, and I managed to become indifferent to my future.

Near mid-day there came an old one across the swale, wrapped in a brown cloak with a large brown hood that put the face in deep shadows. Out of that cavern of black came a voice weak and quavery enough to go with the bent back, hobbling gait, and large staff.

"Young man, I thought I saw those cursed Druids. Were they here?"

"Old one, I cannot say yes. Druids were here, but I do not know they are cursed."

"Aye, cursed, fair lad. Know you not that here abouts is Blood Spring."

"Blood Spring?"

"Blood Spring! It is so named because they lure young hopefuls into the maw of that bloody cistern for Sacrifice to red-chopped Hu, their god, and the blood-stained goddess Ceridwin. Hear me, fair lad. Many go in as men. But I give you my word, I have never seen a man return."

The bent one hobbled away, muttering querulously against the Druids and their human sacrifice, and climbed back up the swale and over the lip of the hill. On the sinister warning I had much time to ponder, for the day was slow until sunset when I placed the 148th stone and sat at my lonely meal before going to my pallet of rushes. Contemplation upon the meaning of the things that had happened to me, and meditation upon the spirit of man, soon gave way to the daily kiss of my beloved Golden Girl, and then deep sleep.

I was roused by the thin, plaintive piping of a sad tune. I listened to the sad song almost as one who dreams. It approached my hut, and I rose and went out into the night. Far across the swale came a single piper and a Chief Druid. They paused to pray before the Oak, then came toward my hut and they were lighted by a single taper. When at last they stopped before me the piping died in a crying mood and the Chief Druid spoke.

"Boy, Joseph of Arimathea, holder of twelve hides of lands around this vale of Avalon, bespeaks your desire to risk your life in our initiations. Say you aught for your own interests?"

"I want to know that which is needful to my destiny, Sir."

"Will you risk your life? Will you sacrifice yourself?"

"I will risk my life, but hope to cling to it."

"Hear well, Boy. Many do not live through the ordeal of our initiation. Upon your decision hangs your life. Will you come into Blood Spring, or will you stay upon this Island?" He did not wait for my reply, but turned away, and to the plaintive piping marched thrice around the Oak.

I stood in indecision for the first circuit. Then I sprang into action and gathered my bundle and my blanket. I cast out the fruits and berries that would quickly spoil, and covered with baskets the stores of nuts that would last a while. Before the third circuit was complete I stood beside the Oak, waiting for the ceremonial circuits to be ended. Without another word they went into the mouth of the cistern called Blood Spring, and I followed them.

The stones closed behind us by what means I did not know and we were in a wide tunnel which was lined with rough stones. We made our way swiftly now, to the happy pipe, and circled toward the mound beyond Weary-All Hill. At last we climbed stairs, came out upon a trail on the side of that hill, made our way swiftly over the crest of the hill and into a monastery of great size. In the inner court I was left with many others who squatted on the stones. All were older than I. Many seemed frightened or uneasy, or excited and over-eager. My greatest effort was to be calm and detached, but I now know that some of the morning dew I brushed from my face was distilled out of the sighs of leaving my rude hut near the Great Oak in the vale of Avalon.

Before long there came a half dozen Chief Druids, each the master of one of the training and initiation centers round the country side. All those waiting in the courtyard were placed in ranks, instructed to keep perfect time to the pipe and the drum sent with them, and to follow the Chief Druid at whatever pace he should set. We went our several directions. I was in the group of about seventy candidates who were turned toward Kornbrae, the village of the three Perfect Hills. We started at a leisurely pace, the drum beating its cadence. Slowly we increased our tempo until we were moving rapidly through darkness on the uneven trails. I put all discomfort from the jarring and uneven ground out of my mind and fled into the darkness following the perfect rhythm of that commanding and guiding drum. We walked for three hours without stopping. After a short rest we continued on through the night, past daybreak, and into the morning. At last the drum ceased and we sagged on our weary feet to look up from the Salisbury plain at the magnificence of Kornbrae. It was a veritable paradise of beauty, stretching some hours walk in each direction, and designed to bejewel the three perfect mountains around which it was grouped. We then were raced into its walls, and there within that very hour began our studies of every science known to man.

My thirteenth, fourteenth and fifteenth years were spent there in daily studies and recitations that lasted from well before dawn of a summer's day to well past dark. We were regimented, hurried, bullied, confused, and ever guided to new tasks and new learnings as fast as we mastered the first assigned. We were also busy daily with hours of work in the nearby fields to which we ran in step to the endless and unfailing drum. We were taught the use of the long-sword, the short-sword, the curass and the bow, always to the rhythm of the unfailing drum. We were stripped to loin cloths and taught to battle with the hands, and shown ways to maim and to kill. So rough were the assignments that many fell by the way. A few died of over exertion.

At night we were shut up in small cages of stone, not much larger than a pace by three paces, and some men went mad from the confinement. I was lucky. For I had been trained in arduous tasks in the Essene Brotherhood, and was accustomed to long hours of hard work. Learning to kill and to maim was no chore to me. In my mind I reversed the thought, and *created* out of that which was supposed to be used to destroy. Confinement in the cell was nothing to me. In fantasy so real that it was not a dream, I could again visit my rude hut and again and again kiss the willing lips of my Golden Girl.

As time went on, I passed from group to group, until I was soon working with those who had been in Kornbrae for ten, then twelve, and at last nineteen, twenty and then twenty-one years. By then there were only a few, as I remember only nine, who had passed all the tests, endured all the trials, and learned all the required sciences. To my amazement I passed from the class of initiate-candidate to the Class of Eubate. Within a year I passed from Eubate to Bard. As a Bard I could have been freed to roam the countryside as the other Bards did, telling the story of the King of Glory and his twelve knights of the Round Table of Eternity. I chose to stay, and threw all my energy and will into preparing for the last step in the training, the dreadful and sometimes deadly initiation into the Class of Druids.

One morning after our quarterly initiation ceremonies at the winter solstice, I was waked at low noon, and with eight others sent on a run into the night

172

down from Kornbrae onto the Salisury Plains toward the distant and mighty *Caer Gaur*.

Caer Gaur! Could even the most gifted make clear what that name and that place has meant in the development of mankind and the Initiate Man? Could tongue but tell the importance and the antiquity of the symbols and the instruction there all men would fall upon their knees. *Caer Gaur*, "The Great Temple" of the Ancient Druids lay before us, woven about by a veil of mist, yet shining in the first rays of the sun. The temple itself was made of two concentric circles formed of upright stones of gigantic size, rising up to four or five times the height of a man. These enormous stones were connected by cross stones, built, it was said, by mortased stones so carefully selected and fitted that the sound of stonemason's axe or builder's hammer was never heard in the region of The Great Temple. The outer circle was thirty three Royal Egyptian Cubits in diameter. It was made of sixty giant stones, thirty upright and thirty impost. The inner circle was thirty Royal Egyptian Cubits in diameter, and was made of forty gigantic stones.

Within these two circles was the Arch Druid's Sanctuary. It was made of two concentric ovals. The oval shape, or egg-like shape of the Sanctuary was but one of the many symbols which, I was to find, served instead of words for the purpose of teaching the ancient secrets of the Druids. The outer egg-shaped stones numbered ten, and the inner oval was made of nineteen stones. Within this symbol, so carefully designed to tell the world its full meaning, was an altar formed in the shape of a perfect cube. Within that place were enough symbols to occupy a student's meditation for a year!

Caer Gaur, or as a few Britannins called it, Stonehenge, was open to the air, for the Druids considered it the Place Of God. They said that God was too great to be encompassed by roofs and floors, or worshipped in any room that was not open to the sun. Between the circles and sets of stones there was a greensward. Surrounding the entire temple was an enormous embankment beyond which there was a deep ditch; it was said that both were made without any tools stronger than a green reed and that all earth was moved in hands of love. It was said also that the dozens of underground rooms which lay to the north end of the Mighty Temple were dug with loving fingers and with gentle and yielding reeds.

We were all halted by the Chief Druid on a path which led directly into the gateway between the gigantic stones. Looking down that avenue I saw something that was to puzzle me much, almost cause me to fail my final examination, and at last be most significant to my life. Near the entranceway was a single stone, slender and straight, standing upright on the earth. Beyond it inside the inner circle was another similar but much larger stone towering in its loneliness among the other stones that served part of a team purpose of forming a wall. I wondered why these two stones were placed so conspicuously and so uselessly in the great temple.

When the drummer came near I whispered, "Sir, looking down this pathway you see two stones set apart and apparently useless. What is their purpose and what are they called?"

"No one knows, Boy. They are called Phallus One and Phallus Two, but their use and their meaning is not known to any man. Silence!"

I fell silent, but I pondered in my heart. Fleetingly I thought of my wonderful father and how he taught me by use of curiosity, and also of his insistence that there were three ways of virgin birth. But we were soon very busy and the thought faded from my mind. Hundreds of groups of candidates were arriving from all over the land. Within a space of half a sunrise the plains about the deep, wide ditch were dotted with the colorful robes of Chief Druids, and the brown robes of the candidates. Each of the many oaks seemed to have sprouted brown-robed men around its mighty trunk.

Even as the sun was a finger's width above the eastern plain there was a sudden stir among the men, and a sigh went up. The Arch Druid and his train of Druid Priests and followers came slowly down the broad aisle, flowing like gaily colored water around the far lone stone,

174

then past the guardian stone and across the bridge to the moat-like ditch. In that train of men subservient to the will of the Arch Druid were kings, princes, potentates, and masters of commerce and trade. Each man moved, however, with the calm dignity and strong grace belonging to his station. At last the procession fanned out into the plain, forming a veritible rainbow, but a beautiful rainbow that was soon to become menacing and terrible. At a signal all of us were ordered to move toward the Druid Priests, and did so eagerly; but as we approached the rainbow of Priests gleaming swords leaped into their hands and we were stopped by a network of sharp and deadly blades thrust at our breasts. The voice of my uncle came from the Arch Druid, echoed across the plain in commanding and powerful tones.

"Abandon hope, all who enter here, for the death of man awaits you."

Many of the candidates were startled, but none fell back. A line of priests came forward then, bearing in golden bowls bloody looking sticks.

"Open your mouths," commanded the mighty voice, "and take this wormwood and gall. Then you will know what your initiation is to be like."

Quickly the many priests tossed into the open mouths the crimson sticks. I was assailed by the horrible taste of wormwood and the bitterness of gall. For a second it seemed too repulsive to bear, then, to my amazement, the bad taste faded away and my mouth was filled with the sweet taste of apple-blossom honey and sweet horehound.

"If admitted through the guardian blades, you will advance to the bridge and there you will kneel and offer your tongues to be cut out. Within these sacred stones words are not as important as symbols. Look well to each symbol, each stone, for eventually you who live must pass the Final Examination, and in it you must explain every symbol and every stone."

One by one we knelt, extended our tongue, and a symbol stroke was made with a blade that nicked the skin. From that time on we were forbidden to speak inside the sacred area of Stonehenge. However, when we went to our underground quarters north of the Mighty Temple, we were instructed in words concerning the mystical symbols and the meaning of each stone. But this was much later. The first moments of *Caer Gaur* were almost as overwhelming as were the final moments of the dreadful and deadly Final Examination.

As we approached the stone called Phallus One, each candidate was handed a small *glain** (^{E}ditor's Note: A *glain* was a small boat made of glass and never before now was its use, purpose, or meaning explained) probably no bigger than half a thumb, but very trim and strangely iridescent. As I looked at mine I wondered that it should be handed to me in the very shadow of the first of the unexplained stones. I stood in the awful majesty of that Great Temple, and tried to understand the weighty questions that echoed in my brain,.... to take into the unknown future answers for my dreaded Final Examination. But I was not to have time or opportunity. We were soon moved onward toward the second and larger of the unexplained stones, crossing the greensward in bare feet. As each man received his *glain* a mighty voice thundered: "Put off your shoes. This is Holy Ground."

Barefooted, we were then taken seven times around the outer circle, and were shown by signs that we hungered for three drops from the mighty cauldron of the Druids, for those three drops brought great happiness, the ability to tell the future and the fortunes of men, and an understanding of how man might become immortal while still in the flesh. For it was around the everlasting soul of man, and the reincarnation of the spirit into the flesh, that their instruction was based. They taught that the world was saved from destruction because the Nameless Mediator, the Son of God, took the part of man and hid his Godly self in the flesh of man. They taught that all men could know this God-self by inward contemplation and pure faith.

An apparently unrelated offshoot of their belief in reincarnation caused me to think much and to ponder deeply. It was their contention that a great man, a hero, could come back from the world of pure spirit and occupy *any form* whatsoever. A song was sung, in the usual triad

176

so popular with their Bards, of the Prince of Powis, one Owen Cyveiliawy. It said, in metric way, that Owen had appeared in the form of a vibrating shield, a lion before the chief with mighty wings, as a terrible spear, as a bright sword spreading fame in conflict, in the form of a dragon banner before the sovereign of Britannin, and in the form of a daring wolf. To most of the initiates the meaning was found in the symbology of the daring wolf. At all initiations there were men in white ceremonial robes who wore red jewels in their headdresses - these were called the "terrible wolves" who were supposed to kill the candidate who quailed or quit.

I pondered in my heart upon a deeper meaning, a meaning more important to mankind. It was becoming clear to me that there were many levels of their instruction, and Owen appeared in six forms other than his own flesh-self. Besides *Owen* was but a word whose true meaning was *Bright Self*, or *Perfected Self*.

We were taught that no man was truly separate from the Divinity. All upon the earth was one in the spirit, merely separate in the physical. They also taught that the world had already been destroyed by flood, and was - unless man perfected himself - to be destroyed by fire in spite of the Mediator, the Son Of God, and all he could do to save the world. They believed that each individual soul continued after the death of the flesh, and had to face the throne of judgement for all his earthly deeds. They taught also that time was but an infinitesimal fragment of eternity caught in the mind of man, and that there had been and was to be an endless succession or continuing chain of worlds, a continuous creation and destruction of all things physical. The place of punishment for wickedness was a quagmire of never-ending frost filled with stinging insects and deadly snakes.

I adored their teachings regarding TRUTH. They constantly struggled to make each man realize his *divine responsibility* to the absolute Truth, to duty, to love. We were taught that we should more readily give up our lives than fail in duty, in love, or in our adherence to the Absolute Truth. This, we were taught, was not limited to

177

the time of initiation but to all transactions of life in every situation!

In my heart of hearts I knew that this teaching was more beautiful and far more complete than the historical-religious teachings of the Jews. If the teaching and practice of the Druidic Brotherhood was less than that of the Essenes, it was less only in the practice of love and exchange of affection. The Essenes were no deeper in the worship of the Divine; they were more concerned with the group. The Druids created contest and strife, and they caused men to be islolated one from another. But they tried to make of each man a powerhouse, an independent and mighty man, able to walk alone into the thickest battle of either physical, mental, or spiritual enemies. They gave no quarter; they asked no quarter in any contest. Death itself could not shake them in their duty. Withal they lacked, to my mind, the beauty and the tenderness of Brotherly Love.

Eubates and Bards were supposed to be able to foretell the future and exercise charms, spells, and provide entertainments. The Druid was called upon to practice advanced skills in the interest of the State. Neither war, peace, not any State decision was made against the wisdom of the Druids. The lives of kings and princes lay in the power of the Arch Druid and his Council. Thus it was that the States of all Gaul and Britannin, Wales and North Humberland supported the ritual and the training of Druids, for they wanted only the most highly developed performing within their courts. The dreadful Final Examination was designed to screen out the faulty and the frail.

The course of Druidic instruction was based upon symbols and signs, without the use of audible language. In the Final Examination we had to be able to give back what we had learned with unerring accuracy, without fail. We could choose any subject in the arts, the sciences, the laws, or the procedures of the Druids. Once we had chosen we had to be able to answer all questions and then explain everything within the area of our choice to at least three levels of understanding. Failure could mean dismissal. Dismissal meant that you were turned

178

loose without friends in a hostile land, for no man would befriend or help you. Failure was worse than death! Therefore many men continued to study for years.

I could not. After a little more than a year we were segregated into advanced students and candidates for the Final Examination, and I was placed in the latter group. When asked what category I would choose for my Final Examination I heard myself say, "The Sacred Symbols of the Druids, of course!"

"Can you explain each symbol to three levels, without fail?" one of the candidates whispered when we sat at food. When I did not answer he added, "It will be bad enough to be set adrift in a *coracle* upon the sea. But how can any one explain Phallus One and Phallus Two, when even, the Chief Druids say the meaning is lost to history."

"Perhaps I will not be asked about them," I said, and my heart was heavy with my rash choice. But it was part of the discipline of the Druids that no man could change his pledged word. I was bound in duty to attempt this impossible task! The news was whispered from cell to cell in our underground chambers, and soon it was known in all Britannin that Jeschuau of Nazar, in four years of study, would try to pass examinations which most men required twenty one years to master, and that he had chosen the Sacred Symbols of the Druids for his dissertation. Weeks before my Examination, caravans began to arrive from all lands, and one came in the most colorful feather robes. I was told that these were the Jaguar Priests of a Brotherhood Colony upon a far continent, and that they were called *Caribes* after the *Sea* near which they lived.

The morning of my Examination was clear and cold. The assembled visitors waited a little impatiently while I made the ceremonial walk from east to west by way of the south, seven times around the inner circle. At last I walked toward the Arch Druid, who was Joseph of Arimathea, and knelt and handed to his assistant my golden sword. If I passed the test it would be returned and I would wear it in the physical trials which were to follow. But if I failed my Examination, it would never be

179

returned. Or, if it was the order of the Drudic Council, it would be buried to the hilt in my heart. To such things did one bind himself in taking the Oath of Initiation of the Druids!.

"Jeschuau of Nazar, you understand that you must answer all questions to the full satisfaction of every Druid, and on three levels of understanding?"

"I do."

"You certify to all assembled that you have chosen for your dissertation the Sacred Symbols of the Druids?"

"I do."

"First Question, Masters?"

The first question came from one of the castrati Druids, who personally destroyed their manhood in order to become more sensitive to the powers of the Divine. "Explain the *glain*."

"The *glain* is the physical symbol of the goddess Ceridwen, keeper of duty and truth. It is handed to the candidate as a token of his readiness to begin work on the Druidic Degree and is, therefore, the symbol of mental and physical readiness and truth. But a grain of sand might have these symbols, and there would be no need for the work of making an iridescent glass boat representing great care, much preparation, and exacting skills. In this lies the third level of understanding. This easily crushed but brilliant *glain* is in truth the symbol of the eternal spirit, the soul of man. When it is handed to the candidate it represents the moment of birth, when the soul parts from the Supreme, imparting to man the living flame of life."

I would have gone further, but there was an angry murmuring among some of the Druids from Egypt. After a while they were quieted, and a Caribe, a Jaguar Priest asked, "What is the true meaning of *Spica*, the ear of corn?"

"It consists of many grains, representing abundance or prosperity. It is grown of the earth, representing the fructifying of the earth forces for the use of man. In the spiritual sense it is the growing of the stalk that is important as a symbol, and the ear merely represents the entire process. As the plant unfolds it sends forth its leaves and its tassels, even as man unfolds spiritually he sends forth healing power and the silken blessing of love."

"Explain the symbol of the Straw," a distant Druid commanded.

"The straw is the symbol of agreement between men; the breaking of the straw is the symbol of the breaking of an agreement. Straw itself molds into many shapes and forms, when formed into a dart it is said to have the ability to destroy wild beasts. The true, spiritual symbol is found from this: the thought of man is like many straws in the wind. When it is fashioned into a single form it has surpassing power! Especially, it is able to subdue and destroy the wild beast, that is, untamed and undisciplined man. Thought can be as powerful as the dart represented by the straw, or it can be as flimsy as the breakable straw."

"What is the meaning of the Rainbow Symbol?"

"The rainbow is a symbol of protection, because it is said to be the promise of the Divine never again to destroy the world with water. The rainbow is also said to be the belt of the successful candidate, protecting him from all evils. This is merely the symbol of the many-colored dresses of the Druids in which each man finds personal safety. The spiritual meaning is this: There is a radiant being within each and every man, a rainbow of great brilliance, and it – somehow, just how I do not yet know – can bring him safety and protection from all things."

Even as I finished talking an angry murmur came from the Egyptian Druids, and one even drew his sword and would have come toward me, but was seized by the Jaguar Priests and thrown to the ground. His headdress was knocked away, and as he rose, struggling against the *Caribes,* I recognized the fury and contempt on the face of Nicodemo. His distorted face was like the face of death, for a vote against me could come from any Chief Druid and he wore the colors of a Master Priest! When at last he was quieted and placed back with his group, I felt the pounding of my heart in my throat, and a strange fear was crawling snake-like up my cold spine. The next question had to be repeated. I heard it, but my mind was too much in turmoil to register its meaning. I fought to control the mind within me, to fashion the straws of my own passion-tossed thoughts into a cutting sword.

"The symbol of the Wheel, what is its meaning?"

"Sir, I am sorry that you had to repeat your question. The symbol of the Wheel is based upon the astronomical cycles and represents the precession of the equinoctial point. On a higher level it represents the cyclic returning of the earths of time, that is, the rebirth time after time of the world out of sleeping matter. However, this is not its highest meaning. It also represents the rotation of the cross, upon which, time after time man must crucify his physical self in order that the spiritual self may find its full release."

I was breathing hard, knowing that I was not doing a good job with my answer. The distraction had thrown me out of rhythm with the crowd, and out of contact with my own inner self. I was stumbling in my words, halting in my decisions. But the answer was not challenged and I waited with my breath coming sharp and hard. I had expected severe questioning, but I was not prepared for this open hostility – not against my answers, it seemed, but against me as a person. I was confused. I was worried. I was in great danger from an unknown cause.

"Explain the symbolism of the Reed."

"The Reed is a symbol within a symbol. It is said to be a symbol of deceitfulness, because it bows before the wind from any direction and because it hides the stealthy and deadly water snake. By reverse thinking, it is also the symbol of patience and persistence against any adversity, because it rebounds from any wind or storm. On the spiritual level it represents the eternal contact between the Supreme and man, the ever-pliable cord of love that links man to his God."

"What say you of the symbol of the Oak Tree?"

"The majestic Oak is the symbol and the visible representation of the Deity. It is also said to be the place where the Supreme resides. Yet a higher level of meaning comes from the belief that the largest and most centrally located Oak should be formed into a cross by cutting away

182

the unneeded branches. The Oak Cross is considered most important and most holy; the cross is more important as a symbol than is the tree itself. The cross thus made is a living cross, the residence of the Supreme. It is the symbol of the eternal sacrifice. The Oak Cross becomes the symbol of the Supreme, or the Mediator Son of God, and of the force of the eternal Mother, the earth. It is the symbol of the sacred trinity toward which man struggles with much sacrifice and in which he may at last have eternal salvation."

"Then what is left for the symbol of the Mistletoe, the All Heal?" It was the rasping voice of Skakus, and it seemed to come from within the hood of one of the Egyptian Chief Druids.

"Sir, All Heal is the symbol of the perfect medicine of high esteem, said never to fail as a remedy for disease, in counteracting poison or in preventing sterility. On a broader basis it is the symbol of protection against all dangers and difficulties, the grand preserver against all evils, moral and physical. Its spiritual meaning can be understood only if you consider the ritual by which it is collected. The *Tola** (Editors Note: The *Tola* was the Druids name for a Chief Druid who was temporarily the leader of a ceremony and was, therefore, an Arch Druid for the moment.) is purified by many cleansing baths, by fasting and by rituals, and he is also purified by means of the *Tolmen*.* (Editors Note: The *Tolmen* seems to have been a hollow stone which was very sacred and used in purifying and cleansing all candidates.) Two snow white bulls who have never been secured by the horns are made ready for the sacrifice. A golden scythe is forged of newly mined metal, and made sharp without the touch of common earth. Then the *Tola* is dressed in a white robe with a red tiara. Barefooted he climbs the oak and holding the scythe in his awkward hand must cut free the All Heal with a single stroke and catch it in his new-spun *sagus* so that it is never touched with human hands. The bullocks are then sacrificed amidst rejoicing."

The angry murmurs rose to where I could not speak until they were stilled.

"Spiritually, then, the All Heal is the divine minister

which comes from the Oak Tree, the abode of the Supreme. It is therefore the symbol of the spiritual Son Of God, of the Supreme All Healer of man's ills and man's corruption. But his Supreme All Healer is acquired by man only by great and carefull preparation, by careful and practiced disciplines, and by the use of the *Tolmen* or sacred rock of faith. The symbolism of the white bulls completes this.... the bull represents the sexual and physical vitality of man. A white bull represents these vitalities purified. A white bull represented as never to have been tied by the horns merely symbolizes the fact that man has learned to control and purify his own physical passions, and is willing to sacrifice them to receive the Supreme All Healer into his breast. The symbols are all now one. The Mistletoe is the symbol of the Son Of God made manifest in the breast of every man by discipline, sacrifice, and purity. Mistletoe is the symbol of spiritual and physical immortality acquired by man through worship and devotion."

Pandemonium broke loose and groups began to struggle with other groups. One of the Egyptians ran toward me, but was tripped by a Caribe, and they fell to blows and then to drawn swords. The clang of metal was great as more and more began to fight. The voices were heated and harsh and the place seemed filled with hatreds, with strife. It was midmorning before the dissention and the argument was stilled and I was ordered to continue with my examination.

"Can you explain the Beehive as a symbol?"

"Yes, Sir. The Beehive is but a cube with the sign of activity. The Cube symbolizes perfection, truth, and also the inviolable and sacred inner self of man. The Beehive represents the collection of many sacred selves within the confines of perfect truth. It is said to represent the Druids. This is true: but not, as some may think, on the physical level only. It also represents all of the perfected souls of all time. The Beehive is the symbol of the Masters Of The Ages, the Teachers Of Man, the Source Of All Knowledge. The Druids themselves become merely a symbol of this Higher Order!"

"Must we listen to him bemean the holy Druids?" It

was the voice of James of Bruton. "I say, kill him now and cleanse the name of our Order!"

There was much growling and much argument before I was ordered to continue, but with due respect to the Druids.

"Proceed now to the symbol of the Chain," my uncle commanded.

"The Chain is a hidden symbol, too. It appears to be the symbol of the candidate's willingness to accept confinement and restriction and endure the rigors of preparation and initiation. But it is not merely a symbol of patience, fortitude and perserverence. Each link in the chain represents a perfected life, a master raised above the human level. The chain circled about to link to itself represents the binding of all masters of all time into a unity or enduring truth, an order above the physical."

"Would you say, an order above the Sacred Druids?" It was the harsh and angry voice of Skakus who stood to his feet with sword half drawn.

Before I could answer my uncle's voice stopped me, and he sounded quite angry with me. "Jeschuau of Nazar, you have been warned not to bemean this supreme and sacred order of Druids. Watch your tongue if you wish to live."

I bit my trembling lips and stood with bowed head. But I could not answer except in truth as I saw it. Knowing that my answer might bring the wrath of the Druids upon me, I still could answer only to the truth I saw.

"It is a higher order than the Druids, Sir."

Half of the Druids were now against me, and they were only partly restrained as they shoved and battled against my defenders until I was surrounded by a threatening ring of swords. But at last order was restored, though with much difficulty, and the highest Jaguar Priest spoke to the group.

"Brothers, we must make allowances for this boy's extreme youth. Like you, I am much disturbed by one who can take of our goods and our substances and yet feel no loyalty to our Druidic Order. I am disturbed by one who knows that the Druids have the best and

185

greatest teachings of all eternity - yet dares to say that there are higher orders. Perhaps, however, he does not understand the treason within his mind that makes him say such things. Let me then ask him a question concerning a symbol which we all know to be purely of the Druids. Let him guard his answer. What say you, then, about the symbol of the Serpent entwined around the World?"

"Sir, such a symbol worn as an amulet is said to gain favor and to protect the wearer against mental distress. But it is in truth a Serpent entwined around the Egg. The secret Druidic meaning is that this symbol signifies the care which the Serpent of the Ages, that is, the Supreme Being, gives to the Druids who worship him. But"...

"Boy!" the Caribe said, "watch your tongue that you do not bemean the Druids."

"Sir, if I bemean the Druids it must be sorry indeed that they are so easily bemeaned. For I say to you no Order is higher than Truth, and I am sworn to tell Truth to the limit of my knowledge and belief. The Serpent represents the vitality of man raised to the spiritual level of God. It is the sign of man made like unto God. The Egg is the symbol of the ever-fresh source of man, the body or physical self. Together they have a meaning even higher, for they symbolize the protection of the ever-abundant egg or the physical by the ever wise spirit of the everlasting God, showing that the physical is the source of all-power, the fountain of Godhood, the Temple of The Everliving God. The symbol, in full truth, is not limited to the Druids, but concerns all men of all races, everywhere in the world. Within each man is Divinity! Not within Druids alone!"

The Caribe fell back in astonishment, and his Jaguar Priests rose with an angry shout. But at last he calmed them and whispered: "Quiet, Brothers, he will be in the Tomb for three days before being set loose upon the sea in the *coracle*. We will stealthily weaken the skins of his boat and let nature dispose of his hateful mind."

Skakus was on his feet, shouting, and was at last recognized by the Arch Druid, my uncle, who seemed

186

little pleased with me indeed.

"My question is this, simple and direct, and you must answer that which no man knows. What is the meaning of the symbols of the useless stones, Phallus One and Phallus Two?"

There was happy laughter among the Druids, and someone said, "Ah, now we have him. No man can answer that! No answer is known, hah!"

I stood with head bowed, the very weight of the failure already upon me.

"Well, Boy, can't you answer?" Skakus taunted.

"According to the Druid tradition there is no answer. The Druids have never caused me to believe there is an answer. But I have pondered much upon the apparently useless stones, and much upon the excellence of the training of the Druids. It seems such a waste of effort to place such singular stones in such conspicuous places unless they have a very important meaning."

Sarcastically Skakus cut in, "Boy, are you trying to repair your boat when already at sea?"

"Sir, if my boat must sink, let it be! This I must say. I believe the Druids do not know the meaning of those two stones. I believe that there is a race that does, a Brotherhood that not only knows but teaches an important and eternal principle by those stones."

"Oh, so the Druids are not as great....."

"Sir, will you be silent! I say there is a Brotherhood who knows the meaning of those two stones, but I do not say it is a greater Brotherhood than the Druids. I do not know. I have thought much and concluded that they must be Egyptian in origin."

"Why?"

"*Caer Gaur* is built on the basis of Egyptian Royal Cubits. Blood Spring, it is said, is built to the dimensions of the Royal Chamber using the Royal Cubit as the base of measurement. Look you, sir, down into the giant ditch. Even there at the bottom of a ditch dug by reeds and loving hands is a greensward which is 105 sandal lengths across, that is to say, thirty-four Royal Egyptian Cubits. Even within the Sanctuary of this Great Temple is an altar of perfect cube – and it measures one

Royal Egyptian Cubit and not a hair's breadth more."

"Answer the question, Boy! What is the symbol of the stones?" The command or the question was flung at me from hundreds of voices until the shouting echoed from the distant oak grove, and I stood helpless before an angry mob in whose hands my life had been placed. At last the shouting was quelled and I could not help but answer.

"I do not know the meaning of the two stones. But, if I live, I shall some day find out!"

"Kill him! Kill him!" Skakus yelled, and charged at me with drawn blade.

A Caribe stepped in front of him and a moment later I found myself surrounded by Druids who led me away. A few minutes later I was in the stone crypt known as the Tomb. It was no larger than an ordinary stone coffin. I could barely lie straight and could not sit up. I was literally laid into the tomb as one dead. My guides admonished me to think carefully upon my life and my future if I lived, for I would be set adrift on the Northern Sea on the 29th of April, to live or die by the will of God. Perhaps, they suggested, I would prefer to drown rather than to face the punishment of angry Druids. With this dire thought they left me, closing the tomb with a large slab of stone.

I was weary beyond speaking, and collapsed gratefully upon the firm stone. Surely for a moment I lost consciousness in the upsweeping waves of utter fatigue. Then I lay in the absolute darkness, letting my mind drift to my home, to my interest in healing, to my quest for the White Brotherhood and the Order of Melchizadek – and I could not feel that all these years had been wasted. Why I had become so unpopular with the Druids I did not know, and I could not explain no matter how hard I pondered upon the possible reasons. Then a golden light began to glimmer in the darkness, until the beauty of the glorious Golden Girl was before me. As I approached to kiss her willing lips, she came toward me, but I was pulled backward with a compelling force. No matter how she hurried toward me, I was pulled away even faster. I cried aloud and broke out of my reverie to find that I was sweating and shivering. I forced my mind to think upon the ordeal before me, but I knew, no matter what the punishment, I would never be sorry for having told the complete truth as I saw it.

On the third day – the time seemed very short to me – the stone was rolled away from my tomb and I was told to come forth from the dead. I was then hurried to the sea, and set adrift at midnight upon the treacherous waves. The sea tossed and pounded the small, skin covered boat. I found that it was not as violent as in a *scull* in a windy sea. Battered and bruised from the beating upon the black waves, I saw at daybreak that I was but a few hundred yards from the headlands. Before sunrise I had managed to guide the *coracle* to the beach.

I saw the Druids there waiting for me. I knew that I had just enacted the key role in an endless drama. I had been made dead, buried, and resurrected on the third day. Then as the new-born, I had become the infant in the basket, and had been forced to trust the Divine with my new life by being set adrift upon the treacherous sea. At last I was lifted from the water by the hands of many cheering Druids and carried back to food and to rest, and to magnificent festivities of the May Day.

But in my heart I pondered. What was the greater meaning behind this ancient play of being dead, buried, reborn, entrusted to fate, redeemed, and at last allowed to stand as conqueror of time and fate before those happy Druids who now addressed me as "Thrice Born Jeschuau of Nazar"? What was the deeper mystery? What was the third meaning? Why could I not separate from my mind the two Useless Stones and the vision of the Golden Girl? What had these to do with my wonderful father? What had all this to do with the White Brotherhood and the Order of Melchizadek?

Yet, even as I pondered thus, another channel of my heart and mind asked an even more urgent question. Would I ever again see and truly kiss the Golden Girl?

189

11

MYSTERIES

OF THE ORIENT

The fun and happy frolic of May Day was not over before I knew that I must go and live among these peoples. I was to perform for at least one year the duties of the Druid, the Bard, and the Eubate. My task was to tell fortunes by many ways, especially by tossing the 147 apple twigs, to counsel with the leaders of tribes and villages, to show by example and teach by concept the glory of God come into the form of man. After the ordeal, when I was at last handed my sword with a golden blade, I found I walked with a firmer tread, and kept my mind upon ways to ennoble mankind. Truly, I became in some subtle way a better man. But living among those simple folk in Sommersetshire, and along the River Brue, tasting of their daily joys and sweet loves would have made any man a better man. Their food was simple, their life was joyous, and they turned to me, the Druid, for advice on all things of the heart and the soul. Among them I found the true reputation of my Uncle, Joseph of Arimathea. They called him "The Man Of Tin", for he came often among them to buy handicrafts, and most especially he bought any tin they had mined. His ships plied constantly from the Orient to Britannin, carrying tin and grain one way, carrying marble and fabrics the other.

We Druids were taught to tell of heroic deeds by the Knights of the Table Round, and their king whom we named Author Of All, but whom the simple natives called

Arthur, King Of The Round Table. Into these heroic deeds we wove the story of the moral precepts which were inculcated by the Druidic ceremonies and studies. Each Knight was given one of the twelve virtues which the initiate had been taught to strive for. The King, of course, was but the symbol of the initiate. *Mer-leen*, god of the sea, was made into the worker of miraculous things - even as the sea brings on a sea change in all things - and he became Merlin, to the natives.

Sometimes, for a few glorious days, I could retreat to my rude hut on the Isle of Avalon, near the Mighty Oak beside Blood Spring not far from the River Brue. Oh the joys that were there! I walked about the swale, keeping in my mind the hope that someday the most glorious Temple in the world might rise on that ground, for it seemed so peaceful, perfect and sacred. Sometimes I would let it be known that I would talk to a group of native Cornwallians under the boughs of the Mighty Oak, and many would come. Sometimes the swale was filled with serious faced men, handsome women, and beautiful children - all fair and slender and tall. They sat to hear me talk, and sometimes for half a day I would spin the tales which taught morality and fortitude. Thus in the place I had come to love most dearly, with a people whom I dearly loved, I spent most of my seventeenth year. Many came for healing in mind and body, and I healed.

Though I was happy in my usefulness and popularity, I was lonely in my body and in my soul. For my body yearned for more than a thought-caress of the Golden Girl, and my soul yearned for more than a hint of the existence of the White Brotherhood and the Order of Melchizadek. I yearned with a strange soul-hunger for knowledge of them, for more knowledge of the things of the spirit and the mansions of the soul.

Trouble came into my Paradise by a line of Druid priests who came out of Blood Spring early one morning. They surrounded me without the usual salutation of Brotherhood, and drew their swords. Skakus then came forward his hand outstretched.

"Give me your sword, the symbol of belonging to the Druids." When I refused he took from his robe an edict of the Arch Druid of all Britannin and read it to me, his voice mean and triumphant.

"By this edict I command Jeshuau Joseph-bar-Joseph, man of Nazar, to give up and abandon his symbol of belonging to the Druids. I command that he yield it unto Skakus, the Egyptian, and I further command that it shall not be returned or touch his flesh until he has deserved the highest award man can possibly receive.

"Thus further do I command. Skakus, the Egyptian, shall keep this same golden sword and return it when it has been re-earned.

"And yet further do I command. Jeschuau Joseph-bar-Joseph shall leave this land before the sun sets this day, and this sacred land is forbidden to him until he has deserved to receive the golden sword."

Skakus laughed harshly, and the ring of bared swords closed in upon me until I could not move for the blades.

"But why, what have I done?"

Roughly Skakus grabbed the sword from my scabbard. Then he shoved me over his leg and threw me to the ground, and my heart was heavier than my body. Within seconds the Druid Priests had thrown out of my hut the perishable foods, folded my bundle, and were marching me rapidly across the swale. We crossed back to Weary-All Hill, then down the path toward the distant wharves. I was hustled below the prow of a ship on which I could read "River Hindus", shoved across the gangplank with such force I fell into the arms of an Indian Captain whose name, I later found, was Bomachari Ramanchana. Captain Ramanchana set me to my feet, but Skakus threw my bundle so violently I was almost knocked over in catching it.

"How violent are the Druids," Captain Ramanchana said.

"But how wonderful, too," I said. Skakus heaved at the gang-plank and sent it aboard the "River Hindus" with a clatter and a mocking laugh.

"Why is he so hateful to you?"

"I do not know. But perhaps I have deserved his

hate."

"Are you saying, Jeschuau the Outcast, that hate lies not in the actions of the active, but in the passions of the passive?" His slender face was neither serious nor smiling, mean nor disapproving. In his dark eyes there was no hint of passion, no suggestion of emotion. They were deep pools of understanding that mirrored back to me the essence of my own self.

My assignment on the ship was to be officer's aid, and I reported directly to Captain Ramanchana. Before we had glided down to the sea over the same route as the Golden Girl, I knew he was beloved by all his men, and was a man of great development and high skill. He was not only Captain, but also spiritual healer and personal teacher to most of the men on the ship. He was, in fact, their *Guru*, which means an adept who takes students to teach. So much was he loved that he never gave an order. His merest suggestion was carried out by a crew that vied with itself only to carry out his wish. The second day at sea I dared ask if he would become my teacher, my Guru, and teach me of the Indian philosophy.

"I will teach you, Jeschuau the Outcast, with this agreement, that you will take the first three of the Four Steps of our secret religious initiation as soon as we think you are ready."

I bound myself by my pledge, and he began to open to me the strangest and sweetest mysteries of belief. The Essenes filled their teachings with mental and physical work; the Druids filled theirs with strain and terror and the triumph of the individual against all odds; but the Indians filled theirs with the triumph of the individual by passive acceptance of fate and the yoke of the Supreme. The whole purpose of life, so I was taught, was to yoke the soul of man with the Supreme Soul of the Universe. This could be accomplished by thirty three paths including Mental Study, Perfected Training, Physical Efficiency, Adoration of the Supreme, Love of Fellowman, Service to Fellowman, Acts of Devotion, and Acts Without Attachment to the End Result. There were special breathing exercises and daily meditations that were supposed to help speed this *Yoking* with the Supreme,

193

which was called *Yog*, or *Yoga*. He who is thus coupled with the Supreme acquires many special skills, among them healing and levitation, and when he has advanced to adeptship is called *Yogi*. Again I was taught that God Supreme, the All Pervading Spirit was in everything and in every act.

"We Hindus believe that God Is All and All Is God. We are said to have three hundred and thirty three million deities – one for each breath we draw in a life time. But this is not enough. We have one also for each breath we exhale. For God is everything, even the breath and the used breath," my gentle *Guru* said one night on watch. "The problem we try to solve is how can man unknow his separateness from God, how can he know he is God and nothing but God."

In the many weeks before we sailed into the mouth of the Hindus River, I was specifically taught for at least sixteen hours a day. When the *Guru* was busy elsewhere he turned me over to one of his advanced students and they taught me concerning the subject he assigned. Never were there more thorough teachers, for they were taught, as a prelude to attaining a wonderful state of consciousness known as *Samadhi*, to contemplate any subject to its uttermost completion and in the minutest detail. Thus, in my teaching, no detail was missed and no remnant was left out.

"The body," my *Guru* said one watch night, "the human body is the temple of the Supreme Spirit. It must be adored and cared for. Sensible exercise, sensible food, cleanliness – all are essential. But it is the mind of man that makes the animal body do those things which it must. Therefore before the body can be made the pure temple of the Most Holy, the mind must be curbed like a wild horse to obey the bit."

Once when I came to him concerned with the theory of Karma we had quite a long discussion. I began "Karma, I was told is the inevitable repayment for any act, and it holds through the cycles of lifetimes. That is, what I do *or do not do* in this lifetime may be caused by something from my most recent incarnation and may influence my life a dozen incarnations from now. This is hard to believe. For if God is good he must be just. What justice can attain to punishment for acts many births ago?"

"Justly reasoned, Jeschuau the Outcast," Ramanchana said gently. "But *Karma* cannot be understood apart from the Law of *Dharma*. *Dharma* is the true and inevitable law of the Universe, and all things happen according to the rule of that eternal law. Truly, he who would kill by the sword, by his very thoughts, sets into play the Law of *Dharma*, and the inevitable result is that he who would kill by the sword may die by the sword. It is inevitable that love shall be repaid with love, hate with hate, emotion with emotion, good with good and bad with bad. Yet there is nothing good nor bad but that the mind works to make it so. *Dharma*, when disturbed, seeks again its inevitable equilibrium and *karma* is the resultant movement. But it should not be understood that there is no changing *karma*. Indeed, man can change his *karma*, else what is worship for? He who worships superbly well, who becomes an adept, who is a true *Yogi*, that man is beyond *karma*. So great is he that he may undo the bad *karma* of lesser ones. *Karma* presupposes some *maya* (ignorance), the Adept has risen to enlightenment and the removal of all lack of knowledge. It is said in the *Upanishads*, our treasured teaching, that even if an Adept should murder it would not be murder nor have sin or *karma* attached."

I was taught the Hindu trinity, Brahma, Vishnu, and Siva. Brahma was said to be the creator, Vishnu the preserver, and Siva the destroyer. But I was taught to think of the three as but one. Their highest priests were called *Brahmins*, or Learned Ones. One day, almost five months later we sailed into the harbor near a city on the west coast of Hindu's Land and after we had tied to a wharf my beloved *Guru* sent me to gather my bundle and follow after him. This I did without hesitation or question, although my heart was heavy at leaving so many sweet comrades as were the sailors on the "River Hindus". We made our way by boat and on foot for several hours and rested overnight. Then we continued on until at last we stood at the entrance to the cavern of

195

Elephanta, ancient and sacred cave of Initiation.

Guru Ramanchana stopped and pointed at one of the small stone houses near the entrance to the cavern. "That will be your home. Go there and wait. And if the waiting seems long, look up at the lip of the cavern. See how it is worn by the feet of many who have gone before you. See the two giant statues that guard this entrance, so bare to the sight of God except for the jewels which they wear. Six others guard three other entrances, each decorated with jewels even more beautiful, and those entrances are deeply worn. For we believe that within this cavern one hundred and thirty feet square, and eighteen feet from floor to ceiling is the oldest temple in the world which has been fashioned by the hand of man. So old is this temple that its origin is veiled in mystery, and so patient was the love of man for its rituals that it is carved out of solid rock, supporting its roof on four massive pillars. Wait, and contemplate the passing life of man and the enduring life of God. Wait, and set your heart right with God, for many are called but few are chosen, and many die before they come out from this dreadful ritual." He walked a little way and then turned. "Let this be my final lesson. You must be attached in detachment, and detached in attachment. When the moment comes...though I love you, I may have to kill you. Though I kill you, I love you not one whit less."

I moved into the small stone hut near the foot of the giant statue on the right hand of the eastern entrance. Each morning I found on my stoop cooked rice, fresh fruits, nuts, and sometimes rich stews of vegetable along with a pot of water. Each day at noon I walked down through the village and to the river where I bathed and swam, rubbing my skin with the fine, white silt from the bank of the river at that place. Men, women and children came to me with problems and for healing. Many times I was brought the victim of the deadly cobra, but in rare cases did they live. Since my clothes were not those of the region they called me "The Holy Outcast", and they sought my help and council on many of the problems of the village. Thus I spent two years and a little more until a note came from my *Guru* which read:

196

"Make ready. I have asked for you Char Asherum (the four initiations) in one of our secret religions. May you live through them to attain equality with the gods."

The next morning there was neither food nor water on my stoop and a white cord had been tied across my door, a signal that I should not pass. All that day I waited, past nightfall, and into the night. The following morning there was a half gourd of water, about three swallows for a thirsty man. I waited all day and into the night again. Just before midnight there was the sound of footsteps outside, and the light of tapers. A silent signal caused me to follow in the steps of the processional of priests. Ahead they carried the statue of the goddess Durga, and by this I knew it was the ninth day of the decrease of the moon. With much lamentation they took the statue to the river and let it sink slowly below the waves. After an hour of silence they brought it up again, and began to sing glad and happy songs, praising God in the highest, and spreading joy amongst all men.

We went briskly back to the entrance of the cavern, and for the first time I was permitted inside. How can I say what I saw? Statues of gold, giant gems of ruby, amethyst, diamond and jade, enormous figures with four, six and eight arms, each holding a bejeweled symbol. I was quickly bathed and then invested with the sacred *Zennar*.* (Editor's note: The *Zennar* is a sacred cord of three threads said to represent the elements earth, fire and air. Water, the fourth element in some religions is considered by the Hindus to be condensed air.) We then made sacrifice to the Secret Sun behind the physical sun, and I was dressed in a garment without seams of any kind. Then, after a long lecture on the importance of morality in human relationships, we rested for a time to signify the closing of the first degree. It had been easy, but I was not unwary nor unprepared for the ordeal that came next.

The *Gerishth* began when I was enclosed on all sides by intense fires and burning brands were held over my head. Then the sign of the Cross was marked on every part of my body, I was cautioned to make no sound, and told that I was dead. Then I was sent to hours of

197

probation in *Pastos*, said to be the doorway of *Patala* (hell), and told that if I even moved so much as to blink I should have failed the test. I was admonished to keep my eyes open at all times during the entire ceremony, for the God Vishnu would surely appear to me and I must be ready to kneel before him and hold him with my adoration. I have no idea how long I was cooped up in that small tomb, for my mind raced outward to the past and to the sweetest companionship, the Golden Girl. I think it was a full day later that the small crypt was opened and I was hurried from the darkness into the blazing light of the cavern. I was met by the point of a knife, and on pain of death commanded to take an oath in which I promised to be tractable and obedient, keep a pure body and a civil tongue, be passive and attentive in receiving the doctrines of this Secret Order, and keep inviolable and secret from all men the hidden and marvelous mysteries.

The cavern was a mass of majesty and color. Each participant wore a pyramidal cap, symbol of the flame of the sun and the spiritual flame within each and every man. One hierophant approached me and sprinkled me with water, and whispered into my ear: "Let this water make fecund your mother-body that you may receive the eternal birth from the virile God." When I was allowed to rise a voice commanded, "Put off your shoes, that is holy ground." Then I was hurried to the very center of the enormous cavern and there began about me a spectacular and gripping drama of dance and mantrum. The hundreds of participants moved with flowing grace and in intricate but perfect time and they chanted a mantrum as a song to the Spiritual Sun behind the Physical Sun.

> "Almighty, Indwelling, Perfect Being
> Greater far than majestic Brahma is
> All *knowing* men bow down before You
> As the Pure, as the Prime Creator,
> Eternal God of all the Gods,
> Ever enduring Mansion of the Worlds.
> You are the incorruptible Being that is
> Distinctly separate from all things transient!
> You were and are First of all Gods
> Indwelling and ancient Purusha*

198

* (Editors Note: Purusha is the
Supreme Self of the Universe
made individual in man)
Supreme Cause of all the universe
You are the Greatest Mansion
In the Mighty House of Eternal Life.
The Universe was formed by You alone,
Yet I am You and You are me,
Almighty, Perfect, Indwelling God."

As the gentle voices rose and fell, in cadence with movement, ever climbing to a climax, I felt a stirring in my heart that was both anguish and sheer joy. The emotional pitch was increased. I was placed in the center of the cavern and told to meditate upon the perfection of the deity and learn to pronounce His Name in such a way that I would be given the ability to see into the future and bring to any man the greatest wish of his heart. Upon this I pondered while the ceremony went on, and I was deeply curious as to the meaning - for there was no name by which the supreme could be named except *Perfected Self*. Before I could reason on this important concept I was hurried to the Eastern end of the cavern where I took the part of the Physical Sun in a mime, and traveled three times from east to west by means of the south. Almost exhausted, I was then placed beneath the statue of *Sita*, Goddess of Perfection, and the heavy statue was gently lowered upon my back. I became the *Mahadeva** (Editor's Note: *Maha* is "Great", *Deva* is God) in the mime, and was told that I could be free of the burden of my love only when with my mind alone I could shatter the body of the goddess upon my back. I began the circuits of the cavern, and with that weight upon my famished and trembling body. Each circuit felt as if I had indeed carried the body of my dead consort around the periphery of the world. With each step I took the din of howling, shrieks, and dismal lamentations grew. Wailing and keening rose to an earsplitting intensity and by the time I had circled the cavern seven times I truly knew the pain of all the world and bore the burden of eternity upon my back. At last a hierophant stopped me and demanded:

199

"Say aloud, what two great concepts does this drama personify?"

"Sita, known also as the Eternal Woman, is goddess of love, and love of good. When she is dead the whole world weeps and there is blackness upon the souls of men." I was too tired and weak to think or speak more.

"That is true. Also, when an aspirant to the Greatest Mysteries loses his faith in the endless quest, he weeps ever more bitterly and knows the unspeakable anguish of the Black Night of the Soul. Now say aloud the second concept."

"I cannot say. I do not know."

"That is true. You do not know because you may not know yet a while. But remember and ponder this: Until the God-aspirant can change the form of Sita, Woman Eternal, with the force of his mind, his love and his will, he cannot be accepted into the highest Order, he may not step through the barrier between man and God. Watch now for the meaning!"

The statue of Sita was taken from my back and placed upon a golden altar at the south of the cavern. One of the hierophants strode toward the east, and mounted a throne. All sounds died, even the breathing of the participants was stilled, and my own breath ceased to flow. How long did we stand thus hushed in awe? Sharply the sound of thunder came from the roof of the cavern, and the Master in the East suddenly was luminous with a golden light. From his head floated a slender tongue of blue-white flame. Slowly, as if with reluctance, it extended its arc through the cavern and touched the statue of Sita. There was an explosion, a burst of light, and the statue of Sita opened and from her womb there came a figure looking like Sita but dressed in the manner of the Master of the East. I looked on, stunned, confused and bewildered – for I did not know the meaning of this strange event, and none was given. Indeed, no explanation was given to relieve my fascinated mind!

At the urging of a Hierophant I was taken through seven fantastic mimes. Each told a story of special moral, social, or spiritual value and told that story in a way no words could convey. First I was dressed to personify the

God Vishnu the preserver, one of the many Avatars.*
(Editor's Note: An Avatar is a highly evolved form of
either man or God, existing temporarily in a different
mode of being.) This Avatar was that of the life of
Vishnu as the fish-god. The story told was that Great
Brahma was distracted or asleep and the demon *Hayagriva*
stole the sacred Vedas, without which mankind could not
live. Without the scared books for instruction, mankind
fell into vice and universal corruption so great that the
world had to be destroyed by flood. Only one pious
monarch and seven others were saved in a vessel
constructed under the direction of Vishnu who strives to
preserve. When the flood was at its height, Vishnu
changed to the *Matse Avatar* and plunged into the flood to
seek and slay the demon at the bottom of the ocean.

I was told to go into an enormous tank of water and
bring back the three volumes of the Vedas hidden at the
bottom, and was flung into the water. As I came up I
found the water was only chest deep, and facing me was
my beloved *Guru*. So great was my joy that I moved
toward him in delight. Suddenly his fist lashed at me, he
grappled me and bore me backwards, and held my head
under water. Surprise gripped me, and then terror, and
then an intense anger. Suddenly, as my breath was
expended and drowning was near, I felt the inrush of an
enormous power. I fastened my thrashing feet upon the
bottom, struck his hands from my throat, and grabbed
him by the middle. With maniacal strength I rose out of
the water bearing him in my hands aloft. As I gulped for
air I strode near the edge and thrust him into the air
toward the hard stones. He was caught by a dozen hands,
and tried to get back into the pool, but could not do so
before I had dived and found the three Vedas and
brought them up.

"What two concepts?" a Hierophant demanded.

"That he who would be as God must always strive to
serve his fellow man, even at risk of death. Second, that
in things of God, no man can be your teacher or your
priest; there comes a time when man must strive against
the very ones who first taught him, lest in their love
they destroy him."

201

Next I became the Avatar of Vishnu as the pious King Satyavrata who as a fish warned the world would be destroyed by flood and all men with it who had not drunk the water of immortality or rebirth called *Amreeta*. A conference of Great Seers on Mount Meru, the Spiritual Mountain, could not produce the *Amreeta* for men. But they discovered that it could be produced only by violent revolutions of *Mount Mandar*, the symbol of the physical world. But even the Devas could not spin the physical mountain, and Vishnu came to their aid. The Serpent of Wisdom, *Vasookee*, wound his powerful body round the physical world like a cable, and I, Vishnu turned myself into a tortoise and took the world upon my back. It was then spun, the waters of reanimation or new life given forth.

Tired as I was from supporting the heavy, gyrating world on my back I had to explain the concepts to the demanding Hierophant.

"First, life cannot be improved from the spiritual plane alone. Human life is improved by human qualification of divine energy. Second, agitation or emotional force is required to cause the human body to change the energy of the divine into a force acceptable to the physical world. The spiritual energy must be qualified by the human mind agitated by great emotion to bring about curing of disease, or raising of dead nature."

As a third Avatar I was forced to charge into a lower cavern on all fours through passages scarcely large enough to permit my body. Here I pursued the monster *Hiranyakshana* through all the regions of the seven lower worlds. I did this as a boar, a form taken by Vishnu. We met and fought, and I was at last triumphant. Immediately I was attacked again by the brother of the giant who had been promised by Brahma that no being of any known form could have power to hurt him. I was placed within a marble pillar, and caused to burst forth as living flame, defeating the giant whom no thing of known form could harm.

"Give the concepts!"

"The giant of the passions of man burrows into the

202

seven caverns of his being, and must be ferreted out and destroyed by the inturned and relentless boring mind. The second giant, fear, cannot be controlled by any known thing, but only by the destroying flame of courage."

I was then taught to take three steps at right angles, representing the story that Vishnu became a small Brahmin and demanded of the tyrant *Bali* as much room as he needed to place three feet upon for the purpose of holy worship. The giant granted the demand, and Vishnu took a step to the east and a step to the south. When the giant came near to ask about the third step, Vishnu brought forth a third foot from his belly and crushed the skull of *Bali*.

Tired as I was I could not miss the meaning here. *Bali* was the tyrant of the physical mind, embroiled with the things of the physical world. The room to worship could be none other than a purified and holy body. The step to the east was the effort to acquire spiritual enlightenment from the glorious sun of eternal God, the step to the south was the effort to acquire learning to support this enlightenment in the body of man. The third foot had come suddenly from the belly, and was used for nothing else than to destroy the tyrant. It must then represent the pure and undefiled will which conquers *without struggle* the physical mind.

Almost before I had finished these ideas, a sharp sword and a strong shield were placed in my hands and I was told that I must fight my way against all odds through the seven caverns beneath the upper cavern. I was literally plunged into hell. The noise of combat was deafening in the narrow confines of the space. As I advanced along the corridor, I was attacked by many with mean and cutting swords, and was wounded many times before I could beat off or escape the fury of the combat. As the Seventh Avatar I was the fabulous Rama, and had to prove that I wanted to be equal to the Gods by doing what they had done; by undergoing the same tiring trials and exposing myself to the same dangers. Slowly I advanced down the deadly corridor which was stained with the blood of those who had sought to pass here

203

before. At any moment I was viciously attacked and mercilessly set upon by any odds. I battled seven times the length of the cavern, and came to a closed door. Beyond the door I could hear the fury of battle and the cries of wounded, and it seemed that some were dying. Suddenly a Hierophant appeared near me.

"Hearken. You have fought the good fight through the seven caverns of hell. You have outlived the allusion to reincarnation of the spirit of the Avatar in human flesh. You have seen the seven places of reward and of punishment which the many nations have taken into their creeds, for it should be clear that the Supreme Abode contains many mansions which are but degrees of reward made proportional to the measure of man's faith and obedience. Now, one last act of faith and obedience must lead you to *Cailasa** (Editor's Note: *Cailasa* cannot be translated, but it means both spiritual and physical paradise) or to sure and certain death. You are instructed to go through this door."

In the blink of an eye he was gone. I stood panting, fatigued beyond all feeling, drugged by the weight of my bones and muscles. I heard behind me the urgent whispering voice of my *Guru*. He came up to me out of the corridor and seized me firmly and desperately.

"They have gone mad," he whispered. "Two factions are now battling and killing each other because one says you should never have been made to suffer the four initiations at one time and should be let out of the final battle because you are consumed and impotent with strain and fatigue. The other will battle to death to see that no initiation is ever interrupted. If you wish I can guide you to another way and you will not have to face the task beyond this door." He pointed to the left where a narrow corridor led upward to a turn, and I could see the deep purple of a royal colored door.

He stood back and left the decision totally to me. Could I escape the final trial? Could I survive it if I did not escape? Was he truthful, or was the Hierophant right? I could not decide. But in my confusion I felt the urge to go through the door ahead. Yielding to that pull, I flung open the door and leaped up an incline, turned hard left and raced on. Suddenly I stopped, sword at ready, and crouched behind my shield. My eyes were fixed upon the juggernaut before me, and I was unable to draw my attention from it although around me there was the furious sound of combat. For the juggernaut, a wheel of stone, was poised at the top of a steep incline running straight down between stone walls to the purple door. It was stopped only by a hinged lever which was attached to the frame of the purple door. Had I pulled open that door, the trigger would have released the stop, and the enormous stone crashed down the narrow passage with an irresistable force and speed. A horrible death would have been almost certain beneath that massive stone. Above the purple door was a simple sign that made clear every concept of the initiation: "Choose Duty *Or You* Choose Death".

Dimly in the recesses of my tired mind I noticed that the sounds of battle had died away. Suddenly a voice echoed in the cavern: "Whatever is done without firm faith, whether it be sacrifice or service to man, fasting or purity for God, or Duty to one's assigned task, the results are not for this world nor for heaven." Even as I was groping with the enormity of the message, I heard the tolling of a lovely bell. I stumbled toward it, and burst through doors to the sound of a conch. Suddenly I was in an apartment of the Cavern so brightly lighted that it seemed more brilliant than day. Within my sight were beautiful statues, rich with gold and jewels. The pillars were covered with plates of gold, set with stones of fantastic price, and from the open bellies of gold and silver statues flowed rivers of diamonds, rubies, emeralds and pearls. Through all this and through the rich vestments of the priests and Hierophants my eyes were drawn directly to the sacred adytum and the simple marble altar. It was flanked by twin pyramids from whose tops fires blazed, and upon the marble lay a single perfect golden lotus.

Perfume touched my being with a new dimension of emotional experience, for the fires were of incense. I stood utterly struck immobile, and then the most amazing thing happened before my eyes. My tired heart seemed to stop, to swell until it reached the bursting point. It then exploded upward and shattered the base of my brain. But I was too tired and too moved to feel or to care that I felt. Then there rose out of my physical flesh a radiant form. It moved from me to hover over the four petals of the lotus. There it stood, and I could see my ragged and bleeding physical self looking through haggard and hungry eyes at my radiant form hovering over the golden lotus. I was in two places at the same instant. I was myself, my flesh self. I was also some radiant body able to travel through space and see as with physical eyes.

Oh the joy that flooded through my being. I understood then the story told of Brahma! When Brahma assumed mortal form, from one half of his divine being was born *Satarupa*, a goddess so beautiful that Brahma fell instantly in love with her. But since he deemed her his daughter he was ashamed of his passion and in his conflict between love and shame he stood motionless. The goddess saw his quandary and stepped aside from his desiring gaze. But suddenly a face appeared to gaze upon her, though Brahma did not move. Dutifully she stepped aside again, but another face appeared. Yet a fourth face appeared, so that Brahma could look upon the perfect beauty of his thought-born goddess at all times and in all directions.

Magic music ran through my nerves. I understood the symbol of the lotus. It was said to be the symbol of the soul's freedom when liberated from the earthly body. The lotus takes root in the mud, grows by degrees from germ to perfect plant, and then rises proudly above the water, floating in air as if independent of any outside aid. The lotus of my radiant self was now floating above its own golden symbol and every cell of my body was filled with light, music, and the fragrance of perfected life. In this divine moment I was certain that the Supreme God and the Supreme Universe were one, without beginning and without end, and that God was omnipotent, omnipresent and omniscient – and I was part of, yet not separate, from the Godhead. I knew that I was immortal and had existed since time began and had been reincarnated through a thousand forms, even as had every other man upon earth. I knew, in that exultant moment, that man could choose the habitat of his soul; that he could change his abode as one throws away old garments; that he could quit the old mortal frame and enter into others that were new or more perfectly purified and made useful. I knew too that at the last, man who was sufficiently trained and purified could be physically absorbed into the eternal. During all of these thoughts I knew the most supreme bliss.

Guru Ramanchana appeared at my side. I could see him from two sides. I could see his front facing the golden lotus. I could see his left side facing my bleeding and battered form. I saw upon his face the look of reflected glory, the momentarily recaptured perfect bliss which he must have been able to know upon his initiation into this advanced and secret training of the Hindus. Though he had tricked me and fought with me, and had almost been my death, yet at that moment I loved him more than anyone upon earth – even more than my own self. I knew that but for his dedication and love of me, his willingness to risk my ruin or my illumination, I could never have come so swiftly to this magnificent moment of sheer delight.

Then the magic moment passed. Someone moved and my radiant body slammed back into my physical body with a force that jerked my frame and almost threw me to the stones. My body tingled all over as if it had been asleep and was now awakening to the flowing of new blood and new life. It was then I felt the blow and heard the sound at the back of my head, as if someone had struck my neck with a light club – but I knew it was caused moments before when my radiant body had surged out of my physical body. Only when the nerves and the tendons were again awakened from the stillness which was like unto death – when the muscles of the body became as stone – only then could the physical sensation be brought to consciousness. Only then could the full beauty, the full bliss, the full significance be recognized by the physical brain.

My beloved *Guru* took my hand and led me gently to a high throne. There I was enfolded in the embrace of each of the mighty Hierophants, and given the secret and sacred name of God. It was the mantrum *AUM*, said in my mother tone with mind and body perfectly composed. I was told that any time I said this word the world would be shaken to its foundation and all the gods would hurry to obey. Then I was bathed in curing ointments, robed in magnificent clothes, rich and stiff with fabulous jewels. I was offered the sacred cord and the Jewel of the Master of the East provided I would go forth for a year and teach among the people of Hindusland. I was then called "twice born" and "thrice born" and urged to go teach the Glory Of The One. But my *Guru* asked that I be given fifteen days to rest and think, and this was granted.

When at last the ceremony was over I stumbled to my cell. I was so tired that I fell over the low stoop. There beside my bundle was a great variety of tempting and delicious foods, looking colorful and bright in the morning sun. But I ate only a little before I fell asleep. I waked to remember the Magnificent Moment, to eat a little more, and to look at my cuts. But soon I was asleep again.

When I fully waked - three days later - my wounds and gashes had all healed without a scar of any kind. Then I sat down to food of the body that was plentiful and a delight. But I knew that nothing could equal the food of the soul I had known in the Moment of Magnificence when my radiant body floated like the many-eyed Brahma above the Golden Lotus in the cavern of Elephanta.

The mystery of the Master who changed the form of Sita with his mind was fresh and keen, and I pondered much. But even that lack of knowing could not dim the memory of the Glorious Moment when I became one with the Universe and all men. How I longed to reach that Moment of Bliss again - and how long I was, perforce, to wait!

12

MYSTERIES OF THE MAGI "

Within a week after my initiation I was fully recovered and strong again, and in my self there was a strange and consistent joy. This joy was so intense that at times I felt that I could not breath deep enough to engulf all the joy of the world. It was during this time that there was brought to me a victim of the deadly King Cobra. He was already beginning to stiffen, and about him was that blueish white palor that announces quick death. The weeping procession stopped in the shade of a *bodhi* (tree) not far away, and his wife came weeping and wailing to me. In my state of radiance and bliss I felt annoyed at such disturbance. Do these foolish people not know that the bite of the King Cobra is sure death? Do they never learn? Why will they bother me with the impossible? But in the cycle of an instant I was chagrinned with the wild horses of passion that tugged at my inner thoughts. I rose and went toward the *bodhi* at her request and her urging.

I was happy to feel that the sense of supreme joy had not been shaken out of my consciousness by the anguished and futile wailing, or the intense passions of my inner-self or of these simple folk. As I looked down upon the Hindu I saw that he had been a young man of the merchant class, prosperous and handsome, with everything in the world to live for. His wife was beautiful, young, and from the five children hovering in tears around her I gathered she was also fruitful and dutiful. But in some strange way I felt no pity for either the dead or the living. At that moment it seemed to me, death was the greatest joy. Death was the sweetest passion. Death was the perfection of life, the continuum of the state of beauty of soul. Death was but the moment of life extended beyond the human senses into a boundless eternity of perfect bliss.

That one was dead was of no consequence. He would in a while come again to the learning and joys of life. What matter then that he ceased this life a whisper of time earlier than was possible? Would he not come again even more quickly, recompensed by the immutable law with time which these events had taken from him?

Thinking this, I was somewhat surprised to see the form of the young man sitting upon the limbs of the *bodhi* as well as lying cold and stiff at the gnarled roots.

"Murthi was such a wonderful man," the wife cried. "Oh, why should he have to die?"

"No man dies until he wills it," I said, and was surprised at my own words. I was more surprised at the look of consternation and guilt which came upon the sensitive face of Murthi in the *bodhi*. Thus did I know that my tongue had been guided. I sent all the crowd away a distance of two hundred paces that I might speak with the spirit of the dead.

How simple was his story. He was a man of intense passion, wanting his woman every day. She was tired and repulsed him, and he turned to a younger woman, more willing if not more beautiful. He had felt that he had done great wrong. Seeking to punish himself, he had grown careless and did not watch his path, and had been bitten by the deadly cobra. Why did he think he had sinned? Because he had been taught so! Why did he not want to live? Because he owed his duty to his wife, and his love to the younger woman. In my moment of utter joy I could see nothing wrong with this and told him so.

Then I beckoned the family and friends to return. I stood over the prostrate form of the man Murthi and took him by the hand. "I forgive you of all your sins. Forgive yourself and rise up and walk and continue to do as you

210

have done while living!"

The spirit of Murthi trembled in the limbs of the *bodhi*, then came down to fall backward into the flesh body. Murthi on the ground shuddered as the flesh took home the spirit, groaned, and began to rise. Consciousness came as he gained his feet, and he looked from soft brown eyes at me. For a moment his spirit spoke to my spirit by means of sight, then the veil of forgetfulness came before his eyes. I knew that Murthi would live yet a while. But he would be caught and ground to death between the demands of his flesh and the teachings of those who never understood or knew such demands.

Even this was of great indifference. In my state of bliss, death and life were one, morality of man was of no lasting consequence; only the eternal law of God was important, and it had nothing to do with the petty foibles and worries of man.

Soon I lost the feeling of bliss, and though I tried to heal other cases of snake-bite, I failed. Sometimes men would live, but I never felt that I had done anything to cause them to live. For I was in, and concerned with the passions and the cares of the too, too solid flesh. Sometimes I even worried that I had advised Murthi to live happily in defiance of the mores of the society in which he was raised and the teachings of the priests of his religion and the family to which he owed his allegiance. Gradually I became more and more convinced, however, that the Laws Of God had nothing to do with the morals of man. Morality and goodness were akin but morality and Godliness were not akin in the same manner. For morality had to do with the needs of man, and Godliness had to do with a higher, more supernal power and force. In a dull and muddling way, I was certain that I was on the path of a great truth. But my mind was not ready to receive it, or my training was not enough to make it clear and serviceable. Slowly I lost hold of this concept and became again enmeshed in the cares and the toils of the flesh – mine or others.

Upon the fifteenth day I was visited by the Hierophants, and agreed to go throughout Hindusland in

211

the yellow robe of the mendicant, wearing as my only ornament the Jewel of the Master of the East. I was to teach the concepts of Brahmanism, and live the life of a beggar monk. In this manner I made my way across to the Ganges, and followed down through that beautiful country. At first I taught the concepts of Brahmanism, but in a little while I began to see how the concept of karma and of the four castes was used to make a few incredibly rich, but most people incredibly poor - even untouchable. I saw the stupidity of carrying the idea of non-harm to the point that one let serpents harm oneself! I began to see that the idea of blissful meditation was a way to pleasure of the cell-self as surely as a pathway to the contact with The Supreme. Slowly I began to include some words on these ideas in my daily talks before the people who came to hear me. Soon I was visited by a group of Brahmins, wrathful and demanding. They insisted that I must stop teaching the ignorant people to rebel against those things which were the way of the land. They argued that it was custom, and without custom the people would become confused and violent, and in violence the people would come to great harm.

"What you mean is that if the people become wise they will throw off the yoke of you who wish to keep the *status quo* for your own ease and enrichment, is this not so?"

"Perhaps we gain a little," one wily Brahmin said, "but we pass it on to the glory of God and to the comfort of our fellow priests. You benefit by this simple generosity."

I did benefit. I was well tended in the monasteries throughout the land, and given all needed creature comforts. But it seemed to me that my personal comforts were of small importance to the creature comforts, manly dignity, and human rights of millions of Hindus. I prayed for several days upon the matter, then spoke out specifically against such beliefs. Within a week those common folk who came daily to hear me talk had grown from about a hundred to well over two thousand. Word spread, and men came from every surrounding village to hear my message simple as it was. I told them:

212

"No man can serve two masters. Is not your body the temple of the Supreme? Should it not be kept in cleanliness? In health? In good condition? Well fed? Shall you, then, let this temple of the Supreme be the servant of custom? Will you say that your own divine self should not eat the sweet herbs which are cropped by the cattle you drive not out of your garden? Should not your pathway be cleared of the deadly serpent you will not harm – is the snake more divine than you yourself? Shall there be ranks of divinity? If one of you is divine, are not all of you divine? How can one divinity be untouchable to another divinity? Can you answer me that?

"It is true the meek shall inherit the earth, but the stupid shall perish. For the meek are of the earth and understand it and live from it and love it. But the stupid defy not those who would defile their sacred temples, and drive not out those noxious and harmful creatures that would kill the body."

Within three weeks I was talking daily to three thousand, then to five. A giant meeting was being readied for the celebration of my twentieth birthday, for the common men had come to love my words, and had sent my fame before me upon my path. But daily the Brahmins became more threatening. First I found no lodging in the monasteries, then no friends at the wayside. So I turned to staying in the homes of those who invited me, no matter what the caste. Thus it was that I was arraigned before the angry Hierophants and accused of these great crimes.

(1) "In defiance of God, he has taught that all men are equal.

(2) "In defiance of Custom, he has taught that animals are not sacred.

(3) "In defiance of Reason, he has taught that Untouchables are as divine as Brahmins.

(4) "In defiance of Truth, he has taught that *karma* is not ever enduring.

(5) "In defiance of Love, he has taught that Brahmins are not pure and perfect.

(6) "In defiance of Training, he has taught that all men have a right to life, liberty from caste, and such happiness as the flesh may know.

213

(7) "In defiance of Teaching, he has taught that a *Guru* is not essential to help man reach to the Supreme.

(8) "In defiance of the Vedas, he has taught that there is not one single law which is sacred and divine.

(9) "In defiance of the Law of the Land, he has taught resistance to authority and breaking of castes.

(10) "In defiance of Justice, he has taught the taking of food from the lands of Brahmins to save lives of common people at times of famine."

When the howling priests had quieted after the reading of this bill of charges, a Hierophant rose and said: "Now, let us mete out his punishment."

"Wait," I cried, "you have read the charges, but you have not proved them. Bring witnesses to support your preposterous position."

"See," cried an angry voice, "he rebels against even the law of the priests. It is known that when we have spoken a thing, it is true and no man may speak against it and live."

A surge of fury filled me with great power, but I stood quietly while they made a sham of justice and a triple sham of humanity.

One Hierophant said, "We will take from him the Master's Jewel, but in pity, we will not turn him over to the law of the king to be tortured and slowly killed. Mercifully we will stone him, here and now, and great reward shall come to him who throws the killing stone."

But even as hands were raised to hurl the stones, there arose three of the Hierophants each dressed in the robe and the cap of the Magi. One advanced before me, his arms held high, asking for silence and attention. When the maddened priests had quieted he said, "I am Melchior. Here is Caspar and also Balthazar, and we are come out of Persia to see this man. If what you accuse him of is true, your wrath still cannot be justified. If you stone him, do you not break your own law, do you not bring upon each of you the bad *karma*? I plead not for him, I plead for your eternal souls – let him go free into the arms of the secular law."

Caspar and Balthazar had moved so that they stood as points of a triangle opposite Melchior. They made an imposing and commanding sight, but they made no impression upon the priests. In spite of the plea, the Hindus were determined to kill me of their own hands!

When this intent was clear, each of the Persians raised a jeweled scepter and spoke three commanding words. Instantly the angry voices of the Hindus were hushed, and they seemed to be gesturing so menacingly in dumb show. Then Melchior took my arm and led me through the midst of the angry and gesturing priests, but no one looked upon us, and no one spoke. At the edge of the circle I looked back to see the priests hurling stones viciously at nothing! When we were a hundred paces away in the forest I suddenly could hear their murderous yells of triumph and hatred, and could even hear the awful clatter of stones striking upon stones.

The three Persians walked swiftly, leading me to safety. Though we passed many priests along the trail, not one noticed or spoke to us. When we had hurried along for many hours, my physical limbs were growing too tired to respond. Melchior took his wand from the pocket of his robe, closed his eyes in intense concentration for a moment, then touched me with its tip. The touch was light, and seemingly only at the very center of my forehead. But a warm glow of golden light seemed to diffuse itself into every nerve and every cell of my being. I felt radiant, buoyant, and strong. The energy which had been drained from me had returned a thousand-fold. Tirelessly then we hurried on through the night, a day, another night, and made no stop for food or water. The swift pace did not drain me, and my silent companions seemed not to know the meaning of fatigue.

What was the magic they worked? My curiosity and my mind worked with this question. They had made us invisible to the crowd of angry priests, and brought me to safety. They had made us invisible to those we passed on the trail, thus leaving no way for us to be followed. They had filled my body with endless energy, even the energy of the universe. Even more, they had left something before the stones of the angry mob of priests that satisfactorily represented my physical form. It must have been thus, for otherwise no stone would have been

215

thrown, and there would have been a cry of pursuit. How had they worked such wondrous magic?

We hurried on and joined a caravan of merchants ready to leave for Persia with rich goods for trade. Then I found that Melchior was the owner of the caravan's richest contingent, and they waited by the river for his return. We were soon placed in carry-tents to rest – and perhaps to be hidden – while the caravan got underway and out of Hindusland. When we were safe, the caravan stoppcd, pitchcd magnificent tents, we were brought together at the big fire, and I had an opportunity to thank them for saving my life.

Balthazar was a tall, lean man, very dark of complexion, with piercing eyes, tawny in color. Caspar was a short, broad man, much along my stature, with a broad forehead and the look of great wisdom. His eyes were dark brown, but pierced one to the soul as he looked. Melchior was big, big in all senses, with a barrel of a chest, a high forehead over wide-set black eyes. While not as tall as Balthazar, he was much heavier. In the intensity of his manner and the fervor of his expressions he reminded me of my beloved cousin, John-John, who, I knew, had now retreated to the desert of Paran and was living the life of a holy hermit. Melchior was emotionally at constant explosion, and had to be active. His mind, like lightning from wind-driven clouds, leaped and sparkled in all directions, seeming virtually to devour whatever it touched upon.

"In saving me you used a magic which made us invisible and changed the seeing of that violent mob. By what method could I learn that magic?"

There was a long silence. Then Caspar spoke, his voice so pure and resonant it was like to sweet music. "Jeschuau, the Nazar-Essene, such knowledge is available only to those who have passed through the external religion of the Zarathustrians, and entered into the secret religion which is behind the outer. Then only may one be ready to be told where, how and when he may learn such magic."

"In a few days I shall be twenty. Are there enough days left in my life?"

"Yes. – There is much danger!"

Balthazar's voice was deeper, with a hint of a dialect which made every word he spoke seem most important.

"I have faced some dangers," I said, "neither wisely nor well. But if a river must be crossed in the quest, it must be crossed."

"Let it be so!"

No other words were spoken, but as the days grew into weeks, we four grew to commune by the sweeter voice of thought.

My false trial by the Brahmins had been held in the Monastery of Benar, near mid-length of the Holy Ganges, at the confluence with Benar Creek. In the weeks that followed, we turned southward in a loop and back to the Ganges. We followed it north of westerly to Kanpur, then another ten trading days to Jaipur. We took the rugged pathways to Lahore and bore northward across the mountains and into the Indus River Valley west of Kashmir. There we spent many days at Peshawara, a trading village on the Indus. We then turned down the Indus and followed southward. We left the river valley at the end of twenty days, and I knew that my initiation into the Persian Mysteries must soon come about or be denied. When at last we left the caravan, taking to foot, I knew that we were headed for the Sacred Cave of *Bokhara*.

These days had not been wasted for my training. When Melchior or one of the other Masters was away with the trading or loading, always one was with me. When we were on the march, Melchior spent much time with me. My instruction was continuous. It was impressed by thought, and by the use of only a few well chosen words – and it continued throughout the hours of sleep, whenever they might be. Many times we traveled at night either to escape the burning sun or to be in a trading village on a special market day. But at last we were hard upon the path toward the Sacred Initiation Chambers of the Mysteries of Mithras, Son of God, born of a virgin in a lowly manger of stone. Much, much had I learned in the many weeks of our travel and my training, and I knew that great effort lay ahead. Yet I was not quite expecting what happened when we had left the pleasant valley for

217

the high mountains, and came suddenly upon an amazingly deep crevice. Melchior stopped facing the cleft in the mountain, a thousand feet deep and so steep and rocky that not even moss grew on the vertical sides.

"Jeschuau, the Nazar-Essene, in your initiation you will come face to face with the mighty crevice called *Chinvat* which no human being can cross. How will you cross it?" Without waiting for my answer he moved ahead along the trail. I stood contemplating the question, looking into the depths of the chasm before me, my head slightly dizzy from the thought of trying to cross such physically impossible obstacles. Puzzled, I turned to follow along the trail, and I heard Balthazar laugh behind me.

"It can be done," he said. "Fairly easily. Look! I will show you."

The rocks under my feet were not sure, so I took three paces to solid rock, and turned. But Balthazar was not on the trail. A new kind of emotion struck me, something near to panic and confusion. But his deep laugh came from the far side of the chasm and I looked in amazement across the space. He was walking along a trail on the other side, looking at me with a wide grin upon his lean face.

"I don't think you were watching," he said gaily. "Man may miss the road to heaven by watching the rocks beneath his feet. Now watch carefully."

His body seemed to vibrate and to glow, then it virtually disappeared like a flame that has been slowly blown out. I was looking at bare rock where moments before my beloved and merry friend had stood. He spoke then, behind me, and I whirled to see him twenty paces above me on the trail, between me and Melchior. "You see, it is fairly easy."

With a merry laugh he turned and walked briskly along the trail. I followed after my three Magian tutors, my heart pounding both with hope and despair. I had learned much, but there seemed so much more to learn! And much indeed there was to learn in the months ahead.

There was a familiar basis between the thinking of the Persians and the Druids. They believed in common that their mysteries ran back to the very earliest times of man, but the Magians accepted a special development made by a supposed human being called *Zarathustra** (Editor's Note: *Zoroaster* is the Greek translation of *Zarathustra*). The Magians worshipped in the open air, contending, as the Druids, that God was an immaterial Being and could not be confined in a building created by man; and the heavens were a sublime covering for a temple for the use of their deity. The Magians put their temples on the tops of hills, and built their temples of irregular circles of stones which had not been hewn or shaped by human hand. Fire was sacred to the Magians also. Once when Balthazar's robe caught fire over the camp fire, I tried to put it out. He stopped me with a command, stepped out of the robe, and left it to be consumed by the flame.

"But you could have stomped it out!" I cried.

"Fire represents God. It must have its will in all things."

In all our travels they never put fire out, allowed water to fall upon the fire, and no man ever dared spit in the direction of the flames! For the Magians, like the Druids, worshipped the Sun as the representative of the Spirit of God. Earthly fire they adored as the representative of the Sun. No fire could ever be put out by any means whatsoever.

On the night that we camped before the massive opening of the Cave at *Bokhara* I was told that I must be tested on my readiness to enter the initiation into the Secret Persian Mysteries, and that I must satisfactorily answer all the questions asked by the three Masters. I was wary, for though my friends were gentle in their physical manners, they were fierce in their spiritual force. I knew that while they would give me anything I wished in the physical, they would demand the most specific and spiritual answers to their probing questions.

Caspar asked the first question. "Who is Zarathustra and what is his importance to the Magian Belief?"

Before I could begin to answer I saw the silent groups of Magian Priests closing in around our fire. They sat in absolute stillness all through the night, all the next day and even through the following night. By my estimate there were more than nine hundred who listened to each word of my detailed answers.

"*Zarathustra* is said to be the man who established the Sacred Magian Rites known in Persia, Media, and Ancient Chaldea. He is said to have lived about a thousand years ago. But this cannot be fully true. Such a *Zarathustra* may have been the end of a long series of inspired beings, for in the *Sesatir*, the oldest collection of Magian books, we are taught that there are fourteen great prophets of Magianism, and Zarathustra is the 13th on that list. Who then shall be the Fourteenth? *Zarathustra* must, therefore, have been the name given to a whole series of divinely illumined law givers. He may have been made one mythical and mighty figure by a composite of many historic figures, but at least he is superbly metaphysical. For his very name means many things, such as, "Worshipper of the stars", "Image of Secret Things", "Fashioner Of Living Forms From Hidden Fire". Of all these I like the last, for within man is the hidden fire of the Divine Self. He who can fashion living forms from this fire is worthy of worship indeed.

"*Zarathustra* was – in the most recent physical form – born to *Pourushaspa* and *Dughdhova*, and was the third of five sons. He was called *Spitama*, and was said to be born by immaculate conception because *Pourushaspa* while performing a sacred rite drank the Holy *Haoma** (Editor's Note: *Haoma* of the Magi was the same sacred drink as the *Soma* Juice of the Hindus, and was said to be a mysterious drink of the gods, forbidden to man) and *Dughdhova* conceived without knowing a man.

"All nature rejoiced at the birth of *Spitama Zarathustra*, knowing that he was to become a divine being. He himself laughed at the moment of his birth. For he alone of all men saw at birth his *Fravashi*, his spirit form, his etheric double, and standing face to face had learned divine wisdom from it. He brought about the divine books. The *Gathas* contained the hymns and chants of the most ancient sages, and the *Vendidad* gave the story of creation, and in greatest detail showed how the priests and the people must perform the religious

220

rites.

"At the birth of this divine *avatar* his baby head throbbed so hard it pushed away any hand placed upon it. All the evil ones sought his destruction. A cruel *Katrap*, using his kingly powers, ordered that all new-born infants in the land be slain in order to destroy the infant whom prophecy foretold would destroy idolatrous worship and the priest-craft of sorcerers. But even the most crafty demons were unable to destroy the divine infant, and the *Katrap*, *Dursarobo*, was stricken dead by the very thought he sent forth for destruction.

"By seven he was a precocious and amazingly brilliant and learned child. He was given into the keeping of the Magi and educated in the mysteries of the True Religion, and at a mere fifteen years of age was initiated into the True Faith of the Ages. At twenty years of age – strangely my age – Zarathustra went to fast and meditate in the vast Persian Desert. Here he was fed by the invisible masters, and lived upon a mysterious cheese which never grew old. He lived in a deep cavern on a sacred mountain – perhaps this sacred Cave of *Bokhara*. There he was surrounded day and night by rings of flame, through which only the prophet could pass.

"After trials and testing he began his ministry at the age of thirty. He healed many, and in one of his miracles caused the sea to part so that his followers could pass through on dry land to escape the wrath of a *Katrap*.

"It is said his first vision came at dawn on May 5th as he sat beside a beautiful river. He was commanded by celestial *Vohumano*, messenger of the High God, to cast aside the physical body and follow unto heaven. This *Zarathustra* did, and he was lifted into the presence of *Ahura-Mazda*, Eternal God, and from His lips received the eternal truths and exact doctrines which he was to teach. After six more such visions he was initiated into all the Divine Mysteries, and was then left to face every temptation. At last he arose victorious and after 12 years of his ministery converted to his Religion King *Vishtaspa*. This he did by appearing into the great court through the roof, holding a cube of fire in one hand and a

221

scepter of cypress wood in the other. He was examined by the priests and philosophers for three days, and from all this questioning emerged victorious. Finally he converted the entire country, and wandered in Egypt, India, Greece where he performed many miracles especially curing blindness. He was at last killed as he was performing the sacred rituals in the temple of *Mush-adar* by a ruthless Turk. It is said that a Great Flame came down from the constellation of Orion and took up the mortal remains of *Zarathustra* and took him back to the starry heavens from which he came down to suffer and die for all mankind."

I stopped and waited and after a moment Balthazar asked softly, "Did you purposely leave out the books written by *Zarathustra*?"

"No. There were four books written by the Great Prophet of the Magi. One was the Mystery of Astrology, one was on Morals, one was on Political Obedience, and one was on Spirit and God. It is said that the mystic seers know that these books are put away in a great cavern at the summit of a high peak in the inaccessible *Thian Shan* mountains. The original writings are preserved on stone tablets, and were secretly and mysteriously inscribed by tongues of sacred flame. At some far time when the world of men is wise enough to live by the Religion and can interpret the Sacred Message, the tablets will come forth, and be the law of the land. Even so, it is said, these writings were in truth the law of the Medes and the Persians which does not change."

I hesitated a moment, and a tongue of blue-white flame lashed out of the priests behind me - exactly as had happened so many times with my beloved father, Joseph of Nazar. I felt the surge of joy, but knew I must rush on to fill the void of knowledge.

"It is said *Zarathustra* brought from angels the divine *Gathas* of the *Avesta*, the sacred book. Originally they were written on twelve thousand hides in a secret and sacred language of the angels, and they were bound with golden bindings. These, it is said, brought man from the time when he dealt only with narrow and literal

222

physical codes, and it became the law of moral and spiritual development."

"Name the Gods, define them in your own words, and explain the philosophy of the Magians of the World." It was the voice of Melchior out of the blackness of the second night of questioning, for there had been many questions in between.

"Let us then begin at the beginning. To the Magi all is explained in the life of man by Good Thought, Good Deed, Good Word and the Sacredness of Fire. While to the common man these seem limited to man's estate, in the mind of the true Magian they are but symbols of Divine Estate. Divine Thought is the extension of life of the Divine essence into all things and all life. Good Deed, or creative activity is symbolized by a line which extends in indefinite union with its own self, that is a *circle*. Good Word is found in the creation of a Master God which I shall explain. Behind the philosophy of the Magi is the proof of the Good Thought, the absolute extension of Divine Being, which becomes God In Space, or the Boundless Circle of That Which Is Unknown and Unknowable. Yet, that man may have a name by which to signify this Unknown and Unknowable God, this Unchanged and Unchanging FIRST PRINCIPLE, it is called *Zeroana Akerne*.

"Out of this unmanifest, this eternally unknowable, comes the physically manifested creator, the glorious, radiant, powerful *Ahura-Mazda*. He is space made objective, visualized as a gigantic physical entity. It is believed that *Zeroana Akerne*, the unfathomable abyss, the unknowable, the thrice-deepest darkness has within itself eternally the power of turning outward and manifesting as nature – even as the thought of man turning outward becomes manifest in activity. Out of this eternally unmanifest, from time to time, comes magnificent *Ahura-Mazda*, also known as the Logos or the Word Made Physical or Word Made Flesh. But after a time he must retire into the eternally unknowable. Thus it is said that when the world is unmanifested it is *Zeroana Akerne*, and when manifested it is *Ahura-Mazda*.

"If we would understand the Unknowable, we must

make it yet more visual for man. *Ahura-Mazda* is therefore pictured as a trinity – a triangle blazing in the eternal darkness of the Eternal. In this symbology, *Ahura* is Wisdom, *Mazda* is the Vehicle that carried that Wisdom. When they are combined they represent the Light Of Knowledge manifesting before the Created World. But when Light manifests in darkness it creates the combat and strife of contrast. Thus does the principle of evil arise, for eternal darkness must always seek to devour eternal light. Thus it was that *Ahura-Mazda*, the radiant and glorious, moving in space or darkness, formed the greater universe and incarnated himself into the luminous parts of the whole universe. Finally he manifested as the sun, which the Magi call *Ormuzd*.

"When *Ormuzd*, the sun, as objectified light, fights with darkness to sustain light and the life of the world, both matter and spirit are brought into being. When spirit unites with matter, forms are created – but the eternal conflict, the combat of eternity, must be found in all forms, including mankind. In man the conflict is between the higher self-of-light and the lower self-of-flesh.

"*Ahriman*, the serpent of destruction, is born of this lower, grosser, elemental and material world. When *Ahura-Mazda* creates, *Ahriman* counter-creates. When *Ahura-Mazda* makes living things, *Ahriman* creates shadows or bodies into which the eternal and luminous principles of spirit are imprisoned. A trinity is formed of *Ahura-Mazda* (or that which is radiant and spiritual), *Ormuzd* (that which is radiant and material) and *Ahriman* (that which is shadowy and physical). Thus we have the trinity of man as the creator, preserver, and the destroyer.

"It is said that *Ahura-Mazda* created out of his spirit-nature and his substance six secondary beings, who, combined with him make the Great Seven, the Septenary. These are called *Amesha-Spentas* by the Magi, but in other religions they are called such names as The Seven Gods Of The First Dawn, Dhayana Buddhas, Elohim, World Builders and such. In all religions there are seven. These seven gods created the world of being.

224

They are the spectrum. They are the seven planets. They are the ones who built the seven heavens as well as the seven earths – one for each of these *Amesha-Spentas*.

"*Ahura-Mazda* incarnated in the first heaven and sent out his six regents. He then incarnated in the lowest of the worlds and sent out six manifestations which created each one a continent. The *Amesha-Spentas*, therefore, are the Divine keepers of the earth, lords of time, and lords of the divisions of space.

"But *Ahriman* sent out a shadow each time *Ahura-Mazda* sent out a power. Thus were created six demons to act as absorbers or adversaries of the six godly principles; thus seven deadly sins were issued forth to oppose the seven cardinal virtues.

"The *Amesha-Spentas* or attributes of *Ahura-Mazda* are these: First, *Vohy Manah*, Good Thought, sometimes said to be kindliness. Second, *Asha*, that is to say Right or Divine Perfection. Third, *Spenta Armaiti*, Piety or Divine Harmony. Fourth, *Haurvatat*, or Salvation by Divine Grace. Fifth, *Ameretat*, Wisdom which brings Immortality. Sixth, *Xsathra*, Magnificent Sovereignty. Though not named as one of the original, there is a seventh Mighty One, the Mediator God, *Sarosh*, who is Divine Obedience, a spirit messenger. *Sarosh*, son of *Ahura-Mazda*, is the messenger between man and God, the Messiah, the Savior of the World. He guided the learning of the *Avatar Zarathustra*. Thus was formed a new trinity: *Ahura-Mazda*, Manifesting Logos, First Principle of the new triumvirate which is a Creating Triad of Power; *Sarosh*, the Messiah, the Word Made Flesh, the mouth-born son of the breath of the First Principle of Creation, who is also the second Logos within this Trinity of Creation; And *Zarathustra*, into whom the Word Made Flesh is incarnated, upon whom the Word Of God, the Messiah, *Sarosh* descends, thus making fleshly man into the Perfect Image of God.

"Man was created out of the Celestial Virgin in the original six days of creation. The world is periodically created and lasts twelve thousand years. At the end of each Great Period of Time the Deluge comes, and *Ahura-Mazda* draws all things back into Primitive Nature,

225

into unthought Thought, into inactive Deed, into unmanifested Word. There it sleeps and floats in the eternal abyss serving as the base of the resting *Amesha-Spentas*, for the Universe is then absorbed back into Eternal Darkness, *Zeroana Akerne*.

"When they manifest, the Seven *Amesha-Spentas* incarnate in man. This they do as seven mystic bodies, as seven master organs, as seven ever-enduring principles.

"How long shall the combat of good and evil last? Until Truth shall be established in all things for all time. Though mankind grow very great in wisdom, still shall there be combat until Truth comes to abide. Wisdom is the mysterious fire within the thought of man, symbolized by the flame on the *Zarathustrian* Altar, ever kept alight. Truth as a living flame consumes all lower elements, like fire set free upon wood and material things. When at last Truth reigns as free as fire the lower elements will be consumed and the work of *Ahriman* will be eternally destroyed."

I stopped at last, after three days of constant mental effort, and allowed myself a fleeting thought that there had been signs of pride and approval on the faces of Melchior, Caspar and Balthazar. But my feeling of elation was shortlived and broken by the harsh laugh and raucous voice I knew too, too well. Skakus called from somewhere in that vast crowd, "About the Celestial Virgin...tell us about the Virgin Of The World."

I was startled - nay, verily, stunned. For I knew nothing about this symbol which had passed so easily in my learning and had been accepted without question and without probing. After a long pause I said wearily, "I know nothing really about the Celestial Virgin Of The World."

There was a murmur of agreement from a thousand throats. There was a look of annoyance upon each of the faces I could see. But the snarling voice cut back across them all and struck my inner responses to a crippled resonance, like a rude hand upon a half-finished harp. "Why not? you devoured her with your eyes from the deck of the 'Britannin' as you sailed into the River Brue. Why don't you know all about her?"

Those nagging questions left me hopeless, shivering with inner confusion and frustration, though the Persian sun seared me with heat. But Melchior came toward me as if he had not heard the words of Skakus, the hateful words that probed into my dreams of the Golden Girl.

"You have passed your three day test, Jeschuau, the Nazar-Essene. Now it is your turn to be tried and sorely tempted in the desert, as was every great Candidate before you. You will go for eighty days into the desert, there to face fifty temptations irresistable to man. If you return victorious, you may then enter the Sacred Cave of *Bokhara* to undergo the trials of our Mysteries. Give me your cloak, your bundle, and all your belongings. Speak not a word, for these eighty days must be passed in absolute silence while you search for the meaning of Being to the limits of time. Turn now, go forth. If God wills, you shall find water and food. If God wills it not, no man will succor you."

I turned and stumbled blindly into the desert hills of that wild place. My confusion was not over the possibility of living those eighty days, but over how Skakus – Skakus of all people – happened to be here and came to know my innermost secret. In a short while I was crouched against the trunk of a juniper in sick despair, and I wept. As I wept I reviewed my life and its wasted moments, its bitter cruel moments. For all my struggles and all my trials, was I nearer to the Truth? Was, indeed, my mother right when she insisted that I was not the son of the flesh of Joseph? In truth I did not know the answer. What was the third manner of virgin birth? In truth I did not know. What was the meaning of the Useless Stones in *Caer Gaur*? In truth I did not know. Why could I heal the dead of the king cobra one time, and fail another? In truth I did not know. Why had I given up the Master's Jewel of the Nazar Essenes, why had the Master's Sword of the Druids been taken from me – by that Skakus! –? Why did he hold so much of my rights, and why did he hound me around the world? Why had I been so cruelly treated on the ship – with my uncle's tacit permission? In truth I did not know. Why had I been brought before a mock trial of berserk monks wanting only my death? In truth I did not know. What had been the meaning of the Hierophant who burst the form of Sita and produced his own image - what, what indeed? In truth I did not know.

In a most perverse turn-about of emotion, I suddenly didn't care. I hated the things I had wanted, I hated the wasted time. I did not even care to learn how man crossed the impassable crevice! I wanted only the animal pleasures, the physical things of life. I became cunning and crafty. With the overbright cunning of a lion, I followed a valley until I came upon a spring gushing from the lip of a cave. I lighted a dry stick with a friction stone, and made a fire, and used a taper to explore the shallow cave. I chose my spot and using sharp stones cut saplings to form a crib, which I filled with green twigs from the pinion trees. This would serve as my bed and as my warming cover. I then found a nearby grove of breadfruit cacti, and a cluster of Desert Honey Trees, which in the early morning before the sun dries the dew, puts forth a rich, sweet sap to protect its slender branches from the damage of moisture. Close by down the hillside was a growth of hollow-berry, so called because the kernel in the dried pod rattles in a wind like a hollow shell. But the green pod and the dried kernel are both good to eat and nourishing. Before sundown I had taken care of my physical necessities, and had broken and carried into my cave enough wood to burn night and day for a full month. Then I sat down to enjoy my physical ease - and burst into tears.

How soon the physical was satiated and complete! But, oh, how long, how long did the spiritual make claim upon my heart, my mind, my life!

Bitterly I wept, until I fell asleep in the spicy fragrance of my leafy bed and dreamed of the Golden Girl. But even my dreams, my precious moments with her, were now turned about! I dreamed that I was ill, ill unto my very death with a fever that raged in my blood. She came to me, tended me, and gave me foods and the warm healing of her love. When I waked she was gone, perhaps she had never been there - yet, much of the wood was gone. The green leaves upon which I had lain down were turning sear and yellow - as if with age. How long had I been ill? Had the Golden Girl in truth been there? Even this I did not know!

For many days I sat in the sun as much as I could, and ate and ate and ate. During those days I was a mental nothing, a damp rag fallen upon the earth. Slowly my strength came back, and the sounds of birds were sweet rather than annoying. At this thought I sat upright with a sudden mental clarity. The songs of birds had not changed - only my reaction to those songs! Yet they seemed to change from annoying, discordant sounds to sweet concord and harmony. Upon this I pondered, and turned slowly back to my burning zeal for the knowledge which was to come from initiation into the Persian Mysteries. I meditated much on the events of my life, and upon God The Eternal. I was surprised when one came to summon me back to *Bokhara*. From the seeming short time before he came - 34 days - I concluded that I must have been in a fever for forty six days! Forty six days of illness for one who could heal others? Forty six days - why? Why? Why? In truth, why any illness at all? Should not the healer heal himself *before* the illness?

Without a word I followed my guide down from the cave, for silence was imposed upon me until I had passed the initiation at *Bokhara*. Melchior, Caspar and Balthazar met me at the lip of the giant, circular cave, and caused me to be bathed in water, fire, honey, and then water again. I was clothed in a simple white robe. The sandals were taken from my feet, for this place was holy and not to be trod by feet shod in skin. When ready, the flutes and drums picked up a cadenced air, and we moved as a procession into the Sacred Cave of *Bokhara*.

Bokhara! Such a delightful feast of power and beauty to desert-weary eyes! The cave was an enormous circle, and it represented the universe as being supported on three great pillars which were named Eternity, Fecundity, and Authority. The entire underground paradise was gold covered and encrusted with gems so marvelous that even my guides stopped in awe. Brilliant lights bounced a million beams from the sparkling gems, and bathed the marble fountain at the center with a changing rainbow of colors. In the very center of the keystoned arch of the dome-like roof was a gem so large and beautiful that it hurt the eyes to look upon it. This was the symbol of the Sun, and it shone almost as brightly. Around this center the heavenly planets were shown in gold against a background of empyrean blue. Upon this colorful expanse the entire circle of the zodiac was outlined in embossing gold, and I noted that the signs of Leo and Taurus were dominant, while the Sun and Moon stood out even above them. Around this starry heaven, organized for the knowledge of man, was a decoration made of symbols representing every known element and principle in nature.

The procession disbanded into the cavern, leaving me standing at the top of the steps with Melchior. He moved inward and I started down the steps, but was received on the point of a sword penetrating the skin of my chest on the left side. I looked down in surprise, to see blood seeping from around the sharp blade. A voice commanded: "Stop here and wait a time with goodly patience. No one may pass who is not possessed of virtue which can resist the allurements of the world."

"Melchior, King Of The Fabulous Mountains, Am I. I speak in behalf of this candidate, and vouchsafe for him such virtue."

"Stay, wait yet a time. No one may pass here who has not capacity and will to devote himself to the study of True Philosophy."

"Balthazar, King Of The Serpents, Am I. I speak in behalf of this candidate, and vouchsafe for him such dedication to Truth and Philosophy."

"Stay, wait yet a time. No one may pass here who does not live with heart, mind and soul fixed upon the Supreme Deity and His Supernal Works in unmixed and continuous contemplation."

"Caspar, King Of Initiates Of The Eagle, Am I. I speak in behalf of this candidate, and vouchsafe for him such continuing adoration of God."

"Stay, wait yet a time and a time. For such a one must perforce be armed with an enchanted armour through which nothing of any kind whatsoever can

pierce. If he is as you have vouchsafed he is impregnable, and this sword cannot touch him, pain him, or make
him bleed. Therefore the test shall be this – if one drop of
blood falls upon these gleaming marble steps, he shall be
refused and you three driven from this Sacred Place
where lie was never before spoken without punishment."

One after another the solemn voices repeated three
times: "He is as we have vouchsafed. He is armoured in
impregnable armour. He cannot bleed. No wound will
show, no blood will fall. Withdraw your sword!"

Each time the words were said I looked down upon
the blade penetrating my skin and flesh, I could feel it
grating against my ribs over my beating heart. But I felt
myself being raised up by the sound of the words echoing
in the vaulted cave, and seeming to repeat the same
message of my impregnability a thousand times. Suddenly
the sword was withdrawn and I looked down into the slit
in the flesh which was bubbling with blood. But even as I
looked I felt the power of my own mind commanding the
cut to heal and the blood to be absorbed. I watched the
healing take place. As I raised my eyes I saw the sudden
withdrawal of the familiar blue-white flames into the heads
of the three Persian Masters. I wondered if it was my
healing skill, or their Master's Power which had healed
my bleeding chest.

When the Hierophants were convinced that the
instant healing had been accomplished, a glad song
arose, and I was borne forward by happy priests and
carried with joyful singing seven times around the Cave.
Then I was again stripped and bathed in water, fire,
honey and then water, and dressed for fighting and
danger.

One approached in the dress of a *Simorgh*, a bird
like unto an eagle by the size of thirty such birds. The
Simorgh, I was told in song and mime, had lived several
ages before Adam, and had seen all the many different
species of beings that had inhabited the world since
before the creation of man. The *Simorgh* reigned as the
Queen On Kaf* (Editor's Note: This seems to be a
fabulous mountain upon which all beings live forever)
which I knew meant the heights of being which turned

231

physical things into spiritual essences. Led by this Queen Of Speech Everlasting, I was presented with talismans to protect me from the forthcoming encounters with those hideous monsters which would seek to stop my progress to spiritual perfection. These included the Seal of the Monarch of the World, which gave to its possessor command of all elementals, demons, and everything which was created – and I knew it was the symbol of that gift which made me like unto the sun from which all such creatures were emanated. Another talisman was the *Siper*, a buckler which protected me as a shield against all material things. Also the flaming sword, the Sword Of God, called *Tigh Atish*, the symbol of unquenchable power and unconquerable soul. Thus prepared against all enchantments, and armed against all possible evils, I moved into the underground caverns and went through Seven Stages of Initiation, each designed to raise my spirit self out of my physical self.

I fought my way through the howling beasts which came upon me from all directions, inflicting grievous bites and scratches. The silent guide took me through the center of howling wolves and roaring lions, and I was set upon by a pack of wild and hungry dogs. These I knew represented the beasts of the flesh which had to be shaken loose or destroyed. We raced into blackness and the *Simorgh* guide instructed me that I must now take the part of *Tahmuras*, an ancient Persian King who threw the weight of his combat on the side of Good in the eternal battle with Evil. We battled side by side toward our goal, and at last arrived at the symbol of the mountain *Kaf*, and released from captivity *Peri Merjan* which represented the spirit of man, but the spirit set free of the physical body.

With all the hurry, and the continuous battle, I was soon exhausted, but the pace did not slacken. After hours of strenuous effort, in which I saw clearly that I was the symbol of *Mithra*, Son of God, Born of Virgin, Mediator Between Man and God, Saviour of Mankind. I was *Mithra*, Secret God of the Persians, and I was expected to have all the powers he might have!

After, a long difficult passage through one of the

232

vaults, we came to a fountain bathed in light, and sat to rest. When we had rested a while I heard the sound of footsteps, and Melchior, Balthazar and Caspar came toward us, dressed in wondrous robes and smiling. They spoke words of cheer and success, and Caspar took from his neck the Jewel Of The Master Of Persia and placed it around my neck. I felt an inner rush of sheer joy.

I looked into the eyes of Melchior and he was not smiling. There was something about him that reminded me of Skakus! He took from his pouch an enormous and deadly king cobra, opened my tunic and tossed the serpent into my bosom.

The shock of terror tore through each cell of my being. I could not breathe, I could not move, I could not think. My heart was squeezed until it seemed to move to the center of my chest, then to strike up along my spine, and crash into my head with a shower of blue-white light. I felt the sudden blow on the back of my head which I had felt once before. At that time love, joy, and adoration had held me spellbound to beauty. Now fear and confusion and horror held me spellbound to terror – yet the effect was the same. Suddenly I was above the fountain as well as seated on its step, and I could see myself. Amazement centered upon amazement – for I saw not one of my radiant selves, but two. I was conscious of having vision from three different places at one time! So great was my amazement that I forgot my terror, forgot my fear, and merely marvelled at this wondrous thing. Here was a glory ever greater, here was an event ever sweeter, here was an experience ever more spiritual. And I did not want to let the moment go.

I felt the king cobra crawling across my bosom toward the shoulder, and saw from three directions his hooded head weaving before my very eyes. I did not care. For such an experience as this, let death wait and the exchange was worth it all. Out of my fear and stress I suddenly knew again the same universal love, the overwhelming knowledge that I was serpent and serpent was I, that I was God and God was I. I felt the bliss of all perfection, even as the fanged head wove its pattern a scant three inches before my physical eyes. I joyed in the moment, held it tight against time, wincing not from danger, but glowing with love - love even for the death before my eyes.

Slowly the cobra settled back into my bosom, calmed by the thoughts of love. I watched from two other views as my hands sought him, lifted him out of the confining cloth, and gently set his coiled body on top of my physical head. After a few minutes the cobra crawled from my head to my shoulder and then across to the marble fountain. I knew in that moment a strange sense of loss, tearing at my soul and flesh, and leaving me tearful. At that moment the doors to another vault opened, and the two spirit bodies tumbled back into my physical form.

I was urged to rise and hurry on, and again entered into a turmoil of strain and battle. We at last had conquered all our foes, and were let into the beautiful chamber known as the Sacred Grotto, or as Elysium, the Place Of Peace. Across the grotto was the Archimagus, and he beckoned to us. We watched as the show of the Bridge Of Sighs across *Chinvat*, the eternal chasm, was made before us. Those who had been good were able to cross the swaying bridge, but those who had been bad were shown to have been caused to fall into the vast abyss and the horrors of an eternal hell. When this mime was over, the slender bridge was withdrawn, and the stone door behind us closed. We stood upon the brink of an abyss deep enough no man could climb out and wide enough that no man could vault across. Yet the *Archimagus* beckoned us onward. It was our signal to cross the chasm or die upon the narrow ledge!

Was our situation not like that of the spirit within the physical body? Did it not have to cross the mighty abyss from the material to the spiritual, vault the mighty gap, or die in the confines of the body? The *Simorgh*, my guide, whispered to me:

"As the radiant man is borne within the flesh man, so the physical man may be borne upon the spirit man. Now you know how to cross this chasm."

With that he spread powerful wings, and a moment later was on the other side of the chasm, leaving me alone. Even as I watched, aides were about him, and he was helped out of his weighty costume. Then I saw Skakus, and heard his raucous laughter as he kicked the costume and stepped away toward the entrance of the cave. What a benumbing doubt assailed me! Could his advice be right? Had he not hounded me out of *Britannin*? Had he not jested of my most inward-kept secret? Yet, had he not guided me safely through all the combats and the packs of howling dogs?

I made my mind stand still. Made my heart squeeze over, and willed the ramrod of light up my spine to crash through my brain. The blow on the skull was gentle, but the two radiant bodies floated over the abyss. I willed one to the other side, and one to my side. I willed them to cause me to cross the chasm. With this preparation I stepped from the edge of the ledge into the nothingness of the abyss. I did not fall, but I wobbled drunkenly as I took the twenty three paces to the other lip of the chasm. Then, exhausted, I sank upon the stones, weeping in exultation and in supreme joy. There broke out around me such peans of joy, such songs of triumph that the whole world seemed to be caroling my success. From somewhere – either within the recesses of the Cave or out of the depths of my heart's sweet memory – I heard the voice of my father saying:

"This is my spirit-begotten son. In him I am well pleased."

The *Archimagus* came toward me, his arms outstretched, glowing with his happiness. "My son, my son, you deserve to become the eternal symbol of *Mithra*, Friend, Companion, Spirit Self of Man. Come, anoint his sore and weary limbs with oils and sacred perfumes, and with the sacred oil of *Ban*. Henceforth and forevermore he shall bear the title, The Anointed One."

Even as they were anointing my gladdened flesh with the sacred oil of Ban he stopped by my side and said: "Jeschuau, The Anointed One, hear the last great secret of the Persian Mysteries, the last great enigma of the world. Hear and mark you well these words that have been spoken exactly as you hear them now by men who lived ten thousand years ago.

"In a time there shall appear upon this earth a great prophet, a seer, an avatar of God Himself. He shall be the son of a virgin undefiled who has never known a man. The birth of this Anointed One shall be proclaimed by a new and brilliant star traveling through the heavens and shining with the brightness of a small sun at midday. Look you well, and keep yourself prepared to travel, for this may happen in your day. If you follow this supernatural star to where it hovers in the sky you shall find upon earth a newborn babe. To this babe I command you offer richest gifts of frankincense, gold, and subtile myrrh. This child, grown to manhood, shall be the Savior of the World."

I took each sacred word into the very cells of my heart and the tissue of my mind, that I might ponder upon it long in the strange days to come.

13
EGYPT,
MOTHER OF RELIGIONS

How could one who was never gifted with writing make known the full depth of pleasure that floods the physical being after successfully completing the Persian Mysteries? Through the ages these Ceremonies had been designed to carry a mighty impact. So clear was the message: man has the choice of good or evil within his own heart, mind and will. So beautiful is the realization: the power of thought is the near-divine force in man's life, greater than the power of flesh! So upsurging is the Truth: the pure self is held captive to the base self! So vivid is the picturization: any man is at last fully dependent upon his own will and faith, and must use them to cross the vast crevice from bondage of the spirit to freedom! So obvious was the moral: at last even the divine *Simorgh*, symbol of the eternal urge to human perfection, the source of the power of spirit within mind and body – even this sweet guide and companion must at last desert the one who would achieve the final act of complete faith and belief and move upon the great abyss. So perfect is the example: man who has conquered his emotions, mastered the minions of bad fate in endless battles of will and daring – such a man at last is free of all earthly claims. By faith, duty, and will he can raise the spirit from even the dross of the body.

Yes, it was abundantly specific that he who can make spiritual the body deserves the Holy Unction, the

Christening of the New Born with Sacred Oil and fragrant *Ban*, and thereafter was to be called The Anointed One, The Christos.

I walked from the cave in the brotherly group of priests, the Christs of Persia. I was proud in my inner heart that my beloved Masters, Melchior, Balthazar, and Caspar were pleased with me. Yes, I was proud. How much had I accomplished in the long months now complete! I whispered in my heart. As we walked out into the glory of the morning sun, I heard the song of a lark praising his world. At that moment, that moment of supposedly my highest spiritual elation, my heart was flooded with the sweet feel and warm glow of the Golden Girl. In that moment of religious fervor I felt the unrequited love of man for maid.

Was I an Anointed One? By what right if I could not control my thoughts and my passions? I looked with a little shame sidelong at my spiritually developed Masters....surely they could never have known such longing of the flesh. Was this not the *Maya*, the trap of flesh which the Yogis taught was a bar to all spiritual progress? Was I not accomplished as a yogi, having studied the thirty-three different types of Yoga? Yet the song of a bird could fill my body with a rush of delight and longing too great for flesh to bear! I strove to get my mind out of the clutch of my despair.

I recalled that my three wise Masters had not yet taught me the magic of making myself and others invisible, changing the seeing of other men, and instilling the body of others with great energy and strength. I asked them about their promise.

Balthazar's eyes twinkled with merriment. "Ah, my newly Anointed One, you must remember our words. We promised that after you had passed the Secret Initiation of the Persians we would tell you how and where to learn the science of transmuting flesh and confounding sight."

"True." Caspar was gentle and smiling. "We can and will tell you how and where you can learn this science. But remember, it is not the way of the initiate to assist anyone who does not first ask for help."

"Then I ask you, how and where can I learn this

238

high science?"

Melchior's powerful voice brought the answer. "By seven years of study in the temples of the Mother of Religions."

"In Egypt?"

"Yes. Egypt is the Mother of Religions. Druidism is the Father. All religions took from them their original shoot to be transplanted into alien soil."

"Don't be glum, New Christ. This training to become a Christ of Persia is necessary before you can enter the final school in Egypt. You were not tricked, in truth."

"Seven years! I have been so far and so long from home!"

The very mention of the word made me know how bitterly lonely I was for my family. How I longed to see my sweet and beautiful mother, my brothers and sisters, and my beloved father, Joseph, Secret Master of the Essenes at Nazar. I was almost twenty-one and there was a vast loneliness in my soul and in every cell of my flesh. So great and aching was this loneliness that it made me again aware of my previous thoughts: that I was not worthy to be on the spiritual path. If I were spiritual, how could I feel the tugging of these fleshly things, like the power of a winch bringing home the anchor to set free the ship of self in the gales of passion! Achingly I longed to see my youngest sister, the sprightly, 'Ena, born in my seventeenth year according to letter. Born, indeed, at the time I was being driven out of the Druidic Britannin by angry Priests - for what?

For what indeed! Skakus had my golden sword. What if he was commanded to return it when I had deserved the highest honor? How could I deserve such honor? Had I not passed all the tests of the external and the secret religions? Had I not become Christed, an Anointed One? Surely there could be no higher degrees than that!

Even as I reasoned thus in my mind I was aware of my error. Too many things were not yet explained. Too many powers were not yet mine. Why, though I could sometimes heal, could I not prevent my own illness, or cure it? Was I in truth the son of the flesh of Joseph?

What was the meaning of the useless stones of the Druid Temple? No, though I was not worthy, I had been given some of the greatness of spiritual Truth. What was I but a partly trained Essene hunting the Truth of God? Because of my unworthiness, should I not now abandon the search?

I cried out in my seemingly hopeless despair, and collapsed upon the pathway. Even as I did this I despised myself. First because I showed the emotional weakness of a child. Second, because I soiled the bright ceremonial robe with dirt of the desert hills. No one seemed to notice or to care while I sobbed out my passion and made to my Three Wise Masters my confession of unworthiness. When I could frame the words I cried out again. "How long? How long? Does the candidate ever become worthy?"

"Ask Caspar," Balthazar said. "He is greater and more worthy than I."

When I turned my tear-stained face to Caspar he said in his gentle way, "Ask Melchior, he is greater and more worthy than I."

Before my gaze Melchior shrugged his massive shoulders. "Ask Skakus, he is greater and more worthy than I."

An inner shudder struck through my being. Could it possibly be? Could Skakus the Egyptian Druid, Skakus the cruel and vengeful, – could he be greater than my beloved Wise Men of the East? I could only shudder at the thought!

"Ask Skakus what?" His voice was at my elbow where by some magic he had appeared in less than a wink. Though my very cells rebelled from him, I did ask him. "How long is the training? Does the candidate..., will I ever become worthy?"

He smiled and said in his maddening way. "Ask yourself. You have all the answers."

Even before I could recover from the surprise of such a callous answer he added, "Or ask the Priests of On.* (Editors Note: On is the Egyptian name for the sacred temple at Heliopolis near the Nile. It seems to have meant more than merely a physical temple to the Egyptian.)

I looked around at the Persian hills and the impossibility of his suggestion caused me to roil. I shot the words at him in anger. "How can I ask them.....?" and with my hands and eyes I showed the emptiness and the space.

His harsh voice held a little hint of triumph and laughter. "First get your Masters to teach you the External Egyptian Religion. Then go to *On* and there ask for training in one of the twelve schools of the White Brotherhood."

The White Brotherhood! The very words thrilled me, but even more made me realize how unworthy and unprepared I was. My heart was touched to a furious pounding by my old, inborn curiosity - yet I felt the sickness of fear and doubt.

"But am I worthy of the White Brotherhood?"

The answer was as quick and as piercing as a bolt from a bow. "No. You are not worthy."

In my heart of hearts I knew too well that his statement was true. That of all unworthy persons in all the world, I was most unworthy. When I looked up questioningly he said flatly, "Neither was Joseph of Nazar, Joseph of Arimathea, Ramanchana, Romulo, Nicodemo, The Caribe Master, Balthazar, Caspar, Melchior - or even Skakus. No not even Skakus!" He strode three paces with vicious energy, then turned. "Nor was Tao Te Lin. Therefore you must know that no man is ever worthy of divine initiation. Lest you think women are worthy, neither is *Mherikhu* worthy. But the choice is hers, even as the choice is yours. You must ask, else you may not receive!"

He turned away. I sat upon the ground, bitter, and nursing my strange and undisciplined reactions to one who was apparently a great initiate upon the path of Truth. In every cell of my being I felt the strangest weight, a complete and deadly strangulation of the freedom of self, mind, energy. There was in me an intolerable blackness that grabbed upon and criticised my every breath, deed, act, or thought. It found such fault that I despised myself, and then despised myself for despising myself.

241

"Why am I so heavy, black and glum?" I asked Melchior. "Never before have I known this weight of being, this black doubt, this deep-cell despair."

Melchior sat upon his feet, flat on the trailway, in the manner of the Oriental. "No. Always you have been serenely confident and gay. We of the Brotherhood have waited and watched in concern. Know, until you have passed through this experience you are of little value. At long last you are undergoing this purging of the cellular self — and we are pleased."

Balthazar chuckled and said mischeviously, "Yes, Anointed One, we cannot feel your groans and your pain does not hurt us!"

"We are pleased," Melchior said again to reassure my doubts that this could be part of the Great Pathway. "You are undergoing now part of that great Hell of the Initiate. It is known as the Deep Night of Despair. It is a soul anguish in three parts, but it is only one of the marks and way stations which guards the pathway. It is the reason the Hindus say that every student needs a Guru. Each Candidate must pass through these cruel and destroying experiences. Some are short and intense, some are long and deadly. The short ones cause the most intense suffering. The long ones cause years of anguish, disgust of self, and personal indolence. Let us pray yours is short and intense. Many times the longer ones cause the initiate to depart the path into debauchery, or to lose the path forever.

"You see as your body becomes more and more refined, as it becomes purer and cleaner of dross, it becomes more serviceable to the spirit. But each cell has a life and a right of its own. Though your mind gives up your body to the spirit, the cell may cling to its desire for the familiar dross. There comes a moment when the cell mind fights the system mind for its own self. If it wins, an initiate is lost. If the system mind wins a new Christ is truly born. When the time comes that the spirit would be free of the enveloping body at will, you enter a battle ground within the cell self - you enter a hell, a horror.

"There are three distinct Deep Nights, one each for the Physical, Mental, and Spiritual self. Each of these

242

horrible battles is necessary, it seems, as progress is made toward spiritualizing the flesh. The first is the Physical Deep Night of Despair. This you passed through in the cave of the fountain. Your flesh self was ill for 46 days – a time of despair and near death. Remember this was only the first of three!

"You are now, happily in the Mental deep Night of Despair. We know how futile you feel. You feel that all your emotions are uncontrolable, all your thoughts are stupid or indeed you cannot think. We know that you feel that every thing you have ever done or said was the height of futility – or was wrong. We know that you so analyze and criticise yourself, and hate the fact that your own disciplines have deserted you, that you despise yourself. Then knowing you were supposed to be upon the path, you even despise yourself for being weak enough to despise yourself."

Balthazar chuckled and said as he squatted beside me. "Cheer up. You have not yet begun to suffer! Much worse is yet to come!"

When I shook my head in despair Melchior said, "Yes, believe him. Much worse is yet to come. These experiences are inevitable before the cell self can be made the perfect, obedient, willing servant of the spirit. The inevitableness of this experience by the true initiate is the reason the Hindus – and some others – have taught the inevitableness of *karma*, for they mistakenly tried to apply the condition of the initiate to all men. Mark you well, *there is still a worse time* – a time of spiritual hell and doubt so intense that it will burn the last ashes of the dross from the flesh body and make the body fully serviceable to the mind and the spirit. This dreadful time is yet to come upon you. It will be like the greatest of all calamities. It will be a thousand times worse than the Mental Deep Night, just as the Mental is a thousand times worse than the Physical Deep Night."

"Oh, no!" I moaned, "nothing could possibly be worse than this!"

"Yes. A thousand times worse!" Three loving voices made that dreadful promise. Melchior continued: "Remember what we teach you, for it may mean your very

243

life. You can and will know worse anguish at the time of your Spiritual Deep Night of Despair. At that time, may the Supreme have mercy on your tortured being."

I think I would have doubted even those Three Wise Men but that a Priest of the Persian Christs came by, looked knowingly and said, "What is with our new Anointed One, the Deep Night?" When my friends nodded he sadly wagged his head. "Must be Mental. If it were Spiritual he would be writhing in agony." He turned away, chanting one of the ritual chants, and walked toward the Priest's quarters.

To these quarters we made our way, and I was assigned to chambers. There I stayed for many days, my soul achingly black with sick despair and anguish. And I continued - was helpless to stop - my despising myself. Then I became like a vegetable, sitting out the long, long hours in utter listlessness. Weeks went by, then months, and I sat wasting my life in the clutch of a despair I could not escape. My three mentors left me - which plunged me into ever deeper despair - and made a caravan trip. They came back after about six months, then went again. My mood changed. I began to actively hate my flesh. Many times I walked to high places and the despair bade me throw myself to my destruction. A hundred times I was sorely tempted, but some thin thread of light kept me from doing so.

Still again my mood changed. Once while walking I saw the lovely daughters of a merchant who brought goods to the Priesthood. They were comely, and approached me. I lusted after them in my mind. One I singled out and courted, and gained her consent with the offer of one of the jewels of the Order of Persian Christs. But she was taken on a trip the morning before our proposed night of trysting, and I knew basic hate. I walked and ran for hours in the desert, enjoying the punishment of the heat and the whipping thorns. The Three Wise Men came again, and I was still in deep despair.

For a week or more they tried to talk with me, but I was too listless, too vegetative. Then they came one morning and said "We must be gone two years. We are

244

taking a trading caravan to Egypt. God stays with you."

I could not answer, and they turned away in sorrow and started down the trail. I watched them go with a strange mixture of emotion.

The Deep Night was still in every cell. My body was a heavy, repulsive mass, at least so it seemed. But the word *Egypt* had lighted a single spark of warmth somewhere near the center of my head, right behind my ears. This single bright spark seemed to glow more brightly than the sun – than a million suns! It seemed to feed upon the very blackness of the cells around it. A fire was begun that circled warmly and relaxingly through the cells of my brain, then it ate away the blackness in the cells of my throat, my neck, my trunk, and at last my legs. That glowing warmth seemed to eat away shackles that held me to the spot, as gyves hold a bird that would fly! How long the process took I do not know. But suddenly my whole body was clear, and I was light and free of the burden of hell. I shouted a glad cry, and a hundred priests were soon about me. I cried aloud to God my fervor and my thanks, for I was truly one new-born. The priests all cheered me, comforted me, and dried my tears of joy. The *Archimagus* came and was joyful and filled the air with his thanks and praises to the Almighty *Zeronna Akherne*, the Mighty God.

I thanked the *Archimagus* for his love, for his care. I kissed his feet and begged that he would forgive me, but I must catch my three beloved Wise Men and go with them to Egypt. The *Archimagus* merely nodded in pleased agreement. My departure was delayed, for over three hundred priests wanted to help me and send me rejoicing on my way. Their love for me was clear, and I was at last handed my bundle ready to go in ten times the moments I could have prepared it myself. I started for the path, the priests followed. I knew for them such a love as only he who is released from hell may know for the angels who stood guard at the entranceway praying for his release.

I sped over the trail. My feet were light, my body was swift, my mind was alive and alert. Hour after hour I raced along, without stopping until I overtook the long caravan. I raced ahead until I caught up with the Three

245

Wise Men. They dismounted from their carts and stood near each other as I came up.

I raced to them, fell upon my knees, and embraced the six legs.

"Oh, Masters of Wisdom, take me with you to Egypt, and teach me the knowledges of the Mother of Religions."

Soon happy tears were mingled from cheek to cheek as we embraced, and we went about the business of our lives. During months of travel I was taught the religion of Egypt by the Three Wise Men. I was compelled to learn well, for I knew I would have to pass an intense examination before I could enter the White Brotherhood. Though I sometimes hinted, and once boldly asked, no mention of that Order came from my Masters. It was as if I had dreamed a dream of hearing the name, and they did not even recognize the sounds! But they taught me night and day. Even when I did my work around the caravan, repairing and making saddles and carts, sometimes trading for special goods - even then one of the Three Wise Men was with me. They let no minutes go by when they could teach me that they did not do so.

During the months of my twenty-fourth year we moved slowly in a westward direction, crisscrossed the lands of each country, searching for unusual treasures of every sort. Sometimes the main caravan layed over at a town or city while smaller components set out to distant villages to buy or barter. At one time we sent 600 cartloads northward toward Jerusalem, thence by ship some would go on to Rome.

We came to the shores of the Red Sea. We turned northward, and inland, and spent several weeks at an Arabian town called Medina. Hundreds of tribesmen from twenty desert tribes roistered, gambled, drank until besotten, and fought and died in this town. Some few Arabian tribesmen were pious. They worshipped idols and images of all sorts. Their only pure worship was of a black stone called Kaabah, which they believed came from the heaven of the supreme God, Al Ilah. Their religion was confused, much like the ancient men of Judah. When they were pious they were fierce and fanatic in their faith, and would suffer any pain for their beliefs. Of such emotional fanatics are prophets born.

From Medina, "town of Prophets unborn" we called it, we turned northward to skirt the end of the Red Sea which separated the Arabian desert from the border lands of Egypt. After several days of long marches we cleared the end of the long sea and turned northwesterly toward Cairo and a nearby sea-town with all its wharves and piers. While some of our caravan traded with the natives for special Egyptian cloths and other goods, we made heavy sea-worthy crates. We soon had our material packed and ready for shipment to Rome, Athens, and even my beloved Britannin. Some goods, especially Egyptian punk and golden vessels, we shipped directly to Caesaria for delivery to Mount Carmel Essene Assembly. We were busy checking, building, packing; still my Wise Men lost no moment in which they could teach me more and ever more of the religions of the ancient Egyptians.

At first the study seemed to be hopelessly confused. The Egyptians had a god for almost each hour of the day, and their functions overlapped until it was almost impossible to understand what each truly symbolized. But at last I began to see the mighty religion in all its purity, stripped of its ritual and panoply, stripped to its magnificent heart - a heart so wondrous that truly I knew it could never die. I knew why Egypt was called Mother of Religions. We had been stopped in our travels by Roman legionnaires, burly, over-confident and strutting minions of Caesar and Rome. The Religion of Egypt would stand ten thousand years of Caesar. Rome could never become the center of true religion. For the Mother Religion of Egypt contained hidden in its complicated structure, waiting for the wise and persistent student, all the religions of the world. It was like the religion of the mighty Druids, and in many ways showed those nice improvements which told the serious student that Egypt was a colony and not the original source of Druidism or some religion quite similar in origin.

When at last our vast shipments were sent to agents across the Mediterranean, we gathered our caravan and crossed to the Nile River and moved southward along its fertile banks. Possibly no river in the world is so adored

- and so worthy of adoration - as the lush Nile. I did not marvel that some Egyptian beliefs made the Nile River into a god.

When we left the delta lands of the mouth, we came upon a village called Fayuem, where there were thirty barges and seven swift barques waiting to take the caravan up the long river. I was not to go far. We loaded one additional barge with special reference to my stay at the Temple of the Sun on an Island which was called *On*. This Island was also called *Khusna*, which translates to "Land of God", or "Heaven", or possibly more nearly "Paradise". When we were opposite the Island of *On* our barge left the others and moved straight for a small cove within the Island.

This "Land of God" must have been a paradise indeed! Its top rose about fifty feet above the flood stage of the river. We could see mighty temples to many different gods. In the center we could see the enormous Temple of Osiris, also called the Temple of Thoth-Hermes, for the two great gods were worshipped in the same sprawling complex of buildings.

But of all the colorful buildings, with magnificent statuary and golden towers, none took our attention so much as two small temple complexes of simple white and golden marble. The golden temple was high above the water of the cove, on a small spit of land that was almost an island. The white temple stood on the main island at the edge of the sandstone cliffs, directly across the cove from the golden one. I was caught up in the splendor of that island "Land of God". To the two small temples I reacted with a special pre-knowing of their importance in my destiny.

I stood looking up the river at the temples. Caspar came to the rail beside me. His hand swept out toward the golden temple. *"Hore Kehru.* We call it "Virgin Of The World."

I tried to make a translation of the two Egyptian words, but could not. They meant "Eternal Woman", "Glory of Womanhood", "Virgin Mother", "Eternal Virgin". I too gave up and accepted the name "Virgin Of The World."

"To which of the thousand goddesses is it dedicated?"

"It is dedicated to the Eternal Virgin. It is run as a training school for the Priestesses of all goddesses under the direction of Isis."

"In the thousands of goddesses I have memorized I never heard of the Eternal Virgin."

"She is not named as a goddess. She is the *source of gods.*"

Caspar turned away, almost as if he had said too much. I felt the thrill of the unknown going up my spine, and there was a definite pre-knowing that my fate was involved in that mystery. Caspar stopped as he started into the door of the deck pavilion and waved at the white temple.

"Temple of Horus, son of the Virgin."

I stood in the late sun, watching the island as we glided toward it, borne by the breeze in our lanteen sail, and guided by an enormous oar. I was so enchanted with the island that I did not notice the teak and ebony barque which we had to pass at the tip of the cove, where the mouth was narrowest. But suddenly my body lighted up from within, and each cell of my being became a lute of joyous strings. I heard the love-music of the spheres, I felt the pull upon my being, and my eyes turned toward the deck of the ebony-railed barque. Even before my eyes found her, my heart had sailed to her on wings of adoration. The Golden Girl stood at the ebony rail, one hand raised to shade her eyes from the slanting sun, the other touching the railing. She stood upon a golden rug surrounded by purple cords upon golden stands. She was guarded by two watchful guards, strong, silent and sure.

We glided noiselessly toward our pier, our barge passed only inches from her barque, and we were so close our two hands might have touched had we reached overmuch. I could see the whisps of fine-spun, golden, gossamer-like hair that floated upon the gentle breeze and seemed to surround her head with a golden halo. Her slender body was encased in an Egyptian sheath of sea-green, so finely spun that it seemed part of her flesh.

It was cut so that one shoulder was bare, and over her shoulders floated a thin veil of silk, worn like a shawl, that covered but did not hide the beauty of her neck and shoulders.

Her skin was fair, and so transparent she seemed to shine from within her flesh as a succulent grape reflects the life-giving sun. Her face was slender but strong, her brow was high and made a haven for her wide-set jade-green eyes. Her nose was long, but fine, and flared into dimpled nostrils. Her lips were the richest coral, formed perfectly into an upward sweep, as if she smiled from some constant inner joy. As I looked at her our eyes met, and I plunged beyond the mirror of the surface of green into a ocean-heaven deeper than all the joys of my entire life. Every cell of my being seemed to try to crowd into my gaze, and strive to take root in the highest heaven. The thrill of her passed into my cell-self as water goes into desert sand making it fertile and fecund, giving it the yearning to new life, to push eternity upward into the golden sun.

Her lips parted in a smile of complete recognition, and her hand came forward almost as if she wanted to reach to touch me across the distance. I leaned toward her, for my being adored her, and the blood of my manhood raced and roared its newly-awakening yawns in my ears. I tried to smile, but could not. I tried to speak, but could not. But her smile was radiant and she spoke, and her voice seemed to float upon the breeze like some pure-toned golden bell, perfect, deep and true.

"Welcome to *Khusna*, Beloved of God."

I felt the sweet magic her voice made within me. I felt the pure joy her beauty made within me – and I felt her presence making a true man of me. Though I longed to speak, to answer, I could not do so. My lost voice was hidden in one of the many mansions of my adoring. But my inner being leaped across the space and kissed her coral lips, and she seemed pleased. For her smile grew even wider – wider with tender understanding and friendliness. I sent my adoration by the soul-light of my eyes as the distance between us began to grow. I began to move backward along the rail, staying as near to her as I could. When at last I had come to the stern rail, I was held by circumstance, and carried slowly away from her. My heart was tight with its fast beating, and each cell of me had become a chalice drinking its fill of her golden wonder.

Behind me I heard the swift feet of my Three Wise Men, and then Melchior's voice leading the others in salutation. "*Mherikhu*, how very beautiful you are! My heart sings adoration to you."

Did I imagine that her smile lessened? But she bowed slightly and said gaily, "Thank you, Masters of the Magi. Beauty springs from the soul of the beholder."

Even as they exchanged courtesies the ships drew apart. I wanted to reach and touch her. For ten years she had been the joy of my inner thought. She had been the cause of my rebound from death in the cave of temptations. I struggled to master myself, and put all of my love into my words.

"Thank you." So much more I wanted to say. But how could I say to such a golden one, "thank you for my life" and "I love you, *Mherikhu*"? My two words seemed to be symbol words to her, filled with the meaning of my secret heart. Her smile was again so wonderful, and her eyes were upon mine even as she spoke to the Three Wise Men. Her eyes were upon mine making my soul warm and golden. She stood serenely, almost as tall as I, one hand on the rail and another raised to shield her eyes. With silken shawl and golden hair streaming in the wind, she looked like a soaring angel.

Suddenly there were wild calls for the hurried and precise requirements of landing at our own pier. When I had bound the hawsers to berth the barge I turned to see her moving up the golden stairs that led from the water line to the temple above. How lightly she moved, truly like an angel in flight!

I turned to the business of my visit--the preparation for a seven day long examination of my knowledge of the Mother Religion, by men who had become Masters of the World. Therefore we left the barge quickly, climbed granite stairs which were polished by thousands of feet, and entered the gate of the awe-inspiring temple of

Hermes. It was a sprawling complex of buildings and activities. There were many wings which were complete, self-sustaining little communities. They had pastures, barns, fields. They had rooms and schooling areas for candidates, and temples for priestly functions and for the worship of the gods. We moved directly toward the center of the complex down a corridor of giant granite columns overlaid with gold and precious gems.

In the distance, at the end of this impressive corridor was the entrance to a mammoth temple, the temple of Osiris. On each facade of this giant building were statues and fantastic symbols in pure gold encrusted with priceless gems. As we moved along the corridor, gongs sounded, and our procession was swelled by priests who came into the corridor behind us from the many different smaller temple complexes. The music of lutes, pipes, drums and zinars joined in perfect cadence and sweet melody. We were stopped by a Hierophant at the lowest of thirty three steps which led to the temple. Silently, to the sound of music. I was disrobed, bathed in ashes, manure, honey, milk and then water, and then clothed in a simple robe. It was made like a rainbow, of stripes of many colors, and it fitted perfectly. There was no seam in the garment. It seemed to be made of many patches, not sewn together, but woven together with threads dyed with loving and exacting care.

The silent Hierophant motioned us on into the massive temple of Osiris. We made for the alcove of the nave that opened upon the golden statues of Osiris, Isis, and Horus-The-Hawk-Headed. We stopped before a small rug that compelled one to look and marvel. It was a royal purple, and was surrounded by golden cords supported upon stanchions--it was a small replica and opposite in color to the rug of the Golden Girl, *Mherikhu*. The Three Wise Men knelt, and seemed to worship before that rug. I was led on to a straw mat beneath the statue of Osiris. The procession then slowly passed me where I had been left standing, circled back by the purple rug, and made their worshipful bows before it. No words were spoken, and no one paid attention to me.

Slowly the music died, and the enormous golden

doors to the temple were closed, cutting off the light from the setting sun. I was left alone, without instruction, to prepare myself for my forthcoming ordeal--seven days of examination by the greatest minds in the world. My first thoughts were not of myself or the examination--but of *Mherikhu*. The music of her name kept a melody and a rhythm in my heart.

Mherikhu. In Egyptian it could mean many things and I tried to think of them all. Merry Goddess. Perfected Woman. Eternal Virgin. Mother of God. Mother of the Radiant God. Virgin Mother. Virgin Mother of God Radiant. Yes, her name could mean any one--or all of these at the same time! It pleased me to muse upon the sweetness and the music of the name. It pleased me more to muse upon the glorious person of the living goddess who bore that name.

Before long, however, my mind turned to less hallowed but more structured thinking. I sat upon the straw mat, and began to review in my mind what I knew about the Egyptian Religion. After hours of thinking, I began to imagine that I was in the presence of a mighty host of Priests, and that I was asked questions. These questions I answered in my mind. It did indeed seem that the questions were asked by the whispers of wind in the giant temple. When I answered them it seemed that my thoughts were turned into words by the resounding statue of Osiris. Perhaps it was merely the thoughts of my brain echoing in my head. But I answered questions and still more questions, and here is a summary of what I said--or was it thought--in this the second most important trial of my life.

"The Egyptian religion is the Mother of Religions. It contains in its mystic depths all religions, both exoteric and esoteric. It is the source of all beliefs. Complicated as it seems, it is in reality quite simple. In the outer sense and common practice it is nothing more than a screen for a sacred and secret inner training. For instance, it is said to have many gods--over a thousand gods--at least one for each day three times over! But in truth it has but one God. As proof of this let me quote from writings over thirteen centuries old. This concerns

Amun, the Supreme God. Thus it was written:

"'Amun came into being at the beginning of time. His mysterious nature cannot be known. No god was in being before him. There is no other god equal to him. No one may know his form.

'Amun had no mother after whom his name might have been made. He had no father and no one begat him. He rose out of his own eternal force, mysterious of birth, created by his own radiance, the Divine God who came into being because of himself.

'Amun is not found in heaven, or in hell. He cannot be known. His image is not displayed, his name is not made in the writings, for no one may bear witness to him. He is mysterious and unknowable. His might and majesty may not be disclosed, he is too mighty for men to ask about him or even mention his name, he is too powerful to be known. Whoever utters his mysterious name, wittingly or unwittingly, falls into instant death. The soul in which his name is hidden, too, is mysterious and may not be known to men.

'But let comfort come among men. For though Amun is hidden, all gods are three. These are Amun, Re, and Ptah. There is no second to these. Hidden forever is the name of the Supreme when he is shown forth as Amun, but Re is his face, and Ptah is his body. Though three in aspect, he is but the Supreme One. Amun, Re, Ptah...One Supreme God out of three.'

"Truly, then, the many gods are but adorable aspects or qualities of the One Supreme, Hidden, Unnameable God, who is called *Amun*.

"Egyptian religion teaches of *Sekhet-aaru*, field of reeds, a heavenly homestead which is the death-right of those who have lived purely. Here the everlasting spirit will enjoy in paradise a life of ease and abundance. Egyptians believe the soul to be immortal when pure, and that the soul risen from the dead can recognize family and friends and live happily in heaven after the death of the body.

"Resurrection of the physical and spiritual body is also taught; and the physical body becomes the body or house of the soul after they are both risen from the dead.

Egyptians believe the dead will live again in the identical bodies they had on earth, provided that in the physical body they have lived good, pure lives. They mummified and preserved the physical body so that the spiritual body could germinate or develop itself within that body in preparation for resurrection to live in heaven with other souls equally good and divine.

"Egyptians believe that there shall be a judgment of the soul of the individual by the Mighty God. In this judgment the good are rewarded with everlasting life and happiness. The wicked are eaten by the eater of hearts. But to get to the moment of judgment the soul has to traverse the length of the Underworld or Hell. His way is barred by many avenging gods who will strike him down unless he knows their names, their functions, and words that will appease them.

"They believe in the Virgin Birth of a Mediator between God and man. In not less that seven trinities of the gods they show the sacred aspects of the creation of the Savior out of the Virgin Mother. The most adored trinity is Osiris, Isis, and Horus. Osiris was a human king, killed, and raised at last to eternal life by the love of his wife, Isis, and the power of his Virgin-born son, Horus. Horus, the Hawk-headed, which is but a symbol of spirit-born, is the mediator between Osiris and man. Osiris is but the aspect of the unnameable God, Amun, when concerned with humanity and love.

"Egyptians believe that ceremony and proper words may help to raise a man into favor with the God of Judgment, and therefore into heaven. Much of their ritual is made up for this purpose, and all of their funeral scripts are devoted to this end. This magic is written upon papyrus and placed in the tomb of the dead, and is believed to help his passage through the place of purgation or judgment into heaven. Even in their processions of the dead, the priests repeat the words for the dead, thus helping his spirit in its doubtful journey to eternal heaven. Around these beliefs the priests fashioned a religion that ensnared the mind of the individual and made him obedient to the ways of the people. But these seem not to have been the true priests, for even four thousand years ago the things which were prepared for the dead to say to the God of Judgment shows both external and internal meanings. Let me quote this from the things to be said in the Hall of Truth before the throne of Judgment:

"'Homage to you, Great God, Master of All Truth. I have come, Oh, Lord, to understand your mysteries. I know you, your name, and the names of the two and forty gods who are with you in the Hall of Eternal Truth. I have come to you in Truth, I have brought rightness and truth to you, I have destroyed wickedness for you. In Truth and fear of Judgment I swear;

'I have not done evil to mankind, oppressed members of my family, brought evil in the place of right and Truth.

'I have not done evil, demanded excessive labor for small pay, sought undeserved honors, punished servants unjustly, and I have never even thought ill of the gods.

' I have not defrauded the oppressed one of his property, caused pain, made any man suffer or hunger or any one to weep, nor done anything which is an abomination to the gods.

' I have not done murder or caused murder to be done.

' I have not defrauded the temples of their oblations, stolen the cakes of the gods, carried off the offerings to the spirits of the dead, committed fornication, polluted myself in the holy places of the gods of my temple.

'I have not cheated in measure, stolen land, encroached upon the field of others, taken milk from babes, or driven away cattle which were upon other's pastures, snared the fowl in the preserve of the gods.

' I have not baited fish with their own kind, turned back water at the time it should flow, diverted a canal of running water, put out a light that should burn, defrauded the gods of their meat offerings, stolen cattle from the gods or their priests, or repulsed God in his manifestations.

'I am pure. I am pure. I am pure. My purity is

that of the Bennu.

'Let not evil befall me in this Hall of Eternal Truth. I know the names of the gods, and I believe in the Great God Supreme.'

"Such a confession is but personal testament to obedience to the Ten Great Commandments, and *apparently* has no connection with a secret religion. But even this great statement of morals seems to be part of a total training in secret belief. This secret belief seems to be the core of true Egyptian Religion. If we would understand this Eternal Religion we must understand the secret belief. I shall now try to remove the screen and show the inner religion. Let us begin with the very structure of the Egyptian Empire.

"The Egyptian body-politic has always been like the body of man, while the priestcraft has been like to the mind of man. The body serves and supports, the mind enlightens and enlarges. The relation of both to the Pharaoh is most interesting. The Pharaoh comes to office as a man, but is immediately made into a god. He is then the God of Egypt, and Egypt is the body of the God. As the God he needs no administration of the Priests of the religion - he is above religions of all kind. This very structure seems to me to have been developed by men who understood the relationship of mind to body, and body to radiant being. For only when the mind has been set aside can the radiant being come forth, out of the body; rather, when the radiant being comes forth, the mind must be set aside. Yet at no time can the body be set aside; it must be under the keeping of the guardian mind. These, then, represent a secret belief. The empire becomes the symbol of the True Religion of Egypt.

"Let us see if this thesis can be supported by reference to other facets of Egyptian belief. For instance, let us see what comes to us out of examination of the Egyptian concept of nine bodies. Most other religions conceive only seven bodies, but the Egyptians say there are nine. Each body has a specific function, and also a connection with all the other bodies. These nine bodies are grouped into three units of three, and, as you will see, are for the purpose of eventually producing one

257

perfected body, a radiant god that can dwell with the gods in heaven.

"*Ren* or name is the first of the three physical bodies. It is all-important to the individual, for when it is spoken there is creative power. The name, therefore, is to be preserved, for each time it is said there is new life energy available to the individual.

"*Khat* is the second of the three physical bodies. It is the totality of the physical essence of the individual, with all the raw and untamed forces of creativity.It is subject to decay. Yet it is also the source for a higher body. Therefore it must be preserved as the temple from which grows the higher body at the appropriate moment.

"*Ka* is the third of the three physical bodies. It is the double of the physical body, and is the abstract individuality of the person. It is made of all the acts and deeds of his life, including his name, and is incorporeal. It can dwell in the tomb or the mummy, or the living body. It can wander about at will, and can even dwell in any statue of the individual. I think at a later date than the True Religion, it was said to be capable of eating and drinking, and fed cakes and water as part of the many religious rituals.

"These three bodies make up the physical body. They consist of the father concept, Name; the mother concept, Body or Earth; the Holy Ghost, or double - and the three make one. That one is the basis of higher bodies.

"The second of the three groups of three bodies consists of those having to do with the emotions, the mental-emotional make up of the individual, that is with the Heart.

"Ab, the first of the emotional-mental bodies, is merely 'heart'. It is the center of spiritual-thinking. Whatever good or bad the individual does is written in the Doomsday Book of the heart, according to Egyptian thought. The Judgment has to do with the weighing of the heart against the Feather of Perfect Truth, for each bad act of a life adds weight to the heart.

"*Ba*, the second of the emotional-mental bodies, is the Soul of the Heart. It can assume material form at will

258

- a fact that is shown by the symbol of the human-headed hawk. The Heart Soul is developed out of the fleshly soul or Ka, the Holy Ghost. The Holy Ghost is a support to the Heart Soul, giving it substance and residence.

"*Khaibit*, meaning shadow is the name given to the third of the emotional-mental bodies. It takes its essence from the Heart, and is a duplicate, double, or Holy Ghost of the emotional-mental bodies. It, too, can move and come and go as it wills. We should note that there are now three bodies that raise out of the physical or mental-emotional bodies of man and take an independent movement or action. We should also note that up to now all bodies are mortal, subject to death upon the destruction of the individual's body or heart.

"We turn now to the etherial bodies, those which cannot die unless destroyed by the eternal powers of the gods. These bodies are therefore immortal, if given a chance by pure living on the part of the individual.

"*Sekem* or Vital Power is the first of these spiritual bodies. It is the vital force of the individual which becomes a non-material entity, a personification at spiritual level of human vitality and energy. This vital force raised to spirit dwells in heaven with the radiant gods - but it is not a god. This should be most carefully noted!

"*Sahu* or Spiritual Body is the name given to the second of the spiritual group. It is developed from the physical body, that is, the three lowest level bodies which make up the physical group. It is developed by the means of the Words of Power, the prayers and thoughts of the individual through all his life, and the prayers and thoughts of other persons concerning him. However, once it has been created it takes on an existence of its own, no longer responsible to the physical complex that created it, but subject to the gods and their justice. While it partakes and is created by all the mental and spiritual attributes of the individual, once it is endowed with its own powers, its new life, it takes a nature of its own. It, in turn, is the temple, habitation, or residence of a still higher body.

"*Khu* or Spiritual Soul is the third of the spiritual

259

group. It is an ethereal being, an entity like unto the gods, a radiant being. It dwells in the Spiritual Body, and it is immaterial and cannot ever die, though it can be destroyed. Thus the Spiritual Soul is the last, perfected, radiant body that rises in man. It seems to be the reason for man's existence. It grows out of and is housed in other bodies that have grown out of the physical group and the mental-emotional group of bodies. It is that part of man which becomes an eternal god and dwells in heaven with the other gods.

"It would seem, then, that physical life upon the earth is for the purpose of preparing the immortal and everlasting *Khu* or Spirit Soul. It would seem that every act, every thought, every word and every emotion of the individual's whole physical life contributes to this end. It either hinders or it helps. What is the negative confession above (the restatement of all the things the individual has not done) but a glowing account of the fact that he has conformed to all of the physical and mental mores and morals of society? He has been a moral, good, obedient, kind man. He has, therefore, prepared his physical body and his mental-emotional body for the development of the higher bodies.

"Now we come against an imponderable. The individual has prepared the higher bodies, but they may never pass the barrier, the deadly night or Judgment. Unless they pass that ordeal, they cannot become immortal, and dwell in everlasting bliss in heaven. Rather, they will be destroyed by the fierce thing which eats all bad hearts. What is this fierce thing, this thing that causes eternal death both to the Spiritual Soul and Body, and to the Physical Body? It is a god representing time, confinement, and physical corruption, is it not? Is this not a symbol to indicate that in a bad man the Spiritual Soul dies because it cannot escape the Physical Group of Bodies?

"Let me see if I can document this thesis from the writings of the Religion. Is it not supported by the very papyrus that is left in the coffin or is wrapped between the legs of the dead? This is sometimes called the 'Papyrus of the Dead'. But the Egyptian words are *Reu*

Nu Per-Em-Hru. No person has ever been able to translate those words to modern speech. But they are sometimes translated thusly: 'The Day of Putting Forth One's Utmost Power', 'The Day of Making One's Godhood Manifest', 'The Day of Perfecting The Spiritual Self', or 'The Day of Conquering Eternity'. It refers to the morning after the Night of Journey through the lower Hell, the terrible valley of darkness and desert, through the presence of the awful dead in the world of *Taut*. The Soul emerges triumphant, all conquering, and becomes like Osiris. It has triumphantly risen out of death and the awful grave to morning light and eternal brilliance and bliss. It is clear, is it not, that the soul must have become like The God, become a very God indeed to come forth on that day triumphant? From ancient papyri we have this quotation:

A Triumphant Soul speaking to his God:........
'I came into being from unformed matter,
like the god *Khepera* eternally recreating
himself. I have dressed myself in the hard shell
of substance, and I contain the germ of every
god that was, is or shall ever be. I am
Yesterday of the four quarters of the world,
I am the god *Horus*, virgin born, who emits
light from his divine body. I have come forth
after the judgment night into this day, I am
triumphant, I am a God.'
"From an even more ancient writing we have this declaration of a soul to *the God* Osiris:.........

'I am the radiant Soul of the Supreme God
and have come from the physical body of triumphant
man. I am the creator of the divine food. That
which is an abomination unto me is a sin whereon
I do not look. I speak into being Right and Truth
and I live therein. I am the divine food which
is not corrupted, that is, my body has been good
and served as the feeding ground of my soul.
Thus I gave birth unto myself out of my physical
self; like unto the god *Khepera*, I came into being

261

day by day.

'I am the God made of flesh, and the workers
of iniquity shall never destroy my radiant being.
I am the first born God of primeval matter, that
is to say, I am the Radiant Soul. I have become
the Soul of God, everlasting. My physical self
has been the seed-ground of eternity. My Being
is now everlasting, and is the Lord of Time and
the King of Eternity. I have become Master of
my source of life, and I can easily pass through
the abyss which separates earth from heaven.'

"Some strange inner religious mystery is here! What
is the meaning of so much stress upon mastery of time,
space, and eternity? It is taught in Egyptian religion that
the animal soul of the dead (which has been carried by
the Spiritual Soul into the other world 'above the
heavens') lives on the essences of the offerings which
were made at the tomb where the physical body is laid. It
is believed that the Spiritual Soul may be destroyed in the
other world if it displeases the God or his chiefs. But we
know also that the Supreme God and Osiris, too, were
above this destruction. In our mantra, as quoted above,
the Spiritual Body has become equal to the Supreme God,
equal to Osiris – that is *beyond all destruction*.

"We see also: this Radiant Soul came into being day
by day, creating itself out of the physical group of
bodies and out of the mental-emotional group of bodies?
We must be alert to this: the source of the mantra in the
'Papyrus of the Dead' is said to be the god Thoth, that is,
Hermes. He was the scribe of the gods, he spoke the
creative word of The Supreme God, and whatever he said
was Truth. He spoke and the physical world was created.
His Word was the vital essence of life. From this has come
into the religions of the world the idea that the Chief
Priest is infallible, that when he speaks it is truth. In the
Egyptian religion we also get the strong belief in the
Hekau or 'Words of Power'. It is believed that if anything
– good or bad – is spoken correctly by a person properly
prepared it will come into being. The Word can influence
time, it can erase distance, it can affect all physical and

spiritual things – especially people!

"Let me now develop one last portion of this thesis before conclusion. There seems to be within each individual the ability to develop several non-physical 'bodies'. The *Ka* or Double seems to be a temple for the Heart Soul when absent from its seat in the physical heart. These two, in combination, seem still to be called the *Ka*. This *Ka* has an independent existence and freedom of movement. The *Khaibit* or Shadow seems to reside in the Heart Soul after it has been created out of the physical group of bodies. This seems to indicate a trinity of physical-emotional souls that are one, and can yet be three. We also have another trinity, the *Sahu* or Spiritual Body which is developed out of the physical group of bodies through the emotional-mental group, becomes in turn the temple of the *Khu* or Spiritual Soul. Thus man in his day by day progression develops independent and powerful non-physical 'bodies' that move about under some sort of mysterious control. This control seems not to be centered in the physical mind, the emotional mind, or in the Spiritual Soul. It is a mystery, a gap in my understanding of the magnificent Religion of the Ages.

"However, this condition – or should I say belief? – supports my thesis that the True Religion is secretly hidden in plain sight in the external religion of the Egyptians. Knowing that the *Ka* or Physical Soul and the *Khu* or Spiritual Soul can each have independent movement, let me quote the writing of Thoth – and remember that every word he spoke became reality. The Spiritual Soul speaks:

'I am Yesterday and Tomorrow, I was forever
and forever will be. I have the power to be born
a second time. I am the radiant, hidden soul
which creates the gods and gives vital essence
to the divine beings hidden in the Underworld
(the tomb of flesh), in *Amenti* (the Room of
gods) and in heaven (the Place of Radiant
Beings). I am the Lord of those who are risen
out of the flesh, the Master who comes forth out
of the darkness of the tomb. I work for all the

263

bodies, and we travel on joining hands each to each.'

"May I interrupt the words of the god *Thoth* to ask, is the power which guides the many bodies hidden in the phrase 'we travel on joining hands each to each?' But let me finish the quotation:

'The strength which protects me is the same
that keeps my Physical Soul, my *Ka* under its
protective power. Oh, Gods, you are in me and I am
in you. Your attributes are my attributes. My
bodies are the bodies of the god *Khepera*,
the ever-recreating self. I may enter in as a
man of no understanding. I shall come forth in
the form of a strong Physical Soul. I shall look
upon my form which shall be that of men and
women forever and forever.'

"Masters, I conclude on this evidence that the Egyptian Religion has within it a master secret which is hidden behind master secrets. This must be the True Religion, the Eternal Principle which all men everywhere seek. The partial understanding of this Eternal Principle must be in the outer and also in the hidden and secret religions of all the races – but only here in Egypt can the total Truth and the Final Secret be found."

When I had finished, the thought-voices in my head ceased, and I could not hear my own thoughts echoing within my brain. The sound of the unlocking of the golden doors startled me. The sound of their opening was followed by instreaming sunlight, and my eyes hurt like those that have long been denied the lifegiving light. The sound of music burst through the temple. The priests came in, one following the other, led by the Three Wise Men.

"Jeschuau Joseph-bar-Joseph, you have passed your seven day trial."

It was the voice of Melchior, and there was great joy and cheering by the priests. Then Melchior continued, "you have proved that you can send and receive thought, and that you have passed the highest level of mental and emotional training known to man. Rise up, Master of Men, and receive the sacred jewel of your office."

I rose to feet that stung from long disuse, and legs that trembled for want of exercise. Before the jewel could be placed upon my neck I heard the glorious voice of my father.

"My son, my son, my spirit-born son, in you I am well pleased. You are risen as high as any man has ever risen, and you have earned the adoration and adulation of the entire world. No man before you has been able to take the next step - all have died in the final effort. Knowing this, will you take the jewel of Master of Men and be content? Or will you deny the jewel and strive toward almost certain death to serve your fellow initiate and your fellow man?"

I wanted the glowing jewel. But I wanted to see my beloved father and looked about for him. His voice had seemed to come from beyond the statue of Horus, beyond the Purple Rug. I stepped toward that place. A strange power seemed to force me on, and I could not stop my staggering because my legs were disobedient to my conscious will. I stepped across the golden cord, and came to rest sitting in the center of the magnificent rug. There broke forth around me such cries of joy and gladness, such praises and high hosannas that I thought the angels sang like they did at the birth of Zarathustra or of Buddha. The priests knelt before the Rug and me, and the Hierophants came and knelt. The Three Wise Men knelt, and every person took off his sacred hat and placed it before me upon the floor. I looked at them in consternation, for I realized that I had somehow made a choice that pleased them greatly, but caused fear in some.

14

THE MASTER PLAN
FOR TRUE RELIGION

The glorious voice of my father rang out from the statue of Osiris, filling the enormous temple with echoes. "Call the Council of Mankind, assemble the Masters of the World. Let all interested Masters say those things which are for the good of man. Let this candidate for the Highest Possible Award know all the conditions."

With shouts of joy the priests rose as one man to their feet. They vied with each other for the honor of carrying the frame which supported the Purple Rug upon which I sat. They paraded as if in triumph throughout the vast temple complex. Wherever they went new throngs of priests joined their ranks. Each time the new priests fell upon their knees and performed the unusual ritual of taking off their sacred hats and placing them before me. So great was their joy that I began to awaken from my bewilderment, and my own heart began to know a lightness. My heart began to sing its own joys when we came near to the Golden Temple and I saw beloved *Mherikhu* standing at the rail to the courtyard. She looked with pleasure, and raised one hand in sweet salute. We passed not a hundred feet away, and I felt her body drawing every cell of my being toward her. We were at last circling out of the complex of temples and we went to the Temple of Horus, the White Temple.

I was taken to adequate chambers that opened out upon a courtyard that reached the cliff above the cove.

From the marble terrace I could look across the cove to the Golden Temple, and I did. Beloved *Mherikhu* stood upon her own terrace and still I felt the power of her body in each of my cells. I was fed, bathed, and allowed to sleep. I was awakened before dawn and hurried into readiness for the meeting of the Council of Mankind.

That sacred Council was convened in the central temple of Horus, the Virgin-Born. The vast room was filled to overflowing even when I was borne in upon the shoulders of a hundred eager priests who constantly vied to bear the weight of the rug upon which I was commanded to sit on a golden throne. The air was filled with expectation, for – as the eager priests whispered to each other – the greatest and the brightest Hierophants of all times were assembled here for this conference.

"It could change the course of religious history. It could change the whole course of the world!" the priests whispered, and they looked at me with eyes bright with admiration.

I saw that the place was aglow. It literally beamed with the radiance of the auras of men developed beyond the physical. Beyond the Jade Statue of Isis and Her Child, I saw the Jaguar Priest and his retinue. Then in a quarter circle of the altar of the Virgin Mother, I saw the Arch Druid and fifty or so of his Chief Druids. Within the Altar of Love, near the Golden Statue of Horus, I saw the *Archimagus* and the priests of *Bokhara* who had suffered so long with my Deep Night of Despair. Grouped before the Eastern Altar were the greatest men of Brahmanism, the Magnificent Yogis, and they were led by my old master, Ramanchana. Ramanchana was not now a simple monk, but was robed in the splendor of the Great Yogi, Supreme Ruler of the men of Hindus. Near the base of the Eastern Altar I saw my own beloved father, Joseph of Nazar. He was in the robe of the Supreme Secret Master, the leader of all the Essenes. With him were my beloved old teachers from the Essene Compound at Nazar – all in the robes of Masters. There were even representatives from China, and Buddhism was well represented. Such men of magnificence and learning had indeed never been assembled in the world of my day!

My bearers placed me down at the center of the temple. All of these mighty Masters rose as one man in deference and respect – and love! My heart made my eyes misty for beating with too much pride. I mastered the sudden and unruly passion, and bowed my obedience before the Council. The leaders of the twelve great religions of the world began their deliberations. My father rose, moved to and stepped upon the magnificent Throne of Jade at the Eastern Altar. An instant hush settled on all in that sacred temple.

"Beloved of God. Masters of Men. Masters of Religions. My beloved spirit-born son in whom we are all well pleased. This Council is met to make clear to the candidate his contract and his responsibility, and to thank in the name of mankind this Supreme Master. Time after time he has forgone his immediate ease and reward to struggle onward in the service of man and God. Always he has chosen the harder, shorter path to eternal service."

My heart would have had me cry out to him that I had never chosen but had been chosen, but he hurried on. "In only twenty five years he has mastered the skills of both the external and internal secret religions of the Seven Great Religions." A murmur of approval and consternation went through that vast assembly of trained men, and proud blood must have flushed my face. "This feat no other man in all history has ever accomplished. But his trials are not through, and the most deadly is yet to come. He has chosen to attempt the Supreme Sacrifice, that initiation for the glory of mankind that no other man has ever been able to live through. Therefore, we of the Council must make clear to him that eternal principle for which he attempts the almost impossible. It is now time all the mighty, ancient and secret scheme should be made clear to him. Let each Master speak to explain the Secret of Eternity, the Great Cabal of Basul. Let the pattern of the past and the future be made clear."

The Masters spoke then, each helping the other. They fitted together from different parts of the world a story so marvelous that at first I – even I who was involved – could not wholly believe it. The story was so simple that it must be doubted even at this late date, yet the story was so great that it must be believed. It came to me from the lips of Initiate Priests who were under binding oath never to lie for any cause whatsoever. Thus they said:

In the beginning of time man was born from thought, the creative word of God Almighty. All things that were, were of the essence of God, and man was chief of these. Man was God, with the creative fiat, the mighty word given into his keeping. Man was designed by God as the supreme and eternal temple. Man was made as body, mind and spirit. Fleshly body was the physical temple. Mind and emotions were guardians and administrators to the welfare of the body. The spirit was the radiant essence of God Almighty qualified for the use of man and resident in his flesh. Man then could exist either as human animal, as mental man or as vital and creative Spirit. Man then created his own kind by this Spirit-self. For the Radiant-self could be externalized out of the temple of the body. Man could produce at least seven radiant bodies out of his fleshly self to serve man and God. The highest of these, the most difficult to externalize, contained the creative essence by which man could reproduce his own kind by the power of thought. By power of thought and desire he could implant into the womb of his beloved the fertile seed of birth. In those days all men lived in radiance and splendor, and knew neither want, disease, nor sin.

Proof of man's ancient capacity to create his kind by thought-force is found in every religion under the story of virgin birth. Proof of man's ancient well-being is found in every religion under the story of the "garden of paradise".

However, man is (for he became) a thousand time more sensitive to stimuli of the flesh than to stimuli of the spirit. Gradually he turned from the pure but slightly felt joys to the sensations of the flesh self. He fell further and further from the Radiant Self, more and more out of contact with God, until at last he lost touch with the creative God. His Radiant Self, his God Energy, was trapped in the body, entombed in the flesh. This

Radiant, Inner, and Perfect God Self was ever longing for freedom, which explains the search of all men for the meaning of existence and God.

Religions of the world grew up around this inner yearning. In early times all religions were one - the simple methods of raising the Radiant Self to contact the Supreme God. But catastrophes of nature spread man from his ancient Island Paradise. Then all but the mysterious core of religion was forgotten, and even that sacred core was perverted by false leaders to increase their power. Each false leader claimed to have the only true secret, the direct Word. The ancient procedure for the rebirth of the God-self out of the flesh-self became meaningless ritual.

Yet, as most men turned outward to the sensations of the flesh, some few turned inward to the quiet, creative word, and clung more fiercely to the True Religion. These men gathered and guarded the sacred secrets more and more, and became a living secret within the heart of every culture, every religion, every people. But the physical and mundane ever pressed harder and harder upon them, until at last they were driven completely underground and threatened with extinction forever.

Thus it came to pass that each great religion had the external show of ritual, pomp, pageantry - those things which would appeal to the flesh and the emotional bodies of man. Slowly even the inner and secret religions lost the true knowledge and real meaning of these rituals. Even the rituals themselves decayed, and their true meaning was lost to many.

To this point the Jaguar Priest spoke, and I recall his words: "Such a ritual is in evidence in the practices of the Caribe. For thousands of years our priests practiced the sacred ceremony with full knowledge of its symbology. We prepare the sacred food, the sacred wafer which is the symbol of the body of our God. We prepare the sacred drink, the sacred wine of life, which is the symbol of the blood of our God. We also prepare the sacred incense, the perfume which is the symbol of the spirit of our God. We eat, drink, and inhale the body, blood and spirit of our God. By this act we - by the use of

270

mind - turn ourselves into the very essence of our God. Thus we make ourselves God-men on earth.

"But many priests have taken to the practice of making the sacred food and hiding it in a casket upon the *patache*, the low altar of the Caribes. Such false priests then claim the sacred food becomes the body of the God only if the priest blesses the food and passes into it some of the sacred power given to them alone. They also claim that the sacred drink becomes the blood of God only if they bless it and pass into it some of the sacred power given to the priest alone. Thus they stand between man and God. They assume false powers that no man can have, for in things of God all men were created equal. But the common man is in awe of ritual, and stands down from his birthright. Thus the priest becomes the block; he makes man ever less divine than man was created. For it is an initiate and holy truth that each man must be his own priest and make his own contact direct from his God-self to God."

In such vein the great story continued, told by many Masters. The rituals, as has been noted, were originally merely sacred exercises, methods by which man could re-spiritualize himself. But was it not clear that religious rituals were now only for show? Even the secret rituals did not specifically show how man could recharge himself with the divine spirit and externalize his own radiant body at will! Yoga had a little, by mainly merely not-doing, creating of the self a world of nothingness - without feeling, thought, sensation. The Druids were more direct, they brought about a magnificent ecstasy by action, fear, and stress. The Magi taught much by the development of thought-force. But all of these depended upon hunger, thirst, sleeplessness, abstraction from the world, and utter fatigue to weaken the tissue so that the experience of ecstasy could come with sufficient force to be felt by the candidate.

Several segments of religion used natural drugs to produce visions; the Egyptians used a golden mushroom, the Chinese used the bud of a golden flower, the Caribe knew of those who used the buds of cactuses - at least seven kinds of cactus, each effective in producing the

271

religious ecstasy. Was it not evident then that food could create some upset in the chemistry of the body that brought on the ecstasy. Also that weakened tissue suffered some chemical change that brought on this ecstasy. Yet each chemical means lasted only a short time.

Glorious as the moment was, it was the fault of the rituals of religion that they did not produce the eternal kinship with God of which man was capable. True Religion had the power, the purpose, and the techniques for doing this. The True Religion could produce and sustain this ecstasy without weakening the tissue by fatigue, fasting or thirst; or by long diets – such as meatless ones – which deprived the body tissue of certain chemicals; or by the use of powerful natural chemicals from certain plants to upset the balance of the body; or by the use of chemical drinks – no matter how sacred – which intoxicated the mind by upsetting the chemistry of the body. True Religious Exercises strengthened the tissue, made firm and keen the mind, gave endless energy, made man drive into the problems of the world rather than seek escape in the elusive and short-lived ecstasy known to the weakened tissue.

True Religion had these Sacred Exercises – had had them through centuries. They had been tested on many who became advanced priests and performed the miracles of ages. But the techniques were hard to learn, requiring time and dedication and a careful mastery of each exercise so that others could be begun. These Sacred Exercises at last became that specific exercise that caused the changes in body chemistry which brought man into prime and permanent contact with the Supreme God. Only the most dedicated man was sufficiently strong in purpose to master this work through the many years of training, the seven years required for body tissue to become purified. Common man had no drive to success, no emotional attachment to the outcome, no firm belief and faith in the benefits to come from seemingly endless effort, no personal mind-set, no spiritual challenge.

The reason for man's gradual fall from Truth had been realized some 4000 years before when the Council of the World met at Memphis. They had then planned the first step in the long program which might possibly bring mankind back to Truth. Then the Hierophants had decided to create and foster throughout the world the concept of a Single God, warm and loving, pure and fatherly, concerned with the welfare of each individual. Thus they hoped to put away from the mind of man the confusion of many gods which were in truth but special or negative aspects of the Supreme God.

They also tried to circumvent the strangling power of the secular kings, and laid out simple laws for man's relationship to man. These became the Commandments, the Moral Precepts, which are found in every religion. After many years of selection and training the Hierophants at last produced the mystic and initiate Pharaoh, Amenhotep IV, who became Akhnaton and began the World Religion of the One God. Akhnaton, the Initiate, gave mankind the concept of One Loving God. It cost him his life. The entrenched priests cut down his reforms made for the betterment of man. They were angry that the priests were no longer made necessary as the intermediary between mankind and this One God.

Another part of the long-range cabal had been begun about a thousand years before my time. The Council of the World had planned to slowly insert reforms into the religions of all lands that would make every man know that he was himself of singular worth and special value, and the true Son of God. At that time the Twelve Orders of the White Brotherhood were brought together and formed into a secret weapon for the betterment of mankind. Each order was purged of the indolent, purified by increased disciplines, and given the new dispensation of Eternal Truth to teach under great secrecy to all men who could qualify. Each of the Twelve Orders were headed by mighty avatars. They were to train and encourage the training of mankind in humanizing concepts and moral truths. This training stressed obedience to the community of interests, that is commonly called "morality"; stressed honor, truthfulness, tolerance, understanding, love, and a great personal inner worth. It also taught that each and every man was a part of God, that he could, by special worship make direct contact with God.

Man was, in short, taught that purity and selflessness leads to contentment and peace, that contentment and peace lead to blessedness, blessedness to ecstasy, and ecstasy to a state necessary for individual union with God.

From these special schools (always secret and for the man who most strongly yearned for enlightenment not found in orthodox religion) the redemption of man slowly spread throughout all the lands. The methods and concepts were magnificent, yet if the shools were to endure under the secular laws of kings and priests, they had to be secret and hidden. But these hidden schools helped stay the rush of man to his final degradation, to his abject and spineless acceptance of the false idea that he was not his own priest, his own pathway, his own bright spirit.

Out of this movement grew changes in many religions. Some of the stranglehold of the old line priests was loosened. In five hundred years or less there had risen strong groups that turned the teaching outward in some degree. Brahmanism was refined by pious Yogis. Buddhism arose to sweep the world with its sweet message of personal grace through quiescence and worth. The 13th *Zoroaster*, or *Zarathustra*, reformed the Persian faith, making all men obedient to the needs of the community, and instilling love and consideration into a wild, fierce peoples. Even the secret *Mithraism* was purified and turned outward to more people, and thus paved the way for the conversion of many Roman legionnaires within the last fifty years. Druidism was changed and improved. Even the Caribe cultures on a continent far away had felt the impact. *Tao* had risen in China. *Jainism* had been founded and grown. All of this had come about within a span of some 150 years, ending five hundred years before my birth.

Each and every reformation led man toward his final goal, realization of his own divine powers; acceptance of the sacred fact that God was in all things and in every man; that each man could walk with God and work the

274

magic of God if he but disciplined himself to let God have full sway in body, mind, soul, and spirit. Indeed, much had been done. Yet there were some few things that needed improvement. The World Hierophants had not given to man then the True Religion's sacred and secret methods – for these had to be eternally guarded from destruction by jealous priests who held secular might. Good as the training was, it was not the Truth. It trained to quiescence, and such training appealed to the weaker man, the one who sought retreat into religious ecstasy. What was needed was a training in Truth, which was the religion of robust men, the doers and thinkers of the world who conquered but did not retreat. The Twelve Great White Brotherhoods had asked for a new plan to release a stronger training for the good of mankind.

The bulk of mankind still tended to drift away from man's divinity. The orthodox teachings made men believe that he was unworthy of divine grace, and needed the intermediary of a learned priest between himself and God. Man, in general, had no mind-set toward achieving the Divine Moment. The Great White Brotherhoods found that even initiates often would not believe that man could cross the great abyss – for they felt that no man had ever truly done so.

They even doubted that any man ever could!

Once the great Osiris had been adored as a man who had risen to eternal life. Then he had served as the symbol of the Great Initiate, a goal toward which every man was willing to strive, for he had an example. Now the miracle of Osiris (man becoming a radiant god) was lost to the minds of men, lost in the mists of antiquity. Osiris – once a symbol of great sacrifice – had become a myth, without immediate meaning in the life of man. For the good of mankind, for the good of the Great White Brotherhood, a new Osiris was needed, one known and adored by many – who had risen from the dead and crossed the great abyss to become an eternal God.

Yes, there was great need for a man who could cross the great divide from internal man to external God. This had been the decision of the Council of the World in Extraordinary Session at Basul near the Arabian desert.

The Council had met at Basul one hundred and seven years before my birth. There they had taken the third great step in recovering fallen mankind. This was their Great Cabal - to produce for mankind a new Osiris, a new symbol of the Candidate in the Eternal Mysteries. They had planned then to produce and give to mankind the eternal Mediator, the Saviour, the Guide to Eternal Life, a Redeemer who could transcend death and prove that man could reach Life Everlasting. Such a Saviour of Man would become an example for faith, the symbol of love and sacrifice, patience and power, beauty and truth. Such an example would give to mankind a mind-set to strive for Godhood.

Many candidates had striven for this, the worthiest goal in all the history of mankind. Each had failed at the final moment. Why had each failed at the final moment after each had passed every preliminary test? If he could transmute his flesh under the strain of initiation, why could he not do so at the crucial moment of trial? The Leaders of the Great White Brotherhood had concluded that it was because he had not been sufficiently trained, or had been trained *too long* in the weakening methods. Even he who could transmute his flesh at will in peace or quiet, or at the extreme high-moment of initiation, could not bring about such transmutation at the exact moment required in the final test. Perhaps with time, each would have succeeded, but death from secular execution does not wait upon the subconscious force or will. Therefore the Great Initiate Candidate must be one trained swiftly, trained fully, able to meet the high moment and transmute his flesh into spirit under the greatest stress, the most fearsome conditions, and at the command of his conscious will.

How could such a candidate be produced? What training would he need? What would be necessary to prepare his way? What tests should he pass before he was committed to the final test? What should happen afterward? Each of these had been considered by the Council of the World. Each would be placed before me for my judgment and agreement. Should I object to any, or should I wish at any time to cease my training, I could do so by leaving the Sacred Island of *On*.

How should the candidate be produced? The plan of the Council to bring about a suitable candidate began with consideration of the end to be achieved. The last was first. The Council had decided that if the common man was to love the symbol and make it his own, the symbol must be of the common man. The candidate must be of lowly trade, deeply attached to family and home. He must be of a family beloved in the community, yet one that was distinctive and progressive. He must have brothers and sisters who loved him well. He must be schooled in orthodoxy until he knew all its wisdom, and be able to break with it in such a manner that he could lead the minds of common men to the glory of revolt without hatred. The candidate must, therefore, come from a small village, yet be of a blood-line famous for kings and promising kingly quality.

So that his spiritual development might possibly be accelerated, the candidate should be born of a man who had become a Supreme Master, sired by mental conception in the womb of a sacred Virgin, who was pure, trained and willing. Her willingness was all important, for without her complete understanding no such conception was likely. Time was right when there came a Supreme Master from the lineage of Jesse, King of the men of Judah, who was Joseph of Nazar. There was a woman of his choice, Mary, who had betrothed herself to him. She was of the line of the priests of the Jewish Religion, and had been dedicated to God's service. Thus had my birth been planned even before my conception!

What training would the candidate need? Again the last was put first. The candidate must be able to undergo any stress of physical punishment *without resentment*. He must be able to tolerate, nay, even be indifferent, to any treatment without imputing sin to those who took the action. He must be of pure mind, strong body, and trained thoroughly – as the first step at least – in all the teachings of the Great White Brotherhoods and the external religions of the world. Therefore, I, the choice of the Council, had been trained carefully. First, in the Essene Brotherhood I had been trained in orthodox religion, and in love and kindness. Upon the ship of the Masters, the *Britannin*, I had been trained in the viciousness of fear and punishment and physical aggression. In the lands of the Druids I had been trained in ancient wisdoms through symbols, through regimentation, action, fear and stress. In the Lands of the Hindus I had been trained in the aspects of withdrawal, tenderness, and peace. In the Persian religion I had been trained through the use of thought-force, wisdom, and good deeds. In the Egyptian religion I had been trained by suggestion and thought-force.

My mastery of these trainings showed my versatility and brilliance, but even yet my training was not complete. As planned by the Council, it would require yet another five years of hard work to acquire the Sacred Exercises of the True Religion. It would require not less than seven years in all for the training to ripen within the cells of my body and rechemicalize my being to the point that I could step forth as a God upon the earth. If I chose to undergo this sacred training, I must expect constant effort, intense hours of seemingly endless practice, and great personal difficulty in mastering the work. There would be difficulties I could not even imagine and no man could possibly fore-tell.

What would be necessary to prepare the way of the candidate? To be effective, the candidate must be heralded in his land by a forerunner, one who announced his coming and his purpose. This must be done in a manner that would give prestige and authority, status and power. The candidate must be noted at his advent into the work - noted indeed by all the peoples of the land. In addition to a popular forerunner, there must be ready for service to the candidate strong and powerful men who were of common occupations, beloved by their fellows. For the report of these strong, simple men must be believed by men in every walk of life in all lands everywhere. Furthermore, the candidate must be able to win his way into the hearts of men. They must enthrone him there, adore him there, and make him king in their hearts, not in their land. The candidate must be to all men and all women a symbol of themselves one step further along on the pathway to Everlasting Life. They must feel, understand, believe - nay, they must *know* - that all that he did they could do and yet more! He must be so beloved that they would willingly die for him; nay yet more - he must be so beloved that all people would willingly live for him, in his manner, for his purpose!

What tests should he pass before being committed to the final effort? Skakus stepped forward at the command of my father and said: "You must father a virgin birth.

"You have touched upon the matter in many ways. It has been thrust into your life also. Your own virgin birth forms part of the final test. The third manner of virgin birth is the final test. It was symbolized in the apparently useless stones, the phallic uprights, in *Caer Gaur*. It was shown to you in the next lowest grade by the bursting of the statue of Sita in your initiation at *Elephanta*; there thought-force was used to create a ceramic form and to burst the statue all at the same time. You detected it in the nine bodies of the Egyptians, for it has been hidden in plain sight of man since they fell away from the True Religion. You noted that the seventh body in the Egyptian belief was the *Sekem*, the incorporeal personification of the mind.

"You may be trained in the Sacred Exercises of the True Religion. You will find that you learn to raise the bodies in order from three to nine. Before you can raise the *Sahu,* the Spiritual Body, and the **Khu,** the Spiritual Soul, you must be able to raise the **Sekem,** the Power Body. Through use of this body you can create, you can transmute. Much less skill is required to create *things* than life. But you must so learn to command this seventh body that it is obedient to you, and goes forth at your command, carrying in itself the *Sahu*, the Spiritual Body, and the Radiant *Khu*, the Spiritual Soul. You must be able to create life, your own kind, in the virginous body of a willing woman by means of this Mental Spiritual Power. You must prove your lowest Godhood before you are allowed to try an even higher power. Before you can hope to transmute *yourself* you must be able to create. Even more, you must be able to create in your own image,

279

which is the function of God.

"To prove your readiness, you must find a pure virgin who is willing to become your wife. You shall then be betrothed, even as your mother and father were betrothed. You shall then prove your lower Godhood by creating in the body of this Virgin Of The World, this Eternal Woman, your own image in new life. This willing woman has been symbolized in the stories of the goddesses of all races, in the endless patience of Isis in searching for all the parts of the mutilated body of Osiris – and the story of the Birth of Horus by immaculate conception. Her symbol is found in every religion, and in every tongue. She is always called Mary the Great Sea of Creation. She is the eternal Virgin Mother who willingly helps man prove his readiness for re-ascension to the throne of his Godhood."

Even while he continued to speak my imagination was aflame with a sweet vision that churned my blood. But I was also plunged into despair. For in my mind I could not see why my beloved *Mherikhu*, My Golden Girl, should wish to spend her life with one so short, broad, redheaded – one so little schooled in the ways of love and women. Surging blood made my ears hot, but my attention was grabbed again by the Council.

What should happen after the final trial? My father stepped from the altar in the East. "My beloved son, the Council first considered what should happen in case of failure. These are the paths open to us: First, your followers, your disciples will write such works as will make the whole world believe you died for man alone. Thus, even in the case of failure you will greatly benefit mankind. Second, we will call upon the Order of Melchizadek, those Masters of Eternal Life, to invest your body with life and raise you from the dead at least long enough to reappear as living. You shall be risen from the dead. Thus even in failure of your greater goal you may become a symbol to man, a testimony that through love and sacrifice any man may attain to immortal life and become the son of God.

"The third path requires explanation. Should you fail, the Council could not possibly immediately make known to all men the Sacred Exercises of the True Religion. It would be necessary to proceed with caution lest the men of knowledge of Truth should be ruthlessly hunted out and Truth crushed forever from the earth. It would be necessary to allow time for the new faith of Love and Sacrifice which you establish to permeate to all areas of the world. This, we believe, would require two thousand years. Only then would man truly be ready to believe in the singular worth of each individual, and be willing to come to know God as a direct experience. Only when this mind-set has become a part of the life experience of strong men everywhere, will it be safe to bring the True Religion forth again.

"But there is a fourth choice. Should you fail or succeed, you will be made a symbol of the Eternal Candidate in all of the Mysteries and Inner Teachings of all the religions of all lands everywhere. Thus, though you fail, you will help all common men and all Initiates by becoming the symbol of success - for you already have known more Initiate success than any other man your age upon the face of the earth.

"But let us not take our mind-set toward failure, though we plan the alternate choice. Let us know you shall succeed, as indeed you shall! Upon your success a pathway to the hearts of all men shall be made. Every heart will become a believing heart, every man will follow after you. Then man can be shown the True Religion and put upon the path of his redemption. In a very short time, the True Religion may be brought forth for every man, and no secular or orthodox group will have power to destroy or harm it. Thus, quickly, every man may attain to that condition which is known by the Supreme Master. Each may become a Supreme Master by his own will. Then the earth will return to the days of Paradise, and each man shall live in peace, in duty, in love, and in constant contact with the Supreme God.

"This, my beloved son, is the Great Cabal of the Council of the World. What say you to this ancient and secret plan to aid your fellow man?" My father stopped speaking. Echoes of his voice slowly died away in the vast temple.

I rose from the golden throne upon the Purple Rug

to look across to my magnificent father.

"Beloved Master of my Youth, Eternal Masters, Council of the World. But for the greatness of the trust you place in me I should deny all hope of being successful in such a venture. Surely I would be presumptuous to assume that I can be totally successful where so many have failed. Your choice of my inept self as your candidate makes my heart bold and my determination great. So wise is the plan of the Council, so carefully considered is this Great Cabal of Basul, that even in failure I cannot but help my fellow man. Therefore even the most dismal failure must be a great success.

"I see no fault in your plan. Were you not so powerful, and so wise, however, I might question your judgment in the choice of myself as your candidate for so wonderful a work. Further, how would I — so unprepossessing in looks and so inept in the art of women — how indeed would I become the choice of a woman worthy to be the Bride of God, the Virgin Of The World? But I shall search for her, praying my love may be returned, and I shall ask the one I adore. This is to say: Unless you of the Council in your wisdom shall decide to abandon your choice, I pledge my soul that I will never abandon you, the Great Cabal, nor the plan of the Council of the World. I am ready. Let my final training begin that I may know and serve mankind through the True Religion of all time. My life is yours alone."

At first there was a stunned silence. It was broken first by Masters of Men sobbing their joy to God. Then the assembly came alive like some one-lunged monster so filled with joy its peans shook the world. Hymns of love and joy rocked the statues in the temple. Music rose until it became happy pandemonium. Men wept for sheer joy, and my father's embrace proved that there were tears of joy upon his cheeks. His voice rose and brought its message through the temple.

"This is my spirit-born son in whom I am well pleased."

15

SOUL FLIGHT "

The Three Wise Men, my beloved Father, Ramanchana, and The Jaguar Priest were assigned to the staff of my college of teachers in the Temple of Horus. But Skakus was the master teacher, and I was not altogether pleased. Skakus was like a hornet to my consciousness - he stung and prickled me. I wanted the gentle persuasion of my father, the patient instruction of Ramanchana, or the mentally stimulating outpouring of knowledge of the Three Wise Men. But Skakus!

Balthazar said in his humorous way, "Jeschuau, Joseph-bar-Joseph, you are lucky to have Skakus as your teacher. He'll be the first to tell you that he doesn't know what to teach you, but he knows what not to teach you. He failed in his attempt to interest the Greeks in Truth and deep ethical morality about six hundred years ago."

Skakus confirmed this with his huge body standing spraddle legged, his small eyes ablaze with that strange look, and a smile on his almost ugly face. "Listen to me, Boy, the only one who's gone further than your father. I had the glorious experience of failure. Almost made it. Had thousands of Grecian boys following Truth. What could be better? Know how the orthodox priests got me? Charged I was corrupting the youth who followed me by teaching them to honor false gods. Hah! Taught them to honor the Daemon within themselves - the Eternal God. But the Greeks were having no change in their old and

283

foolish beliefs. Made me drink that hemlock. It is bitter, Boy, but not a painful death. Like going to sleep from the feet upward. I failed as Socrates, but I did some good. Gave the world a philosophy which men can follow even while professing the beliefs of the Church that rules them. Gave them a concept of the Eternal God, Inner and Perfect: Plato spread the idea, especially after he was trained here at *On*. Aristotle – he never had the inner vision and turned all the inner teachings from the Heart Soul, the *Ba*, to the Mind Soul, the *Ka*. He made man into a mere-animal-with-mind – that could become a very popular concept. It's easy for man to deny the existence of all things that are beyond the five most primitive senses. Plato kept the Heart in his teaching, he knew the divinity of direct contact with God. Aristotle made obedience to authority a must, and put prisoner's gyves on the minds of men for a thousand years. Hah!"

Though all the others treated me with deference, Skakus called me Boy. His instructions were direct, simple, charged with importance, and usually based on some question that created a vast field of unexplored information. I remember his raucous voice lashing at me such questions as these:

"Boy, what is the purpose of life? Why are we here?"

When I patiently built up an elaborate and structured reason why we were here – to serve God, to perfect ourselves, to serve our fellow men – Skakus would scowl and snap.

"Good. Good. Well reasoned, but coming from your teachings. Boy, you are a Master now. You must teach from within yourself. You must assume the role and the power of a Master – or you will never truly be one. Search for the answers *within yourself*. Now, try this for a start. We are here to serve the purpose of life, that is, to train the Radiant God within us to step forth under our conscious control. We are here to raise the Radiant God from within this tomb of flesh. We are here to become immortal, and have life everlasting."

Another time he snapped at me, "Boy, what is God?" He stood before me flat footed, weight evenly set upon his feet, like a gladiator nearing combat!

"God is the Creator, All Love, the Great Architect!"
I would have said more but he stopped me with a hand
upraised.

"Orthodox. Look, Boy, look inside your Master
Heart. There lies the true answer. It is not any of the
answers you have been given in your trainings. Try this:
God is eternal, unqualified, perfect Divine Energy. God
is not love. God is all things, and is no more love than
hate, no more tenderness than fury. God is Creative
Energy, in but not of earthly and physical things. God is
not anything that is less than the totality. Especially God
is not a high-tempered, punishing, potent old man in a
white robe riding on a big cloud surrounded by angels
playing on golden harps such as your Jewish prophets
have pictured. God is Perfect Energy, Perfect Radiance.
But He is unnamable. That is the meaning of the Jewish
JOD, the Egyptian *Re.*, *the Caribe* Kak Och. He is The
Way of *Tao*.He is not definable. You know God only when
you have the divine experience, when you raise out of
your own flesh the Radiant God that is entombed there.
For you, within yourself, are God indeed."

Skakus had the energy of ten men, and the eager,
inboring drive of an anxious young puppy after a bone.
He was merciless as a pouncing hawk. Training me
seemed to be more important to him than life itself, and he
acted as if his future was at stake, not mine. One day,
even as I was thinking this he snapped.

"Boy, it is my future that is being poured into you.
My future, and the future of man's true freedom upon the
face of the earth. Not yours, alone, Boy. The life of men
yet unborn, the freedom from mental tyranny, man's joy of
knowing God in their own flesh!"

At yet another time he stopped me in the middle of
one of the exercises and yelled at me: "Concentrate!
Hear me? Concentrate! You've got far by trusting your
unthinking mind. But you must now make your soul selves
obedient to your conscious mind. Boy, you've got to be
better than I was, than I am. I failed. You must not.
Work!"

We went into the Temples of Sleep, the healing
centers of the god Osiris. There we spoke the sacred

incantations that raised men from pallets of death. Healing pleased me, and I took great joy in being able to heal and in learning the more advanced art of healing. Skakus was a master healer, equal, or possibly a little superior to my magnificent father. Yet when he saw my pleasure in the art of healing he snapped at me as we walked toward the White Temple in the early dawn from the hospital: "Boy, healing is good. But it is the very lowest of the divine skills. Soon I will show you. Healing is the Divine Trap, the side-path. It is not the purpose of life, or of study. It ruins the progress of many who come upon the path."

Skakus was abrupt, and insistent. He was my daily companion, many times usurping the sweet hours I had with my father and the other Masters. For if I had not progressed under his direction to the point he desired, he continued the lesson. He waked me before hours, kept me up after hours, sometimes came in the middle of the night to work me. He kept at me endlessly, relentlessly, until my flesh was heavy with weariness, and my brain seemed dull.

"You are here to learn to transmute your flesh into godly and radiant energy, and then back to perfect flesh again. My job is to see that you are brought to that point. You can hate me, you can despise me, but unless you leave this island and break your contract with the Brotherhood, you cannot escape me."

He kept me at the exercises endlessly. And he never ceased to work with me. He coaxed me, he flattered me, he cajoled me, he bullied me. He teased me tenderly and ordered me arrogantly. He kept me in a ceaseless emotional turmoil, and yet above it all was his incessant insistence upon my working at the Sacred Exercises. Even when he was lecturing me upon some point of understanding or philosophy he would stop to say: "Boy, are you building your Radiant Temple? Are you filling your cells with peace and power each time you breathe? Each time you breathe you either add to or detract from your Godhood!"

Control of the breath was his subject for almost all of the five years. During the first five months I was drilled endlessly upon the exercises which relaxed the cell-body.

These were based upon control of the breath. Sometimes he would shout, "Not the Yoga Breathing Technique! That is for beginners, that is for those less than True Masters. I know, you have been schooled in thirty-three of the Yogas. You are a master of Yoga. But you must now learn that which is beyond Yoga. You must not use their breathing methods, but these I teach. You will find that when you are ready for them - and you'd better be soon, Boy! - we will teach you more with five of the Sacred Exercises than you learned in all thirty-three Yogas."

I doubted him. In fact, I was repulsed by his presumption. Had I not done wonderful things with the Yoga breaths? Yet even as I thought this , he flared: "Doubt me! Good! I don't care whether you hate me or love me, just do the exercises the way I give them to you and let your own judgment tell you who is right and who is wrong. You don't have to love, admire. You can hate and condemn - it is the rechemicalizing of your flesh I am after, not your emotional attachment to my person."

Later I realized that he had merely stated truth. When I was ready, five exercises took me beyond all the trainings of all the Yogas. I tried to love him for his sincerity. But he would have none of a tender emotion. He was neutral, as neutral and as detatched as God could be. He was so filled with knowledge and ability that it crackled from him like lightning from a cloud. He seemed above caring about human attachments of any kind. He cared only for one thing, teaching me to transmute my flesh at will, and to pass my Final Examination.

Never once did he relax that amazing discipline which I came to know he had insisted upon aboard my training ship, the *Britannin*. He ran the temple like a ship, driving even the great Masters to greater effort, and all was directed toward hand-tending my teaching that I might learn the Sacred Exercises, the Religion of Truth, and how to transmute my flesh and then restore it again. One day, in a moment of despair, I dared say that I was not of much promise. Skakus flashed a look at me from those inscrutable eyes. "Boy! How dare you doubt your Godhood! Of course you have great promise. Only for one of great promise would I have worn that repulsive bear grease on the *Britannin*. Don't you ever doubt your ability. Do you hear, me, Boy? Don't doubt yourself, ever! Doubt of self is the hand-hold of the Deep Night of Despair."

The training Skakus gave me covered every aspect of raising the Radiant Self out of the flesh. Starting with breath and physical relaxation, it went into mental and emotional development and control, and then into the spiritual exercises. The relaxed and obedient body became the cup of eternity, filled with golden light, relaxation, and divine energy. One day Skakus took me out upon the terrace for his lecture, and I saw across the cove the lovely form of my Golden Girl, standing lonely upon the terrace of the Golden Temple of the Virgin Of The World. My heart leaped with its secret joy and Skakus said with amazing softness in his voice. "Boy, you color like a man in love. It is good. A good sign. No man should ever be without his mate, without that physical delight of manhood. Why, the Hermetics say that a man who dies without bringing forth at least one child must be returned to the earth as neither male nor female – they must mean some of those orthodox priests who do not believe that men should know women," Skakus snorted. "Such presumption, that God would make male and female so perfectly mated, and then deny the divinity of each by making the priests abstain from such felicity. They bemean God's goodness, they impugn His glory!"

Suddenly he shot at me. "Boy, what is sin?"

I was so excited at the distant vision that I answered badly. But it would have made no difference. I had never come to know sin as he now explained it.

"Wait, Boy. You do not bring the answer from within your Master's Heart. Sin as you are defining it was the work of the minds of men, making clever snares for the minds, freedoms, and purses of mankind. Sin, Boy, is only this: That which stops man's progress toward union with the Radiant God, toward eternal bliss and life eternal. That only is sin which stops man's eventual union with God. If this is sin, then all man's morality has to do with ideas that control man's actions, and can have nothing to do with sin. For morals are concerned with man's relationship to man – not with man's relationship to God. Don't tell me God is concerned with man's relationship to man. Do that and you lower God to the status of a slave.

"You may sin when you break a moral code, but not because you break it. You sin only if you let your mind involve you in the act, if you let your thoughts cause you to stop in your struggle toward total union with Divine Radiance. When you have reached such a stage that you can do anything without being sidetracked into the attitude of negation, it is impossible to sin. Your Yogins say that when the Yogi is in the state of bliss, even should he murder it would not be sin. This is a step toward truth. So, will you quit blaming yourself for the holy impulses you feel when you look upon that magnificent woman. Will you learn to forgive yourself all your unruly and divine impulses, for then you will find that the whole world is without sin.

"Now, tell me. Boy, how does God come to be in man?"

His sudden question caught me off mental guard, and I stammered, "Why, by Divine Grace."

"True – partly. But if by Divine Grace only, what value all this work we are doing? Eh, Boy? It is true that man is born of both physical and divine essence. The Divine Central Atom of his being is given him at his birth as the seed of his Godhood. But it is up to man to make that seed flourish and ripen. Divinity comes not by Grace alone, but by the development of the God-self within to reach, touch, and be absorbed in the Eternal Energy which is God. Your development of Divinity is not up to God, it is up to you. He gave you the seed. You must grow the fruit.

"How is it grown, this Divine Stuff of man? One of the ways is courage. Boy, this you have. You have the courage of ten. I knew that as I watched you bring Nicodemo down from that wreck-scattered bow of the *Britannin*. You were demonstrating your quick mind, your sturdy body. We watched you figure out the many forces, and master the problems. But most of all you were showing us who watched with such apparent helplessness that you had courage beyond measure. Courage that did not fail your will under stress. Such courage is needed to develop the divinity within any man - yet so few have that courage."

A thrill of pleasure shot through me. Skakus had paid me a compliment, and I could not help but respond. But even as the pleasure mounted, he slashed at me with a question.

"How does man mature his inner divinity?" He watched me closely from behind those veiled eyes. "Thank you for not answering, Boy. If you knew the answer to that you would be my teacher. I propose to teach you now the true meaning behind the Nine Bodies of the Egyptian religion. Would you like that or would you like better to go to the Golden Temple and see that sweet goddess?"

He stood waiting, and I was unable to speak. Did he really mean for me to answer such a question? But when the silence grew, I knew he waited for an answer. I smiled, but he waited, looking hard at me from those strange eyes.

"I would like both. But first I would like to ... to ... talk to her."

"You'll do, Boy. Your father taught you well never to lie, not even about your feelings. Come, let's call upon the young lady to pay our joint respect--ah, and to have words with her priestess intructress, of course!"

I felt the shaft of a thousand arrows of doubt within my heart as we walked toward the Golden Temple. We came at last to the terrace, and *Mherikhu* was there, so golden and beautiful that I could see nothing else but her glory. Skakus left us, and I stood upon the same earth as that of my beloved. It was rapture, and I could find no words to speak. But she smiled and there was music in every cell of me.

"At last you've come." So simple were her words, but they filled me with a flood of warm delight. She held out a hand to take mine, and draw my awkward bulk after her. She went toward a seat within the shade of an arbor in the terrace. There we sat, and her fragrance was like that of wild honey and ginger flowers. Sitting close to her I could see the endless beauty, the depth within lustrous depth of her skin. I dared to reach my fingers to touch her wrist. Her breath came in a catch of astonishment, and my fingers tingled. Though I felt over-bold I held to her wrist, and let my fingers drink the delight of her warmth. Slowly her fingers opened, her palm came up to touch mine, and we sat enwrapped in my delight. We scarcely spoke, for my breath was too much in my throat for speech, and my brain was too much in whirl for sense. Somehow in that joyous hour, I came to know that she was in training as a priestess of Isis, had been trained as the daughter of Ceridwen, that is, to the highest possible learning of the Druids. She also had been trained in Yoga, and was now taking more advanced training.

There were many things I wanted to talk about, but when I *thought* I could not enjoy to the fullest the touch of her hand, the fragrance of her presence. So I stopped asking questions, just to enjoy her. Then I found that I talked, and she listened, so intent upon my lips that I felt her eyes like a kiss. When Skakus and the Priestess of Isis came out upon the terrace, we whispered our enjoyment of the afternoon as if it were a treasured secret. I boldly asked if I might come again, and she blushed with her delight. I blushed with my own feelings even as her eyes sought mine.

"Oh, I so hoped you would want to come again," she breathed.

We stood facing each other in the arbor.

My inner self leaned from my body and kissed her coral lips. She knew it, and she was pleased.

On the way back to the Temple of Horus, Skakus was silent until we almost reached the terrace to the quarters assigned to me. Then he said, "Boy, you are in love." When I stopped in agitation he said sharply, "Don't deny your man-self. Could you deny your man-self without also denying the Wisdom of the Divine? But know that even love must be forgone in your final test. Cling too tightly to love--love in any form--and it may be the death of you."

We walked onto the terrace and he snapped. "Now, we will work all night to make up this time. Our purpose now is to teach you the Truth behind the nine bodies, and to make each body obedient to your conscious will. Are you ready?"

We did work all night. And we worked incessantly for many days, while he lectured to me, proved to me by examples from history, and at last even demonstrated the things he said. His lectures were spaced over weeks, but at last made one magnificent totality of knowledge. Even in my sleep I could hear his harsh voice, spurting out infinite truths in short and direct sentences. His lectures came down to these concepts, but repeated in myriad ways until the knowledge was buried into my being: "Nine bodies. You must consciously be able to control each one. Nine bodies, and each is a little more important than the other--yet each is dependent upon the other. Nine bodies, each a cup, each a golden chalice for some divine energy that is specially qualified for man's use. Nine bodies, each a carrier, each as serviceable as a chariot--yet each as hard to drive as if that chariot were harnessed to wild elephants with tigers leaping upon their backs. Our job now is this, to raise each body. To raise each of the bodies one after another, to discipline them, to stand them up like centurions and make them march to our mental drum.

"Now, back to your feelings of the importance of these bodies. You were right--far more right than even you at this moment dream. Why have you been so carefully disciplined? Eh, Boy? Why the many years of intense training, and then this last nine months of constant study, starting all over again with the breath and the physical body? Because of the *Ren*. The Egyptians indeed mean more than 'Name' by that word! The *Ren* is the record of all your life--more Boy, it is the record of all your *lives*! Every thought, every act, and even every lack of action, all become part of this *Ren*, this Name. Every thought is part of your permanent record. Those who claim to read the Great Record are actually reading the *Ren's* magic store. The *Ren* waxes and grows as you come by experiences. It expands as you

292

are active. Your 'Name' develops and contains the totality of your lower than human self. Into it are wound your animal soul and the race-soul, each fed upon your own experiences. This animal soul grows obedient only if you compel it to do so. This is possible only by living and thinking in ways that make you acceptable to the racial pattern, to the mores and morals of your age. If you are unruly, obstreperous, mean, your animal soul follows each mental suggestion that is implanted long enough and clearly enough. Therefore, if you would have a good and obedient animal soul you must train it by thinking and behavior that shows it how to be good and obedient. This is the training that you get in preparing for most religions and is the cause for many religions teaching only the basic morals and a little dogma of belief.

"Fortunately, Boy, you have a strong lead in this direction. You have a good animal soul. Your race memory is excellent. And you have had a little training, eh, Boy? A little, most of it either confused or in error--but for the animal soul even this training is good. Very good.

"You must always remember that this soul is balky, unmanageable, and will resist training with a fierceness that seems to make it independent of the body in which it grows, from which it takes its being. Listen, I give you a great secret: You can control it by intense desire. You can control it by very great force of will. Until you can control this unruly *Ren*, this animal soul, you cannot safely and permanently raise the Radiant Self.

"The special breathing techniques you have had are a specific harness for this animal soul. You are now ready for further instruction. It has to do with the Physical Body, the Temple of Flesh, the storehouse for all of these different bodies and Souls we are about to master and control.

"The Physical Body is of special importance, for it is the fulcrum upon which all the other bodies are moved. It is--as you said--the Temple Center, the rudder to the Ship of Eternity. The Egyptians make every effort to preserve the body, believing it is the place where the Soul resides even after death. This is only partial knowledge. The body is the most important element of all the nine elements until the Spiritual Body, the *Sahu*, has been rooted in the heavens, as you will see in about two years. Until that consummating moment in the struggle toward Godhood, the Physical Body is the home of the other bodies and souls. If it is destroyed so is the individuality destroyed. Once the Spiritual Body has been built, that glowing temple not built with hands, secure and eternal in the heavens--then *it* becomes the most important. For out of it grows the Body of Primal Energy, the *Sekem*, and the Soul of Radiant Energy, the illustrious *Khu*.

"You have spent these months mastering the breathing technique which relaxes the cell-body, and at the same time instills into it the greatest power known to man. You have filled it bursting-full with the power. You have done all you could to make your cell-self obedient to the requirements of spiritual growth, and obedient to any mental or spiritual command. Such obedience must be instantaneous, unquestioned. Once started it must go to its completion automatically--that is, without further thought. It may seem impossible to you now, but it is not. It can be done, and you of all people have a good start.

"You, luckily, have a good, strong body. You are healthy and will never allow weakened cells to bring forth involuntary bodies like some do who speak with familiar spirits. Will you, Boy? No? Good. You are disciplined, but you will be more disciplined in a while. Wait and see. Oh, after this lecture I wish you'd work with the Jaguar Priest. The Caribes have a way of mastering the cell-body so that they can sit three hours in the noon-time sun and not sweat. You need such control of your inner body.

"Now we will begin a new series of Sacred Exercises. You will find that they give peace and strength to each and every cell. They also change the chemistry of the body toward that moment of divine fulfillment. Work hard on these exercises. So great must be your controll that not one cell of your body places stress upon any muscle or nerve when you will it thus. At the moment the Spiritual Body rises from the cells, there must be no tensions of any kind whatsoever, not even in the brain or the viscera. You must be able to reach such a depth of quietude as this even in the midst of stress and strain. It is not enough that you reach the quiet of Buddha. Remember it is said that he reached such a peace that five hundred ox carts driven by him did not disturb him? Well, you must reach such a point of inner peace and quiet that even ox carts driven over you cannot disturb you! Then from this point you must be able to train each cell of you body to turn obediently to the sun of your mind, as flowers follow the physical sun. You must be able to go from the highest physical emotion into this Ocean of Peace. You must be able to immobilize all tissue, every cell, every thought--and all this you must not only do, but do in the space of seven breaths.

"When you have reached this stage of training, you then give a twist to your will but without disturbing thought or emotion. This pure will ejects the Human Soul from the placid and willing body. When you are able to externalize the Soul at will, you begin higher training. Mark you, Boy, I'll stand no falling away into the pasty white, indefinite forms which weak cells, sick bodies, and weak wills develop. I want none of that lower level tissue of milky white, that spiritualistic whitewash of energy. Hear me? I want only that firm, bright violet soul-stuff that is the mark of strong tissue, strong mind, strong will! Do you hear me, Boy? Good.

"Sounds impossible? Sounds long? Well, it is long, but not impossible. The control of the Animal Soul and the Physical Body is probably the hardest. It could take many lifetimes without guidance and help. Fortunately two things are in your favor. You have already worked many years in disciplines. Also, once you can externalize the Violet Soul and clothe it as you wish, you are well on the pathway. Well along, Boy! You know it is possible, for you have already externalized the Violet Soul three times--or is it five- I forget how many initiations you have undergone. You know it can be done. We want to see you do it under control, fully conscious of the steps by which you achieve this apparent miracle, and fully able to keep the Human Soul externalized and obedient to your conscious will for any length of time under any circumstances.

"Great care, Boy. Great care! The Violet Soul tries to escape from the body on its own terms, without burden. It then leaves the lower bodies and the higher souls in a state of immobility, a sort of paralysis. This you have experienced, eh? Know why? Well, the capacities of the total mind were developed during the maturing of each of the nine bodies. Some capacities are carried in one body, some in another. Sight, for instance, is carried in the Violet Soul. The first thing that happens when you begin to externalize the lax and lazy Human Soul is that you seem to see from two places at once. Dual centers of seeing! But, the other capacities--the other four senses and much more--are found in other bodies and other souls. The lazy Violet Soul carries nothing it is not forced to carry. It is therefore like an automaton, a walking energy without full mind, memory, and speech. Spooky, Boy, spooky! Ah, but...

"Ah, yes, once it is disciplined, it becomes a workhorse and carries all bodies until the Spiritual Body has been developed fully. Then it is the source of higher bodies--but only when it has been carefully trained and made obedient to your will. Then when the higher souls are available to help, the Violet Soul can clothe itself and even assume the solid look of human flesh. Here, let me show you, Boy."

Skakus lay down upon the smooth stone wall around the terrace, his white robe bright in the mid-afternoon sun. In three breaths I saw his body start, as if the force of his energy of thought switched from the front to the back of his head. With seven breaths he seemed to be asleep. Then there appeared above him a violet or blue-white mist or light. In a single breath it took complete form and moved away, to hover out over the cove. Then it came back and stood on the far side of the terrace from the still, white-robed form of my Master. Slowly this new form clothed itself with color, flesh tones, hair, and at last even a robe--a pale blue robe that looked exactly like the white one in style and form but not in color. He beckoned me across the terrace and while we sat on the far wall continued to lecture and seemed to forget the reclining white-robed body.

"Come to me here, Boy. You will find later that it is hard to stay very close to the body when externalized. There is a hungry pull of the cell-body that entraps the Violet Soul whenever it can. You see, at a distance from the Physical Body the Human Soul becomes a thing of use and service. You could, for instance, when you had mastered this technique, be listening to me here and also sleeping in your chambers--or even out swimming in the cove--or doing any other thing you might wish. Of course I know you could never wish to do anything more than you would wish to hear my lecture. Now could you, Boy? Hah. He blushes like a man in love! Good. Good. Now, let us go for a swim, shall we?"

We hurried down to the water by way of the steps. After the first few steps, Skakus appeared to be fully in the flesh. Had I not been able at all times to see his body on the wall above, I would have believed he was in the full flesh beside me in the warm water. We swam out to the center of the cove and Skakus said:

"Boy, want to race an old man for shore?"

He began the race, and I swam ahead of him slightly. But suddenly he came striding by me, walking on the water. Thus he moved to the shore and was waiting for me at the steps, a huge, loud laugh in his throat. He was like a young boy who had just played a sly joke.

"See, Boy. Serviceable! Useful! Helpful!"

Back at the terrace he walked toward the white-robed body, seemed to dissolve the blue clothes and the coloring, then flipped up and over, and fell into the body backward. Skakus sighed, stirred, rose and continued to laugh with his pleasure at the magnificent lesson he had taught me. "You're thinking it would be good to stay in that form all the time, eh? Until you reach complete divinity you will find it almost impossible. It takes an enormous amount of energy, and a great driving desire. No, Boy, this Violet Soul is better for short stays, and for certain types of healing where the power of Animal Soul is needed. You will see.

297

"Now, you have spent months learning about the Physical Self, the Cell-Self as I call it. This Cell-Self is made up of the Animal Soul, the Physical Body, and the Human or Violet Soul. This is the Physical Unit. It is the first and longest of three steps toward divinity, and it is this that most religions dimly hint of, and that most secret rituals boldly train for. But this is only the beginning. The very beginning, Boy. You will see! Though this level is pleasing, it is not really much. You used it at *Elephanta* and at *Bokura*, but under extreme fatigue, hunger, and high emotion. Now, here are exercises that will help you learn to use it under any conditions whatsoever."

Skakus had always encouraged me to more and more work. Now I had a secret and private reason for work. I began to rush the time with impatience, for it had been over a year since I had been permitted to visit my beloved *Mherikhu*. During that year I had looked at her longingly from my terrace across the quiet cove. Each time I saw her my heart grew more and more lonely. I began to dream of the paradise of sitting near her, absorbing the radiant warmth of her beauty, and touching her hand with thirsty fingers questing the draft of life! Though I hinted, suggested, and once even tried a direct request, my Master Skakus put me off for the reason of work to be done. Yet each time I saw her my soul expanded as if I could touch her gentle hand, and my body knew the fierce fire of creation. Now I was determined. I would see her, stand beside her, touch her! I would. I was determined to learn to externalize the Violet Soul under complete control, clothe it in my form, and escape to her. I knew I could not do so often, but even once in a while would surely be enough to keep my soul from crying in loneliness. Therefore I rushed the hours, forced the minutes, and begrudged each passing second.

Skakus was pleased with my redoubled efforts. I kept up the pace with such furious intensity that I seemed to block my own learning. I found that effort is not work, that relaxed effort is more important than scattered force. But I could not stop the frantic pace. I made no apparent progress. I began to be dispirited. One day Skakus said to me quite suddenly, "Boy, tomorrow I must spend all day in the Golden Temple with that High Priestess. Want to stay here and work, or come with me for a dull day?"

I could not hide the joy of my hope and anticipation and he laughed aloud. "We need a vacation from restraint. Suppose I send tonight to ask if four of us might picnic tomorrow at the Strand, where the river joins the cove? If the young one cannot come, we can hold our conversation there while you retire to one of the shelters and do your exercises. Either way the day will not be a total waste for us."

Oh, how long is the night of hope? Is it not as long as the night of despair? By midmorning we were upon the terrace of the Temple of Isis. There must have been others about, but I saw only my beloved who stood in a golden sheath beside a large hamper. She looked up and on seeing Skakus her face was flooded with sweet pleasure. She ran toward us, her toes only kissing the marble of the terrace.

"Lord Skakus, the Lady Goddess sends me to beseech your patience. There is something... I truly do not know what... which will detain her for some time. She bids you go with us to the Strand, there to wait for her."

Skakus scowled and seated himself upon a bench. I thought there was a gleam of pleasure in his eyes as he said, "Drat women. Always something! Well, we can be comfortable here, eh? Or, would you two like to go ahead to the Cove and wait for us there?"

How my heart leaped, I almost ran to pick up the heavy hamper, turning to stammer back our excuse and decision. Yet I was almost certain there was a gleam in those strange, inscrutable eyes!

I was alone with my beloved, my *Mherikhu*. The Golden Stairs were of the softest down so light was my heart. My heart was in my throat, and I dared not try to speak to my beloved. At the bottom of the steps I turned to face her. "I have missed you, Beloved of God."

Mherikhu smiled so radiantly that my ears

thundered. "Oh, I have missed you too, Beloved of God." The warm wind touched the golden strands of her hair, and kept them floating as if loath to leave off touching her. Her eyes were bright as twin suns, and my world was caught up into the universe of her beauty. How long we stood thus I do not know, but at last I managed to whisper.

"I want to be with you often, Beloved of God."

"Oh, how I want you to want to be with me," she said. So intense was my desire that I was leaning forward to touch her coral lips with mine when Skakus called from above.

"Go on to the Strand. We may be hours!"

How joyous was that message. We hurried toward the distant shelters and the wide sweep of sandy beach. We whispered our gleeful words, as if we were conspiritors. Though we could be seen from above, we could not be heard, yet we whispered, seeming to increase our joys by the very intimacy of our voices. We rushed down the way, and well we should, for the day was all too short. We talked and walked in the sand, feeling its hot-cold mold upon our feet and between our toes. Sometimes, with cautious glances above, we even dared to touch hands, and then my body was filled with sheer delight. Thus the joy of the day of coming to know each other sped, making hours into minutes, and filling a single sigh with more feeling than a sacred ritual can contain. How sweet she was, how graceful, and how learned! Her wisdom was greater than mine a hundred-fold.

The day raced by. It was long after mid-day when we decided to eat our part of the lunch, for the other two did not appear. Strangely we found that either our appetites were enormous or there had been little more food than two lusty appetites could master. We sat then in the shade of one of the leafy shelters, and my eyes feasted upon her loveliness, while my soul expanded to the soft-voiced wisdom of her being. It was mid-afternoon when Skakus called from the terrace, and motioned for us to come up. My heart was heavy with the need, yet my veins were more than ever on fire with the desire to master the Violet Soul and be with her more often. As we walked back to the Golden Stairs I whispered, "Will I be welcome if I come again...no matter how?"

"The Temple of Isis is open to all."

"No. I mean if I come to see you. You only!"

"Oh? Does a woman know unless she is told?"

"Would I be welcome?"

"I...I...Yes! In any form and any time you would be welcome but....." She stopped at the foot of the stairs. "...at any time, Beloved of God. But at night and on sacred days I must stay upon my Rug of Promise, and am surrounded by guards over my person. You know that I am promised as a Bride of God, must always be guarded at night and may not step upon ground that is not sacred or has not been consecrated. Except that this island is sacred, I could not even walk about."

I felt the despair that was like lead in my stomach. "Bride of God? Does this mean you cannot marry?"

"Oh? Yes. I *could* marry. I could marry and still keep my vows and the vows of my parents if conditions were right...I could of course quit my vows at any time and marry."

"If conditions were right?"

"Oh, if someone wants me enough!"

I would have asked more, but Skakus called from the top of the Golden Stairs. This interrupted my near-confession that I wanted her enough for anything. We moved upward, our hearts and pleasures still at the Strand. The memory of this most glorious day of my life sank into my physical being. But I pondered deep in my heart over her phrase, "...if someone wants me enough!" Surely, more than anything I wanted to be with her, to boldly touch and caress her, and kiss her with my physical lips, and declare my love that grew within me, and grew and grew.

Frantic and driving hours turned to weeks, then to weary months, and I was ever at work on the exercises. Each day I looked across at my golden beloved and became more determined to rise out of my flesh and be with her. One day I saw her on her terrace, and my desire was like a flame within me. I went to the exact spot where Skakus had lain upon the wall, lay down, and plunged myself deep into my Temple of Peace. Then I willed that my Violet Soul leap forth and go and be with *Mherikhu*.

I felt that familiar blow upon the base of my neck, and with every cell of my body could see the violet mist that formed above me. I was so pleased that my heart raced. The violet body slammed back into my physical body, almost knocking me from the wall, and setting every nerve to burning.

I lay down again, and this time brought forth the Violet Soul and held it from me at twenty paces. Then I tried to walk, but found that I wobbled and was pulled back toward my cell-self with an almost irresistable force by a silvery cord that ran to the base of my brain. I held the Violet Soul away by the sheer force of will, and made it walk down the stairs to the cove. The further it got from me the easier it was to keep erect, and at last I sent it around the line of the cove and made it climb the Golden Stairs. There at the top I stopped and looked at my beautiful beloved. I saw in her eyes that she saw me and was not frightened but well pleased. Though her lips formed words and I read them saying how pleased she was that I had mastered this technique, I could not hear her. When I tried to speak, I could not make sound. I feasted my lonely sight upon her beauty until I began to tremble from the exertion. Then I let go and hurtled back across the cove and slammed into my physical body with a force that jarred me from the wall.

I was triumphant. I had seen my beloved. I could now go and look upon her and drink deep the joys of her beauty. Strangely, each day I found that my Masters had to be about some other temple business at the time when *Mherikhu* came forth upon her terrace. So daily I lay upon the wall and sent my Violet Soul to be near her and to look upon her and to feast upon the glory that was the sight of her beautiful form. This continued daily for three months or more. I began to long to feel the warmth of her, enjoy the honey-gingerblossom fragrance of her, hear the beauty of her voice, and touch her. Though I hinted that another visit would be well, and even asked Skakus if he had business at the Golden Temple, I was

302

never released from restraint long enough to go physically. Therefore I decided to let Skakus know that I could externalize my Violet Soul so that my training would progress to the point that I could clothe this externalized self with all the senses and the appearance of a real man.

Skakus stopped in the middle of instructing me in an exercise, looked at me through those strange eyes and snarled: "You have something to tell me?"

I knew what he meant and confessed that I had become able to send forth my Violet Self and keep it forth, but was not able to clothe it or to put the senses therein. He seemed greatly pleased and said. "Boy, you are doing well. Now it is time we leave the exercises for developing the physical selves. We now turn to the raising of the Mental-Emotional Bodies, the development of the *Ab* or Psychic Heart, the *Ba* or Heart Soul, *Khaibit* or Blue Self, sometimes called the Shadow Self. Mind you, Boy! You do not cease your exercises, you only add more. You will have less and less time. The exercises you have been doing must be continued to make your Cell-Self grow and to train your Violet Body to come forth easily from the flesh. Continue. Work. Work!

"Now I shall forget that, and we will turn to the Mental-Emotional Bodies. In the teachings of an ancient sect known as Hermetics is a saying: 'Concerning thing of divine nature that which is above is as that which is below, that which is below is as that above!' The structuring of the Mental-Emotional Bodies is the same as the Cell-Bodies.

"The Heart, or rather the Psychic Heart, is the center of the Mental-Emotional complex of bodies. In the beginning it is most important. As the physical heart comes to know the basic emotions, the energies are transmuted into the Psychic Heart. It contains all the emotions refined and purified. It contains the vital spark of life, the seed-atom of divinity which is the root of Godhood planted into the cells of every man. As it grows it becomes like to the living heart, then like unto the entire individual. When externalized it seems to be made of rays of Ruby Light, and is sometimes referred to by those in our Secret Brotherhood as the Ruby Soul or

303

Ruby Body. At this level all bodies are souls, and conversely all souls are bodies when qualified. The Ruby Body becomes the center of all spiritual and mental growth. It grows as your mind grows, not in brilliance, in deep 'heart-felt' understanding. It is the seat of wisdom and the power of reasoning in abstract areas. The Ruby Body grows with every thought, good or bad, and at last is truly the full measure of a man's true goodness.

"Here a man's integrity is most important. His own opinion of himself is vital. For if he doubt himself in any moral thing his Ruby Body cannot grow to full stature as swiftly as it should. Fortunately, Boy, you have a good development. You have the experience of tenderness, love, honor, and a strict truthfulness. These have been trained into you through years. You will have no trouble with the Ruby Soul. You will see."

He smiled at me a strange smile and added. "You will know when you have mastered control of this body. It contains the sense of touch, the sense of feel, the sensations which are needed for true emotion in the externalized body. Now, here are the exercises you are to do first."

The exercises seemed to do nothing for me. Yet each day I could go and see my beautiful *Mherikhu*, and, strangely, found time to do so when all the rest of the day was rushed. Day after day I feasted upon her beauty, and as I looked my love grew. Then one day as I was looking at her in my projected body, I felt the ache in my heart like a twisting knife. Slowly it spread outward and my entire body became sensitive. I could feel the stones beneath my feet, I could feel the warmth of my beloved. Gently I reached to touch her beautiful hand, and she looked up and smiled. Oh, how great was my joy. Each day I hurried to my "Period of Aloneness" that I might be near her.

One day Skakus began his morning's instruction. "Boy, now that you can feel and know you are controlling the Ruby Soul, shall we go on to higher things? The Heart Soul, or *Ba* is the next we will master. This grows out of the Ruby Body and out of the Human Soul. It is built by the power of every thought which you have ever said, heard, or has ever been spoken about you. It is grown directly by emotional words, and develops most swiftly under the power of prayer. It is, therefore, for the development of this Heart Soul that the Yogins chant their Mantra and the Buddhists spin their prayerwheels. The Heart Soul is pure yellow. When externalized alone it is a resplendent color of the mid-day sun upon a white cloud--only more transparent than even the reflected light. As I said, the Yellow Soul is housed in the Ruby Body until it has grown to magnificence and power. It takes its power from the Human Soul, the Violet Body, and qualifies and expands the powers of that body. It adds to healing. It is the source of healing of almost all diseases. It is greatly active and is the base for the sensory facility of smell. You will know when you have mastered the externalization of this Yellow Soul, for you will have the sensation of smell. But I warn you, the fragrances will be powerful beyond belief.

"The Yellow Soul can be either material or immaterial. At first this is at the will of the Cell-Self. But later it takes on a will, almost a mind of its own. When all of the Bodies have been mastered and brought under control to this point, the symbol is that of a risen soul, of a hawk that is human headed, that is, a developed soul risen from the body but obedient to the mind and will. Here is the series of exercises that will help you externalize, master and control this Yellow Body. They start with learning the value of sound. Every word you say, the very vibrational energy of every thought you think will aid you in this. Begin with chanting this sacred mantrum."

I worked hard indeed. In my daily visits to my beloved I waited with great impatience for more than three months. Then one day the fragrance of my beloved touched my senses. I was overwhelmed with the tantalizing and invigorating aroma. Daily I went to see, touch, and enjoy the fragrance of my lifelong beloved; but soon I longed to hear her and speak to her. I longed to tell her of my endless love.

A few days later Skakus merely began a day of instruction thusly: "In the Yellow Soul, there is a finer

305

and more perfected essence. It is the powerhouse of the Mental-Emotional group of bodies. It grows directly out of the Heart Soul, but the force for this growth comes from the Animal Soul. Yet this force is qualified by passing through the Cell-Body, the Violet Body, the Heart and the Heart Soul. This is the Blue Soul, the Shadow Body, which the Egyptians call *Khaibit*. In the beginning it is dependent upon the *Ba*, the Heart Soul. When nurtured and grown by prayer, pure emotions, and great physical care, it becomes independent. In it are carried the sensory elements of hearing. You know when it is developed and obedient, for it contains the ability to hear. The exercises you have been doing for the Cell-Self are to be increased. The exercises for the Heart and the Heart Soul are also to be increased. Now we will add yet other exercises, including rhythmic sacred songs, and the force of the Radiant Temple applied to each cell of the body."

How I worked then. The thought of hearing my beloved's voice was rapture enough to make twenty hours a day seem like minutes. Truly, it proved this way, that to him who desires greatly things will be given swiftly. For in less than two months I had the pleasure of standing in the arbor beside my love and hearing her as she spoke to me. As the days went on she knew I could hear her, and she sang me pretty songs in a pure, low voice. But soon I longed to be able to speak, to tell her of my joy in her. The very day I resolved to speak to Skakus, he came to me and said bruskly, "Boy, it is time you chose a wife. Your case has been placed before the Council. They have directed the Lady Goddess of Isis to determine which of her priestesses may be willing to work with one so advanced as you are, to become your betrothed and finally your wife when you have proved your brotherhood to the creative God."

Three days later a delegation from the Temple of Horus went to the Temple of Isis. All was pomp and ceremony, with royal courtesy extended in all ways. The formality was overwhelming, and I stood with a committee while one after another the young priestesses were allowed to come into the courtyard. They were beautiful,

306

they were gay, they were enough to turn the head of any man. But as the long day dragged on I looked in vain for my beloved *Mherikhu*. She did not come, and at last Skakus snapped at me, "Boy, will you offend the Temple of Isis? Choose one of these beautiful girls *soon*. The High Priestess grows inpatient."

Suddenly I pulled away from the committee, but Skakus seized my arm.

"Come back, where do you think you are going?"

I pulled rudely away from my strange Master and hurried to the committee of priestesses across the courtyard. With hardly the patience for civility I asked, "Lady Goddess, where is *Mherikhu?*.

She threw a strange look toward Skakus who came quickly upon my heels. "Why, Beloved of God, she is a Bride of God. She is under vow never to marry, well at least only under the most unusual conditions."

"What conditions?" I was rudely impatient.

"That she be chosen above all else in the world. That the man who chooses her be willing to prove his Godhood. And other conditions."

"Where is she?"

"I do not truthfully know!"

She did not lie, but the eyes of all the priestess-committee turned downward to the shelters at the Strand.

"It is no matter, Boy. Your Betrothal Committee has chosen a lovely priestess for you. Lady Goddess, we of the Temple of Horus thank you..."

"Betroth her to yourself, then, you of the committee. I will marry but one woman!"

I think they barred my way. I was conscious of the contact of my body with others, and that my tunic was torn. There must have been a blow to my face, for my nose was bleeding ruddy drops upon the Golden Staircase. But I tore through them, and ran like a crazed and wounded thing toward my beloved. I saw her when I was half way to the Strand. She was huddled in the furthest shelter, small and crumbled, and lonely beyond words. Even as I ran I scooped handfulls of water from the cove, and washed my face and dried it, and stopped the bleeding. But my robe was splashed and wet, and my churning feet threw wet sand all over my robe and my head. What an apparition I was as I burst into the shelter and skidded to a stop before my beloved. She looked up in sudden fear, and her eyes were sightless from being too full of tears. Perhaps that was my blessing, for she could not see my wild and disheveled look. She stood, poised as if to flee from me in terror.

"Will you marry me?" I demanded.

The tears from her eyes welled out and I thought she must be able to see me for she startled and caught her breath. "Why... why should I?"

"Because I love you more than myself! You know that!"

"How should I know, you never told me?"

"You knew when first I saw you. You are my life. With you I am a God, without you I am less than no thing at all!"

"I have taken a vow....."

"So have I, Beloved. I have taken a vow to aid all mankind if it lie within my power and it be the will of God. But without you life will have no meaning. Without you I shall surely fail, for I shall not care. Without you I have no hope, no place, no anchor of love. If you will take me with my vow, I will return to you. If you wish, I will disclaim my vow and leave the Order, that I may be with you for all the days of my life."

"I have waited all my life for you." Her words were so simple that at first I did not understand their meaning. Then she was in my arms, and I held my Beloved to my breast. Her lips were sweeter than the wild honey, more exciting than the ginger flower.

When at last we were calm enough to face the angry Priests and Priestesses of *On*, we walked back up the stairs and came out into the terrace hand in hand. Stormy faces were there, clustered groups, whispering and chattering. Many an eyebrow was raised at the way I looked in my wet clothes, with sand on my person, made dark by the tears of my Beloved upon my cheek. But holding her hand I faced my Master defiantly and said, "Lord Skakus, Lady Goddess, I thank you both for your efforts. But there is but one woman I can love. This one is now my betrothed."

Skakus advanced upon me with an angry countenance, and the High Priestess advanced upon *Mherikhu*. "What if this means your dismissal from the Order?"

My arm stole around the trembling frame of my Beloved. "Let it be as God wills it. This is my decision," she said firmly.

"Mine, too!" I said.

Skakus turned on his heel and strode toward the terrace wall.

16
" LOVE MAY KILL YOU "

Skakus turned from me and strode to the terrace wall, and stepped upon it. His hands went over his head and were crossed three times. From the steps of the Temple of Osiris the enormous gong was sounded three times. Suddenly the voices of all the priests and priestesses were raised in rejoicing. So suddenly and forcefully did they cry out that my Beloved shrank to me, and I knew the manly joy of protecting the one I loved. Suddenly the priestesses were around us, all gay and happy. From their chatter we soon learned that we both had been on trial. Had we not been willing to forgo all for each other, the Order would have stopped the program upon which we were embarked.

"Love, Boy! It is wonderful. It may kill you, but it is wonderful. The test was that you love her more than your own self. You've proved that. Now we can tell you, she, like yourself, is a member of the Order. She, like you, is born of a pure virgin by Creative Thought. She, like you has gone through all the initiations and has lived as a pure and perfect virgin awaiting your development to this point. Know, too, that she was part of your training. She shortened your efforts by years, for you desired her presence strongly enough to rise out of the enfolding arms of your cell-self. She is the daughter of the Lady Goddess, and the Arch Druid, Camus. She was as carefully prepared for this day as were you."

There was a joyous week in which our betrothal was re-enacted in state and pomp. We were carried upon our Symbol Rugs to the Temple of Osiris, and there we were placed side by side. With great ritual one of the guarding strands was taken from the side of her Rug and woven into the strand of my Rug. The same was done on the other side, thus weaving the symbols of our oaths and our lives into one. Oh, how sweet and wonderful was that moment when she was declared my betrothed by act of the Order.

Yet in all that stateliness and pomp I found my beautiful wife-to-be was filled with a deep humor, a pixy-like mind that made hearts laugh. When it came time for me to officially ask her to marry me - after I had officially asked permission of my Masters, her mother, and also her Order of Priestesses - she looked at me with great joy mingled with sheer laughter in her eyes. And when the chance came she whispered to me: "You were more forceful with blood on your face, water on your robe, and sand and sun in your hair!"

Oh, how we laughed! How the Island celebrated. How nature stood still to hear our joy! It was my wonderful father who gave the Sacred Lecture to us in which was summed up the Order's philosophy on love and marriage!

"Hear all men! Hear all nature! Let creative nature rejoice. True love is seldom found, and when two beings truly love their marriage is made in heaven. Such a marriage let no man put asunder for it must endure for ever and yet a time. Eternity waits upon such union, and it may not be broken, nor put aside. For then each creative act is the sin of fornication, and the joy of love is a scorpion's sting.

"True love comes not in spirit, not in mind, not in body alone! For he who loves in spirit only will be weak of body, changeful of mind. He who loves in mind only will be careless of spirit, animal in body. He who loves in body alone will rut and fornicate and be lower than the worms. Yet he who loves not in the body will never know the upsurging, creative love that makes his manhood akin to Godhood. He who loves not in mind will never know the upsurging of wisdom that raises him out of dross into pure and golden thought. He who loves not in the spirit will never know the upsweeping spirit that joins him with the laughing gods and welds marriage across the break in time.

"He who truly loves, loves equally in spirit, mind and body. He who truly loves, loves proudly in all three levels, fiercely in all three levels. Yea, he who truly loves, loves all ways, always!"

In our celebration week I came to know my Beloved yet better, and to know the depth of her wisdom indeed. At the end of the week we were again put back to the routine of training, and I could only see her in the externalized selves. Then I could not speak to her. I could not tell her of my joys and my love, and whisper rough and pleasing words about her beauty. This I longed to do with every fiber of my straining heart.

Skakus was before me early on the morning after our betrothal feast in the Temple of Hermes-Thoth. My eyes were still heavy, but he was alert and there was again in him that fierce and driving energy – that power of ten men and a handful of hornets! His raucous voice stung me to resentful wakefulness, and my day began even as if the most wonderful girl in the world were not now my promised bride! But the lecture began as if we had never interrupted our efforts.

"Boy, you have mastered the body complex, and the mental-emotional complex. You can externalize your bodies – as far as you have gone – with precision and ease. But – have you noticed that you cannot remember with clarity that which you have done while projected? And have you noticed that you cannot speak? Well, Boy, would you like to remember clearly, not as if seeing through a glass darkly? Would you like to speak? Good. You must now begin those exercises which will bring forth the Spiritual Body, the *Sahu*. It is – as you said – the first of the trinity of spiritual bodies. It grows out of the Cell-Self, all three of the Physical Bodies. It takes its force for growth from the Physical Body because of the final obedience of the Animal Soul and a creative exchange between this so-called 'low' soul and the Heart

312

Soul. Here it is born. But it is nurtured by the human Soul, the mobile and moving Violet Soul. It feeds upon each thought, word, idea, sound or particle of food or drink which comes into contact with the individual during all of his physical life. Although it takes its birth from the Animal, its nutriment from the Human, it cannot fully develop without the combined creative force of the trinity of Mental-Emotional bodies, and here seems to be cradled. Therefore the Hermetics say it is cradled on the wind...that is, upon emotion and thought combined. Indeed it is incubated by the heat of the passions of the breast, and suckles the nutriment of the Heart Soul from whence it takes all emotions. But these are, through the continuing change in the chemistry of the bodies, purified and uplifted until they are finally perfected.

"You spoke of the Tree of Life being upside down, with the roots in the heavens and the branches upon earth? The *Sahu* must be that which is intended by such a verbal symbol. When it is at last rooted in the Soil of the higher heavens, or the upper souls, it becomes a new plant. Then, slowly it begins that divine cannibalism which is so much shown in the god-structures of religions. It takes its own growth by absorbing and purifying its parent stock, refining it, raising it, uplifting and supporting it in a new dimension and a new realm. When the Spiritual Body at last becomes deeply rooted in the heavenly world, its growth is so swift it is seemingly instantaneous. This strange and important complexity you will understand later. But the Spiritual Soul must undergo much growth before it becomes firmly rooted in the higher bodies *which grow out of it*. Indeed this is the Serpent of Wisdom which grows out of itself and yet feeds upon itself.

"When the Spiritual Body has grown a while it begins to become evident. Even as a youthful thing it can be externalized. It can be made material. It may also be made immaterial when it is obedient to the will. It may clothe itself with material aspects of nature so well that it will escape detection. It may be as thin as the mists of *Amon's Gas* (Editor's Note: Amon's Gas apparently means *ammonia*. Ammonia was developed by the Priests of the temple of Amon, Thebes. The fumes of ammonia are light, misty-white, thin enough to be almost invisible, and they are very pungent.) or it may be as solid as a bar of iron. It has, in the right stage, an enormous speed and energy. Therefore it may penetrate into anything whatsoever. It is much like unto a light which cannot be contained, yet may be qualified and solidified by pristine will. It may then be fashioned by thought into a barrier through which nothing can penetrate, not even the Kings Arrow! It is at last indestructible, the essential body for protection, and it is the energy source, the carrier of the two higher essences. It is the support of eternal life, the boat of *Re* riding eternally in the heavens.

"This magnificent energy at about mid-stage suddenly develops the vital air of memory. Until you reach this half-stage of development, the point of semi-divinity, the bodies may be made to go, do, see, feel, smell. But all of nature is reflected as if through the ripples of a muddy pond. For the seed of memory must grow. It is thrice wonderful when the bodies are supported and made sure in all things by remembrance of things material and immaterial. Also, this spirit contains the seed of time, and when developed to the half-stage it is the seat of prophecy, and reading the future times. This half-stage is found in the symbol of the Centaur – half animal and half human-divine.

"Despise not the long period of time which you will spend at the half-stage. For this is the time of the rooting of the Spiritual Body in the heavens. This is the time of the growth of the higher bodies into eternal life. Once rooted firmly, there is a single moment when all jumps into eternal life with a mysterious suddenness. From that moment on divinity and life everlasting are *known*. From that moment on, that moment of sublimation into Godhood, the tissue may be made invisible, transported, and again assembled. From that moment on two other bodies are full grown. They are the *Sekem*, the Vital Body, and the *Khu*, the eternal Radiant Body or Soul.

"Hear me clearly, Boy. When you have full memory and clear recall of your externalization, you must tell me.

Then time may be counted almost to the day when your Moment of Divinity will arrive. It requires thirty-three months almost to a day, nine hundred ninety days – perhaps a little less if the individual is a woman with the twenty-eight day cycle setting a rhythm power of its own. About a thousand days, Boy. This seems to be automatic.

"Now, for your future safety, let us discuss even now what will happen after that moment of glory. Growing out of the Spiritual Body, is the Vital Body, the *Sekem*. It is brought to seed by the advancement of the energy of the Human Soul. It is incubated by the Animal Soul, and carried upon the creative mental energy developed in the Shadow or Blue Soul. Yet, when rooted, it takes its being from the Spiritual Body, and is enshrined there. Once rooted it is divine. Yet until rooted, it, like the Spiritual Body, is carried by the mobile Human Soul.

"This Vital Soul is all but invisible, having not much more visible substance than a heat wave rising from the burning sand against a blue sea. It is commonly called 'blue-white' or 'silvery' – yet in truth it is neither. However, in it are contained the creative energies of man, world and heaven. It's vast energy gives it a capacity to perform greatly, and create at the command of thought. It is, when only partly controlled, the source of angels or independent entities who are not obedient to the will of the individual. Angels are obedient to the Radiant Soul, but entities are not. Do you mark me, Boy?

"The Vital Soul serves in its turn as the body for the Radiant Soul. In this Vital Soul are found the magnificent Word, the Creative Energy. It is the seat of speech, the Creative Fiat, the Word of God that can be made manifest.

"Though time is essential for the development of this Vital Body after the half-way stage of the Spiritual Body, great care must be given so that both creativity and speech are developed. Speech in the externalized body is much easier than creativity. In this slightly delayed creativity there is incorporated an automatic development of the Radiant Soul. Let us now turn to this final Spirit and understand it clearly.

"While the Vital Body is growing beyond the stage of

315

speech to creativity, the Radiant Soul is rooting itself for the surge to eternal dominance. During this time both are cradled in the Spiritual Body. But when creative energy is attained, the Radiant Soul suddenly assumes command. It instills into all of the permanent bodies the eternal energy, the power ever lasting, the eternal life. It purifies and spiritualizes the *Ka* and slowly absorbs its energy into eternal glory, raising the personality of the individual into everlasting life.

"Then the individual may exist as human, or as divine spirit. Then the power of dissolution at will and recreation of self at will is known. But mark well, Boy. There is a half-way stage in even the development of the Radiant Soul--and this is important to all the world."

Skakus stopped and was silent for a long while, then he fixed me with those inscrutable eyes and suddenly demanded. "Boy, did it not strike you strange that you took no oath of secrecy before you began this training? Know why? Because I insisted on trusting you. I am now going to trust you with a great secret. I do not want you under oath to never reveal it. I want it revealed to man. Not now! Man has not the mental training yet to understand and use it. He would destroy himself. But there will come a time, and I charge you now to know and use that time for the good of men.

"At the time of the half-way stage of the development of the Radiant Soul there is a barrier. Mark me, Boy, for words cannot explain fully this barrier. But at this point - so near to eternal divinity - there is a pause, a gap, a mighty abyss. Those who do not leap the abyss are the mighty God-Men of the Order of Melchizadek. These men have all the powers of creation except this: they do not seem to be able to transmute their own bodies. Mark this, Boy. They can transmute the bodies of others, but not their own. I know not why this eternal mystery - but such is the will of the Supreme God whom all things material and immaterial must obey. This mystery, indeed, gives rise to two strange things. They are the Legion of the Living, and the Order of No Name.

"The Legion of the Living is a body of individuals

who have, in the prime of physical life, quitted their bodies untimely. These good bodies the strongly developed members of the Order of Melchizadek do - with permission of God and of the departing soul - invest and use. Thus there is no waste of time, and no need for retraining. The White Brotherhoods train those born into the flesh and prepare the way for final illumination. This they do with the ministering help of all Orders. The Order of Melchizadek invests individuals with new life, new personalities, new strengths, and a new concept of divinity. Thus it is that many who seemingly die come back to life, and are changed thereafter. However, sometimes the Order of Melchizadec may, for a short time, when the need is very great, usurp the voice, brain, heart, limbs or other functions of a willing body and use it for the service of man and God.

"Those who can attain to dissolution of their own flesh are of the Order of No Name, until now so secret that they have not been mentioned. It is the purpose of the training of all men under these divine Temple Exercises to bring about this divine condition, this eternal life within the unresurrected flesh! You are not under oath of secrecy. As a Master you may choose the time you think mankind is ready, and then you may make known these sacredly guarded facts. I will even give to you the name of this Transcendent Order. You know that in your exercises you have used the scarab upon the green wall. Do you not wonder that the Spiritual Soul, the eternal Radiant Self, is in fact golden-white in color, so clear and translucent that it is indeed more radiant than the sun. But the source of power, the eternal energy, comes from a small green disc - more radiant than a thousand suns - which grows into the seed-atom space of the Divine Heart. For want of a better name it is called the Divine Jade - meaning the heart so purified and disciplined that it has reached beyond the limits of all the bodies. From this the Sacred Order takes its name. It is known as the *Order of the Jade Sun*.

"The training of the Order requires the individual pass through at least seven of the White Brotherhoods, then enter the Sacred Training of the Order, such as you

317

have been given here. Yet when mankind is ready and the time is right, the training may be made direct. When the minds of men are broadened by education, by confidence in self, by belief in individual worth, by mutual trust and confidence – then the training will be shortened and the pathway made direct. This is your task. This is your future.

"But back to the now. When the Vital Body has been developed to the mid-stage, its energy, corporeal or incorporeal, can be qualified by another body. The unmanifest can be made manifest by the magnet of a developed soul and a willing mind. Therefore the Vital Energy may speak the eternal creative word. When this is qualified and materialized by another body, the spiritual force may be made the creative seed and blossom in the flesh. It can be made manifest only by the force of will and warm desire of both the sender and the receiver. By this fecundation through space and time you will know that you have attained to the moment of decision: which shortly will show if you are to be of the eternal Order of Melchizadek or the eternal Order of the Jade Sun. At that moment, when you know positively that you can sublimate and raise your physical body, you must be ready for the final initiation. From that moment there must be no swerving aside in your great work. You must know you have attained the pure essence of God, and direct the final efforts to begin.

"All the orders, all the Brotherhoods, all the religions within the core of great religions will be readied for your word. When you speak that word the juggernaut will begin to roll and no man will be able to stay it. No man shall move until you give the order and the code shall be when you say. *That which must be done, let it be done quickly!* Before you speak these words know you have the powers of the Eternal, that you can make mountains to remove themselves, that you can turn stone into gold by the power of your divine will. Know that you can make deserts to turn green, green things to instantly sear, and clouds to assemble and give off lightning – all at the order of your divine will. Know that you can absorb the flesh, turn it into pure energy, then reassemble that energy into your fleshly form again. Know all this beyond all possible doubt. Only then can we attain to that great success which will change the path of mankind."

Back within the Temple of the Virgin-Born Horus my Masters all began to work harder and longer with me, and my time was consumed. Many days I could not be alone long enough to visit in mind and spirit with my Beloved. Sometimes I would be upon the terrace and could see her across the cove. But I was allowed no time to visit her in my person. Now that the final goal was in sight, now that my mind had seen what I thought was the totality of the pattern of my life, I rose to new strengths and new understandings and increased efforts. Slowly a great resolve was forged into my very being. Now, above all else I wanted to complete my work for the Brotherhood and rejoin my beloved bride for all time. I realized now that my love for her had been used by my Masters as the strongest possible motivation for the externalization of my bodies, for my desire for her was like the pull of a running elephant. Though I knew it was rushing me toward possible death--in a form I could not possibly foresee or know--still I wanted the final test to be made.

Once in a rare week I would have time to externalize and spend a few moments with my darling. But now that I knew what to note, I was aware that my memories of those precious seconds faded even faster than the memory of a dream. I willed to have permanent recollection of those sweet moments, and not the reflected memory of a cell-mind recalling pleasure. I wanted clear memory, I wanted to be able to speak to my love. For these near goals I worked endlessly, knowing that the final goal would then be but a pace away. But strive as I did, it was at the very end of my fifth year that I thought I found myself remembering exactly those rare moments. For a few days I was silent, fearing lest my cell-mind was becoming filled with the confusing fumes of my desire. I *was remembering* the most recent moments when my externalized self touched her warm fingers, or she touched the fringes of my auburn hair, or a strand of silken-gold caressed my forehead as I sat beside her. The day came when I clearly remembered the rosy petal that

319

fell from the flower in her hair upon my palm. Then I was positive.

That day I rose from my place upon the wall and ran to find my Master.

"I now remember!"

Skakus turned his eyes to heaven in praise. "One thousand days!" His voice had a new timbre, and almost exuberant surge. Yet he was impersonal and distant--an enigma to me.

For three days I worked incessantly with my Masters. Each one rechecked my knowledge of the work he had given me. Each one questioned me to be certain I knew the meaning of his teaching upon all three levels. Then for three additional days a committee of Hierophants tested me by putting different items on the holy altars of the temples. I was then required to go, see, return and report, for they wanted to test fully my remembrance. Then I would be questioned on what I had seen the day before.

This testing was extended to nine days, without end. I made thousands of trips in projection to prove that I could positively remember what was strange or rearranged upon the altars of the Temples upon the Island of *On*. I was so busy that I had no time to see my Beloved, and when they were finished with me in a day, I had no energy, but collapsed into fatigued insensibility. On the twelfth day we were upon the terrace and I could see her staring across, trying to see against the sun. It was that very hour that the Committee of Masters assembled, completed their plans, anounced my definite success, and set the day of my departure.

I was to leave in three days to go back to my own land. Great were the tribulations of the Jews under the Roman heel, and each day they spoke more openly of the Messiah who was to come. Their Redeemer was sorely needed and eagerly awaited. It was to Israel that my ship was to take me, there to begin and conclude my final teachings and test. Those three precious days I spent half in final instruction and half near my beloved *Mherikhu*. Skakus encouraged me in this saying in a rough voice, "Boy, if you enjoy not the sensations of flesh, how can you enjoy the more subtle sensations of mind and spirit fully. Only the weak and the falsely-holy deny the joys of earthly love!"

Oh, how I obeyed my master then! *Mherikhu* and I spent the hours on the Strand, and so intense was our pleasure that time, though speeding by, seemed to endure forever. Sometimes we planned what we were to do after my return. We decided to return to the swale of the River Brue – for a joyous time at least. This pleased her greatly, for she was of that country.

Somethimes we sat in that silence which is truly the sweetest communion of love. We joyed in every thing, especially in the sounds of river larks calling their joys to heaven. Once *Mherikhu* touched my palm gently with hers and said, "My Mother, the Lady Goddess, has told me much of the high meaning of the symbol of the serpent that eats its tail. I think the highest symbol is this – it is the lovers touch. For does not the touch feed upon itself, devouring itself, yet growing ever stronger through eternity?"

We were happy, with a strange content that seemed to place time and distance away from us. We formed our only reality within the confines of ourselves. Therein no thought of possible failure and my bodily death was allowed to come. We did not even plan for failure, for we saw the final hurdle completed and my return as man.

The morning of my departure came all too swiftly. My ship was at the dock, near the river-side of her barque of the ebony rail. She was upon the barque, seated upon the Gold and Purple Rug, the two rugs interwoven, which were now our mutual promise. Yet one guardian strand was woven into the fringe of the new rug, a symbol of her willingness that I should share the hallowed and guarded area of her world. It was a symbol that broadcast to the world her desire to accept and share my Creative Word and make spirit blossom into flesh. I stood with her as the ship was made ready. At first we could not speak for the love that flowed within our beings.

She spoke gently, her words hanging like silver sound above the Nile. "All is ready. The entire universe waits the fulfillment of the ancient plan, the completion of the Great Cabal. You have behind you the greatest secret army that ever has been assembled for the good of mankind. But, oh, my Beloved, to me it seems a sad war - for the only soldier is my own sweet love.

"I would tell you this, though perhaps you know. I have waited for you all my life. I too have been trained in this grand army. But I do love you beyond and above duty. An hour of waiting for your caress is surely more blessed than all the kisses of all the kings of earth. I have joyed in even the waiting and the hoping. I shall wait in pleasure the coming short while. But, my Beloved, if you should at any time even faintly doubt the outcome, or if you should merely want to return without the final trial - know I love you with a passion only a woman's self can understand. If you wish, now, this very instant - or any other time - we shall forego our vows. We will leave this sacred island, leave this holy war for the good of man. We will go arm in arm into any land where I may hold your sweet body, and know your love as maid knows man."

I stopped her sweet mouth with a gentle finger. "Hear me, Beloved. I will return. I have this 'soldierly duty' - sweet, I like that phrase - and it I will perform. But I will return in my flesh, and we will test the treasury of love. I have loved you, and you only, and I love with a passion which struggles now against the traces of the heavy load of necessity. I shall be faithful to my vow, and I shall return this same body to meet your most fond caress. Believe me."

"Oh, Jeshu, my husband! I do believe you. But woman knows no such inner compulsion to duty, only the pull of her yearning self. Believe me, Love, that flesh alone is hard enough for woman to conquer and subdue! I shall wait - in joy and pleasure - but with every wish of my heart and every fibre of my being I shall draw you back to me. Then I shall pounce upon you and hold you with the hungry talons of my eagle-fashioned soul!"

I kissed her then and held her close for those last few seconds. She whispered. "I love you higher still, beyond the touch of soul. Man may know the eternal pleasures of duty, brotherhood, and ordered things - and to him they may have purpose. Woman truly never knows such communal joys. Hers are all private, secret joys of her creative urge. How can such joys be shared? I would have you win the highest award in the history of Men. I would have you change the course of the history of man - but not for me! I would have you do it for your own duty-sense and your own pride in accomplishment. Such things are not for me, they stand arms length from my inner heart. There, in that secret place, I would have you in my arms, sire of strong sons, father of my children, lover of my willing self."

The time was ripe and the ship ready. I said, "I shall come to you."

Her head came up, and her eyes were clear. "Yes! Beloved, my husband, I shall welcome you and proudly bear your son."

As I turned to go she said. "When you come, come for love of me, dear. Not for love of duty or spirit, but love of my fond flesh. And remember this, even if God shouts while her lover whispers, a maid in love hears not God's word. No radiant, shining God can take the place of warm and vital flesh in a girl's heart - or her life."

I left her then, my bright eyed Golden Girl, my joy, my life - my hope for eternal bliss!

The ship I boarded was bigger even than the *Britannin*, with wider beam and higher sails, and it was called *Galilean*. Skakus and the other Masters met me as I went aboard. The other Masters embraced me fondly and spoke to me, proud of their love for me and mine for them. When at last Skakus only was left he stood away, and this I could not understand.

"Final thoughts! You are said to be a Master, ready to start the True Religion in the hearts and minds of men. Remember, Boy! No man is a Master though he act as one and is believed by others to be one. He is a Master only when he himself knows he is one."

He stood aloof, not offering to touch or embrace me. In my mind I charged him with indifference to human emotions. He looked at me from those inscrutable eyes and said harshly:

323

"Love! It is in your heart, it is in your mind. Love may kill you! The moment may come when you must choose between love or physical death. I know, Boy! Had I been wise and strong enough to give up my love for the beknighted youth of Athens, I might have succeeded. Had I been great enough to give up the youth of Athens, you would not now have this chance at glory!"

He waited for a moment then went on. "The plans are made - plans which you must not know until they are upon you. Your final test is planned. All the world is in readiness. You alone, however, may set the final days into motion. I gave you the code words to say, for there will be one of our brothers always ready to bear the word that you have ordered the juggernaut to roll. But hear me. Your order to set the juggernaut into motion must not be given if you fall into the terrible despondency of the Deep Night of Spiritual Despair. Mind this! How long it will last no one knows. How terrible it is the anguish and cries of a million initiates will testify! When that black hand is upon you, not even the Supreme God could force you to succeed. Your very will would be set against it. Therefore *always*, *always*, *always* you must watch your energy. Often you must retire to exercise and restore your self. Hear me, Boy?

"When your final goal is in sight you may become over eager, even over confident. This can lead you to defeat - as it did me with the hemlock which I thought I could overcome. God is you, Boy."

Thus saying, Skakus, my strange inscrutable Master, turned and moved away and the waves of the Nile seemed to crackle with his furious energy. I looked at him, hoping he would turn and show his love, let me understand him. But he did not even seem to hear my heartfelt thanks which I called after him for his years of effort in my training. Why did he so deny my love? Why did he hold himself away from the emotional self? Why could I never come to know and to understand him? Why could I not really love him?

Even as I pondered thus the stubby nose of the *Galilean* moved into the current of the Nile. I looked back at the beauty of my bride and she was again standing as I had first seen her there, an angel ready for flight.

I knew the secret, inner joy of beginning my final adventure, my greatest test. Was there ever a soldier better trained, was ever an army more carefully prepared, more safely supported. Gratitude was in me, and compassion for all men – and my boundless love. I was glad and I knew no fear, no doubt, as I moved towards my homeland and my destiny.

17

JOHN JOHN AND BAPTISM

Oh Israel! When Tiberius Caesar came to rule as the Regent of conquering Rome, Israel and the stiff-necked Jews reached the all time low in their history. This cruel despot was not a religious man, yet he hated the Jewish religion with all his heart, and raised his armed heel to stamp it out. Under this awful shadow the Jews crouched, disbanded of their unity, disabled in their spirit, stupified in their meaningless ritual, rebellious in their baseless pride, hopeless in the sight of God. Their punctilious observances of their "Sacred Law" was a mockery of God's Graciousness, their ritual was but meaningless mime dryer than the dead branch of the tree of life! Truly I say to you, there can be no spirit of God when Priests perform dead rituals, and such are but profanation of God's promise of divinity in every man.

Cathedrals and churches should never be the repository of God's ordinances, but trained and ministering Brothers who derive neither gain nor livelihood from such training. If you would hear me, let the edifices be taken down stone by stone, let the priests who live upon the desire of men for heaven be put to traces, let the symbols which are used to gather moneys from hopeful, fearing men be melted down. Let men turn inwardly to God, and bring forth that God from himself, manifesting to all men his Godhood. This is the only church! This is the only Salvation! This was ever my way and no other will ever be!

Oh, Israel. Each man was made to go each sabbath to the synagogue. There the endless ritual was followed, with reading from the scrolls of Law and the sermon--but with "one of authority" ever there to see that no thought was expressed but that which was approved by the Elders. Who were these Elders? Who have they been since first the Church was conceived as a way to control man? They are the mediocre, the incapable, the ones so weak in mind and spirit that they will never think or do that which is unpleasing to their own "superiors". Neither originality nor force is within them. God is naught but original force so God is never within them!

Oh, my lost Israel! Tax gatherers were commissioned by Rome, sat at the cross roads, and rifled each load of commerce. Such Publicans were truly sinners, for great was the opportunity for personal profit by cheat and fraud. What man could resist? There was a ten percent tax on products of the field and vineyard, a tax upon the head of all men between fourteen and sixty-five, and all women between twelve and sixty-five. There was a tax upon everything moved, bought, sold. The tax grabber was everywhere to molest, demand, and destroy should he wish--and he was backed by the might of Rome. Tax upon the movement of merchandise, or upon the individual's exertion of strength and husbandry is an abomination to man. That nation which suffers it will inevitably fall, for the individual ability is ever greater than the collective in creativity and new things.

But the fury of the secular tax collectors was nothing beside the insidiousness of the tax levied by the Sanhedrin for the Temple. When, once a year, all Jews were compelled by religious law--except there was good reason--to go in to the Temple at Jerusalem, it was not for God's glorification. No! It was for the treasury of the Temple. There were many coins, but the Temple would accept only one. Each man was compelled to change his coins to that one, and the Temple Fathers made a profit on this exchange. Each man was compelled to offer his sacrifice, and animals and birds for such sacrifice were

327

sold by the Priests--at a great profit. Truly, they turned the avenues and streets, the porticos and courts of the Sacred Temple into an animal pen, filled with exchange booths... all to make money for the family of Ananias, the pompous and stuffed-up priests who knew naught of God.

Oh, my lost sheep of Israel! There was in the temple an enormous curtain hanging five times the height of a man, drawn across the opening into the sacred sanctuary, the initiate chamber, the sekinah. Yet so filled with falsehood was the religion of the Jews that they denied every man right to enter there for his own initiation. They permitted only the High Priest to enter, and kept all others in awe and terror of that supposedly holy place. To me that curtain was an abomination, a sin. For did it not stop man's hope of ever reaching God directly? Did it not forbid him the highest and best in his belief? Did it not make him a physical and mental slave, and a spiritual coward? It was a sin, as such barriers to man's personal contact with God will ever be a sin! Truly I say to you there is no barrier between man and the Eternal God. I bid you destroy every symbol upon the face of the earth that purports to be for the use of one group of specially trained who alone have the key, the secret, the use. Unless the truth is given freely to all men who are willing to take the Oath of Secrecy--Verily it is not Truth. The new age is come! Falsehood even in high places must pass away! Man must not be curtained off from God!

Oh, my confused Israel! The Jews taught each sabbath of the coming of the New Covenant, the Messiah who was to raise up the Jews, the new King of the Jews who was to lead them to victory. But they let factions divide them, let points of doctrine create death-dealing dissentions, let insignificant acts of ritual create civil strife and murders! The leaders of Israel were worse than useless, they were a plague upon their own people.

Within the common man, within the husbandmen, the fishermen, the merchantmen there was a spirit. True it was depressed, true it was sullen, true it was rebellious--but there was a spirit, a desiring spirit! Yet even these good men were confused. The Jew refused even to speak to the Samaritan, and would travel extra days to avoid going into the area of Samaria. Both Judea and Samaria were under the heel of the Roman conqueror, and in truth had no real religious differences of import! In their hearts all men knew that they lived in error, that the Religion was an error of history, that the Temple was run by frauds and cheats, that man was in a quagmire from which only the miraculous would save him!

Such was the condition of Israel when the *Galilean* put me down near the Sea of Galilea and I was turned out to find my own way to my final initiation. My course was soon set. In less than a week I was talking with the citizens, learning to express myself in the vernacular of the street which I had never learned and now needed to know very well. I worked as a cargo tender at Caeseria Philipi, and lived with three such others in a hovel which looked up to the Philipian Palace on the hill. My Sacred Exercises went apace, yet I spent much time with these sweating, wine-bibbing, loud-laughing men and they knew me as a meek but willing worker. I think they loved me. One of them came crying of the miraculous man who preached to throngs of startled hearers at the far end of the Sea of Galilea, near the mouth of the River Jordan, at a village called Enon.

"He is big, handsome, with sun-bleached hair. He sacks himself in rough raiment, of camel's hair caught at the middle with a leather belt. His mild brown eyes are wild. Even his followers say he lives on locusts and wild honey and that he has been for twenty years in the deserts of Paran seeking to know God's will. Now he comes forth with his divine message. And when he speaks--such a voice as God's messenger must truly use! The voice that cries out in the wilderness of man's doubt and his fears and commands to be heard. When he preaches, all the world must needs listen, and men flock to follow him. Yet he is not puffed up, but is humble, and he cries to all: 'Follow not me, for I am but the forerunner of Him who is to come. Come unto me and repent and make straight your path to God, for the Kingdom is near at hand. I am sent but a pace before as the prophet of Him who is to come! Come, repent your sins, take of me the symbol of new life and be baptized in this living water!'

By the mystic tie that had bound us through the years I knew that this must be John-John. Surely he was keeping his promise to me in our youth! He had made a cleansing sacrament out of baptism as an honor to me!

I took my roll and began the journey to find my big cousin, for his work was but a testimony to his belief in my own divinity. I found him at the ford which crosses the Jordan near the village of Enon, and he preached to an enormous throng. Though he made his message captivating by his big voice, his stories and his sweet humor, yet he preached nothing but this: "I am the forerunner of one to come. Repent, be cleansed by baptism, set your world aright. The time is at hand." I thought to surprise and please him, and tried to go through the crush of the disciples around him. But at last I stepped into the line of those who were coming down into the Jordan to be baptized at his hand.

He did not at first see me, even when I stood at the water's edge. When I stood before him his eyes opened in recognition, then closed in that look of awe and respect which my mother had drilled into him. He saw not his living cousin, but some potential me! "Oh, Jeshuau, why come you to me? I baptize but in water, you baptize with Holy Fire of Life."

Turning to those assembled upon the River's side he said, "Behold, one comes who is mightier than I. One the latchet of whose sandals I am not worthy to unloose."

He would have turned aside reverently, but I came upon him to show my remembrance of our past and my love for him. Then did the mighty preacher embrace me. Reverently, with tears mingling with the flowing water, he did baptize me in the River Jordan. And when I was raised out of the water he fixed me with those eyes that saw not me but some potential me, and said in a loud voice filled with joy:

"Behold, a spirit like unto a dove settles down upon him. In my heart I hear a great voice crying, "This is my beloved son in whom I am well pleased." Hear well you

330

who have flown from the coming wrath, you new generation of wise and wily serpents, for I have said that the time is near at hand. Surely when he speaks he must tell you that the time is fulfilled."

Thus did he clearly lay the scene for me to claim the Messiah's place, an act which all his life he had hoped for. I could not do so.

I tarried with him and his disciples for a few days. In our quiet evenings before and after prayer, I tried to tell them of my times in the Persian Desert, and the trials of the initiate. Some few who were cleansed in spirit by John's baptism understood my higher message, but some misunderstood and thought that I spoke of temptations in the nearby deserts from whence John had come. But John-John would call together his disciples and then urge me to speak before them, and to please him I did. Some who came in faith were healed by my prayers. Even as I tried to follow my beloved John-John I was being made his leader by his own strange will.

When my wish to see my family took me from him he said to his disciples: "You know well that the Paschal Lamb is sacrificed in one Temple of the Jews that it may atone for their sins. I say unto you, this one is come to take away the sins of the world. Behold the Lamb of all mankind!"

John-John! How great was his love, for he made himself nothing more than the tool of my growth. In truth the pathway had been made ready for me by my sweet cousin and he did cause to come to me the first of my personal disciples. They came after me and I demanded to know why they followed me and not their master, John the Baptist. They countered with a wily question, "Master, where do you live?"

I knew they wished to observe me to decide if John-John was right in his insistence to his own disciples that I was He who was to come. "Come and see" was all I could possibly say, and they came and tarried with me at my lodgings for the day, and they eagerly waited for permission to follow after me. I did not encourage them until two days later when I saw them and bade them follow me.

One of these first two of my disciples was Andrew of Bethsaida, near the Sea. The other was John out of Zebedee, and brother of James. When they had been with me for three days and tested me with questions, and probed to get me to admit that I was the son of God--which I could not do (nor yet, for my mother's sake, could I deny it)-- they were convinced and went forth with great energy characteristic of fishers and simple men.

Andrew sought out his brother Simon and assured him that John the Baptist was right and that I was the Messiah. Eagerly he brought the big man to me. Simon was not of the coloring of John-John but of the huge stature, and the firm and unyielding mind. Before he spoke a word I read in his aura his doubt and his probing mind and I said, "You are Simon, son of Jona. You are so big and stubborn that you are unwieldy as a rock until you do believe. Therefore you should be called Petros, that is to say Peter, which is Greek for Rock." The big fisherman smiled his belief and his pleasure, and followed after me, and his conviction swayed hundreds of others who lived near the Sea, because all men loved Simon-Peter. Soon I was moved to his home, and his many friends came because he called them, and believed because he believed, and many healings took place.

John of Zebedee and his brother James then did leave their father's boats and clung unto me. A day or two later we met Philip of Bethsaida and I yielded to the impulse and said, "Follow me." Philip--because of the many healings--tried to convince Nathanael-Bartholomew that I was He of whom the prophets spoke, come to fulfill the law of Moses. Nathanael would not believe and challenged "Could anything good come from the unknown village of Nazar?" Yet by distant sight I had seen him under a fig tree, a devout man, and had read his mind for he was preparing his goods for the Feast of the Passover and was rebellious of the injustice of the Temple taxes. When I told him this he was amazed and cried. "Master, truly you must be the son of God!" I chided him gently and replied, "You believe with such fervor because I saw you in the shade of a distant fig tree. If I am what you say, surely you will see the heavens open and the angels of God minister unto the Son of Man!" They were all convinced by John-John's great voice and his sincere personal belief, and proclaimed in whispers what they believed.

After I had spent a time at Nazar with my beloved family, I returned to Capernaum and the house of Simon-Peter. Nathanael-Barthlomew had arranged for me to speak in the synagogue at Cana. Hearing that I was to be there for a while, my family decided to come from Nazar for the wedding of the daughter of my mother's third cousin. This girl was named Anna, I think a short form of Hannah. She was to wed Aram of Cana a fine man but young and not of a wealth which should have supported a large wedding feast. With my family and my disciples we added too many to the feast.

It was a large crowd indeed which accompanied the veiled bride from her father's home to that of Aram the groom. Marriage was considered a sacrament and brought about forgiveness of sins—and it was a time for great jubilation. We went past the roofed-over breeze-way, each person carrying a torch or a lantern held aloft on poles, and each singing aloud the praises of the bride. We were each bearing a gift, of oil or wine, but mostly we brought oil. In the breeze-way we almost stumbled over six stone jars, about twenty gallons each, which were filled with water for the ceremonial washing of hands and for the actual washing of pans and utensils of the feast.

The marriage contracts were signed, and Aram gave to Anna the expected gifts of money, about $30.00, an enormous and generous sum. When her dowery was named he most generously doubled it, whereas he was expected by custom merely to add one half! I mention this, for it was soon evident that he had not judged the expected crowd, or had skimped on the wines to make such generous gifts to his bride - and I mused pleasantly that I hoped it was the second reason. Soon it was evident that the wines would run short, and that Aram had not the money to buy more. My mother, to whom everyone confided their trials and their joys, assured the worried bride that I would do something to save the wedding feast. Then with that expectant look which contained both pride and pleading, she asked me to do something. I knew that secretly my mother was not as much concerned with the feast as she was hopeful that I might do that which would proclaim me the Son of God.

"Oh, Woman!" I chided, but to the hurt look in her dear eyes added, "Beautiful mother, what has this to do with me! Even if I were the Son of God, has my time now come?"

Yet, even as I spoke, I remembered that Skakus had instructed me to be constantly alert for ways to test my developing skills. I reflected that a little miracle would give people much to talk about for a few days. So I smiled into these dear pleading eyes and my mother walked away confidently and proudly and said to the servants, "Do whatever my son tell's you, quickly in good measure!"

I asked that the stone jars be brought in and filled with water, and too many eager hands were available. Laughing they filled each jar full enough. One burly and scoffing guest urged them to fill them to overflowing so that no one could be deceived, for it was against the known laws of man and God for water to be turned to wine.

I calmed my physical self with seven breaths, then sent forth my Violet Soul and stirred the waters with power. Then I brought to bear the earthy and creative power of the Ruby Soul, seeing it by force of will changing the pure water into pure wine.

Though my eyes were closed the gasps of the wedding guests near the jars told me that the change was made, and the bride wept with her happiness. The one in charge of the feast, one Johan Bessar, a merchant of Cana, cried to Aram upon tasting the wine, "Oh, you wily one! Others put their best wines first, but Aram of Cana saves the best for last!" I was pleased for my mother looked at me with eyes that saw not truth, but a lovely dream - her dream come true! Yet her dream could never contain the Truth of the Initiate Secret, and I pitied her within my tender love.

When I left Cana my mother and brothers came with me back to Capernaum. I loved the sweet air of that new city nearby the delightful and fertile plain called Gennasaret, that is to say, Garden of Princes. It lay near the shore of the Lake of Galilee, about two miles from the mouth of the Jordan. There was a new synagogue, the gift of a Roman Centurion, built of stone and white limestone over a basalt base. I liked the little synagogue. Each time I entered its portal I was reminded of my Beloved. Over the doorway was a symbol of a pot of manna, reminding the Jews of God's graciousness to their race, but reminding me of the ministerings of my Beloved while I was in fever in the Cave of Trial near *Bokhara*. My family came with me. It was but a few days before we should all go on to Jerusalem for the time of the Feast of the Passover was fast approaching. This was in the month of April, in the sixteenth year of the reign of Tiberius. We all were busy repairing roads and bridges and putting whiting upon sepulchers, which was the custom of the Jews before Passover.

In the men about the countryside there was much bitterness. They were all gathering their herds and flocks from which to pay their tithe to the Temple, which they were constrained to do not less than two weeks before the Paschal Feast. Men were coming on pilgrimages from many places, some hurrying on to Jerusalem to undergo purification for all kinds of imagined transgressions. Men grumbled that neither tithe nor purification were for man's needs, but only for the enrichment of the priests.

Then the booths of the money changers began to appear at every synagogue and cross road. Yet another Temple Tax was to be paid – the head tax for all men over fourteen and all woman over twelve. Though the tax could have been paid in equal value with copper or silver coins from the Persian, Tyrian, Syrian, Egyptian, Grecian or Roman areas, the priests insisted upon a still further usury. They would accept only the half shekel. They charged about an additional one-tenth, or even one-fifth of the value for changing to the special money. When my family and disciples, with a large body of followers from the synagogues around about, came to the Temple in Jerusalem to celebrate the memory of God's promise to the

Jews, we found it a noisy and boisterous place. Not only were there cries of anger from the pilgrims filched of additional moneys for the changer's fees, but there were stalls of oxen and goats, and cotes of doves and pigeons. With all the shouting and pushing to obtain these animals for sacrifice, there was no place to worship. Many men cried out to God that it was a shame upon the Jews – but they were silenced by the looks of the priests who profited by the commerce and would not have it disturbed. But the practice was unpopular and most men bemoaned it.

When I entered the Court of the Gentiles, and saw that it and the porch were both clogged with money changers, animals, birds and covetous priests, the divine wrath settled upon me like a giant calm. I knew that which I did, for I thought very clearly, "I will here prove to all mankind that one man can stand against the entrenched priestcraft if he does it for God's glory." In another part of my brain I reasoned that this which I was about to do would bring me great notoriety, and many followers – as well as the hatred of the Sanhedrin which held the power of life and death over Jews.

I calmly took the ropes from the necks of two great bulls, and twisted them into a scourge, and drove the money changers from the Temple. My disciples took the ropes from the necks of all the animals and drove them through the courts, and turned them out the gates of the Temple. We then overturned money pots, and sent the bird cotes out of the sacred area. When it was all done I cried aloud: "This is the House of God. Make not the Father's House a place of merchandise!" The priests were surly and mean, but the people were on my side and brooked no interference. When the deed had been reported to the Sanhedrin, the seventy who ruled the religion of the Jews, they sent their most wily ones to try to trap me. They knew they were in the wrong and dared not approach me with an open accusation.

Ananias, the High Priest came, and he demanded of me: "Show me your authority to do such things. Give us a sign of this authority."

I knew the trap he layed. He wanted me to say that I

was authorized by God, which would have been punishable, whereas the deed was not. So I answered him with a loud voice, "This is my authority, that if you tear down this temple of God, yet in three days shall it be raised again."

But the High Priest answered with cunning not with wisdom and said, "This building had hundreds of workmen for forty-six years - yet you would build it anew in three days!" He dared not stay to argue the point, for many men were angry, and he hurried away. Many followers attached themselves to me, some because they thought I was brave, others because they heard my teachings. I was doubly wary not to permit myself to say anything that would indicate that I claimed myself to be the Son of God. I was equally careful not to deny it and this was for my mother's sweet sake.

My mother and my brothers were a constant problem for me. They wanted to be with me, and followed after us whenever they could. It so happened that they had come from Nazar to be with me, and caused complications the first time that the Council of the World sent a representative. He came to find out how far I expected to disclose the secret and hidden concepts of the True Religion in setting up my new religion. My own disciples caused me to wish to be most cautious. They were much more interested in the phenomenon of healing than they were in the personal disciplines that would raise out of the man-self the Spirit-self. They of course did not have the initiate key - and could not have for a time - therefore I could talk to them of anything and they only heard what they wished to hear.

Thus things stood on that strange, blustery spring night when John of Zebedee came into the *aliyah* in great agitation. The outside stairs leading to this guest room upon the roof of our host's dwelling were hidden from the street. On such a night only a strong man would have been abroad. There was great secrecy in John's urgent whispers.

"Master, a ruler of the Pharisees has come to seek audience, but he must not be known to other Jews."

It was late, and my brothers were already asleep

upon the pallets in the *aliyah*, and the other disciples were sheltered upon the roof. But John was so insistent that I let the visitor be brought. I felt him at a thousand paces, and knew his mission long before he crept up the stairs. Truly he had a double reason for secrecy. Even when he stepped out of the darkness into the light of our fitful lamp he did not betray himself, not so much as by a glance.

"This is Nicodemus, Master, ruler of the Jews." I knew the former master of the *Britannin* by any name, and I knew why he had come. John was much attached to my person and would not leave, and we fell to speaking as if Nicodemo had truly come as a leader of the Jews rather than an initiate.

Nicodemo said, "Master, we know you are a teacher come of God. No man could do these things you do without the aid of God."

I was pleased, for he thus showed that the Council approved of my efforts so far. I knew he was there for the report of what I planned to teach to mankind, and how. I could not yet tell the world of the Sacred Exercises, but I did believe that they were ready to know that man could raise the divine from within, and come to know the new-born, indwelling spirit.

"Sir, truly, unless man be born anew he will never know the kingdom of God." With this single sentence I told him what I expected to teach, but he wanted to know how I would teach this great truth. Nicodemo assumed the role of a puzzled common man, and gave me a chance to answer all his questions. He demanded, "But how can any man be born again. Can an old man re-enter his mother's womb?"

"Sir, a man must be born again of spirit, else he cannot know the kingdom of God. Flesh is born of flesh, spirit is born of spirit. It is nothing amiss to teach that man of flesh must be born anew of spirit." His almost imperceptible nod told me that he wanted to know how I expected to make this concept of spiritual rebirth understandable by man, so I hastened on. "The wind blows where it will. One may hear the sound and yet not know from whence came the wind, nor where it goes. It is ever thus with those who are born of the spirit."

"But how can such a thing be?" Nicodemo asked the question in the tone of a puzzled man.

"Those who know by direct experience may speak of what they know and have seen. Those who have not such experience cannot take the word of those who have. Some are doubters, even the Jews. If I tried to tell of earthly things and you could not accept them, would you believe what I said of heavenly things. Truly no man can know heaven unless he has been in heaven, even as the divine spiritual being. As Moses lifted up the serpent on a staff in the wilderness so that those who looked thereon might be saved from snake-bite, now this new-born man, this spirit self must be raised up. So that whosoever believes in this New Born divine self may come to have eternal life. In the beginning God so loved the world that he gave his essence into man. He who *knows* this Son of God shall never perish but shall have eternal life."

There was a stillness in the *aliyah*, except for the breathing of the sleeping ones. I did not know then how very much asleep the entire world had become!

"Surely God would not send his Son into the world to condemn the men thereof." (It is against the initiate's oath to condemn at all!). "But that the men of the world might learn through the Son to save themselves. He who inwardly knows the Son of God cannot be condemned. He who does not inwardly know the Son of God has condemned himself already - because he has denied the inward knowledge of the eternal spiritual self. Yet, it is the shame of eternity that when divine light comes into the minds of men they refuse it. For they have been taught to keep their minds in darkness by these whose deeds and thoughts are evil in the sight of God."

Nicodemo knew I was talking of the orthodox priests of Judaism when I said, "For many who do this evil to mankind hate this inward light, and dare not allow men to see this glorious light lest their false teachings should be rebelled against. Only he that knows Truth seeks the light in which his every deed may manifest the glory of God."

Thus I announced to my Masters the extent of my

teaching of the ancient truths, and the campaign against the stupidity of the Jews and their controls over the minds, purses, energies, bodies and futures of man.

From Jerusalem we went back to my beloved Sea. I taught many with sermons on this matter, showing that all men were equal *within*, for they were of God. Many flocked to hear me, yet I sometimes thought they came more because of my mother's persuasive stories, the consistent healings, and John-John's testimony than because they truly understood my talks. I came to realize that I could teach only the simplest beliefs, for even my own disciples were not ready for the stronger faiths and could not understand the Temple of the Divine Spirit.

The many healings were possible because I was able to constantly stay in or at least quickly regain that feeling of elevation which had caused me to heal the Hindu dead of the king cobra. This feeling of sweet glory and strength flowed from me like the golden chalice overfilled! Everyone who came was healed unless they were everlastingly pre-occupied with the many "sins" of the Jews. These were endless, these so-called "sins", and caused most grievous maladies by weakening the vital energy to a dangerous point. Surely even God would have been overtaxed to have invented the multitude of "sins" that the priests spewed out upon man! It was even a "sin" to forgive "sin", or to do aught of good on the sabbath. But I continued to heal the sick on the sabbath. That was the time when they had leisure to come. I knew I was endangering the controls of the priests of Judaism, for he who knows the Truth must forever be free of such controls.

It came about that one man rose up against them in defiance - and this is the story. Four zealous men lowered a palsied fisherman, Salim, a distant cousin of Simon-Peter, through the roof where I was teaching. I told him that his sins were forgiven, to take heart and rise up. The Jews demanded whereof I might forgive sins, since that was the right of God, and they began to conspire against me. So that when I had taught in all the country round about, and many followed me, even a mulititude, the Jews became distraught and looked for

340

ways to discredit me and my teachings.

During a feast time we went to the pool of *Bethesda*, surrounded by five buildings in which were many persons of divers illnesses. They all waited for the angel which came down to stir up the waters of the pool, so the story was told, for it was believed that the first one who then entered the waters would be made whole. One man could not walk, but desired to be well. He could not get into the pool before the power of the water was usurped by another. Seeing his longing, I said to him "Take up your bed and walk", and he believed in faith and was made whole. It was the sabbath, and the Jews confronted him, saying that it was not lawful for him to carry his bed on the sabbath! Of such stupidity are some laws!

This man stood against them and cried: "He that made me whole has more of God's power than all your priests! He said for me to take up my bed and walk, and him I obey!"

They were furious and demanded who had healed him. He would not show me to them. I was pleased and did quickly retire, for it was not yet clear when my trial should come.

In the Temple this man came upon me teaching. I said to him, "You have been made whole. Therefore mend your thoughts, lest a worse condition come upon you." When, in his great joy he talked with other Jews, the priests discovered that it was I who had healed on the sabbath, and they tried to entrap me and harm me through guile.

Taking my disciples I went into Samaria and won many to believe because I read the past of a woman in her aura. Now there were crowds around wherever we went. I asked my disciples to use the baptism rite in honor of John-John, which they did, but I refrained from baptizing in water.

We went into Cana again, and there a man of noble birth sought me out, for his son was sick at Capernaum and was at the point of dying. I would not hurry back to Capernaum. Rather, I sent the healing by the Violet Soul and the Vital Body, and told him to go home for the child was healed. Great was the surprise when his servants met

him on the road and cried: "Your son is alive. Yesterday
at the seventh hour his sickness left him suddenly." The
nobleman came to me and cried out that his son had been
given healing at the moment I told him that his son was
healed. Then the nobleman believed in me, and so did his
many relations and servants, for he was a man of great
power. Yet the priests found fault, for they were much
afraid of a religion that freed the minds of men.

The priests stirred up the Jews to try to slay me,
and when they confronted me to accuse me for healing on
the sabbath I merely said, "My father had such healing
powers and now I use them."

The priests urged the people to kill me for I had
broken the sabbath, they said, also I had blasphemed
against God by saying that I was His Son – yet I made no
claim for my sake, and denied it not for my mother's sake!

When they would have advanced against me I taught
them of divine things thus: "You are like unto the Divine
Father, and within each is the Radiant Son. The Son can
do nothing of himself, only what the Father allows. The
true Father loves the Son and shows all that greater
works can be done than these I have done at which you
marvel. That Father can raise up the dead, and that Son
can bring life to whomsoever he will. That Father judges
no man, but permits that Son all understanding and
power. Should not all men, then, honor that Son even as
they honor that Father. Hear me in this! He who
understands my words and has faith in them may come to
know everlasting life, and need never die but may pass
from death into eternal life. For that Father gives to that
Son the power of independent decision and life itself, and
the vital power and authority to live of Himself. Do not be
confused by this: For the time must come when all those
that are in the tomb of flesh may hear His call. Those who
have striven well will raise up into life of the spirit, and
those who have not tried shall remain entrapped." When I
had finished the people would not follow the priests and
no hand was raised against me. Yet, they could not
understand the great initiate truths I taught them!

As Skakus had commanded me, I did. Slowly I tested
every one of the powers of my developed self. Each day,

if possible, I retired from the crush to concentrate upon my exercises, and to look into my heart upon the image of my Beloved. Even as the anger of the Jews was fanned, I used each opportunity to test my advancing powers. The healing of diseases was easy as long as I stayed in that advanced state of rapture. Leprosy was healed, blindness, many loathsome diseases, the consuming cough, and insanity.

But I had not yet tried to transmute and change *things*. I needed to practice the use of this power. Opportunity came on two occasions, and these I will relate. It chanced that a great number of sweet folk followed me over the sea of Tiberias at the time of the Passover. It was not fitting that they should miss this feast of the Jews, so I called John and Philip and asked them where food could be bought for that multitude. Philip was astonished, saying that a small fortune would not buy even enough bread for each of that multitude to have a crumb. Andrew said that a lad had five loaves of barley-bread and two small fishes, but that was all the food among that multitude.

Then I decided to make my first attempt at transmutation of material. I caused the gathering to sit down and to be silent, as if in prayer, and to breathe in rhythm with me. Then I placed the loaves and fishes upon a raised stone, as upon an altar, but in plain sight of all. Then I entered into my sacred exercises, passed through the Ocean of Peace, trod the Pathway of Glory, and brought forth the Vital Soul. With the Animal Soul I instilled energy into every tiny particle, each individual atom. Then with Vital Soul and pristine will I caused these to recreate themselves on the creative impulse from each cell of my body.

The disciples gave loaves and fishes to every person present, and there lacked one for me. For each initiate is taught that he must never profit of himself from the use of any of the divine powers, not even so much as a morsel. When they were much disturbed that I fasted so long I assured them, "I have foods and strengths you cannot yet dream of, but which, with time, you may also have."

When the feast was over I suggested that they gather up all the scraps, and was greatly pleased that there were seven half-bushel baskets of these!

As night came on apace we all went toward the shore of the Sea and were to return toward Capernaum. I tarried behind that I might commune with my Beloved. Before I reached the shore, the disciples had decided I had been taken over by another boat, had set forth and were a full two miles away. But a strong wind was blowing, and they could made little headway in the sea. With the crowd around me, and no boat, I decided to wait a while, then see if I could walk upon water as Skakus had shown me. On my first trial I wanted no public eyes. When it was dusk and many fires were lighted for those who must now stay the night, I walked to the water's edge, and did command my bodies to be light and the water to be firm, and then hurried across the almost three miles to the boat of the Zebedees.

The wind had been hard against them for hours, and with all their rowing they had gained little. As I came near they were greatly afraid, but I reassured them and they took me into the boat, and there was great praise upon their lips. They were tired from much rowing, and I decided to try to sublimate the wind and the sea to propel the boat. By concentration of the energies of the Vital Body I caused the water and wind to fall away in front of the boat, and build up behind. We came rapidly across the sea much to the amazement of those who found they could not dip in their oars for the boat moved too fast.

Those who had remained on the far shore roused early and came looking for me. When they found me not they became quite concerned and hurried to find boats with which to cross the sea, and they came to the house of Simon-Peter to find me. "How did you come here?" they demanded. "There were no boats, and you came not by land." They marveled much, and spoke of it many days – and this was the cause of my talk in the synagogue about the breath of life which caused many to cease from following after me, which shall be told later.

It chanced at an early time that I chose another six disciples that should follow me. They were Matthew,

Thomas of stubborn will, James of Alphaeus, Simon Zelotes, Judas of Alphases, and the other Judas who was a Judean whose surname was Ish Kehrioth, that is to say, a man of Kehrioth. Whereas they were to be the perpetuators of as much truth as I felt they and man could absorb, without harm to the Ancient Sacred Truth, I did teach them carefully. As is required with all initiate studies, I began with the simple and moral things. I taught them to be meek, honest, perservering, and not to worry poverty; to love their enemies, and to treat others in that manner they would find pleasing should they be so treated; to be merciful and never to judge; to give forth of their own selves that they should discharge the initiate requirements for refilling of the self.

Though they loved me well, they could not understand the true meaning of that which I taught them. They often failed in simple faith, or quarreled among themselves over the detail of what I had taught, forgetting in the letter of my teaching the greater spirit of Truth.

I taught them by simple stories, and by veiled stories of my own Initiation, trying to feed them a spark of the Divine. I showed them many things of great import, but they were simple folk with simple beliefs, and could not raise in concept to the sublime. I taught them about the Druids, and about the Tolmen, the sacred stone, the symbol of ever-enduring faith. I explained that even though the stone was hollow, as the center of faith is invisible, and seemed of little strength, yet upon this rock of faith I would build my church and all the forces of men or hell could not prevail against it.

Yet it chanced that I could teach them an important lesson in breaking with the hold of the orthodox. At this time the priests, scribes and Pharisees brought a woman who was bruised and bleeding, and who was forced sobbing to kneel before me. Each man had in his hand a stone with which to kill her. She had been taken in the very act of copulation, and she was married to a Jew.

They accused her of adultery, and then demanded: "Moses gave the Commandment that one should not commit adultery, and it is the law that such a one should be stoned. What say you to this ancient and perfect law?"

I knew they planned to stone me if they liked not my

345

answer. I read their auras, and in each there was visible the knowledge that they had committed adultery, or stolen, or lied, or cheated. I then bent over and made clear a patch of sand, and wrote thereon: "God gave to each man a creative urge, and men who control belief about that urge control other men."

They understood not the true meaning. So again I wrote: "God gave to each man the creative urge, shall men prohibit the use thereof by fiat?"

While they murmured to themselves, trying each to gather courage to cast his stone, I wrote again upon the earth. This time I wrote the name of each of the leaders there in a single column. They crowded around in amazement. Then I put as a heading in another column "The Sin Committed." By looking at their auras I wrote thereafter the sin, and in many cases of adultery I wrote even the name of the woman with whom they had copulated. Then I raised myself and said: "If you think this woman should be stoned, and all who have committed adultery, let him who is without sin cast the first stone." They glowered, but I bent and began to write the names of others and the sins, and the names of their partners in copulation, and they shrank away lest their secrets be made plain. When they had gone I asked the woman where her accusers were, and if no man had stayed to condemn her.

"No man, Sir," she whispered.

"Then go. You cannot truly sin in the eyes of God for acts of the flesh. Would God make into each man the law of procreation and then an even more important law denying its use? I could not believe in such an inconsistent God. But be circumspect. Go now, I do not condemn you."

My disciples learned a lesson in forgiveness that made them love one another more. I taught them out of the initiate's oath, to forgive all trespass even to the seventh time, including moral trespass — yet I taught them that even this is not the law of God and there is no punishment for failing!

Again I say, in truth, John-John gave me my following and my disciples. Even as my following grew apace he came often with his followers that they might hear me teach. Slowly they began to be estranged from him and cling to me. In honor to his faith, I commanded my disciples to baptize believers in water that they might have new life. Such a cleansing is also required before the first step into the initiations of Truth. But I remained away from such baptism, that his promise to his followers might be true: "He shall

346

baptize you with the spirit and with fire."

John-John seemed to desire to grow weaker as I grew stronger. One who was in his presence came to me with this story: When the disciples of John the Baptist complained that he was allowing me to become more popular than he, he smiled a sweet, sad smile and sighed a happy sigh. I knew that he had indeed kept the word pledged in our youth! He said to his accusers: "Can any man use a power unless it is given him to use? I have always told you what I told the officers of the *Sanhedrin*. I am not the Son of God: I came but to foretell his arriving. My joy is like that of the friend of the bridegroom who has not the bride but partakes in the happiness of the groom. That one I have come to foreshadow must increase, I must decrease. For I believe that he is above all on earth, but I am of the earth. In his very life he testifies to that which he has seen and heard. No man yet truly understands the testimony of his miracles – that God is eternal Truth. Surely the Father who loves His Son has given into his hands all powers. He who believes in the Son may come to know everlasting life."

John-John, as he became weaker in following, was troubled more and more by the Jews. At last Herod dared to have him cast into prison for declaring that it was not lawful for him to take as wife Herodias who had been married to Herod's brother. John the Baptist was popular, and Herod dared not harm him, but did keep him jailed in fair comfort. We did not worry, and he was content, for he felt that his work was almost finished, and sent me word. Yet he and my mother were troubled much by insidious Jews and by threatening priests, and were constantly bothered by relays of officials who were angry because they had said that I was the Son of God. Many times my mother was rushed away by "The Law", and suffered indignities at the hands of the priests. She was bullied and threatened, but she clung to her story and would not recant even under persuasive promise of sums of money. It has ever been the habit of "The Law", when entrenched, to abuse the people of less strength and less privilege and protect the strong and privileged.

347

Harassment of my mother became too much to bear!

But her very tribulations caused many common people to flock to me out of protest and sympathy for her. She and John-John in their love and devotion increased my following beyond measure. The pressures of the crowds came to be unbearable, for virtual multitudes were brought daily that they might be healed, and my beloved disciples were busy from early morning until late at night with baptisms and other work. Even those who were converted to believe were interested in what they could receive from the faith, not in the Sacred Way by *which they could become able to do this work.*

We set up a very simple working organization, and I trained the twelve that they might know how to carry on the work. Then we selected seventy of the followers, trained them to act as advance agents for our coming, and sent them by two and two into all the lands adjoining to announce our coming.

Many came, many saw, many believed – only a few wanted more than a small exciting miracle for their delight! We worked diligently to set up the basis of a faith that would break with orthodoxy, teach in the tabernacle of the heart of man, own no properties, train its adherents to serve their fellow-man and spread the faith without edifices and structures, and take nothing of personal benefit but sustenance and shelter. This was our simple work, and truly it foreshadowed no command to construct giant edifices, maintain separate political states, or become the sole religion of a nation.

We worked hard. Once in a rare while we would escape into a desert place that we might rest a while. Daily I tried to retire into my own heart, there to practice my Sacred Exercises, and to be with my Beloved. There was too little time for my own development, and I needed the spiritual influx which comes from physical rest and mental solitude. Therefore I took Simon-Peter, James, and John of Zebedee apart into a mountain, a spur of the mighty Mount Hermon, that we might let our hearts and our souls know each other. Many days we tarried there in brisk sunshine of that high place, and I worked hard and long so that my Vital Soul grew to obey my will and my body came to know the sweet repose of every cell.

Alone in my chambers in a small house that served an upland shepherd, I did my exercises and projected myself to my Beloved. Ah, sweet benediction of love, man for maid. Without it the cell-self becomes void of the juices of true understanding, without it the mind-self goes wildly in one direction like a sailing ship without a keel, without it the spirit becomes as brittle as an ancient scroll of Law. On this night I let my love on three levels envelop my Beloved, and great was my desire to tell her of my love. It seemed that I was in her presence and surrounded with the delight and beauty of her. Suddenly I was speaking to my love and she answered me, and we told our love again, again and again.

Glorious Day. Joy in God. I had spoken with my love. Skakus had told me that when I could speak in my externalized self the long waiting was almost over. Now time was running in my favor. I had reached the mid-point of the growth of my Spiritual Body, my *Sahu*, and my spirit was rooted in eternity. That morning I went early to a distant hillock, praying in my heart my gratitude to Almighty God for thus blessing His servant. Even as I prayed my three disciples sat a distance away in prayer and meditation, and suddenly I heard them cry aloud and opened my eyes.

There was a glow coming from within me, and it shone around me upon the drab rocks, causing them to sparkle like jewels. Every cell seemed to burn with a sweet fire, clearing my mind of strain and dross, and the inner fire cleaned my robe, making it whiter than the snows at mid-day sun. Even as I heard my disciples crying aloud about the shining beauty and whiteness, my own father and Skakus stood before me and we embraced, they in radiant spirit form, and I in shining flesh. Oh, Glorious Day!

Though they greeted me in greatness of spirit, they had come upon the business of the Order, and we conferred upon the general plan. They approved of my delay in trying to give the Secrets of the True Religion to mankind, but insisted that I should now no longer call myself merely Son of Man or a son of God, but should

349

boldly declare my full divinity and call myself the Son of God.

"You have done well. You have trained your people like true initiates. You have proved the value of the training. You have set a new religion in motion and all in seven hundred days. Boy, that is good!" Yet, even as he praised me, I felt that Skakus did not really love me. "Remember, you are to be the final judge on whether or not - or when - the Secret of the Ages shall be given to mankind. Remember the words that set the juggernaut into motion, but speak them only when you are sure *you* are ready."

Then my beloved father turned toward the three kneeling disciples and said in a loud voice, "This is my beloved son. Hear him!"

As suddenly as they had appeared they were gone. When I came down to the three, they exclaimed with great joy at the wondrous experience, and their own blessedness in being there to see it. Simon-Peter exclaimed joyfully, "Master, let us here build three tabernacles, one for Moses, one for Elijah, and one for you to commemorate this day of your meeting." I forbade them not and they built three small hollow altars of stone.

These sit in lonely splendor upon a hillock on the northwest shoulder of Mount Hermon and might even yet be found. Thus they may be known: They form a triangle of equal sides, pointing like an arrow to the rising sun, and each is a perfect cube. As we returned to our labors I charged the three that they should tell no one until I should have risen from death - and they were confused and astonished, and knew not whereof I spoke. Yet at that moment I told the world of my coming trial.

What a turmoil was that into which we returned. A huge crowd had gathered, for a man had brought a son who had epilepsy, and fell at times even in the fire, and foamed at the mouth - and my disciples could not bring him healing. I recognized the difficulty from the months of work in the Temples of Sleep, and healed him. My disciples were stricken in confidence for their failure to do so, and I said: "The only real cure for such a one is in fasting and prayer", and they took heart again. Soon afterwards I announced, "I must teach you well. I may be delivered into the trials of man and may be killed. I shall be raised again to eternal life."

They could not understand what I meant, and fell to disputing among themselves – not upon the religion which I taught, but upon who should be *first* among them if I truly died! At first I was furious with that divine fury, but then called them and said, "Let any man who wants to be first, be lowest of all, the servant of all." Yet, even a little while later John of Zebedee said, "We saw a man healing by the use of your name, but he was not one of us. We forbade him to do this because he did not follow our manner."

Again I was divinely furious, but I calmed myself. "Do not forbid him. No man who shall do a miracle in my name could possibly speak evil of me! If he is not against us, he is for us. Take all that is offered in my name, even a cup of water, and you shall find it good. Offend no one who believes in me, for it were better to hang a stone about your neck and leap into the sea. You are the salt and the savor of our faith, and each has been salted with the fire of spirit. If this good salt is lost in you with what will you be seasoned? Keep the divine salt of spirit, and do not contend one with the other."

Once again we went to Capernaum and I announced my divinity and my forthcoming trials in this manner: "I am the bread of life. He who comes to me shall never hunger, he that believes in me shall never thirst. You who are moved by the spirit of the Divine Father to come to me shall not be denied, for I am come to do the will of my Masters, not my own will. Yet of all that I have when I go through death I shall lose nothing but will raise this very body again on that day. You who see this and believe what I say shall also be able to enter into life everlasting and be raised up on that final day of life."

This was too much for them! Many who followed after me then went away. The Jews and even my disciples murmured. "Do not murmur. Hear my simple message. I am the son of Joseph and Mary whom you know, but the Almighty Lord has given me to know the inner spirit and all men who come to me shall be raised up on that final

351

day. Truly I say, he that understands and believes shall have everlasting life. Each man is the son of God. His very body is the bread upon which the living spirit feeds, and he who eats of this body and drinks of this spirit shall not die but have everlasting life. I come from my Masters and I will give my flesh as the bread of forgiveness. I will give it up for the life of the world."

To my disciples I later said, "It is the spirit that gives life and the flesh is its tomb. In what I teach you is the life of the spirit, for my words bring life indeed." And in my anger I challenged the twelve: "Will you now go away and leave me?" Big and gentle Simon-Peter said with a smile: "Master, where would we go? You have said you have the words which teach of eternal life." I could not help but see the humor of his words and laughed, and he added seriously. "We all believe, we *know*, you are the Son of the Living God." I could not argue but said, "I'm glad I have chosen you twelve, even if one of you is a devil!"

Thus it was, that my disciples were both blessing and plague to me. They loved me well and tolerated much, but they saw only the most orthodox interpretation of all I taught, and could not see the initiate Truth which I dared not teach until they were ready. Sometimes they were most understanding, and sometimes they were blinded by Jewish beliefs, such as in this saying: "The sins of the father shall be visited upon his sons even to the third generation". Thus they could not understand what caused a man to be blind from birth, but asked, "Did this man sin, or did his parents?"

I answered, "Sin is not visited upon man by a just God, neither is punishment. This man did not sin, nor did his parents. This man may be merely an opportunity for us to show the power of God in us. While I am of the world, I will be the light of the world and give sight to all blind men." I made a poltice of mud for his eyes, and told him to go and wash it away in the pool of Siloam, that is a healing water. He went and bathed his eyes and could see.

Yet I had foreknown that this man would be there, and born blind. For it was said that "since the beginning of the world no man has opened the eyes of him that was born without sight" - yet this I had done. When the man was brought before the Jews he told his story, even though his parents deserted him in fear of the Sanhedrin and the priests. The man insisted of me: "If this man came not of God, could he do such a thing?" But they cast him out as one born in the multitude of "sins" which they invented to control man.

The vicious betrayal and death of John-John, however, was the hardest blow to me. It came about in a strange way. Herod promised a daughter of Herodias, his unlawful wife, anything she might ask. For he was pleased with her dancing and was in a drunken feast with his officers. To please her mother the innocent child asked that the head of my gentle cousin be struck off and brought to her upon a silver platter. This vile thing was done, and I knew the pain of the slashing blade, and the severing of the mystic cord that had bound us since early youth. He who gave me credit for saving his life in our youth was ever the greatest of men. He rose not to sublime heights, for he denied his own divinity by believing that others were divine but not he. John-John had loved me well, but not enough to believe my teaching, that every man is capable of the divine and eternal life. I loved John-John, but he had fallen beneath the spell of mother's persuasion that I was the son of a God which alone held the mastery of divinity. No man should ever believe by any persuasion that he is not divine, or at least potentially so! John-John's death was the first signal to me that my time was running out. It was, I believe, the bitter memory of his death that delayed my own development and almost caused complete failure of my mission.

The Jews were slowly closing in upon me, and I had not yet proven my worth as an initiate. This, and my memories of John-John, came often to my conscious mind to annoy, and delay my own acceptance of perfect peace within so that I might externalize my spiritual bodies. I thought to myself, "If I cannot raise to God-level when alone with my thoughts, how can I raise to the highest level when surrounded with the noise and confusion of a

353

final initiation?"

The surly Jews ringed me as I taught on the Porch of Solomon in the Temple, and demanded, "If you are the Messiah, prove it!" I knew they had been sent by the priests to stone me. I did not know then- and did not come to know until the very last hours – what manner the final trial should take. I answered warily, "I proved it to you, but you would not accept. Now let the works I do prove that I do miracles in the Father's name. Yet you may never believe for you are not of my kind. I have given to those who follow me knowledge of how to attain eternal life that they may never die. Those who have known the contact of the Supreme cannot be dragged away from this sure knowledge of God, and the absolute knowledge that the Supreme God and the Internal Christ are one. Is it not written in Jewish law that God said 'You are gods'? To whom did he speak if not to those who accepted his scriptures? You say that these scriptures are all truth and cannot err. Then why would you stone one who believes and accepts that he is the Son of God?

"When I fail to do the work of the father, condemn. But if I do the works of God, believe in them even if you condemn me. For does not such work merely show that God is within the son?"

They were confused and I slipped away. But the danger was great and I was not yet ready, so we went back to the Jordan. We came to stay near the place where John-John had baptized me, and my memories lay heavy in my heart, and I began to know the terrible inner agony of one who doubts and dreads.

When word came that my friend from youth, Lazarus of Bethany, was ill, I did not rise up and go to aid him. His elder sister was Martha, and his younger sister Mary – named after my own mother and it was at their home we often stayed. In my turmoil and doubt I said to my disciples, "Our friend is not sick unto death. His sickness is for the glory of God that we may prove our powers." I could not go, excusing myself with the idea that the fury of the Jews had not lessened sufficiently.

We were brought news that Lazarus was dead, and I was ashamed of my failure and said, "Our friend merely sleeps, but we must go and waken him."

Yet the disciples did not understand that I spoke the initiate mind which sets into motion the thing to be done by visualizing it as finished. When they persisted I said, "Lazarus does not sleep in fact, but in figure. Lazarus is not dead. Let us go to him immediately."

Thomas Didymus, who ever doubted and challenged, rose and said "All of us should go with the Master, for he is going to his death!"

This but confirmed my own conviction that the sands of time were running out faster than the hours of preparation.

But I could not pull back now, I could not admit failure to my Brothers. I could not throw away the time-table of the ages! I resolved to hurry with my own development, to force my will to complete attentiveness and full power. When Martha came I could assure her that God grants whatever is asked of Him, and that the Son of God was in truth the resurrection and the life – and both she and I believed at that moment. When Mary came and I bethought myself of my own mother and her years of travail, I again became heavy in inward spirit and groaned with the pain of doubt and despair. I wept.

The sense of duty pulled me on, and I came quickly to the tomb. There I brought myself to the state of inner peace and tested my ability to transmute flesh from death to life – even as Skakus had directed me to do, I practiced. The Violet Soul churned the flesh. The Ruby Soul gave strength, the Human Soul gave breath, and the Vital Soul, pushed with all the power of pristine will, gave life and power. The hillside echoed with my command as I spoke the creative words. Lazarus came forth from the tomb, hobbling against the grave clothes, bound and masked.

Great was the joy as he was unloosed and found to be well and naught but hungry. Great was my inner joy, for I had now proved that I could sublimate and control the flesh of others. I had arrived at the level of the Order of Melchizadek. But I also feared, for the sands ran swiftly, and the higher Order was not yet mine!

Another reason I could not withdraw now: The

religion that had been built by my efforts had a wide following, and the Jews wished to crush that upsurge of freedom in man. It came to us from one of the scribes that the priests had met and decided that I must die, for the miracles I performed were drawing men from Jewry and threatened the faith.

It was *Caiphas*, the high priest of that year, who urged my death thus with cunning: "If we destroy not him he will destroy us. Is it not more expedient that this one man die than that we lose all who flock to his teaching? If he continues our faith must perish. I shall prepare the people to accept his death. I will prophecy that he shall die for the nation. This supports his contention. I will go even further and prophecy that he will by his death gather together in one body all the children of God, from all corners of the earth. Then even his own followers could not blame us for helping him to such a destiny!"

In my turmoil and doubt I chanced to stop under a fig tree on the Bethany road, and would have eaten of its fruits but there were none. It became the symbol of myself, a tree barren of fruit. As I was to move away I remembered that Skakus had said that the creative fiat came shortly after the destructive fiat – and I turned back and commanded that the tree should be destroyed. As I passed that place again, I noted that the tree was dead and withered in less than six hours, and both joy and dread entered into my being. Joy that I was progressing toward my development, dread lest it not come in time.

The Jews set watch upon the Temple grounds, swearing to catch me. If I showed not courage enough to face them, my following would desert me. I knew I could not turn back. The time of the Feast of Passover was coming apace and it was a time of great danger to me. Yet I must go into the Temple and teach. There was another reason why I had to go. I no longer wanted to live without my Beloved. My desire for her had grown so great that I preferred death and failure to being kept longer from her.

This overwhelming desire was brought home to me at

the home of Lazarus, by the presence of Mary. Much fame had attained to Lazarus because he was raised from the dead, and many people came to see him. This marked him for death by the priests, for he spread my fame. I went to see him to persuade him to tell no one further. When we were at dinner I noticed little Mary came with a jar of spiced ointment and sat at my feet. She was darker than my Beloved, yet she resembled her in many ways, and I knew my heart would break for longing unless I went soon to my Beloved. I knew then that I would go into the trial.

Someone protested that the use of so much ointment was a waste, I replied, "The poor you have with you always, but I will not be here long. She has saved this against the day of my burying!"

Yes. I knew then I must and would go up, and this was but six days before the Feast of Passover!

Many were the things that rushed me on – yet I had not spoken the words to release the juggernaut.

So much to do, and so little time. Daily I worked. Nightly I worked. Every second I worked that I might raise my complete Spiritual Body and speak the creative word. Time flew but my cells were so logged with heaviness and doubt that even my mind would not soar. On the day I left Bethany, many ran before us and threw flowers. As I came near to Jerusalem, many met us bearing palm branches, singing praises, and crying "Praise God. Blessed be the King of Israel who comes in the name of the Lord."

News of the miracle of the raising of the dead ran like a wildfire before me in the crowds which were gathering in Jerusalem.

18

THE LAST DAYS

So much to teach, so little time! The love I bore for my disciples lay like a tight band around my heart. Soon they would be left to carry on the religion I had founded, which only touched the garment of Truth. They would soon have need for sure knowledge, the divine influx. They were so willing, but they could not even remotely conceive that a greater truth lay behind the primary truths I taught them. Behind all lay the Eternal Truth, larger and more beautiful than all the churchified religions upon the face of the earth – even mine; and the immutable law that all men to know God must know Him directly and in their own person. Because even those who loved me could not conceive of the great truths of the initiate Religion, I could only teach them little parts, by example. We went into the Temple and there I taught the crowds who had come to worship, and many worshipped me. Tuesday, Wednesday and Thursday of that rushing week I spent trying to teach my own disciples how to face the coming storm and carry on my religion.

The Jews came tempting to see if I would deny tribute to the Romans. I taught: that which belongs to society must be rendered unto society, and that which belongs to God must be rendered unto God. Those who believed that the grave was the eternal end of man came with a piteous question about whose wife a woman would be in heaven if she had been in turn the wife to seven brothers and I taught that in heaven there will be only those qualified as angels – for how could I say that in the eternal form of spirit man sought after the total good, not personal pleasure? When the disciples admired the building and stones of the Temple, I suddenly saw into the distant future. The Temple would not endure. I showed them then the foolishness of putting Truth into a box. Truly, religion can never be put into edifices and buildings. No box of stone and glass could ever contain even my teachings and certainly not Eternal Truth. I showed them the coming trials and tribulations and forewarned them of the coming persecution. False priests and false people would try to stamp out my religion. I tried to bind them to my faith, to abide in my teachings and not return to Jewry. I tried to raise them from the belief that they were servants unto me to realize that they were equal to me – but this they could not then understand. I said to them, "I have taught you these things that my joy may be yours and remain. This is my commandment, Love one another as I have loved you. Remember it is said that man has no love greater than this: he will lay down his life for his friend. You are of my belief because I have chosen you. You are not of the world, and therefore the people will hate you for they will not understand you. To help in your travail even when I am gone, I will send a Comforter to you who is of the Divine Self, to serve you in the Spirit. I have many things to say and teach you, but the world could not understand them now. Yet when the Truth is ready and the hearts of men prepared, the Spirit shall show the magnificence of the True Religion. Then all things that I have done and known shall be done and known by every man, for my skills shall be shown to them."

Yet, even though the last Thursday was almost gone, and we sat at meat – our own Paschal Lamb – I knew not what was truly to happen. For three days I had been trying to see clearly, and could see a little. The sacrifices at the Temple were moved ahead an hour to make time for the Paschal Feast. I sent two of my disciples into the city to find a certain man which I had foreseen carrying upon his head a pitcher of water. I know not

359

why the vision came, or why I *knew* that man would provide a guest chamber in which to eat the Passover with my disciples. I did *know* that he had a large upper room, ready and furnished, and that it was there we should enjoy our last supper in fellowship. In my doubt and fear I tested the arrangements of the Council. I said to them as we sat at table: "Surely one of you will soon betray me."

I read sorrow and concern in the eyes of eleven of the disciples. In the eyes of one I saw the brighter look of love and duty. Judas Ish Kherioth was the one. Yet in no physical way did he betray himself. Why had I not suspected? Judas, the Judean, the man from Kherioth. Surely he must have been the man of the Brotherhood from the beginning. Surely he must have known! He had been with me three years, and in all those days – despite my teaching – he had never by any recognizable act, word, or thought betrayed his greater knowledge, or his deeper love. How disciplined he must have been, and how at that moment I loved him for his selfless discipline, his service in my cause, his service to the Brotherhood. Judas was surely a true initiate, wiser and more learned than the others, loving me doubly for the work we did together, but ever obedient to the greater good. Judas Ish Kherioth was the truest of all my disciples and surely his name should rank high in history!

So little time, so much to do! We sat at our last supper, but I had not yet given to my religion a symbol of turning man into God. I remembered the ancient ritual of the *Caribe*. They ate, drank and inhaled the godhood. I wanted such a eucharist of special meaning for my own remembrance. I took up the unleavened bread which had been broken once and set aside as the meal began, and broke it into small pieces. "Take and eat. This is the body of the Inner God." I took up the cup which was passed three times at the meal, and filled it and handed it to the disciples. "Drink deep. This is the blood of the Inner God!" There was no incense but the fragrance of roses, but I had built the ancient *Caribe* practice into my religion. In that room only one understood that I built symbols of the mind to help reach the Inner God. My religion was now established, with tenets, ritual, and procedure. I knew that I had woven into it as much of the Eternal Truth as the minds of men could then bear, and though that part was small it would surely endure against all time. Man cannot touch the garment of knowledge or come to know Truth even dimly but that he is eventually clothed and cloaked in Truth. Even with this small start the vine of Truth would sprout and grow and someday the minds of men would be ready for the return of True Religion. One thing yet I needed to teach and that was humility. This I did by girding myself with a cloth and washing their feet, one after another.

Now I had done all that time would allow. My job was not finished, but the hours were flown. Truly I say to you that I was ready, for so greatly did I long for my Beloved that I would hurry myself to death or to her arms! I was ready to die, but not ready to succeed in my assignment. Something prompted me and I raised my voice and said the code, "Let that which you are to do be done quickly!" Even before the lamb was finished, even before the washing of hands after the feast, the Brother from Kherioth left the chamber. I knew that the juggernaut was now to roll, and no man could stay its power.

Even before the meal had ended my inner doubt and terror assailed me so hard that I almost collapsed under the burden. We sang praises to God, and left the guestchamber. Heavy were my thoughts and my steps, for I was not ready and time had run out! We went west beyond the brook *Kitron*, named for the blackness of its wet rocks, turned left for a thousand paces. At a special point we stopped to be certain that no one followed upon the roadway, for the Jews were aroused and could be vile. We then turned right into a narrow path and made our way to the garden of a grape vineyard where there were vats, jars, and a small wine press. For this reason it was called by us *Gethsemane*. Fearing lest we be caught unwary, I left eight at the gate of the garden, and retired with Simon-Peter, James, and John of Zebedee to a far corner of the garden which was beyond the vats. But even as we walked less than thirty paces, the bitter ache of my soul stole my strength and I felt heavy, coarse and mean.

With this realization my breath came in stark terror. I recognized the real cause of my doubt, fear, heaviness and attitude of defeat. I knew now why my heart was craven, my cells weeping, and my soul aching. I was in the dreadful grip of the Deep Night of Despair. It rode like a devil upon my spirit. I grabbed my friends in terror, and collapsed. They clung to me in amazement and I whispered dully, "My spirit is in the clutch of sorrow and death. Wait here and pray for me."

Sobbing, I stumbled forward and fell upon the ground. Truly I had betrayed the order. I had ignored my orders, I had destroyed the Great Cabal. Skakus had prepared me, but I had ignored his words in the press of time and the teaching. For an hour I alternately wept and prayed. For an hour I tried in mounting desperation to externalize my spirit self. At last in hopeless defeat I cried to the starry night, "Oh, God, to You all things are possible. Stay this cup of initiation if it be Your will!"

In my aimlessness I came back to find the three dozing, and my terror and loneliness leaped to anger. Out of self pity, not righteousness, I upbraided them, "Asleep? Can't you stay awake one hour? Wake up, and pray, do not yield to the temptation to sleep. Pray for me! Oh, my spirit is strong but my flesh is weak!"

Weeping to myself I went again to attempt to enter into my exercises, my meditations, my prayers - and externalize my spirit self. But my cells were grapples and would not let my spirit go. I tried ever harder, and as the moments sped by the terror mounted within my dark brain. In search of sympathy and companionship I went again to my friends, but they were stupified by the hour of waiting and dozed even as they manfully fought sleep. I turned away in sorrow and went again to pray and weep for self-pity.

Suddenly I seemed to hear the rasping voice of Skakus. "No one is a Master unless he acts the part!"

Truly I had not acted the part of the Master. I had turned to my followers for human comfort. How patiently they waited, and how great was my injustice to them. They did not know, not truly, that I faced an unknown

362

and terrible ordeal. The days had been long, the work heavy and they were rightfully exhausted in body and mind. They looked with heavy eyes and waited in patient love. I must be the Master. I must not turn to them for solace, but must accept my fate.

Again I prayed, asking that the Cup of Initiation be withheld yet a while, The answer to my prayer came in the faint shouts of voices already upon the path leading from the road to the garden. I tried desperately to externalize myself but could not and let go the fierce determination. For I remembered that the plan of the Great Cabal was so clever that even in failure of my greater goal I should partly succeed. Even as the voices drew closer I felt better, for I had overcome somewhat the overwhelming sense of onrushing failure.

Clearly now I could hear the voices of the party of guards from the Roman Garrison Antonia mixed with Jews from the Constabulary of the Temple. I could guess that they had been sent by the High Priest to seek me out. The sands ran fast indeed, and the time was now come. I rose from the ground somewhat refreshed. In the closing of issues, in the removal of doubt comes comfort and courage. That which is known is never as bad as that which can be imagined. I went back to my beloved friends in that tranquility of spirit that comes with action.

"Sleep on, my beloved friends. Take your rest now. The hour is at hand when I shall be delivered into the hands of false priests." Even as I spoke the voices grew so loud that all the disciples jumped up in concern, and some slipped out of the gate into the night. Before we could reach the gate a great band came into the garden, carrying search-lanterns upon high sticks. The Jewish Constabulary were armed with staves. The Roman guards carried swords. They blocked our path and came swiftly around us. Judas Ish Kherioth came forward with that indefinable look of love which supports duty. He saluted me and then embraced me.

Ah, that kiss! He made it upon all the secret points of love in the manner of the Brotherhood. It was a kiss of love, a moment of uplifting joy. I felt the tears of his love upon his dark cheek, and looked deep into his brown eyes. There I saw the agony of love overshadowed by the greater love of duty, and I knew the glory of selfless love. Yet I wanted physical proof and gently asked, "Do you deliver me up with this kiss?" He did not admit to me that he had done his assignment, but I *knew*. I took some heart in knowing that the Brotherhood was aware of all. They knew also that the Final Initiation was about to begin. For a second more he held me, then turned away and was gone – this dedicated, silent, loving soldier in the army of God.

It gave me even more courage to know that I was not alone in the fight for the freedom of the minds, hearts and souls of men. I was not alone, for I was but the leader of the charge. I quieted my angry and frightened disciples who would have defended me, and dispersed them lest they be harmed by the angry mob. I wanted them to live for my sake.

It was an hour past midnight when I was taken, and delivered to the Chief Priests and the *Sanhedrin* which had been called into session. My cell self was in agony as I was tried. Tried? Is it a trial when false witness comes after false witness under oath, each so false that he makes lies of the other's testimony?

When at last the travesty was played until even the Elders were smiling, the Chief Priest arose and came pompously and stood before me. He drew himself up to the greatest height possible with such a fat belly and short legs and he cried: "I abjure you by the power of the Living God. Say whether or not you are the Son of God."

What a mockery he made of the powers of Eternal Truth when used by a true initiate! He could not have compelled a flea and I almost laughed, as indeed the Elders and Scribes did behind their hands. But I answered, "You have a saying which goes: Hereafter you shall see the Son of Man sitting at the right hand of Eternal Power, and carried by the clouds of heaven."

Was it a trial? Even at that he rent his tunic, for this was the custom of those who heard blasphemy, and he cried out in sanctimonious pity that I had even by these words been witness to my own blasphemy. On this the assembled Priests and Elders did solemnly vote that I was guilty of blasphemy, for which I should die. They then spat upon me, blinded me with a scarf and struck me, laughingly demanding that I prophecy who would strike me next.

In every evil there may be good. The very cruelty reminded me of the initiation upon the *Britannin*, and a faint hope began to grow in my heart. Had I not been prepared for this surpassing well? Yet I knew not what manner my death might take and could only wait. Short, short were the hours, for I tried to make the Sacred Exercises burn into the black ashes of my cell self even as they reviled me and cursed me.

By early morn, six hours after I was taken, I was delivered to the governor of Judea, one Pontius Pilate. But the Jewish leaders would not enter the building of his Hall of Justice, for it was a Gentile building, and would, they thought, defile them and make them impure for the feast days ahead. Pontius Pilate ordered the court removed to a raised pavement in front of the steps upon which he held state functions. He looked down upon me from the dais of marble, gold, and red carpet and asked, "Do you claim to be the King of the Jews?"

I looked up in surprise, and almost smiled. For Pontius Pilate was Romulo of the **Britannin!** Yet I knew that he would not help me, for he was one of the Brotherhood, part of the Great Cabal. "You brought the subject up," I evaded, and he almost smiled.

But the Priests and Elders crowded about to accuse me of ridiculous things that needed no defense. Defense would have been useless, anyway. Who could have defended himself against such varied, such false, such stupid charges? Pilate knew that I would offer no defense, but in Brotherly jest he turned to me and said: "You do not answer? Look at the charges brought against you!"

I thanked him deep in my heart, for there was a mild surge against the Deep Night's grip upon my soul, and for a moment I dared hope. But this hope was not to live long.

It was the custom of the times for the governor to release to the common people a prisoner. Even as we talked the groups began to arrive from all over the city and standing outside the palace they cried aloud for the release of their annual prisoner. Pilate went upon the balcony and asked them, "Shall I release the King of the Jews to you?"

But as one voice they thundered back, "Give us Barabbas! Give us Barabbas!"

"What shall I do with the King of the Jews?"

The words cut hope from me and plunged me deeper into the dreadful Night of Despair. "Crucify him."

Crucifixion was the lowest and meanest of all deaths, used for the foulest criminals. Even Pilate was startled and he called to them. "Why? What vile thing has he done?"

But they thundered back, "Crucify. Crucify. Crucify!"

In my dulled brain I hoped for a day or two. I was not prepared for the fierce onslaught of events and time. I was scourged with the lash upon the steps of the palace. Exhausted with pain I was delivered to the Praetorium Guard. There the soldiers mocked and reviled me and robed me in purple with a crown of rose-bush thorns. Then they marched about me chanting "Hail the King of the Jews". Then in mock worship they knelt before me, and spat into my face. It was great sport to them, though I have enjoyed other initiations somewhat more.

Yet this sport was cut short and thrown into rough confusion by a Centurion who yelled, "Crucify him *now*. That's an order!"

It was not yet twelve hours since I spoke the code words! Time moved too swiftly, events staggered me, punishments exhausted me, and my own stubborn, aching cell self defied my mind and my will. It was all too desperately swift.

I was pushed out of the hall, and a cross was slammed down upon me. I was too exhausted to bear the burden and fell upon the stones of the street. As I lay gasping, the cells of my brain dark as night, I heard the banter of soldiers, and then the usually quiet voice of Nicodemo. He was shouting that he was Simon a Syrian and should not be commandeered by the Roman guard. He was forced to lift up my cross, and as we moved through the streets he whispered to me: "I told you once I would someday bear your cross for you."

Oh, how I loved him then. Oh, how I loved my

Brothers then. How the pain of failing them shot through me, through every cell, through every pore of my skin – like a thousand arrows. My Brother carried my cross and supported my weak steps up the steep slopes of Golgotha. Yet when he was forced away by the Roman guards the grip of the Deep Night upon me returned with terrible force.

Truly I say to you, let no man believe the lash, the thorns, or the nails caused me pain. I knew no pain from these. The only pain I knew was the unendurable agony of my Deep Night of Despair. It made a millstone of each cell, gave the awful power to each cell to rebel and riot against reason, and tear itself from its fellows in searing blackness. I did not feel the physical nails of the cross, but I suffered a thousand deaths of defeat by the false cells of my own body! The nail driving through my right hand – in keeping with the custom of impaling the right hand first – struck a small glow in the utter blackness of my heart. The nail driving through my left hand struck a small glow in my mind. I was then raised aloft. The nail driving through my feet upon the foot-stop struck a small glow in my blood. I could hear the sounds of weeping, but could not see, for my eyes were dark with the millstones of death.

I do not know what happened during that first hour, but it seemed that two others were crucified near me, and one spoke in my behalf. Later I came to know that a sign was put up over me saying, "Jesu of Nazar, King of the Jews." Many who were curious stopped upon the Roman road which ran nearby and those who could read said the words aloud to their companions. Many stood upon the top of the knoll to rail and laugh.

Later came the triumphant Jews, the false priests and the scribes. They mocked me and challenged me to take myself down from the cross, or heal myself as I had healed others.

Some of my followers came to cry aloud and beseech me to descend from the cross that they might believe in me and accept my teachings. I tried with all my strength to externalize, but the hold of my black cells was greater than the iron nails. Yet none of this do I recall perfectly but as if I had seen it through reflections in a muddied pond. Much later I seemed to have rested, to have recovered from the exhaustion of the lash, and my mind began to work slowly - as a cold worm works in frozen earth!

In the third hour I began to try to recall how I had really come to this end. Why? Why? Why? Had I not done all - even more than anyone else? I loved my family well, but had I not given them up willingly for the greater world? I loved each of my Masters, but had I not given them up willingly to advance on the path? I loved each of my disciples, but had I not given them up that I might serve the Brotherhood? I loved life, but had I not given it up for the good of all, as the Lamb of Sacrifice, to atone for the sins of the world? Had I not given up all?

Suddenly my reason thundered "No!"

I was not here to atone for the sins of the world. I was here to fulfill my initiate destiny. If I became a symbol of atonement for *sins*, I forged a link in the chain upon the captive minds of all who believed.

No, no, no! I had not given up all! Slowly thoughts began to writhe in my dark brain, like serpents in black ice, creeping lowly, one by one. No, I had not given up all!

Had I ever given up my secret pride in my ability to learn swiftly? No! In my initiate oath I had solemnly promised to give up pride in all skills, for they came not of man but of God. With a tortured sigh I gave up that lingering, subtle emotion. The glow grew in my brain to a smothered flame on soggy wood - but with promise.

Had I given up my pure hatred for the stupidity of the Jews? True, I had learned not to hate them - but still I held onto the rancor against their endless stupidity as a drowning man clutches even a stone. With a twist of will I let go that stone. The glow in my heart licked at the black cells there.

Had I given up my pure hope to achieve for the Brotherhood? No! For did I not now - in this instant - strive for the high praise? Was it not more for the praise of man than the service of God I sought, truly, in the secret recesses of my heart? Again I breathed away the insidious and pleasing serpent from my flesh, and my mind began to burn away its blackness with a slow and churlish flame.

Had I given up my resentment toward those who tortured me, those who even now taunted me? No! Even toward the Chief Priests, scribes and their cohorts who came to taunt me in my failure, I held a resentment! In my initiate oath I had promised to forgive all things even unto seven times. I heard the sound of my voice and the words, "Father, forgive them for they know not what they do." The flame in my heart became fitful and rebellious, but growing.

Had I given up my love of pity for failure? No! For I still mentally justified my failure because of the adverse events, the crushing avalanche of time. But why, if I was a Master, had I not clearly foreseen this - why had I not been prepared? Had not Skakus warned me? Had not the signs been clear? Had not the Deep Night even announced itself at Capernaum, while yet I had time to see and to escape? No, it was not the fault of an avalanche of time. Had I not sworn in my initiate oath that I would not indulge in the luxury of self-pity? With a mighty twist of my will I set my mind aright, and the flame in my blood grew yet more.

Had I given up my self-will to become a Master? Was not my purpose to master myself, that I might be the Master of all men? In my initiate oath I had promised never under any circumstance to control the mind of man. With a great sigh I gave up even my desire to become the Master of men. A flame licked cherry-red in the black cells of my brain.

Had I given up my desire to bring a new and different religion to all mankind? No! In my initiate oath, had I not promised never under any conditions to undermine the faith or mind-set of any man in his own beliefs until he was ready to give up the old and accept the better? Was the world ready for the new and better religion? No! For man could never be free until the sciences of Egypt's Osiris were married with the splendor-in-lowliness of China's *Tao*, until the philosophy of Aristotle was wedded to the beliefs and doctrines of

Plato. With a great effort I gave up my long cherished dream, and I placed the future of man in the hands of God. For man would *in his time* throw off the yoke of the false beliefs, unloose the chains of slavery upon his mind and being, and rise up to knowingly become as God upon earth. I could but make known the goal – I could only fight the good fight – and I could not even point the path. With this realization a slender flame leaped in the cells of my blood and ran a needle of warmth into every tissue.

Had I given up the delight of dependence upon my Masters? No! Had they not all told me that they taught me only that I in my turn might teach beyond their knowledge? In my initiate oath had I not promised to build upon the skills of those who went before until I was at last skilled and worthy to walk as God upon earth? Had I done so, truly? Had I reached beyond my Masters? With a twist of will I gave up my dependence upon all men and stood alone under the banner of heaven.

Truly, had I given up all men? Had I given up my father? Had I given up my beloved *Mherikhu*? Had I given up my own self? No. Yet had I not promised in my initiate oath to forsake all others and cling only unto God? Had I given up my beloved father? No! Yet I had promised in my initiate oath that I would forgo all family, knowing eternal beauty as my sister, the world as my brother, creative energy as my mother and the universe as my father. My brothers, my sister – even my mother – in truth I had given up years ago. But not my father! I saw that he was not my father, he was the universal father. Suddenly I knew that the three modes of virgin birth were only one. My mother had been right all her days, for I was the son of the Eternal God. What matter it that my father qualified the energy for the use of man...I was and would ever be the direct Son of God.

Even as I thought upon this the flames in my heart, brain and blood began to leap, to glimmer, to glow. There came through my body a stinging warmth. And I began to feel! I could feel! I could feel the blessed nails in my hands and feet, I could feel the crying ache of the muscles in my legs, the thirst of my lungs for air, the cords binding my legs and arms, the tears upon my cheeks. Oh, how lovely to feel!

I could feel the great love I now had for my sweet mother. I opened my eyes against the millstones of death and looked for her. I knew she would be near. My beautiful mother, my paternal aunt Mary, who was wife to Cleophas, and Mary Magdalena stood near the cross. Two were weeping.

But my mother looked proudly upon me, with the joy she would have looked upon a conquering king. How, in the years, could I have been confused with her love? Why did I not see that she loved me all the while – not the potential me, but the real me which was there even then because she willed it and knew it? Had not her love been the strongest of all and borne her up to make her great beyond women? What strength was required to believe that she bore the Son of God, yet live with him as nearly human? What goddess could have done more, what mother on earth could have done half as much? I did not pity her now. Not for her suffering, not for her downthrust hopes, not for her years of efforts – no. I think I envied her then, for had not hers been the better part? Had she not known and experienced the blessings of divinity even before they were given to her? Was not her faith and her love an example to all men for all time?

I smiled down upon her with the old, boyish joy and her smile came back with no sign but pride and love. Here was beauty undiminished, here was courage undaunted, here was *knowing* which made me God. Hers was the gay smile I loved so well, firm and sweet, fresh as dawn. In all the years I had not loved her enough! In those years when I had given her up, she never had given me up, but was constant in her knowledge and her delight. Hers was the truest courage, hers was the larger blessing, let hers be the sweetest rest!

John of Zebedee stood near her, looking up at me with that love he ever bore me. "Mother! Look and behold your son!" My beautiful mother took his hand for he was till now the son of her sister, Salome. "John! Look and behold your mother!" His arm stole about her shoulders and they stood as mother and son looking upon me with hearts undaunted.

371

Thus it was with love for both that I gave up my beloved father and my beautiful mother. They served me devotedly, each in his own way. Thus did I give them up to time and to the world. In a flash of insight I saw them placed in the future. My mother was the symbol of kindly motherhood, the idol of men, the example for women. Yet in a far time I saw my father rise in the esteem of man, and with it the rise of Eternal Truth. In those far off, hallowed days, he was the idol of all men who sought Truth, the Symbol of the initiate. I was not disappointed that my mother would be raised quickly and that my father, Joseph of Nazar, the Master of Ages, would be forgotten even in my own religion until Initiate Truth came at last fully to all men and science and love met and wedded.

Had I given up my Beloved? No! Yet even as I bethought myself of my darling, the desire for her was like the pull of a herd of stampeding elephants. My heart raced with the delight I knew in her. Could I ever give her up? Was she not more than honor, more than fame, more than family, more than life, more than Godhood? Was she not all beauty, all graciousness, all......

Suddenly the raucous voice of Skakus cut into my memory and I was reminded that he had said that love might cause me to die. He had given up all but love for the youth of Athens...yet he had gone through death! Even as I thought upon this my Beloved seemed to run from my mind, my heart, my blood and I cried aloud, "My God! My God! Why have *you* forsaken me!" I do not even now believe I could otherwise have let her go. But with a bitter sigh I let go even my Beloved.

The flames seared through me with an intensity that burned me. The centers of my cells were aflame! The air around me was a living flame! The world was a radiant flame! The flame of my heart rose in a green sun and engulfed the world. The energy of the world avalanched into my brain. The glory and strength returned to me, and peace flooded through my blood. All of my emotions were refined in the furnace of these flames, and they were but ashes until even the ashes were absorbed in the flame.

"I thirst!" The words came to my ears and a moment later the touch of sour wine upon my lips startled me and I lost the glorious flame. But I knew the willing soldier could not have understood that he did me no service at that moment to serve my physical needs.

The flame was gone, and I was conscious of the cross. But there seemed to be no weight upon the nails, no real pain, only a blessed lethargy. And into this came two thoughts. No longer were they for myself, for I was now grown selfless. For all men I wanted to leave a symbol that the secret places of religion, behind the veils and curtains, should no longer be considered forbidden to all men, nor sacred and holy, nor the place where one man could atone for the sins of mankind. I wanted to attain to the highest initiation – not for the pride of self – but that it might be a sign and symbol to all men that what I had done they also could do and more also – even more. I wanted to leave that great symbol that all men may know God directly, and that all men may rise by work and skill to become *Consciously* God.

I reached outward then with every effort of mind and will, and gathered from the world the essence of strength. As the mighty energy came into me, the earth around grew darker, and the sun ceased to shine through the black air. It seemed that I was sapping the strength and light from the air, and that the day became for the world a Deep Night of Despair. It was dark at midafternoon and there was a deadness in the air that made men afraid and birds to fall in midflight. But I continued to draw in the vital power, until the very earth grew weak and began to tremble, to cry with pain and rend itself in its torture.

When I was filled beyond holding with the strength and light, the very life of nature, I fixed my mind upon the giant curtain in the Temple – that curtain which the Jews boasted it took three hundred men to move. And I fixed my mind upon the practice of the Jews – but as the symbol of the practice of men everywhere – to forbid all men to enter save one, and to send him beyond that veil once a year to incense the "Holy of Holies" and thus atone

373

for sin. I willed that this practice be forever removed, that all men might know God directly, and be set free of the chains of "sins" that are invented even faster than they can be committed.

Suddenly the power leaped from my head in a blinding flash of lightning more brilliant than the sun. It struck the curtain and ripped it and tore it, and shoved it aside until it hung in two shreds against each side of the doorway. The inner sanctuary was open, the body of God could no longer be hidden from man - either as a symbol or as a fact. My first truly God-like wish had been granted.

For a moment I rested, hearing the frightened cries of those who had come back to mock me, hearing the curses of the soldiers. Then slowly I began again to absorb the power of the universe and to qualify it to do the bidding of my mind and my will. I turned then to my Beloved. In my mind and heart I fashioned an image. This lovely image was made by the marriage of the picture of my Beloved which was in all my cells with a picture of myself as I had always *wanted* to be. *Mherikhu* became the *Sita* of the cavern, the symbol of motherhood throughout the universe. *Mherikhu* became the Spirit Mother of all creation. When my mental image was complete I flung it across the world with all the force of my being.

Suddenly I left the cross. I was in the arms of my beloved *Mherikhu*, in a heaven of welcome, of merging, mingling, flowing together into a wedding of wills, delights, breaths, cells, souls, bodies and spirits. We were not separate nor could ever be, but were a single unit larger than the world, more beautiful than the Godhood, more wonderful than all life. A million voices spoke the Word, the creative fiat, and every cell of my eternal bodies married those of my Beloved. The Word spoken became flesh, and we endowed it with our energies, our souls, our spirits. In the great mystery of creation they intermingled until the compression of time and space exploded into a joy meant for all eternity.

My Beloved looked upon me with sweet laughter and great love. I looked upon her with pure and perfect understanding - for I knew at last that I had not spoken falsely when I said that marriages made in heaven no man could put assunder. For we were wedded for all eternity – even in the spirit.

Suddenly all the Temples of Secret Egypt rang their great bells, and spirit messengers ran through the secret places of the world bearing glad tidings of great joy. The Great Cabal had not failed. Yet at that moment my Beloved, laughing in her joy said, "Remember, I want not the love of a Shining Spirit, but the solid flesh of my beloved man!"

With those words I was back upon the cross, and the world about was weeping while I knew the ecstasy of success, the power of exceeding joy. Surely I could now transmute my flesh into spirit and move it from the cross. But though I tried with all my will – and now with a selfless will – I could not do so. Yet even as I worked I saw my father and Skakus beckoning to me from beyond the distant cluster of my followers. In my joy I shouted to them my song of triumph, "It is finished." But they beckoned until I left the physical body, taking the Animal Soul, and all other souls and bodies. I clothed myself and we stood together looking back upon the three bodies upon the cross.

"Why can I not transmute my flesh?" I asked.

My father answered softly, "My son, do you really think you have passed the Final Test?"

Had I not passed the final test? I pondered on what more I could do, but when I would have asked them they strictly instructed me to be silent, for it would be many days before I could speak without exerting excessive energies. We mingled with the crowd and walked as men on earth. We saw the Centurion break the legs of the two crucified beside me that they might die quickly by suffocation. We saw the spear thrust into the side of my body because I was already considered dead. Soon Joseph of Arimathea came from the Palace of Pontius Pilate with an order to the Centurion to release my body for burial. Skakus and my father helped to ease the body from the cross. I was told to stay far away until they beckoned to me, then to hurry in and remove the nails from my hands and feet.

This I did, removing the nail from the right hand first. When I was close to the body I was pulled with a mighty force, and almost succumbed to the demand of the cell-self upon my externalized spirit. But I myself used the pry that loosed my hands from the bar and my feet from the upright. Let it be known that I did take myself from the cross - and let this apparently simple statement be heard by every initiate in the world.

At sharp and stinging orders from Skakus I moved away from the terrible pull of flesh and watched Nicodemo come with a clean linen winding sheet. He carried my head while my father carried my feet and they hurried to the nearby crypt newly prepared in the burial cave of my uncle. I stood behind five weeping women, and six of my disciples and watched as the myrrh and aloes was placed so that it would keep away the mice and borers, and my body was wrapped as if in swaddling clothes. At this moment I realized that I was the universal candidate for initiation into the Highest Mysteries. I was the symbol of all initiate learning. I was the eternal babe laid in the eternal manger.

There was an invisible force that held all but those who were of the Brotherhood away from the ritual. They only worked on my body.

It was all done with accomplished skill and great dispatch and in less than an hour I was left in the crypt and the Centurion caused the soldiers to seal the tomb. This was the manner in which it was done. The Jewish Priests had persuaded Pilate that my body would be stolen so that it could then be claimed that I had risen from the dead. A large stone was moved to block the passageway to the cave, and three smaller rocks were set against this stone. They were then each sealed with seals of paper and wax. These would be broken if one of the stones was moved.

When the Centurion carefully affixed the seal a High Priest grated, "Now we'll see if this Son of God can raise himself in three days".

Yet a moment later a runner came with the breathless news that the veil of the sanctuary was torn assunder and that any man might enter the sacred place and all men could see clearly therein.

The Council of the World was assembled in the home of my uncle. I received the congratulations of those Ascended Masters, the everlasting ones. But Nicodemo came in quickly to tell that the Chief Priest had decided to have my body stolen and hidden away. If, on finding the body gone, my followers made it known and claimed I had risen from the dead, the body would then be thrown from the tower of the Temple to prove for all time that no man could be part of God, and crush out my religion forever. The consternation and concern of the council was so great that I wondered greatly.

Skakus said, "Your body should not be disturbed for three days, but you'll have to re-invest it."

Thus it was that Nicodemus joined the party from the Temple who went to steal my body. They found the tomb empty in this manner: I could not yet transmute my flesh. But I could re-enter and animate it. Yet this would leave the flesh body inside the sealed tomb with no way out. However, there was a narrow crypt near the mouth of the cave, and the body of a man would block the view into it. I was to re-invest my body and hide there. Nicodemo was to stand blocking sight of me, holding aloft a light, until some - possibly all - had entered. I was then to come out and join into the group with him.

When the priests found the sealed tomb "empty" they fled so swiftly in the night that I strolled out of the tomb in the early morning and waited in the garden for my Brothers to come. Skakus and my father came and were examining the crypt when Mary Magdalene came weeping at first light. "Why look for the living in a grave?" Skakus rasped at her.

She stood in terror and indecision. I spoke her name and she recognized me. She would have embraced me, but I dared not yet yield to human touch and said: "Don't touch me yet. I have not fully succeeded, but go tell my people that I have proved that each may go to his Radiant Spirit. I to my God, any other to his God."

I was swiftly carried by cart to the Essene Brotherhood at Bethany, and then urged to step forth from my body again. When I had done this I was told that it would now be three days before the tissue again would

377

be able to receive the spiritual bodies without grasping them and binding them. This is a truth known to every higher initiate and is expressed in some religions as a belief in disembodied spirits which haunt the body for three days after death.

Three times more I showed myself, for my disciples needed to see and know that the Inner Christ can be raised from the tomb of flesh. They needed courage for the ordeals ahead. I taught them about the externalization of the Human Soul, and that it came forth from them upon the breath. Thus did they come to see the Holy Ghost.

Yet another time I appeared to teach them to believe upon the Radiant Christ and the resurrection from the dead without being able to see physical proof of one who is risen. I taught them that all who believe that I am a risen Christ and that he may be also, that same may rise to eternal life through my path.

Yet again I appeared that I might teach them forgiveness. Also I manifested for them the loaf and the fish cooked over the fire of will, to be the eternal symbol of the ability of all men by effort to achieve the wedding of the Body and the Radiant Spirit into eternal life. I let them know that even those who have thrice denied me – as Simon-Peter had – were yet to come to my faith, tend my flock, feed my lambs – which are the spirits of all men who hunger for Truth. I taught them that each man was his own atonement for all sin, the fleshly portent of the everlasting God.

More, ever more did I teach. Simon-Peter was the symbol of the plodding, self-satisfied, orthodox – big, strong and grasping. John of Zebedee was the symbol of True Faith attained through mystic love, service, and unrelenting effort. He would eventually attain the higher degree, but in the beginning he would be outdone. I separated the two, showing that the greater must wait my return, and that the lesser would – after serving its time – be destroyed.

This however I did not teach, and never shall: that man must be bound together by strong organizations and central authority. Truly I say to you, no church can

378

contain my teaching, for I taught that the earnest heart of each man was the center of his religion, the church of his soul, the structure of his worship. My religion cannot be contained in things of stone, or wood, or structure, nor taught by paid priests. My religion will come only freely and without tithe or tax from heart to heart, from mind to mind, from soul to soul. Fanaticism of new faith was not of my choosing. It is not my will that the religion I began shall be entombed in a church. That which I most dislike was thrust upon the people for all time!

When at last I had taught them all I could, I had not risen through the last of my own trials. What it was to be I did not know, and I could not get any of the Masters to talk to me about it. I could not leave my disciples but returned to teach them that sin was not of God, but of the mind of man, and they could create it or deny it by their attitude of mind. I taught them that all illness is the result of the belief in sin, and that he who has forgiven the world for its transgress finds no sin or illness in himself.

I taught them to heal by the laying on of hands, and also that healing is the easiest of the mystical skills and becomes the trap in which the feet of those who tread the mystic path are often snared.

But still I did not know what I lacked in my own trials. So I taught them that service to one's fellow man is service to God - one serves one's fellow men not because they are beautiful, deserving or good, - but because it is man's duty to his Radiant Self and to God. In my teaching I came to an end. But still I did not know what remained of my own development and I began to pray.

Suddenly as I prayed before my beloved disciples on a hillock outside Bethany, I realized that Skakus was my final test. Skakus! Indeed he had always been my greatest obstacle even while he was my greatest help. His very indifference, his inscrutability - these indeed had been my final test. They had been as carefully planned as the handy tomb in the garden of crucifixion. He was to teach me that no rule contained total truth, no word could contain the Truth.

I found that I must now give up my teachings - at

least in part. I had said there is no love greater than this, that a man will lay down his life for a friend. Yet men daily lay down their lives for duty only, and do so without thought of heroism. I - who thought I knew all love - went to the cross without knowing the greatest love. Truly there is a love greater than this, that a man will give his life for mankind, for his fellow man. There is a love greater than this, that a man will love his neighbor even more than his own self. Truly I say to you there is a love greater than even this, that a man will love those who despitefully use him, or those who willfully wrong him. It is not always easy to love even where there is understanding - especially spiteful understanding. But the initiate quickly rises above the things he understands, he rises to a higher truth.

Truly there is yet a greater love. From this love comes a commandment for this New Age. A commandment that will bring harmony in the world and peace among nations. This commandment I do now give to you: Love you well those whom you do not understand even as you love your Radiant Self.

This, this was my final test. I had loved all of my Masters well - except Skakus only. He was my test, and his whole life was given to teaching me and testing me. From foul smelling bear grease to raucous voice and veiled eyes of strange content, from apparent cowardice to insolence in the way he said "Boy"; from calculated overbearingness in work to excessive confidence - all were part of my final initiation. Even as I prayed for understanding it swept over me in an ocean's depth.

Suddenly I was surrounded by all of my Masters, and they looked on me with eyes of shining love. Skakus stood and looked upon me, and slowly the veil over his eyes lifted, for I found love in my heart for this Master who would not permit himself to be understood. I saw that in his heart there was a Jade Sun, and Skakus fell upon his knees and gave voice to praises to our Almighty God, saying: "Oh, God, Master of All Godhood, Supreme and Immutable, Indwelling and Perfect. Let us be raised into Your eternal bliss. Accept now this the newest Master of the Universe."

Skakus then handed me the Golden Sword of the Druids. My Masters returned to me the jewels of my Masterships, and the Scepter of the Christs of Persia, and I was exceeding glad. Then suddenly we were surrounded by a great light, and the music of the spheres. Our bodies were raised; and I willed mine to be transmuted. I saw the perfected Souls of my Masters, and in each there shone a glorious Jade Sun, shining for all eternity brighter than a million earthly suns.

As the glory grew around us, I willed myself, and suddenly was upon the Strand. There in the arbor was my beloved wife, and her eyes were raised and her arms outstretched in welcome. She awaited me with the new Son of God, the Avatar of the New Age, beneath her heart. I touched her and was happy.

She touched me and said, "Oh, I'm so glad. My love is not for a shining God, but a lusty man."

Then only did I truly know that I was God.